# MORAL EDUCATION

# Moral EDUCATION

## A HANDBOOK

VOLUME 1
A–L

Edited by

*F. Clark Power,
Ronald J. Nuzzi,
Darcia Narvaez,
Daniel K. Lapsley, and
Thomas C. Hunt*

PRAEGER

**Westport, Connecticut
London**

**Library of Congress Cataloging-in-Publication Data**

Moral education : a handbook / edited by F. Clark Power . . . [et al.].
   v. cm.
Includes bibliographical references and index.
ISBN-13: 978–0–313–33647–8 (set : alk. paper)
ISBN-13: 978–0–313–34646–0 (v. 1 : alk. paper)
ISBN-13: 978–0–313–34648–4 (v. 2 : alk. paper)
1. Moral education—Handbooks, manuals, etc. I. Power, F. Clark.
LC268.M667 2008
370.11′4—dc22       2007033113

British Library Cataloguing in Publication Data is available.

Library of Congress Catalog Card Number: 2007033113
ISBN-13: 978–0–313–33647–8 (set)
      978–0–313–34646–0 (vol. 1)
      978–0–313–34648–4 (vol. 2)

First published in 2008

Praeger Publishers, 88 Post Road West, Westport, CT 06881
An imprint of Greenwood Publishing Group, Inc.
www.praeger.com

Printed in the United States of America

∞™

The paper used in this book complies with the
Permanent Paper Standard issued by the National
Information Standards Organization (Z39.48–1984).

10 9 8 7 6 5 4 3 2 1

# Contents

# List of Entries

# Preface

*Moral Education: A Handbook* offers readers a single source for relevant, current, and practical research and information on moral education, especially as it is presented in various school sectors in the United States. Once thought the exclusive domain of religious and private schools, moral education is today a shared concern of parents, teachers, school administrators, and policy makers.

The organization of the *Handbook* allows both the scholar and the casual reader easy and quick access to pertinent information in the field. A list of all entries is provided along with an historical introduction. This handbook is arranged alphabetically for ease of use and discusses a wide range of topics. Moral philosophy receives attention through entries such as consequentialism and deontology. Major theorists and researchers are also treated as subjects. The work of Edward Wynne, Albert Bandura, Robert Enright, B. F. Skinner, and Stanley Milgram are presented. Other entries include topics such as religion, religious education, and reverence. Civic education, sports and character, respect, and responsibility are also included. Challenges to moral education such as plagiarism and cheating come under review. An extended bibliography of moral education is included at the end, going well beyond the works cited in the *Handbook*.

Entries are designed to provide readers with helpful, current information, offering a one-stop resource for primary research in dozens of areas. Entries are referenced and indexed, facilitating the interest of those who might wish to delve more deeply into the topic at hand. This handbook is an important academic resource for all those who are in search of information about moral education at this critical time in history.

We hope that *Moral Education: A Handbook* fills an important need. It will be a critical source of information for teachers, parents, scholars, and students in a variety of fields, including educational administration, teacher education, psychology and human development, sociology, and political science. As a supplementary reference text, it will be useful to students involved in the sociology of education and the social foundations of education. For religious and private school educators and leaders, it will help to provide a broader, theoretical knowledge base for their efforts. For public school educators and leaders, it offers a quick, but accurate, tool for understanding and appreciating the importance of moral and character development in schools. High school students, libraries, teachers, and administrators will also find the handbook useful for research papers, presentations, and projects, and for understanding emerging moral issues and concerns. It will also be a handy reference tool for legislators, policy makers, churches, school boards, and the general public interested in a variety of moral and social issues.

# Acknowledgments

The writing and publication of any book involves a complicated series of related tasks, managed under the stress of time constraints and editorial demands. A project such as this handbook is made even more complex by its various editors and dozens of contributors. Without focused effort and a high degree of organization, the depth and breadth of this handbook would not be possible. The tracking of submissions, correspondence with contributors, meetings of editors, checking of references, and communication with the publisher all demanded daily attention to detail. These tasks were handled with graceful efficiency and unswerving dedication by our project manager, Julie Wernick Dallavis at the University of Notre Dame.

The editors gratefully acknowledge Julie's leadership in bringing this handbook to publication, managing all of these competing demands while expecting her first child. Our hope and prayer is that all children may benefit from the moral wisdom and insight found in these pages.

# Introduction

THOMAS C. HUNT AND
MONALISA M. MULLINS

The tragedy of the Columbine massacre on April 20, 1999, renewed the emphasis on moral education in American schools. This renewal inspires this handbook, even though moral education has been a priority in American schools from the outset. Historian Michael B. Katz wrote in 1976 in the bicentennial issue of the *History of Education Quarterly* that it would constitute a "minor revolution if the emphasis or primary goal of public schooling shifted from the development of character to the cultivation of intellect."[1]

Katz has ample company in this position. For instance, B. Edward McClellan, in his *Moral Education in America: Schools and the Shaping of Character from Colonial Times to the Present* (1999), presents evidence to support Katz's view. Thomas Lickona's most recent book, *Character Matters,* contains strategies on "How to Help Our Children Develop Good Judgment, Integrity and Other Essential Virtues."[2] The prominence of moral education is also evident in organizations such as the Character Education Partnership (CEP) that recently announced its 11th National Forum, this one titled "Exploring Pathways to Civic Character." On its agenda was a "full-day session on CEP's *Eleven Principles of Effective Character Education: The Who, What, Where, When and Why.*" Lickona was among its featured speakers.[3]

Gallup polls, presented annually in the September issue of *Phi Delta Kappan,* confirm the primacy of moral education in the schools. From 1972 through 1984, for example, the public identified "lack of discipline" as the major problem facing American public schools.[4] Polls in the last decade reveal similar views. "Lack of discipline" has ranked either first or second since 1995.[5] When it was listed as second, either "school funding" (2002),[6] or "drug abuse," ranked first. (The latter from 1986 through 1991 and again in 1996.) It, along with "fighting, violence, and gangs," was judged consistently more serious than items such as "getting good teachers" and "low pay for teachers."[7]

This overview, which focuses almost entirely on public schools, is not a comprehensive history of moral education in those schools. Space alone prohibits such an option. Rather, it is an episodic history that concentrates on selected key periods, movements, and individuals throughout the annals of American educational history from the colonial

Massachusetts period in the seventeenth century to present times that demonstrate the preeminent role of moral education in the history of those schools.

## Colonial Massachusetts

Contrary to popular belief, the schools of colonial Massachusetts were not the first to be established in what is now the United States. That honor belongs to Catholic schools that were founded in Florida and Louisiana. Nonetheless, the Massachusetts schools have been seen as the forerunner of subsequent educational institutions in this country. Marcus Jernegan has observed that these schools were "first in importance" in this era, in their "number, character, distribution, and quality." Schooling was viewed as the responsibility of civil government, as then constituted.[8]

William Bradford, as noted in the *History of Plymouth Plantation, 1620–1647,* reports that the early Massachusetts residents left Holland because of the "licentiousness of youth in that country," which posed a "danger to their souls, to the great grief of their parents and dishonor of God."[9] The first governor of the Massachusetts Bay Colony, John Winthrop, alleged the following as the motivation for the trans-Atlantic migration of the early inhabitants of the colony:

> The fountains of learning and religion are so corrupted that most children, even the best wits and fairest hopes, are perverted, corrupted, and utterly overthrown by the multitude of evil examples and the licentious government of those seminaries.[10]

The noted educational historian, Lawrence A. Cremin, follows this line of reasoning, contending that the Puritans thought it would be different in the New World, where, aided by education, they would seek to

> establish a wilderness Zion, a community of "visible saints" committed to Christian brotherhood and conduct. And within such a society education would assume utmost importance, not merely as an instrument for systematically transmitting an intellectual heritage, but as an agency for deliberately pursuing a cultural ideal.[11]

Edmund Morgan, commenting on the climate that led to the education laws of 1642 and 1647 in Massachusetts, remarks that the "covenant of grace" drove the Puritans, both individually and socially. The Puritans insisted on education "in order to insure the religious welfare of their children."[12] Salvation, the Puritans believed, was "impossible" without education. The very "ultimate purpose" of schooling was salvation, thus the "main business of education was to prepare children for conversion by teaching them the doctrines of moral precepts of Christianity by which salvation could be attained."[13] Learning was thought to be indispensable if one was to "distinguish true from false religion."[14]

Legislation was enacted to support the moral suasions of home and school. In 1648, for instance, the Massachusetts School Law called on the selectmen of towns to keep a "vigilant eye" on parents and masters who were "too indulgent and negligent in their duty" in seeing to the proper upbringing of their wards in teaching the "principles of religion" and "knowledge of the Capital lawes."[15] Schoolmasters were expected to inculcate the truths of religion and the principles of morally upright behavior in their youthful charges. It was their responsibility to check on what their pupils had learned from the Sabbath's preaching and what, if any, offenses that their pupils may have committed on the Sabbath, and then to publicly admonish and correct them for those misdemeanors.[16] Further, the schoolmasters were expected to oversee the prayers of their students, both "morning and evening," and to ensure that they prayed "reverently."[17] Schoolmasters were to utilize punishment, recognizing that all things in the school be ordered for the "glory of God and the training up of the children of the town in religion, learning, and civility."[18]

Textbooks used in schools during this period convey the "values of the society supporting the school." In New England, the "reading materials stressed Biblical themes and conveyed to the child the concept of the righteous life that should be lived by a good Puritan."[19] As Daniel Boorstin has remarked, from the early reading materials, the child learned his alphabet and read the first syllabus in his primer, through which he "was pressed to absorb the truths by which his community lived."[20]

By far the most popular book used in New England schools was the *New England Primer*. It had a number of features. The *Primer* taught patriotism through the alphabet. So, "Our King the good, No man of blood," became in the revolutionary era, "Kings should be good, Not men of blood."[21] The alphabet was used to instruct about biblical themes: "A. In Adam's Fall, We sinned all. B. Heaven to find, The Bible mind. C. Christ crucify'd, for Sinners died," and so forth.[22] Clifton Johnson observes that the contents of the various editions of the *Primer* may have changed, but "for hundreds of years the teaching of religion and reading united" in its pages. Their precepts were "instilled in minds as yet uninformed, and the children were drilled to believe what they were to think out for themselves when they were more mature." The Catechism that was part of the *Primer* was treated scarcely less seriously in the schools than it was in the churches, and the teachers drilled their pupils in it as thoroughly as they did in spelling or any other lesson.[23]

The schools in New England of this era were "designed to create educated Puritans who would perpetuate the religious, social, political and economic beliefs of the adults." All children were to be "able to read and to understand their religion and the laws of the commonwealth"; schooling was an antidote for the children who had been "conceived in sin and born in corruption."[24] It was important, Morgan summarized, to "teach a child good habits, not because they would save him, but because it was unlikely he would be saved without them." An evil nature could be "trained into good habits only if the training started early."[25] Thus it was the task of the schools, as well as that of the home and church.

## The National Period

The link between republican government, democracy, popular education, and virtue as well as knowledge, was present in the educational views of the Founding Fathers, those positions of Thomas Jefferson, Benjamin Rush, and Noah Webster.

A believer in "deistic humanism,"[26] interpreting Christianity as a "humanistic moral code,"[27] Thomas Jefferson looked to schools to provide "educated and virtuous lawmakers."[28] Schools and colleges were to become the "most vital pillars of human happiness and security."[29] Writing to Peter Carr in 1787, Jefferson claimed that the individual is "endowed with a sense of right and wrong" that is as "much a part of his nature as the sense of hearing, seeing, feeling, it is the true foundation of morality."[30] Primary school education can "improve the citizens' moral and civic virtues and enable them to know and exercise their rights and duties," which will bring about individual and social human happiness.[31] Education can improve both the individual and society as it "engrafts a new man on the native stock, and improves what in his nature was vicious and perverse into qualities of virtue and social worth."[32] In the primary schools the children should have the "first elements of morality instilled into their minds" leading to their "own greatest happiness," which is "always the result of good conscience."[33] Universal education was necessary for the development and sustaining of republican virtue and liberty, and for the survival and progress of the republican state.

Though not as well known as Jefferson, Benjamin Rush was a leading spokesman for the role of education in securing the virtues for the survival of the republic. Unlike Jefferson, he called for the instillation of New Testament values in primary school children. Without these values, there could be no virtue, without virtue there is no liberty, and with liberty there is the life of all republican governments.[34] Rush maintained that a Christian "cannot fail of being a republican," because "every precept of the Gospel inculcates those degrees of humility, self-denial, and brotherly kindness which are directly opposed to the pride of monarchy and the pageantry of the court."[35]

Again parting ways with Jefferson, Rush advocated the use of the Bible in schools because "there is no book of its size in the whole world that contains half so much useful knowledge for the government of states, or the direction of the affairs of individuals as the Bible."[36] The system of public schools, infused with biblical teachings, would guarantee that in his native Pennsylvania there would be "one great and equally enlightened family."[37]

Noah Webster's theories should also be considered. Called the "Schoolmaster to America" by Henry Steele Commager, Webster tied the existence of a republican nation to the education given its citizens.[38] Webster's *Spelling Book,* first published in 1783, contained a number of moral precepts, which called for good behavior at home and school, and promised sanctions for evildoers.[39] The *Spelling Book* also included a "Moral catechism" that asked questions such as "WHAT is moral virtue?" and answered, "It is an honest, upright conduct in all dealing with man." Similar, subsequent questions and answers were presented on a number of specific virtues, such as humility, justice, and gratitude.[40]

Composed in 1790, Webster's "On the Education of Youth" is the repository of his views on the critical role education plays in a republican nation. It is an "object of the first consequence" on the part of governments because the "impressions received in early life usually form the characters of all individuals." Education was especially crucial in the United States because the government was "not yet firmly established; our national character is not yet formed." Thus education's charge was to "implant in the minds of the American youth the principles of virtue and liberty and inspire them with just and liberal ideas of government and with an inviolable attachment to their own country."[41] It was not possible to exaggerate the importance of education, Webster affirmed, because the "education of youth" is a matter of "more consequence than making laws and preaching the gospel, because it lays the foundation on which both the law and gospel rest for success."[42] It was in the district schools that the youth should have the "principles of virtue and good behavior inculcated." For, he reasoned, the "*virtues*" of humans are of "more consequence to society than their *abilities*."[43]

There is ample evidence for the vital role of moral education in sustaining the fledgling republic in the waning years of the eighteenth and the beginning of the nineteenth centuries. As early as 1777, Vermont enacted legislation for schools that included the provision that "Laws for the encouragement of virtue and the prevention of vice and immorality, shall be made and constantly kept in force."[44] A decade later Congress passed the North-west Ordinance that proclaimed, "Religion, morality, and knowledge being necessary for good government and the happiness of mankind, schools and the means of education shall forever be encouraged."[45] In 1789, Massachusetts enacted a law that called for each town of 50 families to be provided with a schoolmaster "of good morals," whose responsibilities included teaching "decent behaviour" to his students. The selectmen of the town were charged with ensuring that, to the best of their knowledge, the teacher "sustains a good moral character." The teacher, who was to be a "person of sober life and conversation," was assigned "carefully to instruct" the children in reading and writing, but also to "instill in their minds a sense of piety and virtue, and to teach them decent behaviour."[46]

Concern over education producing a virtuous citizenry, indispensable to a republican government, was not limited to the New England states. As the nineteenth century was ushered in, Governor George Clinton of New York proclaimed that "advantages to morals, religion, liberty and good government" stem from the "general diffusion of knowledge." He was joined by Governor James Turner of North Carolina who urged the establishment of schools to "enlighten the minds of the people, and to preserve the purity of their morals."[47] John Adams, the nation's first vice president and second president, looked to the schools to "Countenance and inculcate the principles of humanity and general benevolence, public and private charity, industry and frugality, honesty" in all of their affairs.[48]

The leaders of American society after the revolution were unanimous in their view that a self-governing people needed "universal education" that would produce virtuous citizens.[49] While there was disagreement over the means to bring about moral education, there was unanimity on its need.[50]

## The Education of the Urban Poor: The New York Experience

Major concern over the moral education of poor children had existed prior to the time of the Revolution. That concern intensified as cities grew and were populated with concentrations of poor children. New York City, with its charity schools, was a prime example of that concern. As Joel Spring has noted, the "charity school movement is important because it was the first major attempt to use the school as a means of socializing children into an industrious way of life."[51] Not only the destitute but also the laboring class were becoming "less industrious, less moral, and less careful to lay up the fruits of their earnings."[52] The Free School Society was created to address these serious social needs.

The application to have the Society incorporated by the state of New York was signed by "about one hundred of the most respectable men in the city,"[53] who "viewed with painful anxiety the multiplied evils which have accrued, and are daily accruing, to this city, from the neglected education of the children of the poor."[54] Not being educated by any of the "various religious societies in this city," their condition was deemed as "deplorable." They were reared by parents who neglected them, and whose "bad example" led to the omission of education that produced "ignorance and vice, and all those manifold evils resulting from every species of immorality." The lack of a *virtuous education* early in their lives was the culprit, and this the Society, if incorporated, promised to rectify.[55]

Following state approval, the president of the New York Free School Society, DeWitt Clinton, pointed out that despite the efforts of the churches, there remained a large number of children living in "total neglect of religious and moral instruction, and unacquainted with the common rudiments of learning, essentially requisite for the due management of the ordinary business of life." The consequences of this indifference, obvious to even the "most careless observer," were children "brought up in ignorance and amidst the contagion of bad example," who were in "imminent danger of ruin," and likely to become the "burden and pests of society." These children must be given "early instruction" combined with "fixed habits of industry, decency, and order," which are the "surest safeguards of virtuous conduct." Absent parental attention, it became the "duty of the public, and of individuals, who have the power, to assist them in the discharge of this most important obligation." Clinton informed the public that care would be exercised in the "selection of teachers, and, besides the elements of learning usually taught in schools, strict attention will be bestowed on the morals of the children."[56]

The monitorial method, named after its founder, Joseph Lancaster, was imported from England to address the situation. Lancaster's method utilized monitors, older boys, whose use enabled the teacher to "teach" several hundred students. Not only was it inexpensive, its adherents claimed the method was effective. The curriculum was designed to "inculcate the values of obedience, subordination, promptness, regularity, cleanliness, thrift, and temperance."[57] A system of emulation and rewards was used to inculcate the desired behaviors in students. Monitors used tickets to reward good behavior, tickets that could be used to purchase toys, and ticket fines were employed to punish bad behavior. For instance, a fine of four tickets was assessed for "Talking, playing, inattention, out of order," and a 50-ticket penalty was levied for "Fighting."[58] Sometimes physical punishment or ridicule was applied. Repeat offenders could have a "wooden log" placed around their necks, and if that failed to change the student's behavior, then his legs were fastened together "with wooden shackles" and he was made to walk until he was "exhausted." Lancaster also used the method of putting misbehaving students into baskets and suspending them from the ceiling while classmates smiled "at the bird in a cage."[59]

Lancaster's backers believed the method was superior to the "divisive sectarianism of the church schools."[60] Its combination of "monitorial instruction and scriptural education constituted a world-wide solution to mass education."[61] The system was not devoid of religious activity. For instance, Tuesday afternoons were set aside for religious instruction. Bourne reports that an "association of more than fifty ladies of the first position and character" who belonged to a variety of religious denominations, "volunteered their services" and taught the children "in their respective catechisms." On Sunday mornings the students met at the school and were escorted by monitors to their respective churches. Additionally, the scriptures were read daily in the schools.[62]

The social situation in New York City in the early years of the nineteenth century was deplorable. Reformers, among whom were the leaders of the School Society, attributed the grinding poverty of the urban working class and the growing crime in the city to "faults of character."[63] The trustees of the Society apparently believed that "scrupulous nonsectarianism, coupled with inculcation of what they took to be commonly accepted moral and ethical values" would enable the schools to "teach children of all religious groups," and hence combat the vices of ignorance and crime.[64] Michael Katz has argued that the system, of "minuscule cost," seemed fitting because the clientele of the schools was lower-class children who were "unfinished products, needing to be inculcated with norms of docility, cleanliness, sobriety, and obedience" that they did not get at home.[65]

The particular form of moral education to be transmitted was founded on military discipline, which, like factory discipline, would "train the children of the poor how to act inside and outside of school." The character traits of which these children were in desperate need were especially promptness and obedience, which were deemed "beneficial to the child as well as the society."[66] The "regimentation of the students" in the Lancaster system was "symbolically and psychologically appropriate to the moral mission of the schools." By imposing order on chaos, it brought the pupils into an "obedient subordination." This "philosophy of order" went hand in hand with order in urban society; indeed it was an "attempt to promote" such order.[67] A student's submission to this "factory system of education" was supposed to indelibly impress the virtues of "orderliness and obedience" on their minds. Then, when the students entered the world, armed with the "virtue of submission, order, and industriousness," they could function in the "world of business." As Spring put it, the "Lancasterian system was supposed to help the pauper child escape poverty and crime by imparting formal knowledge and instilling the virtues needed in the world of work." A child made moral in this framework made him or her "useful to and functional in society."[68]

Moral education was the keynote of the Lancaster system. Free from subservience to any sect, Lancaster argued, and some leading New Yorkers agreed, his system provided indispensable moral education of the nation's urban poor children. It brought to them:

> a reverence for the sacred name of God, and the Scriptures of Truth, a detestation of vice; a love of veracity; a due attention to duties to parents, relations, and to society; carefulness to avoid bad company; civility without flattery; and a peaceable demeanor; may be inculcated in every seminary for youth, without violating the sanctuary of private religious opinion in any mind.[69]

The movement was criticized for its assumption of "exclusive control" over the poor children, not permitting their parents any participation in the "direction of the course of studies, the management of the schools, or... the selection of teachers." The School Society ordered parents with "no action or cooperation" to "submit their children to the government and guidance of others, probably strangers," who were in "no way accountable to the parents."[70] That eminent stalwart of public education, Ellwood P. Cubberley, had a more benign interpretation of the Society's work. He saw it as a "great improvement" over what had gone on before, replacing "idleness, inattention, and disorder," with "activity, emulation, order and a kind of military discipline which was of much value to the type of children attending these schools." Cubberley also saw a precursor role for the Society's schools, in that they "exerted a very important interest in and a sentiment for free schools." They helped people realize the "advantages of a common school system, and become willing to contribute to the support of the same."[71] The movement in New York City died in the 1840s, going out as Kaestle described it, with a "fizzle, not a bang."[72]

## The Common School

The American common school is attributed to Horace Mann, who is called its "Father." Concerned over the growing social unrest in the United States, and especially in his home state of Massachusetts, Mann accepted the position of secretary of the State Board of Education in that state and announced that, "Henceforth, so long as I hold the office, I devote myself to the supremest welfare of mankind upon earth....I have faith in the improvability of the race." Joel Spring comments that Mann believed he was entering a "field of endeavor that promised universal salvation."[73] The priority of the common school under Mann's leadership, a priority that was to remain over the years, was moral education.

Schooling, Mann believed, was to elevate morality, to bring about a needed revolution in character, which would result in the enthronement of the "ideas of justice, truth, benevolence, and reverence...in the hearts of the people and made ascendant over conduct."[74] This moral evolution was necessary for the very survival of humankind; as Mann put it, "I think I restrict myself within bounds in saying that so far as I have observed in this life, ten men have failed from defect in morals where one man has failed from defect in intellect."[75] The mixture of children from all social classes in the common school would bring about the kindling of a "spirit of mutual unity and respect which the strains and cleavages of adult life could never destroy." Hence, social harmony was the "primary goal of the school," which would lead to the larger goal of social progress, brought about by popular education as the "great equalizer," a vivid reflection of Mann's "limitless faith in the perfectibility of human life and institutions." There was "no end to the social good which might be derived from the common school."[76]

Mann's solutions to the question of what can be the moral foundation of a common educational program in a religiously diverse society were twofold. The first of these was to accept "common principles" from all creeds that all could agree with, such as the "Fatherhood of God." The second was to be found in the doctrine of phrenology, which held that 37 faculties make up the mind and these "govern the attitudes and actions of the individual." As a believer in phrenology, Mann held that "morals can be taught outside of their historic context in particular religious doctrines." Thus, common schools can teach such "publicly accepted virtues as brotherly love, kindness, generosity, amiability, and others; leaving to home and church the task of teaching the differing *private* sectarian creeds" that sanction these virtues.[77]

Mann served as secretary for 12 years. Each year, beginning in 1837, he made a report to the legislature. The role of moral education is present in all and paramount in many of those reports. In his inaugural report in 1837, when addressing the role of the teachers in the common schools, he reminded his readers that the law of the Commonwealth of Massachusetts stated:

> It shall be the duty of all instructors of youth, to exert their best endeavors to impress on the minds of children and youth, committed to their care and instruction, the principles of piety, justice and a sacred regard to truth, love to their country, humanity and universal benevolence, sobriety, industry and frugality, chastity, moderation and temperance, and those other virtues, which are the ornaments of human society, and the basis upon which a republican constitution is founded;...and secure the blessings of liberty, as well as to promote their future happiness, and also to point out to them the evil tendency of the opposite vices.[78]

No one, Mann maintained, could deny the "indispenableness of moral instruction and training," by which the "beautiful and sublime truths of ethics and of natural religion have a posing power."[79] Teachers had a divine mission, because "God has so constituted this world, into which He has sent them, that whatever is really, and truly valuable may be possessed by all, and possessed in exhaustless abundance."[80]

That Mann regarded teaching as a sacred calling is clear from his words that "our duty to these children *shall be done,* shall we proclaim, in the blessed language of the Savior: IT IS NOT THE WILL OF YOUR FATHER WHICH IS IN HEAVEN THAT ONE OF THESE LITTLE ONES SHOULD PERISH."[81] Education, he contended, was "such a culture of our moral affections and religious susceptibilities, as, in the course of Nature and Providence, shall lead to a subjection or conformity of all our appetites, propensities, and sentiments to the will of Heaven."[82] Moral education in the common school will

> advance moral and religious sentiments into ascendancy and control over animal and selfish propensities...it will be kept entirely aloof from partisanship in politics, and sectarianism in religion,...commending to practice only the great and fundamental truths of civil and social obligation, of moral and religious duty.[83]

Mann's emphasis on moral education continued throughout his annual reports. For instance, in 1840 he called attention to the "manners of the teacher" for a "right direction" to be given to the children on the "indispensable, all-controlling requisite of moral character." Those who were asked to write letters of recommendation on behalf of teacher candidates had best keep in mind the "moral influence of teachers upon the rising generation," and only those persons with good character should be recommended. Teachers were required to teach the "great axioms of Christianity" and they themselves needed to "be patterns of the virtues, they are required to inculcate."[84]

Mann's fifth annual report in 1841 returned to the theme of approving teacher candidates. The first and "indispensable condition of approval" was "*moral education.*"[85] That same year he lectured that teachers must be moral agents in order for them to cultivate in students a "sacred regard for truth; to train them up to the love of God and the love of man; to make the perfect example of Jesus Christ lovely in their eyes."[86]

Mann's ninth annual report in 1845 focused on the primacy of moral over intellectual education.[87] He credited the State Board of Education with contributing to the moral training of children, and reminded his readers that, "No community can long subsist, unless it has religious principles as the foundation of moral action, nor unless it has moral action as the superstructure of religious principle."[88] As a consequence, moral education must be paramount in the common school. Mann remarked that "however loftily the intellect of man may have been gifted, however skillfully it may have been trained, if it be not guided by a sense of justice, a love of mankind and a devotion to duty, its possessor is only a more splendid, as he is a more dangerous barbarian."[89] To achieve this goal, the first order of business would be to choose school committee members who would "scrutinize diligently the moral character of the proposed teacher and his ability to impart moral instruction." Freedom from vice on the part of teachers was not sufficient; they needed a "positive determination toward good, evinced by his life, as well as by his language." Society, Mann observed, could be "happy without knowledge; but it is not in the power of any human imagination to picture itself a form of life, where we could be happy without virtue."[90]

Mann headlined his eleventh report in 1847 with the title "The Power of Common Schools to Redeem the State from Social Vices and Crimes."[91] Subsequently, he argued that the "redeeming and transforming influences" of the common school system will "expel ninety-nine hundredths of all the vices and crimes under which society now mourns and agonizes." The "crowning beauty" of the system was that "Christian men of every faith may cordially unite in carrying forward the work of reform."[92]

Unfortunately, he wrote, "people did not yet seem to see" the savings that virtue-producing education would provide by eliminating the "cost of legislating against criminals," the "building of houses of correction, and jails and penitentiaries," constituting a "beneficent kind of insurance."[93] Without the moral influence of common school education, the appeals

of advocates of moral reform and missionary societies must fall on "stony hearts" and speak to "adders' ears." But by uniting on behalf of "universal education," only then can the "wheel of Progress move harmoniously and resistlessly forward."[94]

Mann's twelfth, and final report, was the most important, looking back, as it did, on the major issues of his tenure. Never, he wrote, "will wisdom preside in the halls of legislation and its profound utterances be recorded on the pages of the statute book, until Common schools...shall create a more far-seeing intelligence and a purer morality than has ever existed among communities of men."[95] The common school had the potentiality of becoming the "most effective and benignant of all the forces of civilization," especially for a republican government in which the "legislators are a mirror reflecting the moral countenance of their constituents." In fact, he penned, "woe to the republic that rests upon no better foundation than ignorance, selfishness, and passion."[96] Communities without consciences would soon "extinguish" themselves. Pointing to the failings of humankind recorded in history, Mann alleged that "there is one experiment which has never yet been tried, *Train up a child in the way he should go, and when he is old he will not depart from it.*"[97]

Responding to attacks from those who claimed he had removed religion from the schools, Mann pointed to the presence of the Bible and religious instruction in the common schools to deny such claims. Rather, it was divisive sectarianism, not the Christian religion, that he had excluded from the common schools. After all, "wherever the Bible might go, there the system of Christianity must be."[98]

Horace Mann's legacy to the United States was the common school. The "heart of the curriculum" for Mann was moral education.[99] Mann firmly believed that the common school was the one institution that could bring about moral advancement in society, and that advancement was impossible without the common school.[100]

## Nineteenth-Century Textbooks: The Bible and McGuffey's *Readers*

Moral education in the schools of nineteenth-century United States relied heavily on several books, first, the Bible and, second, McGuffey's *Readers*.

As we have seen, the Bible played a central role in the schools of colonial Massachusetts, in the ideas of Noah Webster, and in the common school of Horace Mann. Founded in 1816, the American Bible Society had as a main purpose the use of the Bible as a schoolbook.[101] The Baltimore City Council in 1839 proclaimed that the "chief object in adopting the use of the sacred volume was, to endeavor, by every available means, to imbue the minds of the scholars with that moral influence which its inspired pages are so well calculated to impart." The Council declared that it would never support sectarianism in its schools but believed that the "Holy Scriptures have provided an invaluable blessing to the Christian world" and would provide a "salutary influence" in the schools.[102] The American Bible Societies, first in 1839 and then again in 1840, pledged that the Scriptures would be read in every classroom in the nation.[103]

Confronted by clashes with Roman Catholicism over the use of the King James version of the Bible in public schools, one minister in New York announced in 1840 that "*I would rather be an infidel than a papist.*"[104] Other conflicts with Catholics over the Bible occurred across the nation. In Ohio, the Presbyterian and Congregational Convention declared in 1844 that the

> liberty to *worship* God according to the dictates of conscience cannot, by any principle of legitimate interpretation, be construed into a right to embarrass the municipal authorities of this Christian and Protestant nation in the ordering of their district schools.[105]

It was not the "Protestant Bible," but the "Christian Bible," that was being read in the schools and the "children are to learn piety from it, not sectarianism, or creeds, but pure religion, undefiled before God."[106] The Bible was not considered a sectarian book, and its reading in the common schools did not constitute sectarian instruction. As Wisconsin's superintendent of public instruction remarked in 1858, the people would not consent to its banishment from the state's schools, and thus:

> repudiate its unequalled teachings of virtue and morality as unfit for the instruction and guidance of the children of their love—children who, at no distant day, must become the rulers and law-givers of the State, and custodians of all that we now hold dear and sacred, our homes, our country, Christianity and the Bible.[107]

Several court cases affirmed the legitimacy both of the practice of Bible-reading and of its crucial role in the moral education of children. For instance, in 1870, Justice Hagans, writing for the majority in the case of *Minor v. Board of Education* in the Superior Court of Cincinnati, adjudged that the Bible impresses on the

> children of the common schools, the principles and duties of morality and justice, and a sacred regard for truth, love of country, humanity, increased benevolence, sobriety, industry, chastity, moderation, temperance and all other virtues, which are the ornaments of human society.[108]

Judge John R. Bennett, presiding judge over the 12th Circuit Court, Rock County, Wisconsin, upheld the practice in 1889 as an appropriate book for the public schools. It was, he said, a unique book, a "good, true and ever faithful friend and counselor."[109]

The McGuffey *Readers* were the other books that were viewed as most important conveyors of moral education in the nineteenth century. The famous *Readers* are named after William Holmes McGuffey, though he authored but several of the first edition. McGuffey was a Presbyterian minister who was born in Pennsylvania in 1800 and grew up in frontier Ohio. The estimated sales of the various editions reached 122,000,000 by 1920.[110] John Westerhoff points out that the only edition with which McGuffey was associated—the first—had a vastly different moral view than subsequent editions, which were altered and "severely secularized." Yet Westerhoff argues that each edition continued to "introduce students to the classics, to morality, and to a good character as understood by the emerging middle class.... they strove to unify the nation around a common worldview and value system."[111]

McGuffey emphasized the "values of industry, honesty and morality." He taught temperance in all things, and all moral values constantly extolled that a person should be interested in other people and be ready to give them a helping hand when needed. Religion, as a "guide and necessity for life," was kept before the pupils' eyes "in a most wholesome and enlightened way."[112] The *Readers'* great achievement has been described as the "complete integration of Christian and middle class ideals," and in that respect the McGuffey *Readers* were the "great textbook product of American middle class culture." The *Readers* interwove the social and moral, the Christian and secular, virtues such as kindness, truthfulness, modesty, gentleness, thoughtfulness, control of temper, the love of magnanimity, and a general spirit of happiness and good will toward others.[113]

McGuffey's virtues were closely related to the temperance crusade; he condemned intemperance, gambling, and dishonesty. The social virtues were designed to make a "good Christian and a good citizen," and the *Readers* were to be admired for their "constancy and consistency of purpose, as well as for the charm of many of their stories and lessons."[114] McGuffey warned "ominously of the dangers of drunkenness, luxury, self-pride, and deception and proclaimed handsome earthly reward for courage, honesty, and respect for others."[115]

The long-lasting presence of the *Readers* in the nineteenth-century common schools made ministers happy, because the *Readers* reinforced the Protestant Christian climate of "children in tax-supported schools under the guidance of teachers of sound moral character, who daily led their charges in Bible-reading, prayers, and hymns common to all Protestant creeds."[116] The *Readers* had what has been described as a "special genius" for the American context in the way that they presented American heroes as "exemplars of industriousness, honesty, and intelligence" and were assigned the stature of "Biblical heroes." George Washington, for instance, was compared to Moses. The events of "American history were portrayed as developments in a holy design, Columbus having been guided by the hand of Providence and the Revolution having been brought to a successful conclusion by the intervention of God."[117] The school, fortified with moral agents like the *Readers,* was to be an "incubator of virtue," along with the Church.[118]

The *Readers'* contributions to moral education have been said to be found in the "complete integration of Christian and middle class ideals; and in that respect the McGuffey *Readers* are the great textbook of American middle class culture." They impenetrated "social and moral ideals as to defy distinction" as to whether they were "Christian or secular."[119] Their "moral and ethical influences" over millions of Americans, especially in the Midwest, "is beyond computing. . . . has never been equaled by any school text."[120] Westerhoff writes of McGuffey's impact as follows:

> For seventy-five years his [McGuffey's] system and his books guided the minds of four-fifths of the school children of the nation in their taste for literature, in their morality, in their social development, and [was] next to the bible in their religion.[121]

Called "*the* schoolmaster of the nation" by some,[122] McGuffey "probably did more to mold American thinking than any other single influence except the Bible."[123] The *Readers* provide ample evidence to the nineteenth-century belief that the "primary aim of elementary education was moral discipline."[124]

## The Secular School

The Civil War resulted in an expanded role for the federal government in the country. It led to the industrial development of the North, which was accompanied by immigration and urbanization. The War also contributed to a nationalizing trend that included the public schools. The public school was increasingly seen as the agent by which national unity would be gained. Measures were enacted, such as compulsory attendance regulations, which were aimed at attaining this goal. In this context, the secular public school became the vehicle for imparting appropriate moral education.

The Bible retained its place as a prime agent for moral education, yet as the National Teachers Association declared in 1869, the "teaching of partisan or sectarian principles in our public schools is a violation of the fundamental principles of our American system of education."[125] As the nineteenth century progressed, in some areas of the nation the Bible began to be seen as a sectarian book. The flood of immigrants into the country, especially Catholics, alarmed some Protestants, and the "public schools became the cultural factories of Americanization, transforming the raw material of foreign culture into good American citizens."[126]

The all-embracing national fervor included leaders such as President Ulysses S. Grant, who called on his fellow citizens to "Encourage free schools, and resolve that not one dollar appropriated for their support" be given to "any sectarian schools." Leave the matter of "religion to the family altar, the church, and the private school, supported entirely by private contributors," Grant urged, and make it possible for "every child growing up in the land of opportunity of a good common school education, unmixed with sectarian, pagan or atheistic dogmas." And, finally, he intoned, "Keep the church and state forever separate."[127]

Shortly thereafter, a constitutional amendment was proposed by Representative James G. Blaine that would have prohibited any money "raised by school taxation in any State, for the support of public schools, or derived from any fund thereof,...shall be under the control of any religious sect; nor shall any money so raised, or lands so devoted, be divided between religious sects or denominations."[128] The proposed amendment passed the House of Representatives by the lopsided margin of 180 to 7, but fell short of obtaining the two-thirds majority necessary for passage in the Senate where its margin was favorable by a vote of 28 to 16.[129] Blaine's amendment revealed the nation's mood at that time, as is demonstrated by the 1876 Congress when it required that any state henceforth admitted to the Union have a "system of public schools which shall be open to all the children of said State and free from sectarian control."[130]

More and more Americans looked to the allegedly nonsectarian common school as the lead institution in inculcating moral behavior in the young as the nineteenth century advanced.[131] One noteworthy description of the secular common school's patriotic mission was delivered by the Reverend David H. Greer, an Episcopalian clergyman who would become Bishop of New York:

> My point just now is this: that the public schools of this country being the creations of the state, which is itself secular, must be of a secular character, and that this secular character must not be tampered with or encroached upon by any religious body, Catholic or Protestant, on any ground or pretext whatsoever. They are for all creeds and for no creed, for Catholic, Protestant and agnostic. They are for all nationalities, native-born and foreign,... and their impartial, secular, and comprehensive character...is the only one which can be in this country consistently and safely maintained.[132]

The moral mission of this school, a manifestation of the separation between church and state, that had been decreed by the "Will of Providence" for the advancement of the human race was put forth that same year by William Torrey Harris, who had served as superintendent of schools in St. Louis and later as United States commissioner of education.[133] Harris's moral program for the public schools centered on the virtues of punctuality, regularity, perseverance, earnestness, justice, truthfulness, and industry.[134]

The opinion that the secularization of the public schools fulfills the goal of the founders of the American nation, who wished to separate religion from politics, became more popular. Religion became the province of home and church; morality the terrain of the public schools in this view. The public schools by themselves, without the help of church or Bible, were completely capable of teaching morals sufficient to produce good citizens.[135] Indeed, as an agent of the state that has the right of custody over the child, the public schools were adequately equipped to teach the morals of good citizenship, which is all that was required.[136] Conflicts erupted over the right of the state to compel attendance under the guise of "good citizenship" in several states, most notably Illinois and Wisconsin, conflicts that were laced with ethnic and religious tensions.[137]

The elevated, almost sacred place the secular common school held as the nineteenth century neared its end was widely supported. One of those devotees was Rasmus B. Anderson, a professor of Scandinavian languages at the University of Wisconsin, who put it this way: "Whoever directly or indirectly opposes the American common school is an enemy of education, of liberty, of progress. Opposition to the American common school is treason to our country."[138]

Ruth Miller Elson has documented the manner in which American textbooks of the nineteenth century reflected the moral tone of the common school. "The certainty of progress, the perfection of the United States," she wrote, was not to be questioned or denied. The schoolbooks were "bent on persuading the child that his nation is superior to all others." The child was "expected to develop a fervent faith that the American example will inevitably and gloriously save Europe from its present state of corruption and decline." The books witnessed that "Whatever is good in ideas, behavior, and institutions" was identified with the "United States and its citizens."[139]

The secular common school of the latter part of the nineteenth century taught the sovereignty of God, was morally elevating, and was a form of a common religion that would unite all Americans and fully develop the character of all the youth so they could carry out their duties of citizenship, which were of the highest priority. It was the vehicle to express the will of the people, was the sole way in which the civil state educated to promote the common good, and was, more than any other institution, capable of transforming the young of the nation into morally good, responsible citizens. "The secularization of education," which this common school represented, was, as Ellwood P. Cubberley put it, "an unavoidable incident connected with the coming to self-consciousness and self-government of a great people."[140]

## Citizenship Education at the Turn of the Century

Moral education, under the guise of citizenship education, intensified as the nation moved into the twentieth century, being heavily influenced by immigration. More than 18 million immigrants entered the country between 1891 and 1920, with approximately 11.5 million hailing from southern and eastern Europe,[141] who were regarded as "undesirable" by American nativists.[142]

Schools, elementary and secondary, were exhorted to accept leadership roles in the moral training of the children of these immigrants. For example, Ellwood P. Cubberley, a leading public school advocate of the era, wrote in 1909 that schools needed to address the "evils and shortcomings of democracy that immigration had brought to America, especially in the form of corrupt city government." The public schools were to counteract those problems by instilling "fundamental moral and economic principles" in the "masses." They were to teach a knowledge of values and how to "utilize leisure time."[143] One speaker at the National Education Association (NEA) in 1916 declared that a "revolution" was needed in moral training in the public schools; teachers were admonished to "establish moral and social standards for our time," and they were told they "must help to influence public opinion as to the necessity for positive moral education."[144] "Our work," another speaker stated, was to "make men and women, and character-building is the fundamental, the all-important part of this work."[145] No longer formally religious, yet the school's "curriculum, daily life and goal could be called religious." The public school became the primary institution of American democracy as Robert Michaelsen has observed, and the "cradle and bulwark of its liberties." It became a "prime article of American faith to 'believe in' the public school."[146]

The increasing importance assigned to the moral role of the public school at this time was due in part to what the Cardinal Principles Report would later assert was the declining influence of the home and church in the field.[147] This new role for the schools was described as "one of the splendid new tasks which the school of the twentieth century is to undertake and achieve."[148] In 1907, the NEA created a Committee on Moral Instruction in the schools that regularly affirmed the importance of its topic until it was replaced by the Committee on Training for Citizenship.[149]

The "Syllabus on Ethics" adopted by the New York City public schools constitutes one illustration of the schools' activity in moral education. The document emphasized the centrality of "moral education" in the work of the schools to be accomplished, "not only in formal instruction and training" but also in the "general atmosphere and spirit of the class room and of the school." Relying on the personality of the teacher, it involved such factors as the cultivation of a "sense of reverence" that was "vital to morality" and the development of a feeling of "social membership," and attitude of "loyal membership" in the family, community, and nation.[150]

The NEA's committee on teaching morals in the public schools issued a tentative report in 1911 that described the nineteenth century as the "marvel of the ages" in technological development. Out of this era there emanated "new moral problems of great importance" that required a course of study for use in the public schools. It alleged that to have "strong and beautiful characters in adult life, certain elemental virtues must be inculcated in children and youth." It spelled out a lengthy list of virtues that formed the "very basis of character."[151] Pupils, the committee averred, "should not only have some idea of the meaning of these virtues but they should be trained in the practice of them until they become fixed habits." To that end the committee presented a tentative course, lest moral training "be left to chance," and neglected, which, it claimed, happens "frequently." The school should be organized so that students have opportunities for "moral training daily."[152]

The Cardinal Principles Report of the NEA was a major utterance on educational policy. Issued in 1918, following five years of work, the report set forth seven objectives for which the secondary school curriculum should strive, goals that were determined by contemporary society's needs. "Ethical character" was the seventh and last aim. The committee maintained it was "paramount" among the objectives of secondary schools in a democracy.[153] The ways in which ethical character could be developed included "wise selection of content and methods of instruction" throughout the curriculum, the "social contacts" pupils had with each other and with their teachers, the "opportunities afforded by the organization and administration of the school" in order that students might develop a "sense of personal responsibility and initiative," and most of all, the "spirit of service and the principles of true democracy which should permeate the entire school." "Special consideration" should be given to the "moral values" to be obtained, which included the possibility of a distinct course in "moral instruction."[154]

"Citizenship" was another crucial goal of the Cardinal Principles. The "assignment of projects and problems" to students for "cooperative solution" was cited as a means to develop "attitudes and habits important in a democracy" in order that all students develop a "sense of collective responsibility." The "democratic organization and administration of the school itself" was described as "indispensable" in achieving the goal of citizenship. All subjects were to contribute to the aim of citizenship, but the "social studies—geography, history, civics, and economics" were to have this goal as their dominant aim.[155] The report concluded with the committee's affirmation that it was the "firm belief" of its members that "secondary education in the United States must aim at nothing less than complete and worthy living for all youth."[156]

The "decisive formula" regarding schooling in the early decades of the twentieth century was that the "common school brings common experience which precipitates a common faith which is essential to the common welfare." The public school, elementary and secondary, was deemed the indispensable agency for developing good citizenship in American democratic society, interpreted as moral or ethical behavior. The "common faith" was indeed a "nativistically conceived and religiously buttressed nationalism"[157]; it was the foundation of moral education in the early twentieth century.

## John Dewey

John Dewey was without a doubt the most eminent philosopher of American education in the first half of the twentieth century. As such, his work on the role of the schools in implanting moral values in the nation's youth in schools merits attention, however brief.[158]

Born on October 20, 1859, in Burlington, Vermont, Dewey attended public schools there before enrolling in the University of Vermont in 1875. Influenced by his philosophy teacher H.A.P. Torrey at the University of Vermont, he chose to pursue his doctorate in philosophy at Johns Hopkins University. While at Johns Hopkins he was influenced by George Morris, a German-trained Hegelian philosopher, and G. Stanley Hall, one of the most prominent American experimental psychologists at the time. Following the reception of his doctorate Dewey accepted a position at the University of Michigan, where he stayed for ten years. In 1894, he left Michigan to teach at the University of Chicago, and he directed an Experimental Laboratory School at the University. Dewey left Chicago in 1904 subsequent to accepting a position at Columbia University, where he became involved with work at Teachers College there.[159]

Dewey's work in moral education reaffirms his belief that as moral thinkers we are not simply passive spectators of the world; rather, we are involved participants. His ethical theory recognized that students learn through a variety of educational environments, and that their unique perspectives contribute immensely to the classroom environment. He taught that our moral judgments are constantly changing in the light of our experiences. Education, for Dewey, was a social, communal, interactive, and reciprocal activity.

Critical and reflective thinking were indispensable tenets of Dewey's view of moral education. It was in this way that the students become active citizens who will participate fully in the democratic process as adults. This kind of citizenry will ensure that democracy will remain alive and viable as a working form of government in an ever-changing society. Addressing the balance needed between the individual and society, Dewey looked to moral education to bring about harmony between community citizenship and individual rights. He was the leading thinker of the progressive education movement in twentieth century American education.

## The Educational Policies Commission

The National Education Association (NEA) and the Department of Superintendence accepted the offer of $250,000 made by the General Education Board in 1935 to develop long-range policies for education, and the Educational Policies Commission (EPC) was born.[160] The EPC held its first meeting in June 1936 and declared its purpose to be seeking "agreed-upon bodies of common sense on the social role of the schools."[161] The EPC's life was to span the Depression, World War II, the Cold War, and the early years of the War on Poverty before its demise in 1968. It witnessed the rise of movements such as the Civilian Conservation Corps, the National Youth Administration, wartime curricular reforms, the Life Adjustment movement following World War II, the National Defense Education Act of 1958, and the Elementary and Secondary Education Act of 1965. Meant to be "representative of the full scope of public education in this country,"[162] it was also seen as an "amplification and interpretation of the seven aims" of the Cardinal Principles *Report* of 1918.[163] Throughout its history the EPC held steadfast to the notion that American democracy relied on moral and spiritual values, and that the public school was the leading agent in their inculcation in the young.

Composed of members primarily from the NEA, the American Association of School Administrators, and the Department of Superintendence, it also included prominent citizens over the years, such as James Bryant Conant and Dwight D. Eisenhower. It communicated its positions on moral and spiritual values in a series of publications, especially in its first two decades. Two of these merit special mention here. The first of these, published in 1951, was titled *Moral and Spiritual Values in the Public Schools*. The public schools were the apt vehicle to teach these values, the Commission declared, and if the nation were to "maintain a separate system of religious schools, the common public school system,...with its indispensable contribution to unity and common loyalties, would disappear from the American scene." The public schools were the place where American youth will imbibe "brotherhood, democracy, and equality."[164] The public schools would teach religion, a brand derived from the "moral and spiritual values which are shared by members of all religious beliefs." Education that was "uninspired by moral and spiritual values is directionless," unable to infuse the values of good citizenship "in terms of intelligent loyalty to moral and spiritual values as they apply to political processes and civic issues."[165] The public schools were "indispensable in the total process of developing moral and spiritual values.... Their role is one that no other institution can play as well."[166]

The EPC 1951 document concluded with an exhortation that the public schools needed "partners" in the all-important task of imparting moral and spiritual values. Help was not long in coming. In 1953, the National Congress of Parents and Teachers (PTA) published, in cooperation with the EPC, *Moral and Spiritual Education in Home, School, and Community.* This is the second document that merits special attention. Referring to the 1951 EPC volume in its "Foreword," the PTA noted that it had developed "Action Programs for Better Homes, Better Schools, Better Communities" in 1952, with the first of these being "Emphasize moral and spiritual values to build an America worthy of its heritage of faith in God and of freedom."[167] Local PTA groups were urged to "emphasize moral and spiritual values" through their programs on behalf of the "welfare of children and young people."[168] The nation's world leadership depended not only on production capacity but also "on our firm belief in the worth of the individual, in the concept of institutions as the servants of man, in the brotherhood of man, and in the right of all men to seek spiritual fulfillment."[169] A "system of moral and spiritual values is indispensable in group living," the PTA averred, and nothing can "produce a good and secure society if personal integrity, honesty, and self-discipline is lacking." Our society was in desperate need of adopting moral and spiritual values that "exalt and refine life and bring it into accord with the standards that are approved in our democratic culture."[170]

Under the heading of "Summing Up," the PTA maintained that "perhaps at no time in our history" has the need for a "sturdy morality and a firm spiritual strength...been so great." It fell to the school, in union with the home and community, to see that children do not "grow up morally and spiritually illiterate."[171]

The EPC met its demise in 1968, the victim of the desire to have ad hoc policy committees, instead of a standing committee, on the part of national educational organizations.[172] Throughout its lifetime the EPC had emphasized the crucial importance of democratic moral and spiritual values in the mission of the nation's public schools. Most likely no better description of its work in that arena could be had than to quote from its 1951 document: "There must be no question whatever as to the willingness of the school to subordinate all other considerations to those which concern moral and spiritual standards."[173]

## Moral Development

Lawrence Kohlberg is justifiably associated with the moral development movement that took center stage in the 1970s. Born in Bronxville, New York, in 1927, Kohlberg enrolled in the University of Chicago and did his undergraduate and graduate work there, where he began his work on moral development theory.[174] Following a six-year teaching stint at Chicago from 1962 to 1968, Kohlberg taught at Harvard until his death on April 15, 1987.

Kohlberg's cognitive moral development approach was based on Piaget's stage theory of moral development in children. It was hierarchically integrated, in which the child moves from one stage to the next without loss of insight gained at prior stages.[175] Kohlberg was interested in assessing the level of moral reasoning skills exhibited by his subjects. Using the moral dilemma approach, he classified the various responses to the moral dilemmas into stages.

Piaget had held that changes in moral reasoning skills coincide with the age that a child begins to enter the general state of formal operations. Building upon that, Kohlberg developed his theory of moral development that initially involved six stages of moral skills orientation, which he attributed to three distinct levels of cognitive development.[176] The Preconventional Level was the first level of moral development, which was characterized by concern for the consequences of actions. In the first of two stages of Level I, children were inclined to act based primarily on their perceptions of degrees of punishment or other negative consequences. Moral reasoning was based in the main on deference to authority.

In the second stage of the Preconventional Level, children showed an egocentric preoccupation with meeting their own needs. The children reason from the preconventional perspective of consequences and benefits. According to Kohlberg, children are responding as individuals, not as members of society at this stage. They see moral answers for the most part in terms of what persons in positions of authority say they are to do.[177]

The Conventional Level, the second level of moral development, reflects a child's growing concern for approval from others, and a heightened interest in maintaining social order. In the first stage of this level (stage three overall), children begin to identify as "good girl" or "good boy," based on their perceptions of meeting the expectations of others with whom they identify.[178] At this stage, children believe that humans should meet some set of moral criteria that match the expectations of society by behaving in "good" ways. Children define good behavior as having good motives and interpersonal feelings such as love, trust, and concern for others. The responses in this stage are "conventional" because they have the expectation that their judgments would be shared by the community.

The need to please and seek approval eventually yielded to Kohlberg's fourth stage, in which the child becomes increasingly motivated to act from a sense of duty and respect for social conventions. Actions are now oriented more toward the child's perception of "doing the right thing" even if it leads to conflict with the popular choice of the group.[179] Moral reasoning now embodies an adherence to the maintenance of the social order and respect for authority. In stage four subjects are able to explain their understanding of laws as being necessary for society as a whole.

Kohlberg's final level of moral development is the Postconventional Level. In this third and last level of development, regard for the rules of social order is initially defined in terms of a legalistic or contractual orientation. Children in stage five do not generally approve of breaking laws because laws are "social contracts" that we must honor or change through the democratic process. Thus, in stage five, the standards of right and wrong behavior are reflected primarily through legal and institutionalized rules that have prior interest in protecting and supporting the social structure. At this stage life is deemed of more value than property.[180] Children begin to reflect on the essential elements of a good society, and they make moral judgments based on their conception of a good society. Kohlberg held that in this situation the moral agent is evaluating a response "outside" his or her own community, while still showing concern for society "as a whole."[181]

This preoccupation with conformity to the law will yield to standards of right action in stage six. These standards are increasingly more indicative of autonomous judgments guided by internal processes of rational thought and personal reflection. In this stage everyone deserves full and equal respect. One's individual principles of moral conscience would presumably yield judgments based on the principle of universality. Kohlberg believed that the highest order of moral reasoning is the stage at which one chooses to act in a way that reflects a universal principle of action. Kohlberg attributed the ability to act morally at this highest stage of development to the internalization of universal ideals, such as respect for others as persons with intrinsic worth.

## Values Clarification

The publication in 1972 of *Values Clarification: A Handbook of Practical Strategies for Teachers and Students* by Sidney Simon, Leland Howe, and Howard Kirschenbaum announced a new player in moral education, values clarification, to the educational world.[182] Immensely popular at the outset, especially with teachers, values clarification presented the position that teachers should encourage students to make fully autonomous ethical decisions based on personal choice and analysis of particular situations that presented themselves as moral dilemmas.

Values clarification in programs of moral education may be seen as any process an individual chooses that will aid him or her to better articulate and clarify the values that he or she believes are important. This methodology depends heavily on the assumptions of humanistic psychology, especially the view that valuation involves a process of self-actualization, and the potential to act freely upon one's choices.[183] The values clarification approach attempted to help students use emotional awareness to reflect upon personally held beliefs and to clarify such beliefs by employing their own personal values systems. Objective morality seemed to be a relic of the prescience stages of human development.

The values clarification approach to moral education emphasized the role of teachers as facilitators of discussion. As such, teachers were not to suggest their own personal values, nor suggest shared social values as moral options for their students.[184] Instead, teachers were to help students clarify their own personal values by following a seven step valuing process. The seven steps were:

1. Prizing and Cherishing
2. Publicly Affirming
3. Choosing from Alternatives
4. Choosing after Consideration of Consequences
5. Choosing Freely
6. Acting
7. Acting with a Pattern, Consistency, and Repetition[185]

Students were encouraged to reflect on the significance of values in their own lives, and then assess and prioritize such values based on the utilitarian benefit they have attached to that significance. Consequently, a value does not become valuable until it is chosen by an individual based on his or her assessment of the usefulness of the value. Values have no intrinsic worth, therefore, in and of themselves.

The initial popularity of the values clarification approach in teaching moral education was its strong appeal to neutrality and the nonjudgmental analysis of hypothetical moral dilemmas. This approach appealed to those who viewed "traditional" moral education as dogmatic and insensitive to the expression of different moral values in our pluralistic and individualistic society. As such, values clarification was accused of espousing ethical relativism.

Another objection to the values clarification theory rests on a critical consideration of the consequences of complete value neutrality. By promoting the acceptance of all values as equally appropriate, the method yields the rather bizarre consequence of requiring the acceptance of practices that we would otherwise find to be morally reprehensible, such as slavery, ethnic cleansing, and apartheid. The concept of value neutrality leads to a contradictory conclusion, namely, that we ought not be equally tolerant of *all* values, and that some values are more desirable than others. To remain consistent with the values clarification theory, though, a teacher is not supposed to criticize any moral practice or express belief in a valid discernment between right and wrong moral action. Was Stalin as good as Martin Luther King Jr.? The values clarification method would seem to suggest there is no legitimate answer to that question.

In recent years, the values clarification method has been strongly criticized for its relativistic moral position. In the past decade it has been replaced by an interest in *character education,* a movement that presumably reflects core values shared by citizens in a democratic pluralistic society.

## Character Education

The decades of the 1980s and 1990s witnessed a resurgence of interest in "core virtues" and character education programs that would support them. The American public displayed a strong and growing support for character education programs in the public schools. For instance, over 90 percent of respondents in a 1994 Gallup Poll approved the teaching of core moral values in the public schools.[186] As concerns about crime, juvenile gangs, and drug and alcohol abuse problems increased, interest grew in finding character education programs for schools to combat those social cancers.

One of the leaders of the character education movement was, and remains, Thomas Lickona, a developmental psychologist. He suggested that the crisis in the nation's youth culture was due to factors such as a decline of the family and disturbing trends in mass media programs. In *Educating for Character* (1991), Lickona called for the fostering of core values, "the fourth and fifth R's," respect and responsibility. Schools, he held, should inaugurate programs to develop character by making use of all aspects of a student's school experience. Schools must teach good moral conduct if they wish it to be learned by students.[187] Recently, in 2004, Lickona suggested that schools must play a pivotal role in developing character education programs that offer healthy alternatives to media images that promote behaviors such as drinking, fighting, and sexual promiscuity.[188]

What are the core values that Lickona and his colleagues advocate? He maintained that they are those that promote human rights and affirm human dignity.[189] Thus, a core value would be one that we would want all humans to hold; it must be universally applicable for everyone in the world. Seen in this light, core values justify our civic responsibilities in a democracy and are recognized by rational persons in other cultures as well. Lickona differentiated between moral values such as honesty and responsibility, and nonmoral values such as one's preference for vanilla over strawberry ice cream. Moral values are those that are obligatory to act upon even if we would prefer to avoid doing so. In contrast, nonmoral values carry no such obligation because they simply express personal tastes and interests.[190]

A number of programs of character education have been available for school adoption. One of these is the Center for the 4th and 5th Rs that is fashioned after Lickona's model for the promotion of respect and responsibility as core values.[191] Another, Character Counts!, was also modeled after Lickona's and in 2004 was the largest character education program in the country.[192] This coalition has the most comprehensive program for K–12 education, and in 2004 was used at over 2,000 schools and youth groups across the nation. Founded in 1993 with 27 organizations involved, in 2004 it reported more than 450 such groups. Members learn about the "Six Pillars of Character"—trustworthiness, respect, responsibility, fairness, caring, and citizenship. Congress has designated the third week in October as National Character Counts! Week, in order to focus the nation's attention on the importance of teaching, enforcing, advocating, and modeling good character.[193] The last model to be discussed is the Character Education Partnership (CEP), which is a nonpartisan coalition of organizations and individuals who are committed to developing moral character and civic virtue. Their mission statement declares this commitment as "one means of creating a more compassionate and responsible society."[194] The CEP defines character education as "the long-term process of helping young people develop good character, that is, knowing, caring about, and acting on core ethical values such as fairness, honesty, compassion, responsibility, and respect for self and others."[195]

The character education movement promotes the teaching of core values that can be taught directly through course curricula, especially in literature, social studies, and social science classes. Service learning, which provides students with an opportunity to act on values they have incorporated, is often a component of character education programs.[196]

## Conclusion

Each of the programs or movements described above is a manifestation of the overriding moral purpose of elementary and secondary education in this country. Each has had its adherents; each has also been embraced by controversy as opponents to each movement have arisen, some of whom have been as zealous in their opposition as adherents have been in their advocacy. Given the nature of our society, and what is expected of its schools, especially when it comes to matters of behavior, it will ever be thus.

## Notes

1. Michael B. Katz, "The Origin of Public Education: A Reassessment," *History of Education Quarterly* 16 (Winter 1976): 403.

2. Thomas Lickona, *Character Matters* (New York: Simon and Schuster, 2004), cover.

3. Character Education Partnership, "Exploring Pathways to Civic Character" (Washington, D.C.: Author, 2004).

4. George H. Gallup, "Sixth Annual Gallup Poll of Public Attitudes Toward Education," *Phi Delta Kappan* 56 (September 1974): 21; Gallup, "Sixteenth Annual Gallup Poll of the Public's Attitudes Toward the Public Schools," *Phi Delta Kappan* 66 (September 1984): 36.

5. Stanley M. Elam and Lowell C. Rose, "The 27th Annual Phi Delta Kappa/Gallup Poll of the Public's Attitudes Toward the Public Schools," *Phi Delta Kappan* 77 (September 1995): 41.

6. Lowell C. Rose and Alec M. Gallup, "The 34th Annual Phi Delta Kappa/Gallup Poll of the Public's Attitudes Toward the Public Schools," *Phi Delta Kappan* 84 (September 2002): 43.

7. See the annual Gallup Polls in the September issues of *Phi Delta Kappan* from 1986 to 1996.

8. Marcus Wilson Jernegan, *Laboring and Dependent Classes in Colonial America, 1607–1773* (New York: Frederick Unger Publishing Co., 1931), 64–65.

9. Quoted in Robert H. Bremmer, ed., *Children and Youth in America: A Documentary History, I, 1620–1865* (Cambridge, MA: Harvard University Press, 1970), 17.

10. Quoted in Ibid., 18–19.

11. Lawrence A. Cremin, *American Education: The Colonial Experience 1607–1783* (New York: Harper and Row, 1970), 15–16.

12. Edmund S. Morgan, *The Puritan Family* (New York: Harper and Row, 1966), 6–7, 11, 88.

13. Ibid., 89–92.

14. Warren A. Nord, *Religion & American Education: Rethinking a National Dilemma* (Chapel Hill, NC: The University of North Carolina Press, 1995), 64.

15. "Massachusetts School Law of 1648," in *Education in the United States: A Documentary History, I,* ed. Sol Cohen (New York: Random House, 1974), 394–95.

16. Ibid., 398.

17. Ibid., 399.

18. Ibid.

19. Gerald L. Gutek, *Education in the United States: An Historical Perspective* (Englewood Cliffs, NJ: Prentice-Hall, 1986), 10.

20. Daniel J. Boorstin, *The Americans: The Colonial Experience* (New York: Vintage Books, 1958), 300.

21. Paul Leicester Ford, ed., *The New England Primer* (New York: Teachers College Press, 1962), 19.

22. Ibid., 30b.

23. Clifton Johnson, *Old-Time Schools and School-Books* (New York: The Macmillan Co., 1904), 69–70, 99.

24. Gutek, *Education in the United States,* 6–9.

25. Morgan, *The Puritan Family,* 95.

26. Gordon C. Lee, "Introduction," in *Crusade Against Ignorance: Thomas Jefferson on Education,* ed. Gordon C. Lee (New York: Teachers College Press, 1961), 10–11.

27. David B. Tyack, *Turning Points in American Educational History* (Waltham, MS: Blaisdell Publishing Company, 1967), 90.

28. Carl F. Kaestle, *Pillars of the Republic: Common Schools and American Society, 1780–1860* (New York: Hill and Wang, 1982), 6.

29. Lee, "Introduction," in *Crusade Against Ignorance,* ed. Lee, 18.

30. Thomas Jefferson, "To Peter Carr, with Enclosure," in *Crusade Against Ignorance,* ed. Lee, 145–146.

31. Wayne J. Urban and Jennings L. Wagoner Jr., *American Education: A History,* 2nd ed. (New York: McGraw-Hill, 2000), 72.

32. Thomas Jefferson, "Report of the Commissioners Appointed to Fix the Site of the University of Virginia," in *Crusade Against Ignorance,* ed. Lee, 119.

33. Thomas Jefferson, "Notes on the State of Virginia," in *Crusade Against Ignorance,* ed. Lee, 95.

34. Lawrence A. Cremin, *American Education: The National Experience, 1783–1876* (New York: Harper and Row, 1980), 118.

35. Benjamin Rush, "Plan for the Establishment of Public Schools" (1786), in *Essays on Education in the Early Republic,* ed. Frederick Rudolph (Cambridge, MA: Harvard University Press, 1965), 11.

36. Ibid., 13.

37. Joel Spring, *The American School 1642–1985* (New York: Longman Inc., 1986), 35.

38. Henry Steele Commager, "Schoolmaster to America," in *Noah Webster's American Spelling Book,* ed. Henry Steele Commager (New York: Teachers College Press, 1958), 1–2.

39. Noah Webster, *The American Spelling Book, Containing The Rudiments of the English Language for The Use of Schools in the United States* (Middletown, CT: William H. Niles, 1831), 55–58.

40. Ibid., 169–79.

41. Noah Webster, "On the Education of Youth in America," in *Essays on Education in the Early Republic,* ed. Rudolph, 45.

42. Ibid., 59.

43. Ibid., 67.

44. "Constitutional Provisions for Schools in Vermont" (1777), in *Education in the United States,* ed. Cohen, 2, 794.

45. "The Northwest Ordinance and Education," in *Education in the United States,* ed. Cohen, 809.

46. "An Act to Provide for the Instruction of Youth, and for the Promotion of Good Education," in *Education in the United States,* ed. Cohen, 794–96.

47. Rush Welter, *Popular Education and Democratic Thought in America* (New York: Columbia University Press, 1962), 25.

48. James W. Fraser, ed., *The School in the United States: A Documentary History* (New York: McGraw-Hill, 2001), 18.

49. Cremin, *American Education: The National Experience,* 103.

50. Kaestle, *Pillars of the Republic,* 45.

51. Joel Spring, *The American School, 1642–1996* (New York: McGraw-Hill, 1997), 62.

52. Kaestle, *Pillars of the Republic,* 46.

53. William Oland Bourne, *History of the Public School Society of the City of New York* (New York: Arno Press and *The New York Times,* 1971), 3.

54. "To the Representatives of the People of the State of New York, in Senate and Assembly, convened: The Memorial of the Subscribers, Citizens of New York," in Bourne, *History of the Public School Society of the City of New York,* 3.

55. Ibid.

56. "Address of the Trustees of the Society for Establishing a Free School in the City of New York for the Education of such Poor Children as do not Belong to, or are not Provided for, by any Religious Society," in Bourne, *History of the Public School Society of the City of New York,* 6–7.

57. Carl Kaestle, "Introduction," in *Joseph Lancaster and the Monitorial School Movement: A Documentary History,* ed. Carl Kaestle (New York: Teachers College Press, 1973), 8–9.

58. Diane Ravitch, *The Great School Wars: New York City, 1805–1972* (New York: Basic Books, 1974), 14–16.

59. Joseph Lancaster, "Improvements in Education as it Reflects the Industrious Classes of the Community," in *Joseph Lancaster and the Monitorial School Movement,* ed. Kaestle, 80–81.

60. Ravitch, *The Great School Wars,* 18.

61. Kaestle, "Introduction," in *Joseph Lancaster and the Monitorial School Movement,* ed. Kaestle, 34.

62. Bourne, *History of the Public School Society,* 26–27.

63. Kaestle, "Introduction," in *Joseph Lancaster and the Monitorial School Movement,* ed. Kaestle, 34.

64. Ravitch, *The Great School Wars,* 19.

65. Michael B. Katz, *Class, Bureaucracy & Schools: The Illusion of Educational Change in America* (New York: Praeger Books, 1971), 10.

66. Kaestle, "Introduction," in *Joseph Lancaster and the Monitorial School Movement,* ed. Kaestle, 17.

67. Kaestle, *Pillars of the Republic,* 165–166.

68. Spring, *The American School, 1642–1996,* 66.

69. Lancaster, "Some Improvements in Education as it Respects the Industrious Classes of Community," in *Joseph Lancaster and the Monitorial School Movement,* ed. Kaestle, 63.

70. Katz, *Class, Bureaucracy and the Schools,* 11–12.

71. Ellwood P. Cubberley, *Public Education in the United States* (Boston: Houghton-Mifflin, 1919), 93–94.

72. Kaestle, "Introduction," in *Joseph Lancaster and the Monitorial School Movement,* ed. Kaestle, 44–45.

73. Spring, *The American School 1642–1996,* 100–101.

74. Cremin, *American Education: The National Experience 1783–1876,* 138–139.

75. Mann, in *Horace Mann on the Crisis in Education,* ed. Louis Filler (Yellow Springs, OH: The Antioch Press, 1965), 15.

76. Lawrence A. Cremin, "Horace Mann's Legacy," in *The Republic and the School. Horace Mann on the Education of Free Men,* ed. Lawrence A. Cremin (New York: Teachers College Press, 1959), 8–12.

77. Ibid., 13–14.

78. Horace Mann, *First Annual Report Covering the Year 1837* (Boston: Dutton and Wentworth, State Printers, 1838), 55.

79. Ibid., 62.

80. Horace Mann, "Means and Objects of Common School Citation" (1837), in *Lectures on Education,* ed. Horace Mann (Boston: Ide and Dutton, 1855), 58.

81. Horace Mann, "Special Preparation: A Prerequisite to Teaching" (1838), in *Lectures on Education,* ed. Mann, 113.

82. Neil G. McCluskey, *Public Schools and Moral Education* (Westport, CT: Greenwood Publishers, 1958), 41.

83. Horace Mann, "The Perspective of the *Common School Journal*" (1838), in *Education in the United States,* ed. Cohen, 2, 1080.

84. Horace Mann, *Fourth Annual Report Covering the Year 1840* (Boston: Dutton and Wentworth, State Printers, 1841), 57–59.

85. Horace Mann, *Fifth Annual Report Covering the Year 1841* (Boston: Dutton and Wentworth, State Printers, 1842), 40.

86. Horace Mann, "An Historical View of Education: Showing Its Dignity and Its Degradation" (1841), in *Lectures on Education,* ed. Mann, 263.

87. Cremin, ed., *The Republic and the School,* 57.

88. McCluskey, *Public Schools and Moral Education,* 43.

89. Ibid., 60–61.

90. Ibid., 77–78.

91. Horace Mann, *Eleventh Annual Report Covering the Year 1847* (Boston: Dutton and Wentworth, State Printers, 1848), 39.

92. Ibid., 87.

93. Ibid., 101–2.

94. Ibid., 134–35.

95. Horace Mann, *Twelfth Annual Report Covering the Year 1848* (Boston: Wentworth and Dutton, State Printers, 1849), 84.

96. Cremin, ed., *The Republic and the School,* 80, 91–92.

97. Ibid., 100.

98. Ibid., 102–6.

99. Urban and Wagoner, *American Education: A History,* 100.

100. Robert S. Michaelsen, *Piety in the Public School* (New York: Macmillan, 1970), 76–79.

101. R. Freeman Butts, *A History of Education in American Culture* (New York: Holt, Rinehart and Wisnton, 1953), 172.

102. William Kailer Dunn, *What Happened to Religious Education?* (Baltimore: The Johns Hopkins University Press, 1958), 222–24.

103. Ray Allen Billington, *The Protestant Crusade 1800–1860: The Origins of American Nativism* (New York: Macmillan, 1938), 145.

104. Ibid., 147.

105. Welter, *Popular and Democratic Thought in America,* 106.

106. Henry Durand, in *What Happened to Religious Education?* ed. Dunn, 276–77.

107. Lyman C. Draper, "Moral and Religious Instruction in Public Schools," in the *Sixth Annual Report on the Condition and Improvement of the Common Schools and Educational Interests of the State of Wisconsin for the Year 1858* (Madison, WI: Atwood and Rublee, 1858), 242–43.

108. Michaelsen, *Piety in the Public School,* 32.

109. John R. Bennett, *Opinion in the case of Weiss, et al., vs. the School Board of Edgerton* (Edgerton, WI: W. F. W. Coon, 1889), 69–77.

110. Edward A. Krug, *Salient Dates in American Education, 1635–1964* (New York: Harper and Row, 1966), 58–59.

111. John H. Westerhoff, *McGuffey and His Readers* (Nashville, TN: Abingdon, 1978), 19.

112. Benjamin Franklin Crawford, *The Life of William Holmes McGuffey* (Delaware, OH: Carnegie Church Press, 1974), 86.

113. Richard D. Mosier, *Making the American Mind: Social and Moral Ideas in the McGuffey Readers* (New York: King's Crown Press, 1947), 123, 151.

114. Ibid., 152.

115. Westerhoff, *McGuffey and His Readers,* 25.

116. Frederick M. Binder, *The Age of the Common School, 1830–1865* (New York: John Wiley and Sons, 1974), 71.

117. Cremin, *American Education: The National Experience, 1783–1876,* 73.

118. David Tyack and Elisabeth Hansot, *Managers of Virtue: Public School Leadership in America, 1820–1980* (New York: Basic Books, 1982), 21.

119. Mosier, *Making the American Mind,* 123–24.

120. Hugh S. Fullerton, "Preface," in *Old Favorites from the McGuffey Readers,* ed. Harvey C. Minnich (New York: American Book Company, 1936), v–vi.

121. Westerhoff, *McGuffey and His Readers,* 15–17.

122. Ibid., 13.

123. Henry F. and Katherine Pringle, "He Scared the Devil out of Grandpa," *The Saturday Evening Post* 227, 30 (January 22, 1955): 30.

124. Donna Lee Younker, "The Moral Philosophy of William Holmes McGuffey," *The Educational Forum* XXVI, 1 (November 1963): 71.

125. Nord, *Religion & American Education: Rethinking a National Dilemma,* 72.

126. Ibid., 75.

127. "The President's Speech in Des Moines," *The Catholic World* 22, 130 (January 1876): 17.

128. Alvin W. Johnson, *The Legal Status of Church-State Relationships in the United States* (Minneapolis: The University of Minnesota Press, 1934), 21.

129. Ibid.

130. R. Freeman Butts, *The American Tradition in Religion and Education* (Boston: The Beacon Press, 1950), 44.

131. William B. Kennedy, *The Shaping of Protestant Education* (New York: Association Press, 1966), 27.

132. Anson Phelps Stokes, *Church and State in the United States, II* (New York: Harper Brothers, 1950), 687.

133. William Torrey Harris, "Religious Instruction in the Public Schools," *The Andover Review* XI (June 1889): 582.

134. Selwyn K. Troen, *Shaping the St. Louis System, 1838–1920* (Columbia: University of Missouri Press, 1975), 48.

135. William Elliot Griffin, "The Public Schools and Religion," *The Andover Review* XI (April 1889): 365–66.

136. J.R. Kendrick, "Romanizing the Public Schools," *Forum* VIII (September 1889): 74.

137. Thomas C. Hunt and Norlene M. Kunkel, "Catholic Schools: The Nation's Largest Alternative System," in *Religious Schooling in America,* ed. James C. Carper and Thomas C. Hunt (Birmingham, AL: Religious Education Press, 1984), 48.

138. Michaelsen, *Piety in the Public School,* 119.

139. Ruth Miller Elson, *Guardians of Tradition: American Schoolbooks of the Nineteenth Century* (Lincoln: University of Nebraska Press, 1964), 339–42.

140. Cubberley, *Public Education in the United States,* 173.

141. R. Freeman Butts and Lawrence A. Cremin, *A History of Education in American Cculture* (New York: Holt, Rinehart and Winston, 1953), 308.

142. See, for instance, Cubberley, *Public Education in the United States,* 338.

143. Michaelsen, *Piety in the Public School,* 137.

144. Sara Helena Fahey, "Moral Education: What the Schools Can Do," in *National Education Association Journal of Addresses and Proceedings 1916* (Ann Arbor, MI: The Association, 1916), 638–39.

145. Alice M. Carmari, "Manners and Morals—Our Problems," in *National Education Association Journal of Addresses and Proceedings 1916,* 1011.

146. Michaelsen, *Piety in the Public School,* 136.

147. National Education Association, *Cardinal Principles of Secondary Education* (Washington, D.C.: Government Printing Office, 1918), 7–8.

148. Michaelsen, *Piety in the Public School,* 139.

149. Ibid.

150. Ibid., 137–39.

151. National Council of Education, "Tentative Report of the Committee on a System of Teaching Morals in the Public Schools," *Journal of Proceedings and Addresses of the National Education Association of the United States* (Winona, MN: The Association, 1911), 343–45.

152. Ibid., 345.

153. National Education Association, *Cardinal Principles of Secondary Education* (Washington, D.C.: Government Printing Office, 1918), 9.

154. Ibid., 9–10.

155. Ibid., 8.

156. Ibid., 21.

157. Michaelsen, *Piety, in the Public School,* 156, 159.

158. Dewey was a prolific writer. The authors thank Professor Jim Garrison of Virginia Tech, an internationally respected Dewey scholar, for his suggestions for reading Dewey on this topic. J. Dewey, *A Common Faith* (New Haven and London: Yale University Press, 1934); J. Dewey, *Democracy and Education* (New York: The Free Press, 1915); J. Dewey, *Experience and Education,* in *John Dewey: The Later Works,* ed. Jo Ann Boydston (Carbondale: Southern Illinois University Press, 1939/1988), Vol. 13, 1–62; J. Dewey, *Freedom and Culture,* in *John Dewey: The Later Works,* ed. Jo Ann Boydston (Carbondale: Southern Illinois University Press, 1939/1988), Vol. 13, 63–188; J. Dewey, *Human Nature and Conduct* (New York: Modern Library, 1922/1957); J. Dewey, *Theory of Valuation.* in *John Dewey: The Later Works,* ed. Jo Ann Boydston (Carbondale: Southern Illinois University Press, 1939/1988), Vol. 13, 191–251.

159. For biographical information on Dewey's life consult John J. McDermott, ed., *The Columbia Encyclopedia,* 6th ed. (New York: Columbia University Press, 2001).

160. Paul J. Ortenzio, "The Problem of Purpose in American Education: The Rise and Fall of the Educational Policies Commission" (unpublished doctoral dissertation, Rutgers University, 1977), 5.

161. Edward A. Krug, *The Shaping of the American High School 1920–1941* (Madison: The University of Wisconsin Press, 1972), 252, 249.

162. National Education Association, *A National Organization for Education: Educational Policies Commission* (Washington, D.C.: National Education Association, 1937), 3.

163. Krug, *The Shaping of the American High School 1920–1941,* 253.

164. Educational Policies Commission, *Moral and Spiritual Values in the Public Schools* (Washington, D.C.: National Education Association, 1951), 5.

165. Ibid., 5–7.

166. Ibid., 100.

167. National Congress of Parents and Teachers, in Cooperation with the Educational Policies Commission, *Moral and Spiritual Education in Home, School, and Community* (Chicago: National Congress of Parents and Teachers, 1953), iii.

168. Ibid., 1.

169. Ibid., 2.

170. Ibid., 5.

171. Ibid., 26.

172. Ortenzio, "The Problem of Purpose," 316.

173. Educational Policies Commission, *Moral and Spiritual Values in the Public Schools,* 54.

174. William C. Crain, *Theories of Development* (New York: Prentice-Hall, 1985), 118–36.

175. Marvin W. Berkowitz and J.C. Gibbs, "Measuring the Developmental Features of Moral Discussion," *Merrill Palmer Quarterly* 29 (1983): 399–410.

176. Later in his career Kohlberg dropped the sixth stage of development.

177. Lawrence Kohlberg and Rochelle Mayer, "Development as the Aim of Education," *Harvard Educational Review* 42 (1972): 449–96; Lawrence Kohlberg, "Moral Stages and Moralization: The Cognitive-Development Approach," in *Moral Development and Behavior: Theory Research and Social Issues,* ed. Thomas Lickona (New York: Holt, Rinehart and Winston, 1979), 31–53.

178. J.C. Gibbs, "Toward an Integration of Kohlberg's and Hoffman's Theories of Morality," in *Handbook of Moral Behavior and Development, I: Theory,* ed. William M. Kurtines and Jacob L. Gewirtz (Hillsdale, NJ: L. Erlbaum, 1985), 197–218.

179. Martin L. Hoffman, "Empathy, Social Cognition, and Moral Action," in *Handbook of Moral Behavior and Development, I: Theory,* ed. Kurtines and Gewirtz, 275–301.

180. Lawrence Kohlberg, "Moral Stages and Moralization: The Cognitive Developmental Approach," in *Moral Development and Behavior: Theory, Research and Social Issues,* ed. Lickona, 31–43.

181. Lawrence Kohlberg and D. Candee, "The Relation of Moral Judgment to Moral Action," in *Morality, Moral Behavior, and Moral Development,* ed. William M. Kurtines and Jacob L. Gewirtz (New York: John Wiley, 1984).

182. Sidney Simon, Leland Howe, and Howard Kirschenbaum, *Values Clarification: A Handbook of Practical Strategies for Teachers and Students* (New York: Hart, 1972).

183. Humanistic psychology was strongly influenced by the theories of Gordon Allport in the 1950s, and by those of Abraham Maslow and Carl Rogers in the 1960s and 1970s.

184. Simon, Howe, and Kirschenbaum, *Values Clarification.*

185. Ibid.

186. Stanley M. Elam, Lowell C. Rose, and Alec M. Gallup, "The 26th Annual Phi Delta Kappa/Gallup Poll of the Public's Attitudes Toward the Public Schools," *Phi Delta Kappan* 76, 1 (September 1995): 41–64.

187. Thomas Lickona, *Educating for Character* (New York: Bantam Books, 1991).

188. Thomas Lickona, *Character Matters: How to Help Our Children Develop Good Judgment, Integrity, and Other Essential Virtues* (New York: Touchstone, Simon and Schuster, 2004).

189. Thomas Lickona, "The Return of Character Education," *Educational Leadership* 51, 3 (1993): 6–11.

190. Lickona, *Educating for Character.*

191. See the New Mexico Media Literacy Project at http://www.nmmlp.org

192. Information on this program is available at Character Counts Coalition, 400 Admiral Way, Suite 1001, Marina del Rey, CA, 90202-6610, at http://www.charactercounts.org

193. For information on National Character Counts Week, see http://www.charactercounts.org/aspen.htm

194. For information regarding CEP, consult the Character Education Partnership, 918 16th St., NW, Suite 501, Washington, D.C., or see http://www.character.org

195. Ibid.

196. See Learn and Serve America, National Schools of Character, 202/296-7743, ext. 12, or email geninfo@character.org

# A

## Accelerated Christian Education

Accelerated Christian Education (ACE) is a K–12 interdisciplinary curriculum, rooted in biblical teachings, and used widely in private, Christian schools and home schooling efforts. Founded in Texas by Donald and Esther Howard in 1970, ACE originally grew out of dissatisfaction with public school education, especially the perceived lack of moral education. ACE developed into an educational products company, producing instructional materials for thousands of Christian schools.

The ACE curriculum is highly structured and prescriptive. It is based on series Packets of Accelerated Christian Education, known as PACEs. Each subject area has 12 PACEs per grade level. PACEs are available in the major subject areas, including Math, English, Science, Social Studies, and Word Building (spelling and word usage). Parent or teacher manuals are not published for the elementary grades as all the required material is in the PACEs.

A PACE is approximately equivalent to two weeks of schoolwork. Students set goals for themselves, deciding how much work they will do in each subject every day. The process is highly self-directed. As students work through the PACEs, they do a series of reviews, and at the end take a preparatory test. They then take a PACE test. The passing score for a PACE test is 80 percent. If a passing score is not achieved, then the student must retake the test until he or she attains one.

The ACE educational philosophy is based on what are called the Five Basic Laws of Learning: (1) A child must be at a level where he can perform; (2) He must have reasonable goals; (3) His learning must be controlled, and he must be motivated; (4) His learning must be measurable; (5) His learning must be rewarded. The noninclusive language is standard in ACE materials. Based on these five laws, the ACE curriculum assures parents of a mastery-based, back-to-basics education for their child, a course of study individualized to meet specific learning needs, a program incorporating Scripture, godly character building, and wisdom principles, and a curriculum using advanced computer technology to help ensure the finest education possible in today's high-tech climate.

ACE curriculum materials are widespread and popular in Christian circles. ACE also boasts academic success among its graduates, with competitive standardized test scores, and admission to colleges and universities of choice. However, the content and focus of the curriculum have come under scrutiny and have been the object of criticism from its inception.

Educational researchers have found some aspects of the ACE approach troubling, even incorrect (Fleming & Hunt, 1987). Patriotism, bordering on nationalism, is a common theme. Some schools used desk-mounted American flags that students could raise when they had completed a particular lesson. Patriotic songs are often coupled with Bible readings. The foundations of government are related to Christian values, beginning with the Ten Commandments as a source of justice. Governments, through their laws, are understood to carry out the justice demanded by God's laws.

Because of the reliance on what ACE calls the plenary, verbal inspiration of the Bible, Scriptural passages like the stories of creation in the Book of Genesis are taken at face value and interpreted as literally true and without need of further examination. Much emphasis is given to memorization and recitation of the Bible, given its priority in the curriculum. Such a literal use of Scripture is problematic across a variety of subject areas. Once the assumption is granted that every word contained in the Bible is literally true, application of that truth to instruction in science, history, religion, and moral education narrows the content of the instruction considerably. While ACE proponents acknowledge that theirs is a uniquely Christian approach to education, many of the subject area claims qualify more as faith assertions than fact.

ACE continues to enjoy support in evangelical Christian churches and among those Christian denominations that share the conviction regarding the literal truth of the Bible. Home schooling parents from these denominations also make use of ACE curriculum. National and international conventions are held regularly to organize and support parents, teachers, and students. However, given the strict, literal interpretation of Scripture animating all of the coursework, the curriculum and educational approaches espoused by ACE remain of little appeal to mainstream educational leaders, even those in the private sector.

**Further Reading:** Fleming, D.B., & Hunt, T.C. (1987). The world as seen by students in Accelerated Christian Schools. *Phi Delta Kappan, 68*(7), 518–23. Keesee, T., & Sidwell, M. (1991). *United States history for Christian schools* (2nd ed.). Greenville, SC: Bob Jones University Press. Paterson, F.R.A. (2000). Building a conservative base: Teaching history and civics in voucher-supported schools. *Phi Delta Kappan, 82*(2), 150–55. Peshkin, A. (1986). *God's choice: The total world of a fundamentalist Christian school.* Chicago: University of Chicago Press.

*Ronald J. Nuzzi*

## Addams, Jane

Jane Addams was born in 1860 in Cedarville, Illinois. Devoted to her philanthropist father, she suffered from severe depression and debilitating physical illness after his death just one year after her graduation from Rockford Female Seminary in 1881. After her recovery, Addams traveled to Europe with friends in 1888, where she first visited Toynbee Hall, a settlement house for the poor in the east end of London. Toynbee Hall, named after British social reformer Arnold Toynbee, was associated with both Oxford and Cambridge Universities. Students from both universities were invited to work at Toynbee Hall during their summer holidays. Addams's experience at Toynbee Hall had a profound influence on her later decision to open a settlement house to serve the needs of poor immigrants in the slums of Chicago in 1889. She rented the abandoned mansion of Chicago businessman Charles Hull, from Helen Culver, for the sum of $60 a month. Hull House was located in an area of Chicago where most residents were immigrants who had recently arrived from Germany and Italy. Addams, along with her friend Ellen Starr, worked on behalf of the thousands of poor immigrants who flooded Chicago during the late nineteenth century. Jane Addams was a strong advocate for social justice and labor reforms, especially with respect to the promotion of laws that governed working conditions for women and children.

Addams believed that her education and social status should be put to good use in promotion of meaningful social justice issues. The career choices open to women in the late nineteenth century were severely restricted, but Addams was able to make her mark by establishing the Hull House settlement house and various programs for the poor. She was especially interested in establishing programs that would educate women beyond the narrow bounds of ordinary domestic work. At Hull House, the realm of domestic work was writ large throughout the community. Hull House became a beacon of hope as well as a real home for hundreds of immigrants. For example, during several months in 1893, Hull House served more than 2,000 meals each day for those who had been hardest hit by an economic depression.

Addams viewed moral education as something that must involve direct social action in addition to theoretical studies. This view was also echoed by the pragmatist philosophers who valued experiential learning as an appropriate pedagogical tool in schools. Her tireless efforts at Hull House were supported by John Dewey and James Tufts, two progressive educators at the University of Chicago during the early twentieth century. As a strong proponent of direct social action, Addams was involved as co-founder for two of the most influential reform organizations of the twentieth century: the National Association for the Advancement of Colored People (NAACP), and the American Civil Liberties Union (ACLU). Additionally, she worked for the women's suffrage movement, and became first vice president of the National American Women Suffrage Association in 1911. She also traveled around the United States to campaign for Theodore Roosevelt and the Progressive Party in 1912.

Today, Jane Addams is especially admired by feminists who point to her groundbreaking work at Hull House in furthering the cause of women-centered institutions. Unlike the traditional patriarchal home, Hull House was governed primarily by women. Furthermore, women at Hull House were given opportunities to gain experience in public life that were not previously open to women. The female residents of Hull House were instrumental in creating day care centers, kindergartens, and health clinics. Florence Kelly and Alice Hamilton were two Hull House residents who pioneered social science research through their studies of the exploitation of children in factories and their documentation of the unsafe housing tenements for the urban poor in the Chicago slums.

Politically, Addams aligned herself with the progressives, particularly regarding the progressive view that scientific knowledge should be used to guide social reform for the greater good of society. During her life Addams wrote several books including *Democracy and Social Ethics* (1902), *Newer Ideals of Peace* (1907), *Spirit of Youth* (1909), *Twenty Years at Hull House* (1910), *A New Conscience and an Ancient Evil* (1912), *Peace and Bread in Time of War* (1922), and *The Second Twenty Years at Hull House* (1930). She was also a frequent contributing author in a variety of magazines including *American Magazine, McClures, Crisis,* and *Ladies' Home Journal.* Jane Addams was the first American woman to be awarded the Nobel Peace Prize, which she received in 1931 for her pacifist efforts on behalf of the Women's International League for Peace and Freedom. She remained president of the Women's International League for Peace and Freedom until her death on May 21, 1935, in Chicago, Illinois.

*Further Reading:* Addams, J. (1960). *Twenty years at Hull-House.* New York: Macmillan. Fischer, M. (2004). *On Addams.* New York: Wadsworth Philosophers Series. McCree Bryan, M. L. (1994). Laura Jane Addams. In M.S. Seller (Ed.), *Women Educators in the United States 1820–1993.* Westport, CT: Greenwood Press. Reynolds, M.D. (1991). *Women champions of human rights.* London: McFarland & Company. Rippa, A. (1997). *Education in a free society: An American history.* New York: Longman.

*Monalisa M. Mullins*

## Adolescent Development

Adolescence comes from the Latin word "adolescere," which means "to grow up"; consequently, adolescent development is characterized as the series of transitions occurring between childhood and adulthood. As such, most scholars who study adolescence (e.g., psychologists, sociologists, anthropologists, educators, and health professionals) agree that adolescent development, as the transition out of childhood, begins with the biological changes of puberty. Likewise, as the transition into adulthood, adolescent development ends with the culturally defined indicators of being an adult. Note that, whereas the beginning of adolescence, albeit highly variable, is fairly universal, the end of adolescence is very culturally specific. Indeed, in many nonindustrialized cultures, children become defined as adults during the pubertal process itself, thereby leaving adolescent development to be very short in duration. In contrast, the period of adolescence in most industrialized cultures has become longer and longer as the transitions into adulthood are tied to later occurring events such as the completion of education.

In 1980, the late John P. Hill (1936–1988) developed the Framework for the Study of Adolescent Development. In this model, Hill conceptualized adolescent development as a series of three fundamental changes, imbedded within four evolving contexts, leading to seven psychosocial outcomes. In addition to the major biological changes associated with puberty and the social redefinition of roles associated with becoming an adult, the third fundamental transition of adolescence involves cognitive changes: adolescents develop abstract thought and decision-making skills; they learn to take the perspective of others; and they understand issues of morality and ethics. These biological, cognitive, and social transitions are universal, occurring in all adolescents in all cultures. The variability in adolescents' experiences of these changes, however, creates diversity and individuality in the outcomes of the adolescent period.

The pubertal, cognitive, and social role changes are imbedded within the contextual structures in which adolescents live. These contexts include family, a highly diverse context with powerful influences on the development of values and attitudes; peers, whose increased group structure provides new avenues for adolescent exploration; the school setting, within which societal guidelines are imposed and achievements are manifested; and the work setting, although not experienced by all adolescents, which provides increased interaction with the adult world. Each of these contexts plays a critically important role in the adolescent developmental process, but it is the broader context, defined by society and culture, that most dramatically influences the way in which adolescence is experienced.

While navigating the complexities of this transitional phase, adolescents develop seven important psychosocial outcomes. First, adolescents develop autonomy, establishing themselves as independent and self-reliant individuals. And contrary to the myths of former storm and stress views of adolescence, autonomy develops without the excessive conflict and rebellion once thought necessary to become independent. Indeed, current views contend that adolescents maintain strong emotional ties to their parents during the individuation process, reflecting a transformation in attachment rather than an emotional detachment espoused by earlier views. Upon completing the autonomy process, adolescents become competent decision makers and self-governing adults.

In addition to the transformations in attachment and autonomy, adolescents gain the capacity for intimacy within their peer group, thereby developing friendships that go beyond activities and interests. These relationships include abstract notions of loyalty, trust, self-disclosure, and honesty. Similarly, dating becomes important as adolescents develop the capacity for intimate and loving relationships. Also, within the peer group, most adolescents have their first experiences with sexuality. And despite the struggle among biologically based sexual desires, cognitive dilemmas about morally appropriate behaviors, and often-confusing social expectations regarding sexual activity, most adolescents manage to integrate a healthy sexual identity into their self-understanding.

Adolescents also make measurable gains in achievement, especially in their academic and vocational development. High school provides an enriched context for adolescents to explore their competencies and aspirations. With the help of parents, peers, and teachers, adolescents make great strides in transforming the ritualized process of going to school into a meaningful experience filled with opportunities that enhances one's motivation to look forward. Yet, despite the positive possibilities, some adolescents also struggle with psychosocial problems in development. Within troubled family, peer, and school contexts, adolescents sometimes become tempted by risk-taking, and they engage in problem behaviors like drug and alcohol use, delinquent behavior, and risky sexual activity. Nevertheless, it is uplifting to see that most adolescents overcome these adolescent-limited problems and grow up to be healthy, well-adjusted adults.

Finally, there is the development of what some psychologists might characterize as the ultimate psychosocial outcome of adolescence: identity. Throughout the ongoing series of transformations, adolescents are ultimately seeking their identity, their personal sense of self. It is through the development of autonomy, attachment, intimacy, sexuality, achievement, and psychosocial problems that adolescents come to understand who they are and where they are going. In his Framework for the Study of Adolescent Development, Hill characterized identity as the psychosocial outcome defined by the accumulation of all other transitions of adolescence. It is only through navigating all other changes of the second decade of life that individuals come to fully understand their unique place among others.

Adolescence means "to grow up," but growing up requires a long and complex series of developmental transitions. Although current research has lain to rest many of the myths regarding adolescent storm and stress, the sheer number of transitions within a relatively short amount of time provides for a unique developmental experience. The development of adolescents is fascinating, and it can provide anyone who is interested in this strange and exciting time a lifetime of study.

*Further Reading:* Aries, E. (2001). *Adolescent behavior: Readings and interpretations.* New York: McGraw-Hill/Dushkin. Lerner, R.M., & Steinberg, L. (Eds.). (2004). *Handbook of adolescent psychology* (2nd ed.). New York: Wiley. Steinberg, L. (2005). *Adolescence* (7th ed.). New York: McGraw-Hill.

*Sharon E. Paulson*

## Aesthetics

Aesthetics is a branch of philosophy that is devoted to the study of the arts, beauty, and questions of sublimity and dissonance. Although the ancient Greeks devoted considerable attention to the study of art (which figured predominantly in the works of Plato and Aristotle), aesthetics did not appear as a separate field of philosophical study until the eighteenth century, when it was first introduced by the German philosophers Alexander Gottlieb Baumgarten (1750) and Immanuel Kant (1790). Before Baumgarten's "Aesthetica" and Kant's "Critique of Judgment" explicitly named aesthetics as an independent domain of study, the consideration of aesthetic expression was attached to studies of ethics and religion (Sporre, 2005).

In his "Critique of Judgment," Kant argued that aesthetic evaluations (Is it a beautiful landscape?) must always be considered in the context of a particular phenomenon. In his view, we should not expect to make universal aesthetic judgments about categories of objects, as would be the case in claiming that "all landscapes are beautiful." Instead, the best we can do is to make a claim about this particular object, at this particular time. This criterion of contextualization was an important caveat, according to Kant, if we intend to understand the nature of beauty as sensuous perception rather than an abstract idealized form to ponder. Kant also distinguished between the conceptual categories of beauty, which invoked sensual perceptions of pleasure, and the sublime, which connoted a transcendent quality beyond verbal explanation (Sporre, 2005). Understood in this manner, the sublime reaches into the uppermost regions of Plato's realm of being, taking on a spiritual dimension that cannot be precisely described through language alone.

Aesthetics as a philosophical field of study was met with some indifference during the twentieth century, particularly within the Modern Art Movement that disdained notions of beauty in postwar times. However, there has recently been a revival of interest in aesthetics, as is witnessed by the emergence of aesthetic studies in such varied fields as information technology, industrial design, and gastronomy. Art in the postmodern era is taken to include not only visual arts, music, literature, dance, and architecture, but also photography and film.

These various art forms all have the power to affect our emotions in a variety of ways. Looking at aesthetic judgments in the visual arts revolves around such considerations as the effects of variation in brush strokes, symmetry, repetition, tension, and pattern, to name but a few. For example, an aesthetic evaluation of the visual arts might consider the degree to which a particular painting invokes a three-dimensional representation (an issue that the abstract impressionists pondered). Music, like the visual arts, is also a highly affective art form that causes strong emotional response in the listener. Whether we hate a particular type of music or love it is predominantly an issue of cultural context. Aesthetic judgments in music attend to the issues of harmony, lyricism, resonance, mood, and emotiveness, to name but a few elements.

In the field of literature, authors employ a wide variety of techniques to appeal to our aesthetic values. For example, depending on the type of writing (poetry, short stories, novels, etc.) an author may appeal to the use of fantasy, suspense, humor, hyperbole, and rhythm among many other techniques as effective tools to move the reader to an aesthetic response (Koren, 1994). In literary aesthetics, the study of how we perceive literature at a deep level of "illuminated" understanding refers to the effects of catharsis, kairosis, and kenosis, which primarily relate to how the reader responds psychologically to temporal sequences and feelings of timelessness that is invoked by certain literature.

The field of cognitive psychology has also considered aesthetics through an emerging branch of study called "neuroesthetics." Pioneered by Semir Zeki (1999), neuroesthetics attempts to explain our aesthetics judgments in terms of biological predispositions of the brain to respond to artistic representations of the world. Just as the brain is programmed to respond to the steady stream of sensory input, neuroestheticists argue that the brain can also respond to art as a holistic means of representing essential archetypes of the human experience (Zeki, 1999). Tools such as neuroimaging and genetic analysis are used to research the brain responses of persons during an experience of art in some form, particularly in the domains of art and music.

*Further Reading:* Carroll, N. (1997). *Beyond aesthetics.* London, England: Cambridge University Press. Koren, L. (1994). *Wabi-Sabi: For artists, designers, poets and philosophers.* St. Paul, MN: Consortium Books. Sporre, D.J. (2005). *Perceiving the arts: An introduction to the humanities.* New York: Prentice-Hall. Winterson, J. (1997). *Art objects: Essays on ecstasy and effrontery.* New York: Random House. Zeki, S. (1999). *Inner vision. An exploration of art and the brain.* New York: Oxford University Press.

*Monalisa M. Mullins*

## Affective Domain

In the 1950s, a group of American educational psychologists collaborated in the analysis of academic learning behaviors. The results of this team's research produced what is known as Bloom's taxonomy, named after the team's lead researcher, Benjamin Bloom. This hierarchy of learning behaviors was categorized into three interrelated and dynamic types of learning: the cognitive domain (knowledge), the affective domain (attitude), and the psychomotor domain (skills). The cognitive domain is characterized by a person's intellectual abilities. Cognitive learning behaviors are exhibited by skills such as comprehending and evaluating information, and organizing or classifying ideas. The affective domain primarily addresses a person's emotions toward learning experiences and content knowledge. Affective learning behaviors are demonstrated by the level of interest, attention, awareness, and values associated with various learning experiences. The psychomotor domain refers to learning behaviors characterized by the use of basic muscular and motor skills, coordination, and physical movement.

This taxonomy, divided into the cognitive, affective, and psychomotor domains, lists the skills categories for each domain of learning behaviors hierarchically, moving from the simplest behavior to the most complex. The categories outlined are considered to be guidelines rather than absolute definitions of learning behaviors; however, Bloom's taxonomy is still the most widely used general analysis of learning behaviors, as is David R.

Krathwohl's taxonomy of the affective domain (Krathwohl, 1964). The affective domain includes the manner in which we deal with things emotionally, such as feelings, values, appreciation, enthusiasms, motivations, and attitudes. Learning outcomes for the affective domain are defined in terms of students' attitudes toward particular subject areas, as well as their levels of interest in those academic subjects.

Measuring the accomplishment of learning objectives and learning outcomes is generally more difficult in the affective domain than in the cognitive and psychomotor domains. Krathwohl's taxonomy of the affective domain is based on the principle of internalization, which refers to the process of moving from the simplest and most passive level of awareness about some subject to a complex and active level of awareness that will consistently guide a learner's behavior. Krathwohl (1964) divided the affective domain into five hierarchical levels that reflect this movement from the simplest to the most complex degrees of internalization: (1) Receiving, (2) Responding, (3) Valuing, (4) Organization, and (5) Characterization, as described below.

At the first level of the affective domain, Receiving, the student is passively aware of particular stimuli that exist in the classroom or learning environment. Intended learning outcomes for this level are (minimally) that the student is attentive and focused on the classroom learning activities engaged at a particular time. At the second level, Responding, the student becomes actively engaged with the material and demonstrates a minimal commitment to the ideas or phenomena presented by actively responding to them. Intended learning outcomes for this second level may emphasize participation in classroom discussions and group presentations. Valuing is the third level of the affective domain, and it is characterized by the student's willingness to be associated with particular ideas or learning activities. At this level, the student's value or worth for certain ideas or learning activities is internalized to the extent that the student is motivated beyond required compliance to complete assignments. Intended learning outcomes at this level will demonstrate the student's appreciation of and commitment to particular ideas and learning activities.

At the fourth level of the affective domain, Organization, the student begins to prioritize complex sets of values by organizing and differentiating between them. The intended learning outcomes at this level emphasize the appearance of an internally consistent value system that can synthesize or reconcile disparate complex values. The ability to understand that one's value for freedom must be balanced with the interests of society would be an example of such organization of values at this level of the affective domain. The fifth and final level of the affective domain is Characterization. At this level, the student's value system is consistently internalized such that it may be said to characterize his or her personal lifestyle and behavior choices. Intended learning outcomes at this level involve personal and social emotional adjustments, as demonstrated by pervasive and reliable patterns of behavior.

Educators are cognizant of the importance of the affective domain of learning behaviors; however, there is no general consensus about whether the cognitive or affective domains should be emphasized first in any particular instructional set of learning activities and assignments. Some researchers suggest that the cognitive domain should be the first focus of instruction as a prerequisite for developing positive affective attitudes and predispositions for the subject matter (Barrell, 1995). Others have found that an initial instructional focus on generating interests for a particular topic will better facilitate increased cognitive learning for students (Zimbardo, 1991). For example, many service learning programs are designed to generate students' interest in particular social issues by exposing them in community to practical "real-life" experience, and then presenting the theoretical foundations and statistical data attached to such experience. In any case, educators do generally agree that the most effective instructional designs for the promotion of affective domain learning behaviors will be those that engage students' emotions at all levels of the curricula, as well as providing continuous positive reinforcement for the learner through multiple venues to express targeted attitudes and values.

**Further Reading:** Barrell, J. (1995). *Teaching for thoughtfulness: Classroom strategies to enhance intellectual development.* White Plains, NY: Longman. Bednar, A., & Levie, W.H. (1993). Attitude-change principles. In M. Fleming and W.H. Levie (Eds.), *Instructional message design: Principles from the behavioral and cognitive sciences.* Englewood Cliffs, NJ: Educational Technology Publications. Caine, R., & Caine, G. (1991). *Making connections: Teaching and the human brain.* Alexandria, VA: Association for Supervision and Curriculum Development. Krathwohl, D.R., Bloom, B.S., & Masia, B.B. (1964). *Taxonomy of educational objectives. The classification of educational goals. Handbook II: Affective domain.* New York: David McKay. Zimbardo, P.G., & Leippe, M.R. (1991). *The psychology of attitude change and social influence.* New York: McGraw-Hill.

*Monalisa M. Mullins*

## Affective Education

In 1994 a group of scholars and educators from 12 European countries met at the University of Warwick, United Kingdom, to discuss the affective dimensions of education. It was affirmed that affective education was a prominent goal in these countries and that a significant relationship obtains between affective and intellectual educational objectives.

One outcome of the meeting was the establishment of the European Affective Education Network (EAEN). A second outcome was agreement to use the term "affective education" to describe this affective dimension. Although the term "affective education" is not commonly used in most countries, it was a term understood in all. The EAEN produced a working definition of affective education. The term refers to the significant dimension of the educational process concerned with the feelings, beliefs, attitudes, and emotions of students, their interpersonal relationships, and their social skills. It involves a direct concern for the moral, spiritual, and values development of students, teachers, and parents. The EAEN argued that affective education operates on at least three different levels and has objectives involving different time scales. The different levels are as follows:

- the individual, attention directed to individual students, their self-esteem, emotional literacy, study skills;
- the group, attention to the nature and quality of interactions within groups;
- the institution, a concern for the quality of the climate and ethos of the school itself, its care and concern in relation to students' welfare and mental health.

Work at these different levels may be seen to have both short- and longer-term goals.

This definition provides a fairly clear idea of what should be understood by the term "affective education."

There is earlier work that contributed to the field of affective education. In the 1950s Benjamin Bloom developed a Taxonomy of Educational Objectives that included three domains: cognitive, affective, and psychomotor. The objectives of the affective domain were changes in interest, attitudes, and values, and the development of appreciations and adequate adjustment. Although Bloom did not use the term "affective education," his taxonomy appears to be the first specific identification of a part of education that is decidedly affective. In the 1970s a movement known as Affective Education existed in the United States. J.D. Mayer and Casey Cobb (2000) saw it as stemming from the work of the humanistic psychologists such as Abraham Maslow and Carl Rogers, and as promoting experiential approaches for building students' internal personal skills, improving self-knowledge, and feeling recognition, with a focus on promoting self-esteem and a positive self-image. According to Mayer and Cobb (2000), the affective education movement in the United States has been supplanted by socioemotional learning and character education. It should be noted that both of these would be seen as manifestations of affective education as defined here.

Affective education is of central importance in education, though this is not always recognized. It is important as an approach in itself but also as a dimension of all activities in schools in the curriculum and elsewhere.

Affective education means that the voices of children and young people in our schools should be heard and responded to; they should be involved in identifying their needs, both emotional and academic. They should be encouraged to understand their emotions and those of others as well as how these relate to one another.

There are many strategies for promoting affective education but they all include an experiential aspect. Circle time—classes or smaller groups work in a circle with the teacher acting more as a facilitator than leader—can be very effective when undertaken by sensitive teachers who understand the process. A fairly structured approach can be used with basic ground rules such as only one person speaks while everyone else listens, there are no put-downs of others, and everyone gets a turn but no one has to speak. A safe and unthreatening environment can be created where people share their feeling and problems and each participant gains greater understanding of themselves and of all the others in the group. Role play of various kinds can also be a valuable way of promoting the affective dimension. Both of these approaches can be used effectively in lessons concerned with curricular subjects as well as to engage with moral and values issues.

It is difficult to evaluate the contribution of affective education, though when it is undertaken this should be attempted even if only at the level of the feedback of participants. Of course, it is an aspect of education particularly likely to attract criticism as an unproven waste of time, but it would seem strange to suggest that what has been described above is not important to the development of well-rounded young people and adults.

**Further Reading:** Lang, P., with K. Katz and I. Menezes (Eds.). (1998). *Affective education: A comparative view.* Cassell: London. Mayer, J.D., & Cobb, C.D. (2000). Educational policy on emotional intelligence: Does it make sense? *Educational Psychology Review, 12*(2). Menezes, I., Coimbra, J., & Campos, B. (2005). *The affective dimension of education: European perspectives.* Porto: FCT. Karppinen, S., Katz, Y., & Neill, S. (Eds.). (2005). *Theory and practice in affective education: Essays in honour of Arja Puurula, research report 258.* Helsinki: Department of Applied Sciences of Education, University of Helsinki.

*Peter Lang*

## Agapeism

In *Stride Towards Freedom* (1958), Martin Luther King Jr. describes Agape love, or charity, as a love of one's neighbor in which every person is thought of as a neighbor, even when that person is an enemy. It is love of others for the sake of the other, even when that other does not wish the lover well. It is love based on true well wishing, regardless of what the beloved might deserve according to the world's standards. It is love that is willing to sacrifice, even to the extent of sacrificing one's own life, on behalf of the beloved.

This notion of love had suffered a great deal of scorn before King, in the midst of our most bloody century to date, the twentieth, appropriated and applied it to the cause of civil rights in the American South. With the rise of the Enlightenment, Agape had come to be seen as pure foolishness. For example, Sigmund Freud (1970) strenuously argued that Agape is not in accord with human nature. Love, for Freud, could be understood as Eros, the human being's basic drive for bodily, and ultimately genital, pleasure. Eros, Freud understood, could to some extent be sublimated (channeled) into other activities capable of affirming and sustaining life. In fact, according to Freud, civilization at its very basis is built on the sublimation of Eros into friendship, a bond based on the sharing of a similar aim (e.g., parents' concern for their child), and affection (e.g., the kind of affirmation a parent might feel for his child). Both friendship and affection might then be called "lesser loves." But at higher levels of activity, Eros becomes in the hands of the most talented the force that inspires civilization's greatest fruits, art and science.

In *Civilization and Its Discontents* (1970), Freud traced the crisis of the twentieth century to its failure to understand that Agape had become, and perhaps always was, a dysfunctional coping strategy. Given the violence he had witnessed (during World War I) and anticipated (on the eve of World War II) he felt compelled to postulate a dualistic worldview, contrasting the life seeking of erotic drive with the aggressive, destructive drive of Thanatos. Explicitly referring to the long and brutal history of Christian anti-Semitism and anticipating Hitler, Freud argued that the practice of Agape within communities was possibly only through an equally forceful, although at times subliminal, practice of hateful aggression toward outsiders. In fact, Freud's use of the phrase "the narcissism of minor differences" was meant to refer to the seemingly ongoing practice of hatred between groups practicing Agape love within. Thus, Freud is asking whether human beings as a whole are capable of Agape. Or are they only capable of such love when there exists another group available to hate?

Several other issues arise in this context. The first raises questions about the efficacy of Agape. What good is it? Based on a serious misreading of Darwin, a number of writers had come to claim that Christianity, identified as the religion of Agape, was simply unnatural. True heroes, such as the Homeric warriors, and world shakers, such as Napoleon, affected revolutions of action and thought through a sort of force. But the typical Christian saint is wholly feeble, incapable of affecting the fortunes of the world in any way.

The second has to do with the very morality of Agape. Are my enemies, even those who seek my self-destruction, worthy of my love? Is it morally right to ask Jews to pray for a man such as Hitler, who was striving with all his might to wipe out Judaism from the face of the earth? Freud himself thought that the answer was obvious. What, one might ask, had "turning the other cheek" done for the Jews, especially in relation to the so-called religion of Agape?

Is Agape possible? Is it desirable? Is it useful? In his work, King learned from Gandhi the enormous potential of Agape when organized within a strategy of nonviolent resistance (Fischer, 1954). Gandhi had insisted, in the fight for Indian independence, that his resisters undergo spiritual training with the aim of extinguishing their desire to fight violence with violence. So too did King require that his supporters develop the abilities necessary to practice what he sometimes called "the nonviolent weapon of love." While one can certainly sympathize with Freud's reservations about the possibility of pure Agape, there is also no doubt that Gandhi's rendition of organized Agape has had its victories in the name of truth and justice. It has, moreover, through its use, shown that Agape is not necessarily powerless; it is, in fact, best understood as the true force of love in the search for justice.

But then is not Agape at the very least self-interested? Was it not selfish aims (freedom from the British, freedom from segregation) that fueled the campaigns of Gandhi and King? On the contrary, for both a major assumption of nonviolent resistance is that, in cases of oppression, both the oppressor as well as the oppressed lose their freedom. In the case of King, the segregationist is no less dehumanized by segregation than the segregated.

According to Abraham Joshua Heschel, true love is possible only when we discover, with the prophets, that God is constantly seeking us because he has chosen to be in need of us (Heschel, 1972). Our truest need, on the other hand, is to be needed by him, and it is important to acknowledge that need. As King tried to teach through example, it is in the following of His will, in service of the divine, that we find the highest human vocation. In view of his at least partial success, we might ask whether Agape has failed or whether we have failed Agape?

According to a story told by Heschel, God was warned by the angels not to create man. They cried that he would lie and act deceitfully, irrationally, violently, and that even toward God he would cause pain. This, God finally acknowledged, was the truth. But, nonetheless, God buried truth in the ground and created man out of compassion. Here, according to the story, is the first great act of Agape. Whenever we can slip out of our compulsive need to predict and control, and open our eyes to the sublime present at all times and everywhere, we begin to enact thankfulness for that great and ongoing act. We begin to practice Agape ourselves.

**Further Reading:** Fischer, L. (1954). *Gandhi: His life and message for the world.* Mentor: New York. Freud, S. (1970). *Civilization and its discontents.* Norton: New York. Heschel, A.J. (1972). *A passion for truth.* Woodstock, VT: Jewish Lights Books. King, M.L., Jr. (1958). *Stride towards freedom: The Montgomery story.* Harper and Row: New York.

*Alven Neiman*


## Aggression

The term "aggression" is defined as any behavior intended to harm or injure another human being, physically or psychologically. The criterion for aggression requires the behavior (physical or verbal) to involve harm or injury, be directed toward a living organism, and involve intent. There are many different types of aggression, hostile (physical, reactive), instrumental (proactive), relational, verbal, and social aggression, as well as a variety of theories about why aggression occurs.

Hostile aggression, also known as reactive aggression, indicates that the primary goal of the aggressive behavior is to physically injure or harm another human being. On the other hand, in the case of instrumental aggression (proactive) harming or injuring an individual is not the primary goal, but an indirect outcome of pursuing an aggressive goal (Crick, Werner, Casas, O'Brien, Nelson, Grotpeter, & Markon, 1997). For example, most aggression in sports is considered instrumental, because the primary goal is to win and aggressive acts that injure or harm other athletes occur in the course of pursuing winning. A fight that breaks out in the school yard, however, would be considered hostile aggression because the sole purpose of the behavior is to physically harm another individual.

Social aggression is a very broad form of aggression that includes verbal, nonverbal, and relational aggression. Social aggression is behavior that harms another's psychological (self-esteem) or social (social status) well-being (Crick et al., 1997). Whereas social aggression refers to all social and psychological aggression, relational aggression refers to the intent to damage one's own or another's relationship. Research has shown that relational aggression is more typical of females across the developmental trajectory, while hostile aggression is more typical of males (Crick & Rose, 2000). When relational aggression is included as a type of aggression in research, males and females tend to have similar levels of aggression. Crick and Rose (2000) hypothesize that physical aggression (hostile) decreases with age because it becomes increasingly socially unacceptable the older one gets, while relational aggression increases with age as relationships become more complicated and numerous as individuals age. Also, relational aggression is rarely recognized and, therefore, is socially accepted.

Other forms of social aggression are verbal and nonverbal aggression. Verbal aggression includes threats to another's physical health and verbal insults, while nonverbal aggression includes gestures, facial expressions, or body movements that are perceived as negative and harmful to another's self-esteem (Crick et al., 1997). There are many other forms of aggression within social and physical aggression domains; however, only the major forms are covered within this text.

A number of theories about the origin of aggression exist; four of the most prominent theories are summarized herein: instinct theory, frustration-aggression theory, social learning theory, and revised frustration-aggression theory. Instinct theory (also sometimes called catharsis theory) stems from Freud's psychodynamic approach, which asserts people are born with the instinct to act aggressively. The instinct theory hypothesizes that the need to be aggressive builds up in individuals predisposed to aggression and must eventually be expressed in the form of an aggressive act (e.g., retaliating to an opponent's cheap play) or released "cathartically" in a socially acceptable means (e.g., "blowing off steam," playing an aggressive sport). Overall, instinct theory is not supported by research.

Frustration-aggression (F-A) theory (drive theory) explains aggression as a direct result of frustration that occurs due to a failure or inability to achieve a goal. Frustration-aggression research asserts aggressive acts occur when people are frustrated; however, the F-A theory is critiqued as simplistic, for frustration does not always lead to aggression.

Social learning theory (Albert Bandura) asserts aggression is learned behavior that is developed through observing others who exhibit and model aggressive behaviors, which in turn are positively reinforced. The social learning theory explains that children learn behaviors by watching significant others (e.g., parents, peers, teachers, coaches).

The revised frustration-aggression theory, combines the frustration-aggression theory and the social learning theory. The revised F-A theory explains that, although frustration may not always result in aggression, it increases the likelihood it will occur. Individuals learn when aggression is situationally and socially acceptable; thus, frustration is then channeled into a socially appropriate response, which may include aggressive behavior.

A variety of factors influence the frequency of hostile, instrumental, or relationally aggressive behaviors. Gender differences between hostile aggression and relational aggression were aforementioned. Additional factors that may influence gendered types of aggression include hormones, particularly the male androgen hormones, gender roles or gender stereotypes, exposure to media violence, poor parenting or role models, a predisposed personality characteristic, or troubled families (Berk, 1994).

**Further Reading:** Berk, L.E. (1994). *Child development* (3rd ed.). Boston: Allyn and Bacon. Crick, N.R., & Rose, A.J. (2000). Toward a gender balanced approach to the study of social-emotional development: A look at relational aggression. In K.E. Schlonich & P.H. Miller (Eds.), *Toward a feminist developmental psychology* (153–68). New York: Routledge. Crick, N.R., Werner, N.E., Casas, J.F., O'Brien, K.M., Nelson, D.A., Gropeter, J.K., & Markon, K. (1997). Childhood aggression and gender: A new look at an old problem. *Nebraska Symposium on Motivation, 45.*

*Nicole M. LaVoi and Erin Becker*

### Akrasia

Contemporary discussions of ethics and moral education often use the Greek term *akrasia* (literally, lack of strength) to denote weakness of will or, as it is sometimes translated, "incontinence." It applies to an agent who knows of a better option, but decides not to choose it because he or she feels inclined toward the lesser option. Plausible examples are easy to imagine: consider Claudia, a good student who knows that she ought to study for her exams, but instead chooses to go out to the movies. However, it is much more difficult to explain why such examples are so plausible: how could Claudia make such a choice when she knows better?

This morally nuanced use of the term *akrasia* was introduced by Aristotle while criticizing Plato's equation of wrongdoing with ignorance (*Nicomachean Ethics,* Book VII; see Nussbaum, 1986). Whereas Plato had taught that knowledge of the good logically implies the willingness to do the good, in Aristotle's account knowing the good does not necessarily mean willing to do the good. His explanation of this apparent opposition between intellect and will was that humans are motivated to act not only by reasons, but also by emotions. Aristotle went to great lengths to show that a virtuous life consists in learning to feel in the right way as well as to think correctly. He argued that moral virtue is a disposition of character, developed by the acquisition of certain habits, to have appropriate feelings. Since the crown of a virtuous life is happiness, it follows within the Aristotelian account of moral education that raising a child properly must involve educating the emotions.

As the child grows and encounters different situations, he or she will often need to employ good judgment, and so over the course of time will develop the intellectual and moral virtue of practical wisdom. Since rational deliberation and mastery of the appropriate emotions are marks of human flourishing, the alignment of reason and emotion produces a happy life. However, this alignment does not develop automatically, and typically involves conflict. For instance, deliberation may show an agent that certain actions ought to be taken while at the same time he or she is under the sway of a particular emotion (e.g., pleasure or anger) to act differently. At this point the agent may resist the emotional sway and become "continent" (*enkratês*), or else yield to emotion and become "incontinent" (*akratês*).

As noted above, Aristotle discussed *akrasia* to show that Plato distorted human phenomena, since we do, in fact, frequently act akratically, that is, knowingly and voluntarily, and hence are morally responsible for our actions and liable to praise or blame. For this reason Aristotle went on to discuss why wrongdoers may be motivated to act in a morally inferior way even when they know better. To develop his point, Aristotle described different traits of character that can be set along a continuum, ranging from those characters capable of actions displaying total knowledge and voluntary action to those who act out of ignorance and thus are not liable to blame; the continuum goes from heroic excellence, excellence, strength of will, weakness of will, badness, to beastliness (Aristotle reserved this last term for brutish men who hardly know what they are doing). The akratic person falls in the middle of this continuum, where the agents who fall under the "weakness of will" description act wrongly because (a) they are often misled by pleasure, and (b) because they have carved a character that is easily swayed by pleasure. It is this willful negligence in the formation of character that makes them blameworthy in their actions.

Aristotle's subtle description of the varieties of moral character is extremely enlightening even now, 2,300 years after it was written. For instance, he also distinguished between a thoroughly self-indulgent person (*akolastes*) and the weak-willed akratic person. The former yields as a matter of course to desires for pleasure, such that his or her actions do not aim at a good end; in this way the self-indulgent person shares with the bad person (*kakos*) a misconception of what counts as a good end. But, Aristotle asserted, the akratic person does have good ends and does know how to aim at them. The problem with such persons is that they put themselves into a situation where they will be so affected by pleasure that they set aside their knowledge of what is best. In our opening example of the akratic Claudia, what is important is not that she ignores the fact that she needs to study, but that by agreeing to go to the movies she has put herself in a situation in which she may easily fail to attain the good of doing well in her exams.

It is therefore not the case that Claudia acts out of ignorance or irrationality, but that she acts impulsively, misperceiving the danger of the situation she is entering into or misjudging the relationship between her general principles and the particular case. By placing herself in a particular situation she may forget or be self-deceived about what sort of person she is, and for that reason fail to remember how her actions should be aligned to her ends. Claudia forgets, or deceives herself, about her responsibilities as a student and goes out to enjoy the cinema. The general point that Aristotle wants to make here is not that pleasure is to be avoided, but that akratic persons misplace what is pleasurable about what they do: they quickly and impetuously find pleasure in the wrong activity. Instead of acting, they react, and passion quickly blinds their intellects to their proper intentional ends. Then later they regret their actions.

To expand the example we may contrast the akratic character of Claudia with Sophie, a prudent student who precisely judges the situation, foresees the consequences of placing herself in a situation, weighs appropriately the varieties of pleasures at her disposal, and acts accordingly. At the end of Aristotle's discussion of *akrasia* we see that the English expression "weakness of will" may not be the best translation for what he has in mind. *Akrasia* is not a failure of will, nor a lack of knowledge, nor an excessive love of pleasure (as in the case of the thoroughly self-indulgent person). It is rather a failure of character: our Claudia has created for herself a character that is made up of habits that allow her emotions to blind her reason and to be the primary motivation for both proper and improper actions.

***Further Reading:*** Aristotle. (1999). Book VII. In *The Nicomachean ethics* (Terence Irwin, Trans.). Indianapolis, IN: Hackett Publishing. Mele, A. (1987). *Irrationality: An essay on akrasia, self-deception, self-control*. Oxford: Oxford University Press. Nussbaum, M.C. (1986). The *Protagoras:* A science of practical reasoning. In *The fragility of goodness*. Cambridge: Cambridge University Press. Rorty, A.O. (1980). *Akrasia* and pleasure: *Nichomachean ethics* Book 7. In *Essays on Aristotle's Ethics*. Berkeley: University of California Press. Urmson, J.O. (1988). Strength and weakness of will. In *Aristotle's ethics*. Oxford: Blackwell.

*Marta Sañudo and Thomas Wren*

## Alignment

The concept of alignment, or authenticity, finds its roots in existential philosophy and the writings of theologians. Alignment means that a person's views, expectations, and perceptions, as well as the values by which he proclaims to live, are congruent with how he presents to the world. The old adage "Practice what you preach" communicates this concept succinctly. The antithesis of alignment would be when you see a doctor standing at the side door of a hospital smoking a cigarette after he or she has just lambasted a lung cancer patient for doing the same.

The nature of alignment or authenticity is idiosyncratic in that we define what it means to live authentically for ourselves. Because we all have our own set of values, attributes, and life goals, we have our own criteria for living aligned or authentic lives. Others judge our authenticity by determining the congruence of our words with our actions, and we measure our own authenticity by how we feel about the choices we make. Given the idiosyncratic nature of authenticity, it makes sense that there are often conflicts between the values we internalize from others and the choices that we make.

Existential philosophers, scholars in the behavioral sciences, and theologians have theorized about alignment and related topics such as authentic living, sincerity, honesty, and congruence. Many scholars have debated what it means to live an authentic life; most existentialists would argue that simply going along with what society deems appropriate is not living authentically and that a person should be free to let his spirit guide him without being bound by societal norms, values, or expectations. Some scholars concerned with socially acceptable behavior and ethics would argue that leading authentic lives can pose problems for members of society if the acts of those living authentically lead to the harm of others.

Many philosophers have written essays on the concept of alignment or authenticity. Jean-Paul Sartre uses the term "authenticity" to describe essentially the same concept as alignment. Sartre's definition of authenticity in *Being and Nothingness* (1966) is negative in the sense that one is not aware of the authenticity of one's life until one is no longer being authentic. In other words, one can only recognize the authenticity of one's life when that authenticity is gone.

Georg Wilhelm F. Hegel (1977) criticizes those persons who feel they are living authentically as sellouts or cowards and states that in order for a man to be considered authentic, others must define him that way. Thus, he must be submitting to the social pressures of his historical and social context and conforming to the values and expectations of society at large. Thus, for those who attempt to live authentically, they will likely encounter this paradox: to live authentically means to follow one's personal values, which were likely instilled by others, which in turn means that person is not living an authentic, aligned life after all.

Lionel Trilling discusses sincerity in living as congruence between the values that one avows and what the person actually feels. He discusses sincerity at the societal level, and posits that a society is authentic when the behavior of its members matches the values it upholds. This is societal congruence, or alignment on a macrosystemic level.

Immanuel Kant states that to act for the sake of some virtue is moral, but according to many existentialist thinkers, the act would be unauthentic or unaligned if the person committing the act did so only because that is what virtuous people do, and not because that is what he genuinely believes is right. In other words, he must truly believe in a value and not proclaim to hold that value simply because that is what is expected of him. If he does so and then acts on that value, but does not truly believe in that value, he would not be living an aligned life.

One problem with alignment and authenticity is the degree to which society can allow its members to be autonomous and follow their own guiding spirits. Personal freedom in today's civilized societies is bound by laws meant to protect the common good. These bounds will by definition limit the ability of individuals to lead truly authentic or aligned lives. Philosophers and scholars debate the definition of alignment, the path to alignment, and its implications for the welfare of society.

*Further Reading:* Golomb, J. (1995). *In search of authenticity: Existentialism from Kierkegaard to Camus.* United Kingdom: Routledge Press. Hegel, G.W.F. (1977). *The phenomenology of spirit* (A.V. Miller, Trans.). Oxford: Oxford University Press. Raz, J. (1986). *The morality of freedom.* Oxford: Clarendon. Sartre, J.-P. (1966). *Being and nothingness: An essay on phenomenological ontology* (H. Barnes, Trans.). New York: Citadel. Wolf, S. (1990). *Freedom and reason.* New York: Oxford University Press.

*Michelle E. Flaum*

## American Institute for Character Education

The American Institute for Character Education (AICE) was a nonprofit educational research foundation that developed a K–9 "Character Education Curriculum." It grew out of a charitable foundation, The Children's Fund, established in 1942 by Russell Chilton Hill, in honor of a daughter who had died. Prior to turning its attention to character education, The Children's Fund had provided scholarships to academically talented but economically disadvantaged young people. In 1962, Hill wrote *Freedom's Code,* a book that attempted to describe a nonpartisan, nondenominational code of conduct that would be acceptable for all people in the twentieth century and beyond. The superintendent of the San Antonio Public Schools was impressed by the book, and asked for 2,000 mounted copies of the code. Soon, a collaboration developed that involved the school district, Trinity University, and The Children's Fund to develop a character education curriculum that incorporated the basic elements of *Freedom's Code.*

In 1970, The Children's Fund changed its name to the American Institute for Character Education. In 1974, AICE published a revised version of *Freedom's Code* as a project to celebrate the bicentennial of the *Declaration of Independence.* The revised version of *Freedom's Code* focuses on 15 precepts that summarize more than 80 character traits or principles. The 15 precepts are as follows:

- Be honest
- Be generous
- Be just
- Live honorably
- Be kind
- Be helpful
- Have convictions
- Have courage
- Be tolerant
- Use talents creditably
- Provide security
- Understand citizen obligations
- Fulfill citizen obligations
- Stand for the truth
- Defend freedom

The Character Education Program (or Curriculum) that was produced around the elements of *Freedom's Code* is described by Goble and Brooks (1983). The curriculum included hundreds of lessons, each lasting from 15 to 30 minutes. Topics included self-esteem, self-discipline, decision making, problem solving, attitudes, and character traits such as honesty, persistence, and responsibility. Activities varied across the lessons, with students engaging in role-playing and small groups, as well as artwork, reflective writing, and discussions. Some of these activities were similar to those that had been used in the discredited values clarification approach of the 1960s and early 1970s.

The Character Education Program was widely adopted by schools and districts during the 1970s and 1980s, with AICE claiming that more than 33,000 classrooms were using the curriculum at its peak. AICE received funding from The Children's Fund, the Lilly Endowment, and the U.S. Department of Education. The last of these, in 1985, funded a project in Pasadena, California, administered by the Thomas Jefferson Center for Character Education, which utilized a revised version of AICE's Character Education Program. That project became controversial among social conservatives who were upset that William J. Bennett's education department had funded a program admitting to the eclectic use of approaches such as some (for example, open discussion and role-playing) that had been incorporated in values clarification programs together with a refusal to categorically distinguish right from wrong in all circumstances. AICE adamantly denied that it incorporated elements of values clarification (see Erlandson, 1986), and always attempted to walk a fine line between appealing to the social conservative desire to center moral education on Judeo-Christian values and the public schools' need to avoid promoting particular religious beliefs.

AICE made many strong claims about the program's effectiveness, most based upon anecdotal evidence from teachers and administrators, such as the so-called "Chicago Miracle" of Sylvia Peters's administration at the Dumas School on Chicago's south side. AICE also conducted surveys of the teachers and administrators who used the program, and reported very large percentages of teachers who said that the program improved student behavior (see Hunt, 1990). The effectiveness of AICE's Character Education Program was also evaluated several times by external evaluators. However, Greenberg and Fain (1981) and Keys (1985) concluded that the program had no significant effect on students' behavior or academic achievement, although Greenberg and Fain did find that students enjoyed the curriculum activities.

The assets and materials of AICE were transferred in 1998 to Learning for Life, an entity founded in 1991 and based in Irving, Texas. Learning for Life has incorporated the AICE materials into a comprehensive set of learning materials (teacher's guides, activity books, and awards) for character and career education.

**Further Reading:** Goble, F.G., & Brooks,. B.D. (1983). *The case for character education.* Ottawa, IL: Green Hill Publishers. Greenberg, B., & Fain, S. (1981). An exploratory study of the impact of the character education program within the Dade County public school system. *Conference proceedings.* Austin, TX: Evaluation Network/Evaluation Research Society joint meeting. Hunt, M. (1990). *The compassionate beast: The scientific inquiry into human altruism.* New York: Doubleday. Keys, J.C. (1985). The effects of a character education program in the social studies upon selected self-concept factors of fifth grade students (Doctoral dissertation, Temple University).

*Craig A. Cunningham*


## Aquinas

Thomas Aquinas (1225–1274) was one of several philosophers of the Middle Ages whose thinking was shaped by the thought of Aristotle, even though until the thirteenth century the Aristotelian corpus had been unavailable to the Christian philosophers and theologians of Europe. Arab and Jewish scholars had known of Aristotle's work since the nineteenth century but the documents they had were written in Arabic, not the original Greek and certainly not in the Latin that was the academic language of Europe. All this changed with the translation into Latin of the commentaries of Arab philosophers Avicenna (980–1037) and Averroes (1126–1198), and the Jewish scholar Moses Maimonides (1138–1204), all of whom lived in Spain. One of the first Christian philosophers to take his work seriously was Albert the Great (1206–1280), a German Dominican of extensive learning who was Thomas's teacher in Paris and Cologne; not surprisingly, Albert passed on to his talented pupil his enthusiasm for the newly discovered Aristotelian ideas and their Arab commentators. However, not everyone shared Albert's enthusiasm, and the years of Thomas's greatest productivity were also years of bitter controversy within the Christian intellectual community, which was divided on whether Plato or Aristotle was the true forerunner of Christian philosophy and theology.

Thomas was born into a noble family in the Italian town of Aquino, and at the age of five was placed under the care of the Benedictine monks at the famous abbey of Monte Casino, probably in hopes that some day he would succeed his uncle who had been named abbot there. However, at the age of 17 while studying at Naples he met members of the new religious order of the Dominicans and, to the distress of his family, announced his intention to join them rather than the more established and prestigious Benedictine order. The Dominicans and their friendly rivals, the Franciscans, were a novelty on the clerical scene: they did not live in cloistered monasteries, supported themselves "on the road" by begging, and operated under the direct authority of the Pope rather than the local bishop. Years later, when Thomas was teaching at the University of Paris, he would again have to struggle against those who regarded these "mendicant" orders with distaste. As an adult in Paris he was temporarily forbidden by his bishop to teach; as a 17 year old he was simply kidnapped by his family and held prisoner for two years until he convinced them to let him join the order of his choice. It is an ironic twist of history that after so much opposition from established authorities he would be not only canonized and named "the angelic doctor" but eventually hailed as the official philosopher and theologian of the Catholic Church. Today he is considered one but only one of the major representatives of Catholic thought but, in still another twist of history, he enjoys a new eminence in non-Catholic and even nonreligious circles.

### Works

Thomas's most famous work is his *Summa Theologica,* which as its title indicates is a long, comprehensive, and primarily theological treatise written late in his career. However, mention should be made of an early work *De Ente et Essencia* (*On Being and Essence*), since it goes beyond Aristotle's relatively static metaphysics of form and matter to posit a more dynamic relationship between what a thing is (its essence) and the sheer fact that it is (its existence). Many of Thomas's most important writings are in the form of commentaries on other philosophers, but these are by no means mere derivative studies; the style of the day was to develop one's own thoughts forensically, that is, by imagining what arguments another thinker would muster for and against one's own position. (The usual form of citations, especially to the *Summa,* gives the number of the question under discussion, followed by the article, as in Q.90.4.)

### Philosophy and Theology

Although he was primarily a theologian, Thomas was careful to respect the autonomy of philosophy and the power of natural reason to understand basic truths. He rejected the view of Averroes that there are two completely separate domains of truth, insisting instead that although some truths can be known only by revelation (such as that the world had a temporal beginning or that Christ is divine) there are no incompatibilities between truths that can be known by unaided reason and revealed truths. This point holds for moral truths as well as metaphysical and cosmological ones: for instance, when God gave Moses the Ten Commandments he was only making it easier for ordinary men and women to understand moral truths that could, in principle, be discovered by nonbelievers and, in fact, usually are.

### Teleology

Thomism is every bit as teleological as Aristotelianism, though Thomas did not resort to biological functionality as regularly as did Aristotle. Instead, he laid greater stress on the power of reason to direct our actions, and saw the relationship between reason and action as one of potentiality to actuality. Like Aristotle he understood the "end of man" in functional terms, which is to say that he did not think of the goal of human life as a static state of affairs such as simple satisfaction or contentment but rather as the active exercise of one's powers or faculties, the principal one being reason itself. In this way humans realize their full potential, a form of self-actualization that not only fits into the natural order of things but also conforms to the will of God.

### Morality and Law

Aquinas took over Aristotle's conception of morality as a web of virtues whose exercise led to happiness and human flourishing. One major difference is his treatment of charity, which unlike Aristotle's friendship was a theological virtue. But the most interesting difference between his and Aristotle's moral theory was Thomas's discussion of law, which he defined in the *Summa* as "an ordinance of reason for the common good, made and promulgated by him who has care of the community" (Q.90.4). Thomas went on to distinguish four kinds of law: eternal, natural, human, and divine, which can be characterized, respectively, as God's law, nature's law, civil law, and biblical law. The first of these locates the source of all law in the mind of God the eternal designer, and so in effect includes the other three. These are known by us not directly (we do not have immediate access to the mind of God) but indirectly, by seeing its traces in the world (i.e., the regulative principles that lie behind the way nature and society operate).

The second type, natural law, includes both the descriptive laws of nature (such as the law of gravity) and the prescriptive natural law (such as the law against murder). The last two types of law are also prescriptive and, like natural law, take their names from kinds of traces that give us the above-mentioned indirect access to God's mind. Thus human law is the corpus of man-made laws that, when properly constructed, reflect God's design for human interaction, and divine law, which since it comes from the Bible is always properly constructed but not always properly interpreted, reflects designs that God has that may not be discernible (or at least not easily discernible) from nature or society alone. It is important to realize that these are not purely formal distinctions without a difference but rather alternative perspectives. For instance, murder is clearly a violation of the natural law against needless killing, and this fact alone is enough to motivate a reasonable person to avoid murder. However, an additional reason is available to one who is not only reasonable but also religiously motivated, since a religious person can see that the natural law mirrors eternal law and, consequently, reveals the will of the Author of nature. From this it follows that the natural law should be obeyed out of respect and love of the Author (God) as well as out of recognition of one's natural (i.e., rational) goals and one's place in the larger scheme of the natural world. Or as Thomas puts it, from this connection between eternal and natural law humans receive their "respective inclinations to their proper acts and ends" (Q.91.2).

*Further Reading:* Copleston, F.C. (1955). *Aquinas.* London: Penguin Books. Finnis, J. (1998). *Aquinas: Moral, political, and legal theory.* Oxford: Oxford University Press. McInerny, R., Ed. (1998). Thomas Aquinas. *Selected writings.* London: Penguin Classics. Stump, E. (2003). *Aquinas.* London: Routledge.

*Thomas Wren*


## Aristotle

Aristotle (384–322 B.C.E.) is universally regarded as one of the greatest names in the Golden Age of Greece (500–300 B.C.E.), even though he himself was born in Macedonia. His father and grandfather were personal physicians of the kings of Macedonia, but his philosophical lineage was stunningly Athenian: one of his own teachers was Plato, who in turn was taught by Socrates. Aristotle left Plato's Academy after 20 years to travel and later returned to found the Peripatetic school of the Lyceum. During the last decade or so of his life, Aristotle taught many philosophers including his successor Theophrastus and Strato of Lampsacus, both of whom developed the scientific elements of Aristotle's teachings. For three years Aristotle tutored another Macedonian, the young Alexander the Great, whose greatness consisted in military conquest of the bloodiest sort rather than any philosophical contributions. His association with Alexander was especially problematic because of the hatred Athenians bore toward him as a result of the Macedonian conquest of Athens and the other Greek city-states. When Athens learned of Alexander's death in 323, Aristotle's political situation became precarious; he left Athens to avoid persecution and "to prevent Athens from sinning twice against philosophy." He died after a year of self-imposed exile on the Island of Euboea.

He is said to have written 150 books or treatises, of which approximately 30 still survive. In many cases their authenticity is unclear, largely because some seem to be lecture notes compiled by his students. What is clear, though, is that Aristotle's writing style is much more technical than Plato's (Aristotle wrote treatises, not dialogues) and much less elegant from a literary perspective.

### The Hylemorphic Model

Perhaps the best way to summarize Aristotle's general philosophical approach is to contrast it with that of Plato. Plato claimed that ultimate reality consisted in eternal Ideas or Forms that were not subject to the vicissitudes of time. Thus the Idea of Beauty was more real than beautiful vases and other lovely objects that one could see and touch. Aristotle, on the other hand, thought that the ultimate reality was material, not ideal—or better, that real things are always composed of a material element that has a determinate shape or form, and that this form has no existence in itself. That is, for Aristotle a thing's form was simply its principle of organization, much like a computer program whose details can be known apart from the hardware it controls but has no separate existence. He applied this hylemorphic model (so called because the Greek words for matter and form are, respectively, *hyle* and *morphe*) to the human person in his work *De Anima* (*On the Soul*), with the very un-Platonic implication that since the soul, like any other form, has no existence apart from the body, there is no life after death.

### Aristotle's Teleology

As is the case with his scientific writings, Aristotle's moral philosophy is based on the idea that all action is directed toward a *telos,* which is the Greek word for end or goal. To appreciate the full force of Aristotle's teleological approach, one has to realize that he believed the lives and actions of nonhuman organisms as well as humans must be understood as goal oriented, the difference being that human organisms can act with an accompanying consciousness of the goal, such that human striving takes the form of desire. Thus an acorn's natural goal is to become an oak tree, and under favorable external conditions we may expect it to reach its goal. When it does not, the problem lies outside the organism itself (as when an acorn falls on a stony surface), in contrast to humans, whose failure to reach their natural goal is usually the result of error, either an intellectual error (i.e., a mistake or an error of the will), that is, disordered desires or weakness of the will.

But just what is the *telos* of human beings? It was to examine this question that Aristotle composed his *Nicomachean Ethics*. Here again his answer stands in sharp contrast to the views of his teacher Plato, especially the claim in Plato's *Republic* that the goal of human life is knowledge of The Good, understood as an ideal and utterly general Form to be apprehended though pure contemplation. Aristotle objected to Plato's approach on the grounds that it is useless as an ethical agenda in real life. "I wonder," he said in Book III of his *Nicomachean Ethics,* "how the weaver would be aided in his craft by a knowledge of the form of the Good, or how a man would be more able to heal the sick or command an army by contemplation of the pure form or idea. It seems to me that the physician does not seek for health in this abstract way but for the health of man—or rather of some particular man, for it is individuals that he has to heal."

### Virtue and the Parts of the Soul

The relationship between Aristotle's psychology and his moral theory is fundamentally teleological, as can be seen by examining the Greek word he uses for virtue, *arête.* This is a general term, usually translated as "excellence," referring to any quality that things and persons are expected to have if they realize their natural potential. Thus an excellent knife would be sharp, and an excellent horse would be strong or fast. Accordingly, since a human being is by nature a rational animal, an excellent person would be someone who lives his or her life "in conformity with reason." In his ethical writings Aristotle usually talks as though living one's life is a single activity, in which case the phrase "in conformity with reason" denotes a life lived in moderation, where the balance between excessive and deficient behavior is learned by example. However, he sometimes analyzes life into the component functions of the soul, each of which has its own excellence or virtue. Thus moral virtue is excellence of the appetitive part of the soul (by which we control our actions and passions). In contrast, intellectual virtue is excellence of the rational part of the soul (by which we know things—which is theoretical knowledge—and, in certain cases, how to change them—which is practical knowledge).

### Political Theory

In the first chapter of his book *Politics* Aristotle declares that "man is a political animal," by which he meant that human rationality is inherently social. What he has in mind here is not only simple interpersonal exchanges but also participation in the structural life of the *polis* or state. Unlike Hobbes and other social contract theorists who regarded the state as purely instrumental to the fulfillment of personal desires and goals, Aristotle believed that civic activity was a necessary part of human flourishing, in the same general sense that also applies to the activities of friendship and philosophical conversation. Citizenship was understood as a set of duties (to serve the state), not a set of rights (to receive individual benefits), and fulfilling these duties was to fulfill one's nature. The corresponding civic virtues include trustworthiness, willingness to participate in governance and other political activities, reciprocity, and respect for the law.

*Further Reading:* Barnes, J. (Ed.). (1984). *The complete works of Aristotle* (2 Vols.). Princeton, NJ: Princeton University Press. Barnes, J. (Ed.). (1995). *The Cambridge companion to Aristotle.* Cambridge: Cambridge University Press. Lear, J. (1998). *Aristotle: The desire to understand.* Cambridge: Cambridge University Press. Veatch, H. (1974). *Aristotle. A contemporary appreciation.* Bloomington, IN: Indiana University Press.

*Thomas Wren*

## Aspen Declaration

In July 1992, the Josephson Institute of Ethics hosted a distinguished group of moral educators and youth leaders at a conference in Aspen, Colorado. This diverse group of educators was gathered together to discuss character education, and to devise program and curricula recommendations that could be used in schools across the country. At the end of the conference, they were able to craft a statement regarding their shared values and goals for the future of character education in American schools. That statement, known as the Aspen Declaration, was unanimously endorsed by all the conference attendees. It included a list of seven tenets that gave voice to the special concerns and common language that would become foundational to the Character Counts! Program of character education, started by the Institute the following year.

The Aspen Declaration included the recommendation that character education curricula should embrace core ethical values that could be shared by all students regardless of the complex nature of their individual identities. These core ethical values were assumed to be essential for good moral character and foundational to a democratic society: trustworthiness, respect, responsibility, fairness, caring, civic virtue, and citizenship. Further, the Aspen Declaration stated that the development of good moral character must be nurtured, first and foremost, by the conscientious efforts of the family, as well as faith communities of all religious traditions, schools (teachers, administrators, and staff), and various other social institutions.

The Aspen Declaration was both retrospective and future-oriented in its claim that the character of our youth is a reflection of the character of our society. Thus, an indictment by social critics about the demise of young people today should also consider the implications of that judgment for the adult stewards of their community. As a result of the articulation of six core values embraced by the signers of the Declaration, the Character Counts! Program of character education further developed these as the "Six Pillars of Character." These included: (1) Trustworthiness, which is also described as synonymous with integrity, moral courage, honesty, truth, sincerity, candor, reliability, promise-keeping, and loyalty. (2) Respect, which is synonymous with valuing all persons, living by the golden rule, honoring the dignity, the privacy, and the freedom of others, being polite, and being tolerant of the differences we see in others. (3) Responsibility, described as being honorable as a person, doing one's duty, being accountable, doing one's best by pursuing excellence, and exercising self-control. (4) Fairness, also described as being just, being impartial and consistent toward others, listening and open to differing viewpoints, and following fair procedures toward others in life situations. (5) Caring, which was further defined as compassionate, kind, considerate, charitable, unselfish, and looking through another person's eyes.

The sixth and final "pillar" of character is Good Citizenship, which was explained by the examples of having respect for the laws and customs of one's country, honoring the flag and all it stands for, doing one's share to help the community, playing by the rules of the society, and honoring authority figures and what they represent. What is important to note is that these core values are intended to be representative of values that we would want others to hold as well; they must be universally applicable for everyone everywhere in order to be truly reversible in an ethical sense. Seen in this light, core values not only justify our civic responsibilities in a democracy, but they would also be recognized by rational persons in other cultures as well.

Supported by a strong public agenda to reintroduce so-called traditional character education into the public schools, the decades of 1980 and 1990 saw a resurgence of interest in "core virtues" and character education programs that would support the same. The 1994 Gallup Poll of the Public's Attitudes toward the Public Schools, conducted by Phi

Delta Kappa, indicated a strong and growing public support for character education programs, and a majority of those polled favored stand-alone courses on habit formation of values and appropriate ethical behavior in the public schools. An even more interesting finding of the 1994 Gallup Poll was that over 90 percent of the respondents approved the teaching of core moral values, and two-thirds of those surveyed also valued instruction about world religions. Given the violent and uncivil cultural milieu of our country during these decades, we should not be surprised by this growing public support for character education programs in our public schools. As concerns about crime, delinquency, drug and alcohol abuse, and juvenile gang violence have grown, so has our interest in finding character education programs that work.

The character education movement promotes the teaching of core values that can be taught directly through various course curricula. Core values are embedded in many academic programs through the formal curriculum, especially in literature, social studies, and social science classes. Most of the character education programs promote a strong emphasis on student accountability and hold students to high levels regarding academic achievement. In most schools that have adopted a character education program, service learning is also a major source for delivery of core values instruction for most middle school and high school students. Service learning provides students with an opportunity not only to incorporate values into their own character framework but also to act on those values in socially responsible and meaningful ways. Schools that actively engage students in community and civic service projects may also use those experiences as the source of discussions in the classroom regarding civic and social responsibility in a democratic society.

**Further Reading:** Elam, S.M., Rose, L.C., & Gallup, A.M. (1994). The 26th annual Phi Delta Kappa/Gallup poll of the public's attitudes toward the public schools. *Phi Delta Kappan, 76*(1). Houston, P.D. (1998). The centrality of character education. *School Administrator, 55*(5). Lickona, T. (2004). *Character matters: How to help our children develop good judgment, integrity, and other essential virtues.* New York: Simon & Schuster. McClellan, E.B. (1992). *Schools and the shaping of character: Moral education in America, 1607–Present.* Bloomington, IN: ERIC Clearinghouse for Social Studies/Social Science Education and the Social Studies Development Center, Indiana University.

*Monalisa M. Mullins*

## Association for Moral Education

The Association for Moral Education (AME) is an international organization that fosters international dialogue and research on theoretical and practical issues in moral education. Members include public and private school teachers and administrators, counselors and psychologists, philosophers, sociologists, researchers, teacher educators, religious educators, and graduate students interested in advancing the study of moral education. The AME holds an annual conference in early November or in the summer if the conference is held Europe. Conferences are hosted by universities in different cities each year and feature prominent scholars in moral education and related fields.

Lisa Kuhmerker founded the AME in 1976 and served as its first president. Her goal was to establish an ongoing dialogue about new developments in moral education. The earliest annual meetings of the AME, which were held on the East Coast, focused on emerging research in moral development and education. Lawrence Kohlberg, Ralph

Mosher, Ted Fenton, Norm Sprinthall, James Rest, and their students and colleagues were regular contributors to the early conferences.

Throughout the 1970s and into the early 1980s, the AME was a loose network of colleagues working within the "moral development" paradigm. The AME's only function was its annual conference. Conference fees were minimal and attendees who traveled were usually lodged in the homes of those organizing the conference at the host university.

In the 1980s, the AME held meetings in the Midwest and on the West Coast of the United States and in Canada and slowly attracted an international membership. Conference fees remained at modest levels, but the Association became larger and its governance more formalized. Although the AME's conferences continued to highlight the developmental research of Kohlberg and Rest, they now included many scholars representing increasingly diverse perspectives. For example, the 1985 conference, "Controversial Issues in Moral Education," organized by Dwight Boyd and held at the Ontario Institute for Studies in Education at Toronto, featured an engaging dialogue around Carol Gilligan's feminist critique of Kohlberg's psychology. The next year, the conference "Moral Development and Character Education: A Dialogue" organized by Larry Nucci and held at the University of Illinois, Chicago, brought proponents of developmental moral education, such as Lawrence Kohlberg, James Rest, and Elliot Turiel, together with leaders of the emerging character education movement, such as Kevin Ryan, Herbert Walberg, and Ed Wynne. They disputed definitions of morality and character, the role of cognition and habit, and what constitutes responsible educational practice.

Faced with a growing diversity of approaches to moral and character education, in the latter part of the 1980s the AME attempted to maintain its historical connection to Kohlberg's theory while no longer identifying itself with any particular point of view. The AME clarified its mission as providing "an educational forum" for interdisciplinary dialogue about responsible educational practice. After Kohlberg's death in 1987, the AME established an annual Kohlberg Memorial Lecture in his honor.

During the late 1980s, the AME formally defined itself as an organization with a membership distinguishable from its conference participants. The AME charged dues, which included an annual subscription to the *Journal of Moral Education*. The AME also established two awards: the Kuhmerker Career Award given in recognition of outstanding contributions to the organization and to the field of moral education and the Dissertation Award given to recognize and commend dissertation scholarship in the area of moral development and education.

In the 1990s, the AME widened its international membership to include scholars from Latin America, Asia, and Eastern Europe. Several of the conferences were devoted to international dialogue. For example, the 1990 conference held at Notre Dame, "Values, Rights, and Responsibilities in the International Community: Moral Education for the New Millennium," included speakers from over 20 countries on six continents.

In 2000, James Conroy organized the first conference held outside of North America in Glasgow, Scotland. Three years later, Adam Neimczynski organized a second conference in Krakow, Poland, and in 2006, Fritz Oser held the conference in Fribourg, Switzerland. The AME is committed to meeting every few years in different countries throughout the world.

The history of the AME over the past three decades reflects the growth of the field of moral education itself, and the AME has played a critical role in advancing the field. The field originally established itself around the research of Lawrence Kohlberg and his colleagues, and the AME helped to extend Kohlberg's influence. The field at present, while never losing sight of Kohlberg's contributions, is no longer characterized by a single paradigm, and AME conferences feature a wide diversity of theories and methods. Thanks to the vision and generosity of Lisa Kuhmerker as well as many of its loyal members, the AME today serves as a hub for a wide network of scholars and research centers throughout the world and offers grants to support the research of new and seasoned scholars in moral education.

**Further Reading:** Kuhmerker, L., Gielen, U., & Hayes, R.L. (1994). *The Kohlberg legacy for the helping professions.* Birmingham, AL: Doxa Books.

*F. Clark Power*

## Association for Values Education and Research

The Association for Values Education and Research (AVER) was an interdisciplinary group of educators and researchers at the University of British Columbia in Vancouver, Canada. Founded in 1970, AVER studied moral education, with a particular focus on the role of reasoning in making decisions (Bruneau, 1977). AVER researchers spent time observing moral discussions in Vancouver elementary schools, developed a bibliography on moral education, conducted preliminary research on implementing a moral education curriculum in prisons, and created a curriculum for high school and college students called the "Values Reasoning Series." Members of the group also designed and delivered teacher training through in-service workshops and undergraduate and graduate courses. All of these activities shared the assumption that it was possible to define the attributes of a morally competent person. Another assumption was that it is possible to construct rational criteria for determining which values are worth holding and which are not (LaBar et al., 1983; see also Arcus, 1980).

AVER is probably best known for developing a list of the attainments necessary for moral competence. These attainments, summarized in Coombs (1980), include a recognition that one's actions must be universalizable before they can be considered morally right and a disposition to seek out all available facts—as well as appropriate advice and counsel—in morally hazardous situations. AVER also developed an approach to moral education known as the "values reasoning approach," which placed rationality and normative reasons at the center.

AVER also developed a set of four tests of whether moral principles are rational. These tests include Role Exchange (Would this action be appropriate if it were you in this circumstance?), New Case (If one or more conditions are changed in the posed problem, would it make a difference in your decision?), "Subsumptions" (Can we take a larger principle and see if all cases can be subsumed under that principle?), and Universal Consequences (What would happen if everyone did this? Would it still be acceptable?).

The Values Reasoning curriculum series consisted of a set of booklets dealing with topical issues such as war, peace, population control, prejudice, the elderly, and prisons. The booklets, published by the Ontario Institute for the Study of Education in the mid-to-late 1970s, focus the students on the kinds of reasoning and reasons that are useful in discussing such issues, including making inferences about the missing premises of arguments (Schwartz, 1992).

AVER continued operating until 1990, when it faded away due to a lack of funding.

*Further Reading:* Arcus, M.E. (1980). Values reasoning: An approach to values education. *Family Relations, 29* (April), 163–71. Bruneau, W.A. (1977, September). The origins and growth of the Association for Values Education and Research (AVER). *Moral Education Forum, 2*(4), 5–8, 16. Coombs, J. (1980). Attainments of the morally educated person. In D. Cochrane and M. Manly-Casimir (Eds.), *Practical dimensions of moral development.* New Jersey: Praeger. LaBar, C., Parkinson, S., Lloyd, A., Coombs, J., & Wright, I. (1983). Practical reasoning in corrections education. *Canadian Journal of Education, 8*(3), 263–73. Swartz, R. (1992). Teaching moral reasoning in the standard curriculum. In A. Garrod (Ed.), *Learning for life: Moral education theory and practice* (pp. 107–30). Westport, CT: Praeger.

*Craig A. Cunningham*

## Attachment Theory

Attachment theory is a theory about the role of earliest relationships on social and emotional development. It was originally developed by John Bowlby and Mary Ainsworth in their effort to understand the failure to thrive of otherwise well cared for infants and children who were separated from their mothers. Bowlby (1969/1982) theorized that during the evolutionary time in which humans were hunters and gatherers children needed close maternal care to survive, and thus through natural selection human infants evolved a tendency to bond with their mothers with the aid of a set of behaviors—e.g., crying, smiling, following—for maintaining proximity to the mother and eliciting care. Further, the quality of the child-mother bond depended on the mother's ability to meet the child's needs and affected not only the child's survival but also overall development. Bowlby labeled the child-mother bond "attachment."

Through two basic mechanisms, working models and secure base, success of children's long-term development is shaped by the nature of their attachment relationship with their primary caregivers, usually their mothers. For example, if the primary caregiver is sensitive to the child's needs, the child not only thrives, but also builds working models of himself or herself as worthy of care, of others as trustworthy, and of relationships as collaborative. Such child-mother relationships are labeled secure. If, on the other hand, the primary caregiver is insufficiently sensitive to the child's needs—perhaps neglectful, unreliable, manipulative, overcontrolling, or even frightening—the child builds working models of the self as unworthy of care, of others as untrustworthy, and of relationships as manipulative or coercive. Such child-mother relationships are labeled "insecure"—insecure anxious if the relationship is neglectful or unreliable, insecure avoidant if the relationship is manipulative or overcontrolling, and insecure disorganized if the relationship is frightening (Ainsworth, Blehar, Waters, & Wall, 1978; Main & Solomon, 1986).

Further, when children have secure attachment relationships with their primary caregivers, the primary caregiver becomes a secure base enabling the child to move out from the caregiver to explore and to use the caregiver's help to learn and develop. The sensitive caregiver helps the child acquire optimal solutions to the developmental tasks of childhood, e.g., modulation of physiological arousal, establishment of basic trust, regulation of emotion, and establishment of positive peer relationships (Pianta, 1999). The different working models developed by children in secure versus insecure relationships result in different ways of viewing and approaching the world. Children with secure attachment relationships will "approach the world with confidence and, when faced with potentially alarming situations, (will be) likely to tackle them effectively or to seek help in doing so." In contrast, children with insecure attachment relationships will see the world "as comfortless and unpredictable; and they respond either by shrinking from it or by doing battle with it" (Bowlby, 1973, p. 208).

Over the past 40 years, studies conducted in Africa, China, Israel, Japan, the United States, and Western Europe substantiate the universal existence and importance of the child-caretaker attachment bond. For example, (1) all observed infants were found to be attached to one or more caretakers; (2) the majority of infants in all cultures have been found to be securely attached; (3) secure attachment has been found to relate to sensitive caregiving; (4) secure attachment has been found to result in greater social and cognitive competence, and (5) insecure attachment has been found to predict less healthy development and in extreme cases psychopathology (Lyons-Ruth, 1996; Sroufe, 1996; van IJzendoorn & Sagi, 1999).

Several studies have found that securely attached children are friendlier, more co-operative, and more obedient. For example, Stayton, Hogan, and Ainsworth (1971) found that obedience in infants as young as 9 to 12 months was "strongly related to the sensitivity of maternal responsiveness to the infant's signals, but not to frequency of commands or forcible interventions" (p. 1057). More recently, Kochanska and Murray (2000) and Laible and Thompson (2000) have reported strong positive relationships between security of attachment, mother-child mutually responsive orientation, and moral conscience in young children.

While the body of attachment theory and research provides strong support for the role of the child-caregiver attachment bond in children's moral development, the nature of this relationship does not eliminate the role of other causal factors. For example, mothers' references to feelings and moral evaluations when discussing behavior with their children are positively related to children's moral internalization and to some extent independent of security of attachment (Laible & Thompson, 2000). Nor does attachment theory rule out the role in moral development of teachers and others outside the family (Watson & Ecken, 2003). It does, however, imply that child-adult mutually responsive relationships are likely to be important in school just as they are in the family. It is trusting relationships with caregivers that both provide a vision of morality and open children to their caregiver's moral guidance and instruction.

*Further Reading:* Ainsworth, M.D.S., Blehar, M.C., Waters, E., & Wall, S. (1978). *Patterns of attachment.* Hillsdale, NJ: Erlbaum. Bowlby, J. (1969/1982). *Attachment and loss,* Vol. I: *Attachment.* New York: Basic Books. Bowlby, J. (1973). *Attachment and loss,* Vol. II: *Separation.* New York: Basic Books. Kochanska, G., & Murray, K.T. (2000). Mother-child mutually responsive orientation and conscience development: From toddler to early school age. *Child Development, 71,* 417–31. Laible, D.J., & Thompson, R.A. (2000). Mother-child discourse, attachment security, shared positive affect, and early conscience development. *Child Development, 71,* 11424–11440. Lyons-Ruth, K. (1996). Attachment relationships among children with aggressive behavior problems: The role of disorganized early attachment patterns. *Journal of Consulting and Clinical Psychology, 64*(1), 64–73. Main, M., & Solomon, J. (1986). Discovery of a new, insecure-disorganized/disoriented attachment pattern. In T.B. Brazelton & M.W. Yogman (Eds.), *Affective development in infancy.* Norwood, NJ: Ablex. Pianta, R.C. (1999). *Enhancing relationships between children and teachers.* Washington, D.C.: American Psychological Association. Sroufe, L.A. (1996). *Emotional development: The organization of emotional life in the early years.* Cambridge: Cambridge University Press. Stayton, D.J., Hogan, R., & Ainsworth, M.D.S. (1971). Infant obedience and maternal behavior: The origins of socialization reconsidered. *Child Development, 42,* 1057–1069. Watson, M., & Ecken, L. (2003). *Learning to trust: Transforming difficult elementary classrooms through Developmental Discipline.* San Francisco: Jossey-Bass. van IJzendoorn, M.H., & Sagi, A.

(1999). Cross-cultural patterns of attachment: Universal and contextual dimensions. In J. Cassidy & P.R. Shaver (Eds.), *Handbook of attachment: Theory, research, and clinical applications.* New York: Guilford Press.

*Marilyn Watson*

## Attitudes

Attitudes are positive or negative evaluations that persons have toward other people, things, ideas, and activities. These "objects of evaluation" are present in various ways throughout one's life span and are viewed based on internalized beliefs from experiences. When beliefs about experiences are formed, then meaning follows. Attitudes are important because they influence behavior and are relevant for understanding and predicting social behavior. People have a natural tendency to develop attitudes using thoughts and feelings (Eagly & Chaiken, 1993), which, in turn, can influence behavior. Individuals differ, however, in the importance they place on cognitions versus affect in shaping attitude. This is partly due to temperament. If, however, thoughts and feelings about an object are different, then feelings are often the higher influence on behavior. Another angle explored is the difference between beliefs related to morality and those related to competence. Wojciszke, Bazinska, and Jaworski (1998) found that personality traits related to morality (e.g., honesty, compassion) were more consistently accessible than traits related to competence.

There are several considerations that determine how attitude can shape behavior. The more relevant an attitude is toward a person's life, the greater the influence on behavior. Likewise, the more salient and specific the attitude is, then the greater chance that behavior will be predicted. For instance, if achieving good grades is important to students, then they will favor completing their homework on time versus not. The strength of the attitude, which is common in value held beliefs, can also determine behavior. Although attitude is an internal psychological and emotional process, behavior that follows an attitude can be shaped by outside influences. In other words, the more freedom a person has in making his or her own decisions, the higher the chance of relying on his or her attitudes to make those decisions. However, if outside influences, such as family and friends are strong coupled with the individual's tendency to "do what is acceptable," then there is less reliance on following his or her own beliefs. This is unless the attitudes and beliefs follow the norms of the social group. An example is the formation of stereotypes and prejudices against others.

The strength of attitudes relates to their consistency over time and resistance to change and is affected by education, gender, and race. Attitudes were found to be the least susceptible to change around midlife. Young adulthood and late adulthood were times with the greatest potential for attitude change.

Ajzen and Sexton (1999) suggest in their expectancy-value model that stable and consistent attitudes are supported by chronically accessible beliefs. However, attitudes can shift in their degree of accessibility depending on the context of experiences or decisions to be made. Such factors can cause an attitude to shift between a positive and a negative belief. The original attitude about the object of evaluation may shift back after the behavior is made.

Markman and Brendl (2000) propose the goal compatibility framework suggesting that people evaluate objects in relation to current goals and then base their decision on those evaluations. This concept can also apply to the actual development of goals. Attitudes about work, for example, influence career decisions and occupational choice. A person may value artistic activities and the flexibility that comes with freedom of expression. Because of this value, attitudes toward certain colleges to attend and courses of study to pursue emerge.

Attitudes exist in everyone and are caused by thoughts and feelings that in turn influence behavior. Experiences across the life span can reinforce, challenge, or develop attitudes toward objects of evaluation. Attitudes, therefore, do not exist in isolation and can serve as positive or negative aspects to one's decision making and involvements.

**Further Reading:** Ajzen, I., & Sexton, J. (1999). Depth of processing, belief congruence, and attitude-behavior correspondence. In S. Chaiken & Y. Trope (Eds.), *Dual-process theories in social psychology* (pp. 117–38). New York: Guilford. Eagly, A. H., & Chaiken, S. (1993). *The psychology of attitudes*. Fort Worth, TX: Harcourt Brace. Markman, A. B., & Brendl, C. M. (2000). The influence of goals on value and choice. In D. L. Medin (Ed.), *The psychology of learning and motivation* (pp. 39, 97–129). San Diego, CA: Academic Press. Wojciszke, B., Bazinska, R., & Jaworski, M. (1998). On the dominance of moral categories in impression formation. *Personality and Social Psychology Bulletin, 24,* 1251–1263.

*Scott E. Hall*

## Augustine

St. Augustine, Aurelius Augustinus (354–430), was born in Thagaste, a small town in present-day Algeria, and grew up in the early days of what is now called the decline of the Roman Empire. Only 42 years earlier, the Emperor Constantine had converted to Christianity and made it the official state religion. (The Christian Church returned the compliment, so to speak, by adopting the Roman imperial model as its own political paradigm, a view that Augustine would reject in his later writings on the relationship between church and state.) His father was a pagan, but his mother, Monica, was a devout Christian who was later canonized by the Catholic Church, as was Augustine. At the age of 17 he went to Carthage where he studied rhetoric until he discovered philosophy. He also discovered a woman who became his mistress for 15 years, during which time she bore him a son. He rejected Christianity and began to explore other religions, all to his mother's great distress. For a time he embraced Manichaeanism, but in 384 he went to Italy (he was now 30), where two years later he had his famous garden experience. As he recounts in his most famous work, the *Confessions* (400), while sitting in a friend's garden he heard a child's voice saying, "Take and read, take and read." He picked up a copy of St. Paul's epistles, read a passage condemning riotous living, and was instantly converted. "The light of full certainty" filled his heart, and he was baptized two years later. Only a few years later, after returning to Africa, he became a priest and then a bishop in the town of Hippo.

From that point on most of Augustine's energies were consumed by pastoral activities, but he still found time to engage in voluminous correspondence and compose many philosophical and theological works. His *Confessions* can be read as a personal statement, a devotional treatise, or a philosophical text, since he touches on themes such as grace, sin, time, memory, and knowledge. It is now generally agreed that for Augustine there was no sharp line between theology and philosophy, if only because the neo-Platonic philosophers who most influenced him wrote extensively on theologically charged issues such as creation. He saw philosophical knowledge as anchored in religious belief, or, as he famously put it, the pursuit of wisdom is "faith seeking understanding."

Among Augustine's other writings, the most prominent are his *De Magistro* (*On the Teacher,* 389), *De Libero Arbitrio* (*On the Free Choice of the Will,* 387–395), and his later classic, *De Civitate Dei* (*The City of God,* 413–426). In the first of these works, which Augustine composed as a dialogue between himself and his son Adeodatus, there is a fairly extensive discussion of the illumination theory of knowledge, according to which our knowledge of eternal truths is not a product of abstraction from sensible data but rather a participation in the divine light that is, ultimately, God's own knowledge. Here as elsewhere in Augustine's writings we see the hand of Plato, for whom all knowledge of ideal forms was reminiscence, not discovery.

The second of the works just mentioned, *De Libero Arbitrio,* was more polemical. In it Augustine developed his conception of the relationship between freedom and grace, in contrast to the Manichaeans, whose denial of human freedom entailed that humans are not responsible for their sinful state, but also in contrast to the Pelagians, whose affirmation of human freedom was so extreme that they denied that God's grace was a necessary condition for reconciliation with God's will. Colloquially put, Augustine's position was that we are indeed able to sin all by ourselves, but having done so we cannot "bootstrap" our way back into God's favor. In the course of laying out his case for this intermediate position, Augustine addressed such questions as the problem of evil, predestination, and the relationship between intellect and will.

In *De Civitate Dei* he developed what is sometimes called the first philosophy of history. He replaced the prevailing neoplatonic notion of history as a cyclical repetition of events with a linear view, according to which history began with God's creation of the world and moves forward to the day of final judgment. This movement runs in two parallel tracks, occupied by the City of God and the City of Man. Contrary to the popular misconception of these two cities as representing two institutions, Church and State, Augustine's real distinction was between two groups of people, those who love God and those who love only themselves. However, in this and other of his later writings Augustine did stake out a position on the relation between Christianity and the Roman empire, in which he rejected two contrary views: on the one hand, that the sack of Rome in 410 was a punishment by the Roman gods for having abandoned the old religion, and, on the other hand, that the destinies of the Church and the empire were so closely related that the one could not survive without the other. Augustine's own view was quite the opposite. The Church did not need the empire, and membership in the Church was in itself no guarantee of salvation. In fact, God had lifted only a small number of souls from the morass of original sin, and so the salvation prospects for humanity as a whole were quite bleak.

Among Aristotle's many contributions to moral philosophy and theology is one idea that is particularly relevant to what is now called character education. It is his idea that human desires have a hierarchical structure, such that one can have desires about other desires. A famous instance of this view in his own personal life is the prayer that he uttered during the period between his decision to undergo baptism and the actual event. He understood that to be worthy of baptism he must end his career as a philanderer, and so he prayed that God would give him the strength of will necessary to overcome his sexual desires, which is to say that he had a higher-order desire to be rid of his first-order desires. But he apparently had conflicting higher-order desires, since as he tells us the prayer he actually said was: "O Lord, give me chastity and continence—but not yet." Closing the gap between these two orders of desires is, one may assume, one of the main points if not *the* point, of character education.

**Further Reading:** Augustine. (1990– ). *The works of Saint Augustine. A translation for the 21st century.* Hyde Park, NY: New City Press. (A continuing multivolume series.) Clark, M.T. (1994). *Augustine.* Washington, D.C.: Georgetown University Press. Gilson, E. (1967). *The Christian philosophy of St. Augustine.* New York: Random House. Matthews, G. (2005). *Augustine.* Oxford: Blackwell. Wetzel, J. (1992). *Augustine and the limits of virtue.* Cambridge: Cambridge University Press.

*Thomas Wren*

## Authority

In order to function effectively, teachers, it is often claimed, must be allowed to exert at least two forms of authority. First of all, it is said that they must exert what philosophers call social-political authority. Second, it is claimed that they must be recognized as epistemic authorities within the fields they teach. What exactly does it mean to exert, or claim the right to exert, such forms of authority? Under what conditions can such claims (to authority) be understood as legitimate?

Teachers claim the right to social political authority in classrooms when they claim the right, within an organized set of rules and practices, to have certain of their decisions and commands accepted as binding. Specifically, what is involved here is the idea that in order to teach effectively, teachers must be able and allowed to enact discipline, give grades, in short, to take charge of or to "police" their classrooms. Teachers, given the command to teach their subjects to their students, will try many "nonauthoritarian" ways to do so. Yet, in the end, perhaps after other means have failed, such authority is said to allow teachers the right to enact forms of coercion.

What kinds of coercion does such talk imply? As R.S. Peters (1976) notes, it would be wrong to think of schools as prisons. Therefore, certain coercive measures or even the threat of such must be considered out of place in schools (e.g., electrical shock). But neither are schools to be thought of as a holiday camp. From this point of view, teachers will always want to begin with positive attempts to "turn on" their students to learning. But, it has been claimed over and over again, that learning cannot occur unless certain conditions are set and maintained by an "authority figure" within the classroom.

In recent years the proper role of sociopolitical authority in schools has been much debated. This debate has been part of a larger discussion of democracy and its implications for practice. An important moment in this debate came with Ivan Illich's call to "deschool society" (1971). Whatever claims are made for schooling in the Americas, it has been argued by Illich and some of his followers that what our schools actually do is reproduce existing economic and political inequality. But truly democratic schools must, at the very least, provide its graduates with something resembling a fair chance to compete. Failing even this, Illich doubts the credibility of claims to social-political authority in schools, and thus the whole institution of schooling as it now exists.

While Latin American educator Paulo Freire (1970) was not ready to give up on schools entirely, he did insist, in his famous "pedagogy of the oppressed" on a radical revision of the teacher-student relationship. Freire rejected what he called "the banking model of education" in which students are viewed as passive recipients of the teacher's knowledge and learning. In order to educate students as citizens capable of democratic interaction, authority relationships between teachers and students must change. Thus, Freire insisted on what he called "dialogical education." According to Freire, students could only be taught to be free in situations of freedom, such as, free of the coercive restraints of sociopolitical authority. Yet it is hard to imagine the enactment of teaching or education for freedom totally free of such authority on the part of teachers. I will argue in this essay that freedom is impossible if we define it to entirely exclude the proper role of authority.

A second type of authority claimed and enacted by teachers has been labeled "epistemic authority," or the authority of knowledge. Certain persons are authorities in this or that area of knowledge. Teachers may be certified in one or more subject matters, say literature or history or math. We are tempted to say that we are more willing to grant teachers sociopolitical authority according to such certification. Perhaps then the use of social political authority can be justified on the basis of its value in forwarding the development of such knowledge in students.

Thus, numerous writers in the Aristotelian tradition have argued for a curriculum of studies based on the idea of knowledge that is worth having in itself, such as, by the ideally educated person. Here intrinsic worth is to be understood in terms of what is necessary in order to maximize human potential. To fulfill our human nature, there are things we must know in order to be true to "natural law." One, in fact, might argue that the justification or social-political authority in order to educate students in such knowledge can be grounded in natural law.

John Dewey (1966), rejecting Aristotle's fixed natures yet imagining democracy as an ideal form of living, would tie the justification of both social-political and epistemic authority in terms of creativity and consequences rather than antecedent realities such as natures. For Dewey the exercise of such forms of authority is justified if it contributes to the growth of a democratic society. Moreover, for Dewey democracy must mean more than mere equality of economic opportunity. At the very least, democracy, as Dewey understands it, must create conditions in which human beings in community have the freedom not merely to discover (as in Aristotle), but to some degree create themselves in response to new problems and possibilities. According to a number of recent followers of Dewey, such democracy requires procedures and modes of interaction that are intelligent and entirely open. Here openness means something akin to Freire's situation of pure dialogue in which all participants share authority equally.

Whatever one makes of this idea as an ideal, it is hard to understand how it would be possible in teaching. In order to see this, let us adopt a well known understanding of learning as a process of initiation into various traditions of inquiry. Understanding learning in this way at least suggests that at the beginning of the learning process nonrational forms of persuasion are necessary. For example, initiation into the moral life requires that "beginners" accept various commands, enter into a preliminary process of habituation. We cannot wait for our children and students to become masters of Socratic argument before they begin the path toward the moral life, even if that life in the end requires some such mastery. The justification for coercive elements in education would depend at least as much on its fruits as on its roots (Neiman, 1986).

What those who despise authority forget is that even if everything can be questioned, not everything can be questioned at once. Socrates radically questioned the ethics of his fellow citizens, but did so while enacting some of the same virtues he shared with them. While we may share the ideals of Freire and Dewey, and even sympathize with Illich, a way of keeping authority honest can only be found from within authoritative frameworks of learning and, ultimately, governing. A way must be found within the system to correct errors in the system.

There is no doubt that existing economic and social inequalities multiply our difficulties in finding such a way. Yet it is equally clear that authority in the form of tradition must play a role in reconstructing tradition, even if democracy's past is littered with vast failures to match its promises. As Dewey might put it, it is the self-correcting nature of democracy that makes it our best possible option for keeping authority within its proper bounds, within our educational system and elsewhere.

**Further Reading:** Dewey, J. (1966). *Democracy and education*. New York: Free Press. Freire, P. (1970). *Pedagogy of the oppressed*. New York: Continuum. Illich, I. (1971). *Deschooling society*. New York: Harper and Row. Neiman, A. (1986, Fall). Education, power and the authority of knowledge. *Teachers College Record, 88*(1), 64–80. Peters, R.S. (1976). *Ethics and education*. London: George Allen and Unwin.

*Alven Neiman*

## Autonomy

In common parlance, "autonomy" usually means personal or group independence. Having autonomy or being given autonomy involves having the space to do things for oneself, perhaps cooperating with others, but certainly free of outside constraints or directives. "Autonomy" is another word for freedom or independence in some contexts. "I want to do it myself," and "think for myself" as well.

There are also several distinctly moral and specialized (technical) uses of this important term. In moral psychology, autonomous judgment reflects a stage of personal or intellectual development when we are run somewhat free of the shaping influence of social conventions and social pressures around us. We start to think for ourselves, based on our own standards. We start to develop and use our own measures of what is right or wrong, or how to think about such matters. Usually we need to free ourselves further to think by our own lights through reflective and interpersonal struggle.

In metaethics (the philosophical study of ethical reasoning or theory), "autonomy" refers to the distinctness of ethical thought. Some ethicists believe that true ethical thought and motivation does not mix with practical or aesthetic considerations. It certainly cannot be reduced to such considerations, but represents an autonomous domain of concern with its own logic. Thus, some ethicists feel we should not be credited for acting nobly if a significant part of our motivation was to seek approval or feel good about ourselves, or simply to comply with social norms or practices. They also feel that nondistinctive ethical traditions like (philosophical) utilitarianism, Aristotelean virtue theory, or the ethics of most major religions are faulty, for they mix cultural norms or service to deities with ethical duties. This is especially true if we love and serve God's moral will in hopes of salvation and heavenly reward.

Piaget's and Kohlberg's theories of moral development rest heavily on this logical standard of autonomy, derived from the philosopher Immanuel Kant. Indeed, Piaget refers to adult moral thinking as "autonomous" in specific contrast with "heteronomous" thinking, precisely as Kant did. Heteronomous thinking takes an if-then, conditional form. "If you wish to achieve end 'x,' then do 'y' as means." This includes pursuing the end of doing the right thing as a personal interest you have. By contrast, autonomous thinking requires that you do "y" for its own sake, or for duty's sake. What is right is inherent, categorical, an end in itself.

A part of cognitive science and artificial intelligence deals with ethical software programs. The term "autonomous agent" is used here to describe robots that contain such programs, are able to make choices on their own, and demonstrate behaviors conforming to ethical guidelines or considerations.

Most moral educators seem to be in agreement that the ideal of moral education in the classroom is to achieve moral autonomy for students. Even where we wish students to internalize moral codes of conduct and act in conformance with rules, we wish them to do so for good reasons. And we wish these to be the students' own reasons, generated by student reflection on alterative rationales.

As Kant saw best of all, the study and practice of ethics must be self-determined to be ethical. And there could hardly be a more hypocritical system than an ethic that is unethical. An adequate ethics is designed largely to uphold liberty. To do so via coercion, threat of punishment or other sanctions is self-inconsistent and self-sabotaging. For autonomy buffs in metaethics, self-determination is a prime requirement for any ethic's distinctiveness and adequacy. Ethics is the only system of its kind—in contrast with approved social institutions or traditions, law, public policy, or etiquette that must be voluntary to be what it is. As soon as social pressure, authoritarianism, undue incentives, ulterior motives, or legal rewards and punishments get involved, true ethics goes out the window. That is why even just law is seen as, at best, merely justified ethically, not ethically just per se. It is ethically objectionable because it is backed by threat and punishment, but justified by being necessary to avoid greater injustice.

To achieve such moral autonomy or self-determination seems impossible without critical thinking. At some point in life we must reexamine our moral socialization and challenge our habitual moral beliefs, commitments, attitudes, perceptions, and inclinations. It is morally acceptable to act habitually in fulfilling our responsibilities. But at some point we should play a significant part in determining those habits for ourselves. A real prospect should have been faced when such habits could have been shaped differently or broken, but were not.

This means that autonomy and identity are likely to be partnered in moral education and development. As the research of Augusto Blasi (1984) has shown most of all, it is characteristic of older, more morally developed children, to distinguish their moral identity from other personality structures. Moreover, a key to practicing what they preach is strongly identifying with this moral identity. Such findings help fill perhaps the largest ethical gap in our moral lives—the judgment-action gap—that often renders us hypocrites.

Historically, ethicists pondered a variety of factors that might interfere with our acting as we believed we should. Stemming from Aristotle's discussion of *akrasia,* certain interferences between moral intention and action were considered—the role of ignorance (forgetting), confusion, strong passions and tempting desires, and also conceptual mistakes in applying general principles to particular cases. Alongside these influences, the general lack of willpower or "weakness of will" was considered. This might stem from the general motivational weakness of rational motivations or our failure to rally more powerful emotional motivations or desires behind them. It also might result from an insufficient emotional grasp of a situation, its horrors or evils, perhaps combined with an insufficient flow of compassion or empathy.

Modern research suggests that simply not thinking of oneself as a moral person is more crucial—not counting one's character as highly as, for example, one's business sense and focus, one's success orientation, one's athletic or artistic interests, one's social skills or personality. A "failure" here causes us simply not to care that much about doing the right thing or taking responsibility in the first place.

***Further Reading:*** Blasi, A. (1984). Moral identity: Its role in moral functioning. In W. Kurtines and J. Gewirtz (Eds.), *Morality, moral behavior and moral development.* New York: Wiley.

*Bill Puka*

# B

## Bandura, Albert

A professor of psychology at Stanford University in Palo Alto, California, since 1953, Albert Bandura has become one of the most influential psychologists of the twentieth century. Bandura has helped shape the field of psychology in numerous and important ways, from his classic experiments on social modeling in the 1960s to his more recent theorizing on human agency and moral disengagement.

Born in 1925 in Mundare, a small town in northern Alberta, Canada, Albert Bandura was the youngest of six children, and the only son, of Eastern European immigrants. His father was from Krakow, Poland, and his mother was from the Ukraine. Although his parents had little formal schooling, they highly valued education and hard work. Bandura attended the University of British Columbia (UBC), where he majored in psychology. Surprisingly, this choice of major was more a product of chance than choice. Bandura intended to pursue a career in the biological sciences, but his afternoon job at a woodworking plant compelled him to enroll in a morning section of introduction to psychology. He became deeply interested and within three years earned his bachelor's degree as well as the Bolocan Award in psychology from UBC in 1949.

Eager to further his understanding of psychology, Bandura decided to pursue his graduate studies at the University of Iowa. The Department of Psychology at Iowa offered a dynamic environment to conduct theoretical and experimental work on learning. Even as a young graduate student, Bandura had the insight to think beyond the prevailing models of the day, which emphasized trial-and-error learning. Instead, he was interested in the ubiquitous but more complex phenomenon of vicarious learning, which had its roots in Neal Miller and John Dollard's (1941) *Social Learning and Imitation* and would influence Bandura's research for years to come. Bandura completed his M.A. degree in 1951 and his Ph.D. degree in clinical psychology in 1952. The year 1952 marked another important event in Bandura's life—his marriage to Virginia ("Ginny") Varns, who was an instructor in the College of Nursing at the University of Iowa. The two are still married today and are the proud parents of two daughters and two grandsons.

After completing a one-year postdoctoral internship at the Wichita Guidance Center in 1953, Bandura moved westward to Stanford University, where he has remained on the faculty for over 50 years. In his first few years at Stanford, Bandura was influenced by the work of Robert Sears, a renowned psychologist and then Chair of the Department of Psychology at Stanford. Sears was exploring the role of familial factors in nonaggressive reactions to frustration. Bandura, with his existing interest in vicarious learning, soon began his own studies on aggression during adolescence. This research, which culminated in the publication of Bandura's first book, *Adolescent Aggression* (Bandura & Walters, 1959), highlighted the role of modeling in human behavior. Over the next decade, Bandura would conduct numerous studies on the determinants and mechanisms of observational learning. Arguably, the most famous of which involved the inflatable Bobo doll, which demonstrated that children could *learn* new behaviors without actually *performing* them and even in the absence of direct reinforcement.

Though the present-day reader may find the idea that humans can learn by watching rather obvious, Bandura's distinction between learning and performance represented a major departure from existing theoretical views. Until this point in time, behaviorism had reigned supreme, and it was generally believed that learning was a consequence of *direct* reinforcement or punishment. Bandura's empirical research showed that people could learn vicariously—by observing others and the consequences they received. In short, Bandura was positing the existence of cognition, which had long been derided by strict behaviorists as "mentalisms" and regarded as unscientific speculation about invisible and unknowable processes. Bandura's second book, *Social Learning and Personality Development* (Bandura & Walters, 1963), offers a full account of the cognitive effects of modeling on *acquisition,* and explains the "new" role of reinforcers as motivators of imitative *performance.* (For more on *modeling* see p. 272.)

Through the 1960s and 1970s Bandura continued to break new ground on the role of modeling on human learning, motivation, and behavior. His most important insights and contributions during this period were published in the now classic book, *Social Learning Theory* (1977). One of the critical ideas in this work was the idea that people develop and possess beliefs about their ability to perform certain tasks and that these "self-efficacy" beliefs greatly affect the goals they pursue and the persistence with which they pursue them. A second and equally important area for research and theorizing that Bandura began in the 1960s and developed over time concerned the development of self-regulation; that is, the capacity of the individual to deliberately set his or her own goals or standards, plan and implement strategies to achieve those ends, and monitor and evaluate the effectiveness of strategies. Self-efficacy and self-regulation have become among the most studied constructs in psychology and play a prominent role in Bandura's last two books: *Social Foundations of Thought and Action* (1986) and *Self-Efficacy: The Exercise of Control* (1997).

From the perspective of moral development and education, Bandura's work on modeling offers strong empirical and theoretical support to the wisdom of the ancient (Aristotelian) virtue of emulation and the present-day use of role models in character education (see, for example, Lickona, 1991). Equally important, but far less known, is Bandura's analysis of moral regulation, or, more precisely, moral disengagement. In *Social Foundations of Thought and Action* (1986) and subsequent articles (Bandura, 1999), Bandura describes the psychological mechanisms by which moral control is selectively disengaged by, for example, displacing or diffusing responsibility for one's wrongdoing.

Theoretically, these mechanisms can be seen as the antithesis of Kohlberg's responsibility judgment (Kohlberg & Candee, 1984). Rather than affirming the will and activating the self's sense of obligation to perform the right action, these mechanisms obscure or even negate one's personal agency by attributing responsibility for one's conduct to others or situational contingencies. "Under displaced responsibility...[individuals] do not feel personally responsible for [their] actions. Because they are not the actual agents of their actions, they are spared self-condemning reactions" (Bandura, 1999, p. 196). The propensity to disengage self-regulatory mechanisms may explain, in part, the oft-observed incongruity between moral judgment and moral action.

It is difficult to overestimate the importance of Bandura's impact on the field of psychology. In his nearly six decades of scholarly activity, Bandura has amassed a truly astounding list of accomplishments. In addition to authoring seven books and editing two others, Bandura has published well over 100 journal articles and served on over 30 editorial boards of journals or serial volumes. He has held 15 offices in various scientific societies, most notably, president of the American Psychological Association. He has received numerous awards and honors including the William James Award from the American Psychological Society and the Distinguished Scientific Contributions Award and Thorndike Award for Distinguished Contributions of Psychology to Education from the American Psychological Association.

***Further Reading:*** Bandura, A. (1999). Moral disengagement in the perpetration of inhumanities. *Personality and Social Psychology Review, 3*(3), 193–209. Bandura, A., & Walters, R.H. (1963). *Social learning and personality development.* New York: Holt, Rinehart & Winston. Kohlberg, L., & Candee, D. (1984). The relationship of moral judgment to moral action. In W.M. Kurtines & J.L. Gewirtz (Eds.), *Morality, moral behavior, and moral development.* New York: Wiley. Pajares, F. (2004). *Albert Bandura: Biographical sketch.* Retrieved May 5, 2006, from http://des.emory.edu/mfp/bandurabio.html. Zimmerman, B., & Schunk, D. (2002). Albert Bandura: The man and his ideas. In *Educational Psychology: A Century of Contributions.* Hillsdale, NJ: Erlbaum.

*Jason M. Stephens*


## Behavior Modification

Behavior modification involves the systematic application of learning principles and teaching methods to change overt and covert behaviors. Defining behavior is a very important element, as is measuring changes in behavior in order to assess the effectiveness of interventions. The goal of behavior modification is the same as in any educational enterprise: to help people increase their ability to direct the course of their own life experiences. Some social scientists prefer the term behavior management to behavior modification.

Behavior modification can be summarized in terms of ten phases or procedures. Although they are presented below in an ordered sequence, the number of phases—and even their order—is not sacred. Sometimes the plan can be put into effect easily by simply specifying the behavior (phase two), applying a strategy (phase eight), and noting the result (phase nine). At other times, most or all ten phases may be necessary. Although the procedures are usually applied to change the behavior of others, they can be used by an individual as a strategy for changing one's own behavior. Whether applied to others or self, successful behavior management calls for flexibility in the application of principles and methods.

### Phase One

Conduct a functional behavioral assessment (sometimes called an ABC analysis). This means identifying the behavior to be changed as well as the antecedents that occasion the behavior and the consequences that follow it. An ABC analysis provides an opportunity to determine when and where a behavior occurs as well as the likely reinforcement contingencies maintaining it.

### Phase Two

Defining behavior is fundamental in all behavior change plans. Defining involves identifying the specific behaviors that count as instances of the behavior of interest. For example, if calling people names and making negative remarks about their physical appearance constitute "verbal abuse," then a simple count of the number of times one calls others names and makes such remarks defines verbal abuse. Similarly, "off-task" might be defined as engaging in visual (looking away), motor (playing with an object), and verbal (whispering) behaviors unrelated to an assigned task.

### Phase Three

Observe and measure the behavior of interest. Preferred measures include frequency of behavior, rate and duration of response, video and audio recordings of behavior, and interval recording—determining whether a behavior occurs at any time during each equal interval of time. Data gathered in this phase of a plan are often graphed and labeled *baseline data*.

### Phase Four

Set attainable goals. Being clear about the behavior to be changed and determining its baseline level enables one to consider what the behavior should look like after intervention procedures are completed. Goals should be realistic and in the person's intellectual, emotional, and social best interests.

### Phase Five

Identify potential rewards. Potential incentives can be identified in a variety of ways— by observing what a person does during leisure time and by conducting interviews, for example. Determining whether something really functions as a reward is possible only by noting how it affects a person's actions.

### Phase Six

Select teaching procedures. A number of empirically based strategies are available for strengthening and weakening behavior. Those designed to teach new behaviors include modeling, prompting, fading, shaping, behavioral contracting, creating point systems, and response chaining. Effective procedures for reducing behavior include various reinforcement strategies, extinction, response cost, time-out, and overcorrection. The strategies incorporate the incentives identified in phase five. And it is not unusual to combine strategies to bring about desired behavior change—for example, prompting, fading, and shaping or time-out and response cost.

### Phase Seven

Rehearse key elements of the plan. Rehearsal enables participants to experience conditions much like they will experience when the plan is put into effect. Immediate feedback for participants' efforts can then be provided. Such feedback is lacking when people are merely told what to do.

### Phase Eight

Implement plan. The plan is activated when the above phases are in place. Everyone involved in the plan should know how to contact the lead practitioner when questions arise.

### Phase Nine

Monitor results. Using the same measurement procedures selected in phase three, phase nine calls for collecting daily information to assess the effectiveness of intervention and to make necessary changes in the plan. Behavior managers often track behavior change by employing single-subject experimental designs, such as the withdrawal, multiple baselines, and alternating treatment designs. These designs permit repeated measurements and thus provide constant monitoring of the behavior of interest. Such monitoring is not often found in education.

### Phase Ten

Take steps to maintain and generalize gains. Once behavior has changed for the better, attention shifts to whether the person retains and uses acquired behavior in other places and circumstances. This is called generalization (responding similarly to similar but different stimuli) or transfer of learning. Phase ten is an essential aspect of any form of teaching and learning. Unfortunately, many otherwise effective teaching plans break down at this point. Many things, for example, are forgotten and unavailable for use because they were not learned well in the first place. The remedy is practice and periodic review. Flexible rather than rigid teaching methods also promote retention and transfer.

**Further Reading:** Martin, G., & Pear, J. (2007). *Behavior modification: What it is and how to do it* (8th ed.). Upper Saddle River, NJ: Prentice-Hall. Watson, D.L., & Tharp, R.G. (2003). *Self-directed behavior: Self-modification for personal adjustment* (8th ed.). Monterey, CA: Brooks/Cole.

*Frank J. Sparzo*


## Bible (and Bible Reading)

It is almost impossible to overemphasize the role that the Bible (King James version) and its devotional reading played in American schools from the days of colonial Massachusetts through the nineteenth century. In Puritan Massachusetts people had to learn to read so that they could learn the divinely bestowed lessons in the Bible and thereby be saved, for it was in the Bible that God revealed Himself and His commandments. With the passage of the "Old Deluder Satan" law in 1647, the Massachusetts legislature mandated the teaching of reading to overcome Satan who wished to keep humans from the knowledge of the Scriptures. The Bible was the chief textbook of the schools of the Massachusetts Bay Colony and, along with *The New England Primer,* was to instill virtue in the citizens, young and old.

With the advent of deism, especially as advanced by the educational theories of Thomas Jefferson, the use of the Bible as the chief agent in moral education declined at the time of the Revolution. It did, however, have its advocates and maintained its prominent position. Benjamin Rush, for instance, called for the Bible to be used in schools, holding that no other book had nearly as much useful knowledge for individuals or governments. Indeed, its teachings were indispensable for a republican nation because without it there could be no virtue and without virtue no liberty.

Known as the "Father of the Common School," Horace Mann regarded moral education as primary in the conduct of elementary schooling. Claiming that he supported religion, but not sectarianism in schooling, Mann regarded the Bible as the authoritative expounder of Christianity. Wherever it was, there was Christianity. The allegedly nonsectarian moral enterprise of the common school was founded on the true principles of Christianity, which rested on the Holy Scriptures. Its devotional reading in the schools retained its prominent position as the major infuser of moral truths that led to moral behavior.

The Bible maintained its prominent role in the view of mainstream Protestants as the common school spread and prospered throughout the nineteenth century. Aided by the *McGuffey Readers* (about 122 million copies produced between the 1830s and 1920), it was looked to as providing the moral influence that the students so sorely needed. Regarded as nonsectarian Christian, its teachings were seen as an invaluable blessing to the Christian world. American Bible societies pledged to work to see that the Scriptures would be read in all of the nation's classrooms. Horace Bushnell, a leading Protestant clergyman of the century, declared that securing the proper place for the Bible was a sacred duty to which all sectarian claims must be sacrificed. The Bible belonged to all Christians and of necessity had to be present and read in schools if the youth of the nation were to be moral and righteous.

As the century moved onward, the overwhelming support for the role of the Bible and its reading in schools began to erode, especially in areas affected by immigration, particularly if that immigration included people who were not Protestants, namely, Catholics, who had a vastly different stance on the Bible and its role in schools. The state of Wisconsin was one such place, and it was to be the site of a major conflict over the Bible and its reading in schools in the latter years of the century.

At the time of statehood in mid-century the devotional reading of the Bible was a common practice in Wisconsin's schools and was strongly supported by mainstream Protestants (Baptists, Congregationalists, Methodists, and Presbyterians) as a nonsectarian but religious practice, as advanced by Mann and common school backers. Gradually, the support for that position waned as the state became more religiously diverse. Ultimately, the practice was ruled unconstitutional by the Wisconsin Supreme Court in 1890, the first such decision in the nation, on the grounds that it constituted sectarian instruction and its devotional reading made the schoolroom a place of worship.

The Protestant reaction to this decision was swift in coming and strong. Without the Bible morality would have no shred of authority or directive principle. The school would be unable to preserve society from disaster. The Republic would be imperiled, and the means, next to the Church, of the foundations of popular intelligence, virtue, and freedom in the country would be lost. Moral training would be at best defective, if able to exist at all. The Bible was the book to which the nation owed its liberties, and its removal from school meant the extinction of the only authoritative voice of moral obligation in Christendom in the schools.

Many states, including those in the "Bible Belt" in the South, continued to look to the Bible and its reading in schools as the foundation for morality in the nation. The practice's supporters contended that the absence of the Bible from schools had brought about the increase of crime and other social evils in the nation. Only by its return would evil be eliminated and virtue be present.

In 1962 the Supreme Court of the United States outlawed school-sponsored prayer in public schools. The next year in the *School District of Abington Township v. Schempp* decision it adjudged that voluntary (objecting children were free to leave the room) devotional Bible reading was unconstitutional as a violation of the Establishment Clause of the First Amendment. At that time 37 states permitted voluntary devotional Bible reading in public schools and 13 mandated the practice.

The public outcry that greeted the decision was loud and bitter. Denunciations included allegations of atheism and communism. The public schools were in the protesters' eyes now godless, devoid of the very foundation of moral education. They had abandoned their Christian heritage, which had made them the bastions of morality and virtue in the nation. Baleful predictions of disastrous consequences to befall the nation, similar to those that had been made 73 years earlier in Wisconsin, abounded.

The proper place of religion in the public schools, including that of the Bible and its reading, continues to be an issue as of this writing. There are those who argue that moral education is at best bankrupt without "The Book," the Bible, having its preeminent place in the schools, which would include its devotional reading. Nonetheless, in this religiously diverse country, that practice remains unconstitutional, and other means have been and are being tried to provide moral education for the nation's public school students.

***Further Reading:*** Boles, D.E. (1965). *The Bible, religion, and the public schools* (3rd ed.). Ames, IA: Iowa State University Press. Nord, W.A. (1995). *Religion and American education: Rethinking a national dilemma.* Chapel Hill, NC: University of North Carolina Press. *School District of Abington Township v. Schempp.* (1963). 374 U.S. 203.

*Thomas C. Hunt*

## Bibliotherapy

Bibliotherapy is a technique used by clinical therapists that involves the use of literature to help persons who are suffering from emotional traumas. It has been particularly useful as a therapeutic technique with children, who often relate their own experiences to the fictional accounts of characters they encounter in books. In the clinical setting (or classroom) children read literature that can serve as an entry to a discussion of emotional problems and the possible resolution of such conflict.

In the classroom setting, students are guided through three stages of bibliotherapy known as identification, catharsis, and insight. In the first stage, students identify with characters and events as portrayed in a story. The second stage, catharsis, occurs when students become emotionally invested in the story and are guided to share their own responses through discussion and some form of artistic expression. For example, students might be encouraged to write a poem or draw a picture, for example, as a means to express their own emotional responses to the events in the story (Coon, 2005). In the last stage, the students reach a level of insight about various ways that their own experiences might be related to the fictional experiences of the characters in the story. By brainstorming possible solutions for the fictional characters, students are guided to a better understanding of their own emotional issues and personal conflicts, and how these might be resolved.

Bibliotherapy is often used in the classroom to analyze moral values and to encourage critical thinking skills. Because of this aspect of bibliotherapy as a pedagogical tool, it is important that teachers take care to match students with age-appropriate reading materials. The great potential of vicarious experience through bibliotherapy is best met when teachers and therapists choose literature that mirrors the experience of their students and/or clients. In the classroom, bibliotherapy has been demonstrated to be effective in helping students to develop an individual self-concept as well as in promoting more open and thoughtful self-appraisals (Sridhar & Vaughn, 2000). Additionally, many teachers and high school guidance counselors report that bibliotherapy provides a way for the students to discover interests outside their own limited experiences, particularly with respect to career paths and future continuing education.

Professional journals in education and counseling fields have reflected mixed results regarding research studies on bibliotherapy. For example, Riordan and Wilson (1989) concluded that bibliotherapy may generally be most successful when combined with other therapy techniques. Nonetheless, an interest in bibliotherapy has increased in the past decade, particularly as a classroom pedagogical tool for teachers from kindergarten through high school environments. Perhaps most interestingly, bibliotherapy has been shown to relieve the stress of peer pressures for preteen and early adolescent students by demonstrating that others have encountered similar problems or "life issues."

Educators have always been especially cognizant of the power that reading can exert over their students' lives, but the term "bibliotherapy" as a specific technique was first used in 1916 by Samuel Crothers, writing in the *Atlantic Monthly*. The professional use of bibliotherapy was initially limited to clinical settings such as hospitals, where it was used with much success in reducing post-traumatic stress disorders in World War I veterans. However, by 1940, the use of bibliotherapy had spread to education, especially in those fields related to middle and high school education.

Today, bibliotherapy practitioners in the middle and high school grade levels often collaborate with colleagues to select appropriate literature for their grade level and the interests of their students. Others who typically collaborate with the classroom teachers include school librarians and guidance counselors, as well as community librarians and local authors (Pardeck, 1995). Bibliotherapy practitioners should take great care to select literature that has the potential to stimulate classroom conversations regarding the emotional issues that confront the fictional characters. Working vicariously through the lives of these fictional protagonists, students are better able to reconcile emotional issues and moral dilemmas with which they are confronted in their own personal lives. Classroom discussions provide further opportunity for students to give voice to the issues that appear to be the most prevalent conundrums in their own daily lives.

After selecting age appropriate literature for the exercise, the successful application of bibliotherapy in the classroom requires careful planning and hierarchical procedures. First, the teacher should provide introductory classroom activities that will motivate the students to want to read the selected literature. For example, such exercises might include age-appropriate social studies and geography lessons that are drawn from the literature selected. Second, there should be some classroom time set aside for reading, including both private reading in silence and group readings orally. This stage serves to demonstrate to students the value that has been placed on this activity, and also provides an opportunity for the stronger readers to help encourage their fellow classmates. Third, the teacher must provide adequate time to discuss the selected readings in class. Such discussions may be initiated with basic questions that recall information about the setting of the story. After these brief conversations about the time and place, the teacher may choose to introduce interpretive questions related to the emotional responses of various characters in the story. It is at this stage of the bibliotherapy exercise that teachers usually begin to recognize the power that great literature can have in impacting the emotional lives of their students.

A final imperative step that teachers should include is the opportunity to provide closure for their students. The importance of this stage of the bibliotherapy exercise is critical, particularly in those instances where students have been actively engaged in dialogue about the characters in the story. Students should be encouraged to continue reflection about the comparisons and contrast they might have noticed between particular fictional protagonists and their own real life events at school and at home. Most practitioners consider such closure exercises to be the most significant contribution of bibliotherapy as a meaningful pedagogical tool.

**Further Reading:** Coon, C. (2005). *Books to grow with: A guide to using the best children's fiction for pre-teens.* Portland, OR: Lutra Press. Pardeck, J. (1995). Bibliotherapy: An innovative approach for helping children. In *Early child development and care.* San Francisco, CA: Jossey-Bass. Riordan, R. J., & Wilson, L. S. (1989). Bibliotherapy: Does it work? *Journal of Counseling and Development, 67*(9), 506–8. Sridhar, D., & Vaughn, S. (2000). Bibliotherapy for all: Enhancing reading comprehension, self-concept, and behavior. *Teaching Exceptional Children, 33*(2), 74–82.

*Monalisa M. Mullins*

## Bioethics

Bioethics is the study of morality as it applies to the fields of medical research, medical practice, patients' rights, the distribution of medical resources, and other health care fields of inquiry and treatment. Although bioethics is considered to be a contemporary field of study, its historical roots are traced to the ancient Greek Hippocratic Oath. In today's application of this early imperative to "do no harm" the moral issues and questions that face health care professionals are the subject of considerable debate in the fields of medicine, law, philosophy, and theology, among many others.

In light of recent advances in genetic engineering and reproductive technologies, these moral issues are taken to be of critical importance for health care professionals, patients, and providers of heath care services, particularly with regard to medical treatment and research methodologies. The first official code of ethics, written with the intention to provide guidelines for medical practice, was developed by founders of the American Medical Association in 1846. Almost a century later, as a response to horrific medical research abuses performed by Nazi doctors, the Nuremberg Code would articulate ethical guidelines for research on human subjects in medical experimentation. The moral issues and societal implications of medical research and practice remain prominent topics in current studies in bioethics. For example, violations related to human subjects in medical research at universities in the United States were exposed in 1966 by Henry Beecher, a physician at the Harvard Medical School. Beecher cited a variety of abuses of human subjects, including the use of subjects without their consent and the use of subjects for experimental treatments without their having been offered standard treatment options as alternatives to the experimental treatments. Beecher's publication generated renewed public debate concerning the need for informed consent, and who should be permitted to serve as surrogates when patients cannot provide consent for themselves.

In addition to the issue of human subjects in medical research, bioethics has also addressed issues related to the allocation of health care resources. For example, the escalating costs of prescription drugs and hospital visits have placed a priority on minimizing costs for managed care insurance providers, which contributes to concern by bioethicists that conflicts exist between the need to lower costs and the duty to provide adequate services to those in need of medical attention. In response to the scarcity of organ donations and the concurrent advances in transplant procedures, the United States developed a national program to monitor the allocation and distribution of organs for transplant operations. Considerations that impact these decisions include the patient's position on the waiting list, the severity of illness of the patient, and the likelihood of a successful match between the donor organ and the recipient.

Moral questions related to the refusal of medical treatment and/or consideration of assisted suicide also raise issues of concern for bioethics. Many patients who have been diagnosed with terminal diseases or who may have chronic illness that significantly diminish their quality of life have sought the assistance of health care providers to help them facilitate intentionally ending their life. Opponents of assisted suicide have objected to the practice of euthanasia by physicians and other health care providers by arguing that it violates the most basic moral imperative of the medical profession, namely, to do no harm. Others have expressed concern regarding the potential for abuse of euthanasia should it become legalized. For example, concerns have been raised about how the competency of the patient should be determined and how much assistance should be provided in facilitating the onset of death. To date (2006), Oregon remains the only state to pass a law that permits assisted suicide by administering lethal doses of medications in the case of terminally ill patients who are judged to be mentally competent.

Another interesting moral dilemma for bioethicists is posed by new technologies in genetic research. For example, the Human Genome Project has already been successful in discovering a number of genes that contribute to or directly cause certain diseases and physical traits. These discoveries have vast social implications that are currently the topic of heated debate among genetic biologists and other researchers. Bioethicists are considering whether this newfound genetic information should be the property of the individual person, or whether it should also be shared with one's employer and medical insurance providers, for example.

Even more alarming to some bioethicists is the potential for more insidious abuse of advances in gene therapy, such as the risk of manipulation of human reproduction for eugenic purposes of "improving" the hereditary genetic makeup of the human species. Most geneticists are thoughtful regarding past abuses in eugenics and encourage genetic counselors to be nondirective regarding reproductive choices that families must make. But the availability of genetic testing in the future will increase the likelihood that parents will use genetic tests as part of their family planning regimen. The most critical moral issue, from a bioethicist's point of view, revolves around the question of who will choose the genetic traits that will be tested, and for what purpose? These "brave new world" moral dilemmas are no longer hypothetical scenarios for college philosophy students to ponder; indeed, they are the stuff of new bioethics boards of inquiry across the country. Bioethics, as an emerging field of study, will continue to contemplate these issues as well as many others that present themselves as challenges to health care professionals in the twenty-first century.

**Further Reading:** Beauchamp, T.L., & Walters, L.R. (Eds.). (1999). *Contemporary issues in bioethics* (5th ed.). Belmont, CA: Wadsworth. Caplan, A.L. (1997). *Am I my brother's keeper? The ethical frontiers of biomedicine.* Bloomington, IN: Indiana University Press. Carson, R.A., & Burns, C. R., (Eds.). (1997). *Philosophy of medicine and bioethics: A twenty-year retrospective and critical appraisal.* Boston, MA: Kluwer Academic. Garrett, T.M., Baillie, H.W., & Garrett, R.M. (1998). *Health care ethics: Principles and problems.* Upper Saddle River, NY: Prentice-Hall. Schneider, C.E. (1998). *The practice of autonomy: Patients, doctors, and medical decisions.* New York: Oxford University Press.

*Monalisa M. Mullins*

## Blatt Effect

The "Blatt Effect" is named after Dr. Moshe Blatt and is derived from the results of his dissertation research at the University of Chicago in 1969. Moshe Blatt, an educator in a Jewish Sunday school, proposed to adapt the moral dilemma stories used by Lawrence Kohlberg, his dissertation chair, to be used as educational curricula. Kohlberg had posited a theory of the development of moral reasoning that moved through six stages of progressively more complex and logically adequate ways of thinking about moral issues and resolving moral problems. Kohlberg, however, did not think Blatt's idea was a practical strategy: "I was skeptical that Blatt's proposed verbal discussion of purely hypothetical dilemmas would lead to genuine moral stage change" (Kohlberg, 1978, p. 3). However, Blatt persisted and designed an excellent educational intervention study, which was eventually published in the *Journal of Moral Education* (Blatt & Kohlberg, 1975).

The rationale for the project was to see if developmentally facilitated (often called "Socratic") peer classroom discussions of hypothetical moral dilemmas would stimulate the development of moral reasoning stages in the participating students. Blatt first piloted the intervention in a Jewish Sunday school class, finding that the average stage development for experimental (dilemma discussion) students was approximately two-thirds of a stage. He then replicated it in public junior high schools and high schools. The discussions were weekly for 12 weeks. The results indicated that the experimental group (moral dilemma discussions facilitated according to developmental principles) increased about one-third of a stage from pretest to posttest (and then an additional one-third of a stage from posttest to delayed posttest). The "no discussion" comparison students and a second set of comparison students who discussed the dilemmas without expert facilitation both showed no development from pretest to posttest. This finding of approximately one-third stage change was eventually dubbed the "Blatt Effect" by Kohlberg (1978).

The Blatt Effect, the effectiveness of moral dilemma discussion in promoting approximately one-third stage development in participants, was then replicated in many studies in the 1970s and 1980s, a time dubbed by Jack Fraenkel (1976) as the "Kohlberg bandwagon." For example, Colby, Kohlberg, Fenton, Speicher-Dubin, and Lieberman (1977) evaluated a large-scale high school social studies application of moral dilemma discussions in Boston and Pittsburgh, reporting that students in the 32 moral discussion classrooms averaged an increase of approximately 15 percent of a stage from pretest to posttest. When only classrooms where development occurred were analyzed, the average change was more than 20 percent of a stage. One important difference is that the stage scoring methods were different in the Blatt and Colby studies, allowing for partial stage change to be scored in the latter but only full stage change in the former.

The Blatt Effect is therefore often thought of as either an average of one-third stage development as a result of peer classroom dilemma discussions or as one-third of the students in such classes developing to the next stage. As stage scoring no longer is limited to whole stage scores as it was when Blatt did his research in the late 1960s, the magnitude of change is now more variable across studies. Furthermore, many variables have been identified that impact the effects of classroom moral dilemma discussions: for example, heterogeneity of students, quality of discussion leader facilitation, age of students. Furthermore, the measurement instrument and scoring system to ascertain student moral reasoning stages also impacts the magnitude of measured stage change.

It is therefore best to understand the meaning of the Blatt Effect both historically and flexibly. Historically, the Blatt Effect refers to the discovery that classroom moral dilemma discussions can significantly promote the development of student moral reasoning as defined by Kohlberg's stage theory of moral reasoning development. Flexibly, the Blatt Effect must be understood not as an absolute prediction of the magnitude of stage change, as it originally was understood, but more as an effect whose magnitude will vary depending on a range of variables about the intervention, the participants, and the assessment method. So for contemporary purposes, it is best to define the Blatt Effect as the finding that expert facilitated classroom discussions of hypothetical moral dilemmas with adolescents leads to the significant development of the students' moral reasoning capacities according to Kohlberg's theory of moral reasoning stages.

*Further Reading:* Berkowitz, M.W. (1985). The role of discussion in moral education. In M. W. Berkowitz & F. Oser (Eds.), *Moral education: Theory and application* (pp. 197–218). Hillsdale, NJ: L. Erlbaum. Blatt, M.M., & Kohlberg, L. (1975). The effects of classroom moral discussion upon children's level of moral judgment. *Journal of Moral Education, 4,* 129–61. Colby, A., Kohlberg, L., Fenton, E., Speicher-Dubin, B., & Lieberman, M. (1977). Secondary school moral discussion programmes led by social studies teacher. *Journal of Moral Education, 6,* 90–111. Fraenkel, J.R. (1976). The Kohlberg bandwagon: Some reservations. *Social Education, 40,* 216–22. Kohlberg, L. (1978). Foreword. In P. Scharf (Ed.), *Readings in moral education* (pp. 2–15). Minneapolis, MN: Winston Press.

*Marvin W. Berkowitz*

## Blum, Lawrence

Lawrence Blum is a professor of philosophy and Distinguished Professor of Liberal Arts and Education at the University of Massachusetts in Boston. He is a distinguished scholar on the issues of racism, and his most influential book remains *"I'm Not a Racist, But. . .": The Moral Quandary of Race* (2002) in which he addresses beliefs and opinions that often go unchallenged in discussions about race and racism in American culture. Blum defines racism in terms of the presence of two theoretical constructs: antipathy and inferiorization. He explains antipathy as a strongly held belief that is based on hatred. As such, antipathy does not presume any logical basis or rational analysis; instead, it is based on irrational affective opinions. Inferiorization is defined by Blum as disrespectful and demeaning attitudes or actions. Inferiorization may be based on internalized value systems that support the belief that one's own group is inherently inferior or superior to other groups. When antipathy and/or inferiorization are present, then racism is present.

According to Blum, people are racially insensitive if they are not recognizing the distinction between ethnic groups, such as Korean and Chinese Americans. A second sign of racial insensitivity is not recognizing an individual's distinct ethnic identity, such as Haitian American as opposed to African American. Failing to recognize internal group diversity is a third example of racial insensitivity, for example, asking the single Chinese woman in your class to speak on behalf of all Chinese women with respect to some particular issue. A fourth sign of racial insensitivity is a lack of appreciation for individuality with respect for one's own ethnic group; and finally, a fifth example of racial insensitivity is exemplified whenever we contribute to make ethnic groups vulnerable by continued practice of the four previous examples of racial insensitivity.

Blum defines selective racism as a racially prejudiced belief directed against a subgroup or an individual member of a minority. Selective racism is based on unintentional statistical discrimination; for example, a person might not exhibit antipathy or inferiorization toward all people of color, but might nonetheless view young Black men as violent and dangerous. In this case, the person who describes young Black men as violent and dangerous is being selectively racist. Such examples of unintentional discrimination exist also in various media representations of young black men, which serve to reinforce selective racism. Blum also distinguishes between racism and racialism. Racialism is not based on prejudice toward a group; instead, racialism attaches extreme importance to ethnic identity. For example, members of a particular ethnic group might be inclined to favor the company of other members of their own group based on familiarity of common traits, such as language, shared cultural values, and favorite foods, for example. Other persons outside the group might mistake this association as racist, when, in fact, there need not be feelings of antipathy or inferiorization attached to this selective practice of associating with one's own ethnic group.

Beyond the goal of promoting tolerance and creating an atmosphere that welcomes diversity, Blum identified three additional goals that he argues should guide antiracist education in our schools (1999). The first goal calls for a reduction in racial prejudice and hurtful racial stereotypes. A second goal requires a genuine commitment to racial justice, which not only entails recognizing the structures of injustice but also a willingness to be actively engaged in demolishing those same structures. Blum argues that the goals of moral education about racism must go beyond the hope of simply reducing students' prejudices. Instead, moral education should be teaching students to embrace racial justice as an internalized core commitment not only in their personal value systems but also in their schools and communities. His third goal for education is to promote racial harmony and understanding at the level of community. This goal requires more than tolerance of diverse ethnic groups; it reaches beyond an appreciation of diversity to genuine understanding and valuing of ethnic and racial differences in community.

Blum argues that educators not only must be sensitive to racial differences among their students but also must be aware of how those different identities should influence pedagogical choices regarding racism and how best to approach the topic. He is cognizant of the fact that conversations with students about racism can be emotionally charged. He also acknowledges that many teachers fail to engage their students in meaningful dialogue about this important issue because they see the topic as causing more division than unity, more rage and resentment than harmony. But to those educators who prefer creating a neutral atmosphere that focuses mostly on shared and common values, Blum argues that such an approach is neither desirable (from a moral standpoint) nor practical. The reality is that classrooms typically have a complex variety of racial identities, all of which need to be explored and valued by educators.

Blum is adamant that educators must not abandon dialogue about racism as a meaningful pedagogical tool, and its potential for breaking down barriers regarding attitudes about race. Establishing an attitude of acceptance for all racial identities, and making constructive use of that complex diversity will ultimately serve the purpose of finding our shared and common values. Blum argues that the most successful programs for moral education will be those that are grounded in an understanding that unity arises from diversity.

**Further Reading:** Blum, L. (2002). *"I'm not a racist, but..."*: *The moral quandary of race.* Ithaca, NY: Cornell University Press. Kozol, J. (1967). *Death at an early age.* Boston, MA: Houghton Mifflin. Macedo, S., & Tamir, Y. (Eds.). (2002). *Moral and political education.* New York: New York University Press. Tatum, B.D. (1994). Teaching White students about racism: The search for White allies and the restoration of hope. *Teachers College Record, 95*(4), 462–76. Willoughby, B. (2004). An American legacy. *Teaching Tolerance, 25*(Spring), 40–46.

*Monalisa M. Mullins*

## Bullying

In the broadest sense, bullying is defined as a systematic abuse of power, which encompasses bullying in the school, workplace, home, and various institutions (such as prisons and nursing homes; Smith, 2004). Most empirical research and discussion of bullying has been in the context of the school, which is the focus hereafter. A more specific definition of bullying is offered by Olweus (in Smith, Morita, Junger-Tas, Olweus, Catalano, & Slee, 1999): an aggressive behavior that is intentional and is repeated against another person who cannot easily defend himself or herself.

School bullying appears to be a phenomenon that occurs around the world, including North America, Europe, East Asia, and Australia (Sanders & Phye, 2004). Prevalence rates in various countries differ somewhat, though it appears that anywhere between 40 to 80 percent of students experience bullying at some point during their schooling, and between 5 to 10 percent of students are victims on a regular basis (Griffin & Gross, 2004; Sanders & Phye, 2004).

The behaviors that comprise bullying are varied and somewhat culturally specific. Prototypical bullying behaviors include physical and verbal attacks, such as hitting, kicking, shoving, and name-calling. However, bullying can also take on other forms of aggression (often called indirect, relational, or social), such as spreading rumors about, maliciously teasing, and socially excluding a victim (Smith, 2004). Recently, another type of bullying has been observed: that of sending threatening messages to victims via email, chat rooms, or cell phones (Smith, 2004). In terms of cultural differences, bullying in Western countries tends to be mostly physical and verbal attacks as compared to Japan and Korea, where it more often takes the form of social exclusion (Smith, 2004).

Research in the past 15 years has invalidated some of the beliefs about bullying that have been (and still often are) held by the general public. Though some believe that bullying is related to school or class size or academic competition or failure, research has shown that it is not (Griffin & Gross, 2004). Despite what some think, bullies are not necessarily rejected by their peers; rather, they may have well-established social networks and close friends (Sanders & Phye, 2004). As for victims, the only physical characteristic that has been associated with their victim status is being physically weaker than their bullies (rather than being overweight or wearing glasses; Griffin & Gross, 2004; Sanders & Phye, 2004).

Researchers have also examined the roles of gender and age in bullying. Gender differences have been observed in school bullying, though not consistently. The studies that have found gender differences have shown that boys are more likely to be both bullies and victims (Griffin & Gross, 2004; Sanders & Phye, 2004). However, these studies have defined bullying with the prototypical behaviors of physical and verbal attacks. When defining bullying more broadly to include indirect, relational, or social aggression, mixed results have been found. In some studies, girls were more likely to commit the more covert forms of bullying, while in others boys were more likely (Griffin & Gross, 2004; Sanders & Phye, 2004; Smith, 2004). Thus, no clear gender differences have emerged. In terms of age-related trends, bullying appears to gradually decline with age, though it does not disappear completely by the end of secondary school (Griffin & Gross, 2004). The peak in bullying appears to be between ages 9 and 15. Increases in bullying have been observed with school transitions in some countries (e.g., United States, Australia) but not in others (e.g., Norway, Sweden; Sanders & Phye, 2004).

Four distinguishable roles have been identified in bullying situations: bullies, victims, bully/victims, and bystanders (who may be defending the victim, cheering the bully, or simply watching). In terms of general characteristics, bullies tend to have a more impulsive and dominating temperament and come from a family with harsher child-rearing practices (Griffin & Gross, 2004; Smith, 2004). However, conflicting reports from studies exist on whether bullies have low self-esteem and poor social skills. As for victims, they tend to have low self-esteem and higher rates of depression and anxiety, though it is not clear whether these characteristics are a result of bullying or were present beforehand (Griffin & Gross, 2004). With bully/victims, they tend to be victimized by aggressors but also engage in bullying others and often have difficulty with social skills (Griffin & Gross, 2004).

A multitude of antibullying intervention and prevention programs exist and vary considerably in what they emphasize (Sanders & Phye, 2004; Smith, Pepler, & Rigby, 2004). Elements of antibullying programs may include one or more of the following: training teachers to address the problem; developing a positive classroom and school climate; antibullying curriculum that addresses what bullying is, the harm it does to victims, how victims can seek help, and how bystanders can help stop bullying; and teaching students techniques to counter bullying, such as social skills, anger management, assertiveness, and conflict resolution training. Unfortunately, the research on these programs does not yet point to essential elements of any that are consistently associated with decreases in bullying. The most important factor appears to be the extent to which the school staff takes ownership of the antibullying program so that they persistently and effectively implement and maintain it over the long term (Smith, 2004; Smith, Pepler, & Rigby, 2004).

*Further Reading:* Griffin, R. S., & Gross, A. M. (2004). Childhood bullying: Current empirical findings and future directions for research. *Aggression and Violent Behavior, 9,* 379–400. Sanders, C. E., & Phye, G. D. (Eds.). (2004). *Bullying: Implications for the classroom.* New York: Elsevier

Academic Press. Smith, P. K. (2004). Bullying: Recent developments. *Child and Adolescent Mental Health, 9,* 98–103. Smith, P. K., Morita, Y., Junger-Tas, J., Olweus, D., Catalano, R. F., & Slee, P. T. (Eds.). (1999). *The nature of school bullying: A cross-national perspective.* New York: Routledge. Smith, P. K., Pepler, D., & Rigby, K. (Eds.). (2004). *Bullying in schools: How successful can interventions be?* Cambridge, UK: Cambridge University Press.

*Tonia Bock*

# C

## California Moral Guidelines

In the United States, education is a state responsibility. Approximately nine states have legislation that mandates moral/character education; approximately 11 states plus the District of Columbia recommend moral/character education. California, the nation's largest state, has enacted moral education legislation. Education Code Section 233.5(a) states that students be taught principles of morality, truth, justice, patriotism, equality and human dignity, kindness, and good manners (among others). In addition, the California code requires that students should be taught to avoid idleness, profanity, and falsehood.

That other states do not have similar legislation does not reflect the absence of moral education. One measure is that 48 of the 50 states have received federal funds to support character education through a pilot project.

These data are particularly encouraging during the current standards-based schooling, which has created an environment that makes it more difficult to focus on moral education in classrooms and schools. One reason for the challenge is the emphasis on reading, writing, and mathematics, which has effectively narrowed the curriculum.

California is also one of the states that has received the federal dollars and has legislation supporting moral education. The state has also been assertive in its attempts to integrate moral/character education into the standards-based era. In a notable example, in 2000 the California Department of Education Elementary Grades Task Force, charged with providing guidance to California's schools about how to achieve academic standards, included as one of 15 recommendations that moral education be integrated into the daily school life of children. The recommendation, stated in the form of a quotation from Martin Luther King Jr. is, "Develop and reinforce positive character traits intelligence plus character—that is the goal of true education."

*Further Reading:* California Department of Education Elementary Grades Task Force. (2000). *Elementary makes the grade!* Sacramento, CA: California Department of Education. Education Commission of the States. (1999). *State examples of policies concerning character education.* Denver, CO: Education Commission of the States. Education Commission of the States. (2001). *Service-learning and character education: One plus one is more than two.* Denver, CO: Education Commission of the States. Retrieved April 24, 2003, from World Wide Web: http://www.ecs.org/

clearinghouse/24/81/2481.htm. Elias, M.J., Zins, J.E., & Weissberg, R.P. (1997). *Promoting social and emotional learning: Guidelines for educators.* Alexandria, VA: Association for Supervision and Curriculum Development. Howard, R.W., Berkowitz, M.W., & Schaeffer, E.F. (2004). Politics of character education. *Educational Policy, 18*(1), 188–215.

*Robert W. Howard*

## Care

Inspired by the groundbreaking work of Carol Gilligan (1982) and Nel Noddings (1984) in the 1980s, scholars in the fields of moral development and moral education began to focus their attention on caring as a concept and a phenomenon. The writings of both Gilligan and Noddings represented a fundamental challenge to what they argued was an overemphasis on "justice" as the primary focus in the fields of moral development, moral education, and even moral philosophy—as exemplified by the work of both Lawrence Kohlberg (1981, 1984) and John Rawls (1970). Gilligan and Noddings, furthermore, argued that caring and caregiving were particularly central to the moral experience of many girls and women—thus their work, at a fundamental level, represented a critical feminist challenge to these heretofore male-dominated fields.

Gilligan and her colleagues distinguish between two different moral "voices" or "orientations": "justice" and "care" (see Gilligan, 1982). These two voices represent different ways of speaking about the world of human relationships—different ways of describing moral problems, different ways of understanding such problems, and different strategies for resolving them. Hence they represent two fundamentally different moral languages or forms of moral discourse.

The distinction between the justice and care voices, Gilligan (1982) argues, reflects different dimensions (and different ideals) of human relationship that give rise to moral concern: the justice voice reflecting an ideal of equality, reciprocity, and fairness between persons; the care voice reflecting an ideal of attachment, loving and being loved, listening and being listened to, and responding and being responded to. These ideal visions, furthermore, are experienced as being undercut, in the case of justice, by oppression, domination, inequality, and/or unfairness of treatment; in the case of care, by detachment, abandonment, inattentiveness, and/or lack of responsiveness.

Central to Noddings's (1984, 1992) conception of care is her claim that caring must be understood as a fundamentally relational activity. Both the carer (the "one caring") and the recipient of care (the "cared for") must partake of, and contribute to, this relationship in ways that befit their respective roles, otherwise the relationship cannot be considered a caring relation.

The primary quality of the one caring is an experience of "feeling with" the other that is best characterized, Noddings says, as "engrossment"—where the one caring genuinely hears, sees, or feels what the cared for is trying to convey. This process of engrossment, however, does not simply involve role-taking or projecting oneself into another's place; rather it involves receiving the other into oneself; seeing and feeling with or as the other. This process, moreover, is not exclusively an emotional one. Although an emotional response to another is certainly a central element of the kind of engrossment or reception that characterizes the one caring, cognitive processes also play an equally important role.

The one caring is also characterized by what Noddings (1984) calls "motivational displacement," wherein the one caring shifts all of his or her attention to needs of the cared for, to respond in a way that helps the cared for. In other words, when the one caring truly receives the cared for, and becomes engrossed in his or her situation, there is more than feeling and thinking involved; there is also a motivational shift that necessarily leads to action.

The attitude or consciousness of the cared for, on the other hand, requires both recognition and response, according to Noddings (1984). Just as the one caring must receive and become engrossed in the needs, interests, and concerns of the cared for, so must the cared for receive the caring that he or she is offered. The cared for must also acknowledge his or her receipt of that care—responding, in word and/or deed, in a way that shows that he or she recognizes that the one caring has acted on his or her behalf. And it is this act of recognition and response, finally, that the one caring receives as part of his or her ongoing engrossment in the cared for. Thus the cycle of caring comes full circle, and the process, and the relationship, continue (Noddings, 1992).

One final point about the caring relation: Noddings (1992) assumes that neither the role of the one caring nor the role of the cared for is fixed and static; these are not, in other words, "permanent labels" for individual actors. Rather, in her view, caring relations, particularly in their mature form, are characterized by reciprocity and mutuality, and both parties can exchange places when necessary—both can be carers and cared fors.

So how can teachers help their students to learn both to care and to be cared for? Noddings's (1984, 1992) model of moral education from the care perspective consists of four central components. The first of these is modeling, whereby students are shown how to care by teachers, parents, and other adults acting as caregivers for others. Students do not learn to care simply by being told how to care; rather, they learn to care by example, by being shown how to care, in the context of caring relations with their caregivers (Noddings, 1992). Examples of modeling care include showing children how to care for pets, helping older brothers or sisters to learn how to feed and care for younger siblings, or encouraging adolescents to accompany parents or teachers on visits to elderly friends or relatives in nursing homes.

Dialogue is the second component of moral education from a care perspective. Noddings (1992) argues that genuine dialogue is not just talk or conversation, and it certainly is not an oral presentation of an argument; rather it is open-ended and indeterminate. Dialogue, instead, represents a joint quest for understanding, insight, appreciation, or empathy; moreover, it permits the one caring to talk about what he or she is trying to show or model—engrossment in the cared for, a genuine interest, that is, in what the cared for thinks, feels, and does.

The third component of moral education from a care perspective is practice. Learning how to care takes practice, hard work, perseverance—just as does learning any new set of skills, abilities, and attitudes. Like modeling, the emphasis on practice highlights the importance of the active, engaged, experiential quality of caring and learning how to care.

The fourth and final component of moral education from a care perspective is confirmation. Noddings (1992) defines confirmation as encouraging development of the cared for's "better self." Thus, if a student commits a harmful or uncaring act, a caring teacher must nevertheless respond by giving that student the benefit of the doubt and by attributing to him or her the best possible motive(s) consonant with the reality of the situation.

Historically, the discourse of care, compassion, and responsibility in relationships has not occupied a predominant place in our public moral discourse; and when it has entered into the public sphere, it has often been denigrated and devalued. But the language of care has always occupied a predominant place in private lives and relationships, through the language of caregivers and caregiving as it has been spoken by mothers and others responsible for child care, nurses, social workers, elementary school teachers—roles traditionally occupied by women. One of the consequences of the work of Gilligan, Noddings, and their colleagues and followers, however, has been not only to identify the care voice as a moral language typically associated with women and women's experience but also to legitimize it as a language that has an important role to play in transforming public moral, political, and legal discourse, and in offering a vision of a new and profoundly transformative kind of moral education (see also Blum, 1980; Ruddick, 1989; Sandel, 1982).

**Further Reading:** Blum, L. (1980). *Friendship, altruism, and morality.* Boston: Routledge & Kegan Paul. Gilligan, C. (1982). *In a different voice: Psychological theory and women's development.* Cambridge: Harvard University Press. Kohlberg, L. (1981). *Essays on moral development, Vol. I: The philosophy of moral development.* San Francisco: Harper & Row. Kohlberg, L. (1984). *Essays on moral development, Vol. II: The psychology of moral development.* San Francisco: Harper & Row. Noddings, N. (1984). *Caring: A feminine approach to ethics and moral education.* Berkeley: University of California Press. Noddings, N. (1989). *Women and evil.* Berkeley: University of California Press. Noddings, N. (1992). *The challenge to care in schools: An alternative approach to education.* New York: Teachers College Press. Rawls, J. (1970). *A theory of justice.* Cambridge: Harvard University Press. Ruddick, S. (1989). *Maternal thinking: Toward a politics of peace.* Boston: Beacon Press. Sandel, M. (1982). *Liberalism and the limits of justice.* Cambridge: Cambridge University Press.

*Mark B. Tappan*

## Care, Inventory of (Ethic of Care Interview)

Based on the theory of Carol Gilligan (1982), the Ethic of Care Interview (ECI) was constructed by Eva Skoe (1998) to measure development in care-oriented moral reasoning. The ECI consists of a real-life conflict generated by the respondent and three interpersonal dilemmas involving conflicts surrounding (a) unplanned pregnancy, (b) marital fidelity, and (c) care for a parent. The interviews are audio taped and scored according to the *Ethic of Care Interview Manual,* which contains level descriptions and sample responses for five ethic of care levels.

At the lowest level in the ECI sequence, Level 1, individuals reason about relational issues in a self-protective, egocentric way, and neglect the needs of others. The major concern is survival: ensuring one's own happiness and avoiding hurt or suffering. Level 1.5 is the transition from self-care (survival) to a sense of responsibility. Although aware of the needs of others, self-interest in relationships still is favored. At Level 2, individuals think about issues in terms of responsibility and care for others, to the exclusion of the needs of self. Good is equated with self-sacrificial concern for other people, and right is externally defined, often by the church, parents, or society. There is a strong need for security. Being liked or accepted by others is so important that they may be helped and protected, even at the expense of self-assertion. Level 2.5 is transition to a reflective care perspective, marked by a shift in concern from goodness to truth and personal honesty in relationships. Compared to the more "black-and-white" worldview of the previous level, complexities and nuances are expressed. The goodness of protecting others at one's own expense is questioned. Finally, at Level 3, the needs and welfare of both others and self are encompassed in a more balanced approach to thinking about relationships. The tension between selfishness and responsibility is resolved through a new understanding of human interconnectedness. Out of this realization, the insight arises that by caring for others, you care for yourself, and vice versa. Compassion is twice blessed; it enriches both the giver and the receiver. Attempts are made, therefore, to minimize hurt to all parties (for further details, see Skoe, 1998).

A series of studies has shown that balanced consideration of the needs of self and others appears to develop gradually across childhood into young adulthood. Findings indicate that variations in care levels of reasoning have implications for personal and social adaptation across the life span. The sequence of ECI levels is, for example, positively related to cognitive complexity, perspective taking, identity formation, ego development, and justice-oriented moral reasoning, but negatively related to authoritarianism and personal distress. Thus, it appears that people higher in the care ethic also have a stronger sense of self and social responsibility, a greater tolerance for ambiguity and for people with problems, and a greater ability to see the world from others' points of view (Skoe, 1998; Skoe & Lippe, 2002). Furthermore, with regard to prosocial behavior, higher levels of ECI reasoning are associated with greater volunteer participation in community activities, such as helping elderly people, visiting those in hospitals, and donating money (Pratt et al., 2004; Skoe, 1998).

What kind of mechanisms or factors may facilitate change and growth in care-based moral thought? A recent longitudinal study found that parents' emphasis on caring, as well as the use of more authoritative and autonomy-encouraging child-rearing practices were associated with higher levels of care reasoning in adolescents (Pratt et al., 2004). In addition to family relationships, other factors to be considered are cognitive as well as emotional development, social opportunities, sex and gender role identity, period in life, cultural background, major life events, faith, and spiritual experience (Skoe, 1998; Skoe et al., 1999). Further research is necessary to ascertain whether or not individuals progress sequentially through the ECI levels. Given the positive relations found between sophistication in ECI care reasoning and personal as well as psychosocial growth, balanced care for oneself and others might be a central component of what we call maturity or wisdom.

***Further Reading:*** Gilligan, C. (1982). *In a different voice: Psychological theory and women's development.* Cambridge, MA: Harvard University Press. Pratt, M.W., Skoe, E.E., & Arnold, M.L. (2004). Care reasoning development and family socialization patterns in later adolescence: A longitudinal analysis. *International Journal of Behavioral Development, 28*(2), 139–47. Skoe, E.E.A. (1998). The ethic of care: Issues in moral development. In E.E.A. Skoe and A. von der Lippe (Eds.), *Personality development in adolescence: A cross national and life span perspective* (pp. 143–71). London: Routledge. Skoe, E.E.A., Hansen, K.L., Mørch, W.-T., Bakke, I., Hoffman, T., Larsen, B., & Aasheim, M. (1999). Care-based moral reasoning in Norwegian and Canadian early adolescents: A cross-national comparison. *Journal of Early Adolescence, 19*(2), 280–91. Skoe, E.E. A., & von der Lippe, A. (2002). Ego development and the ethics of care and justice: The relations among them revisited. *Journal of Personality, 70,* 485–507.

*Eva Skoe*

## Categorical Imperative

Immanuel Kant (1724–1804) understood the categorical imperative as the supreme principle of morality and duty as well as the basis of what he called the "good will." Although he wrote several books on morality, the most accessible discussion of the categorical imperative is his *Groundwork for the Metaphysics of Morals* (1785), which was expanded in his somewhat more abstruse *Critique of Practical Reason* (1788). Unlike classical and medieval moral philosophers for whom virtue was the center of morality, in these and other writings Kant grounded morality firmly in the concept of duty. Contemporary philosophers often distinguish these two approaches as the aretaic approach (from *arête*, the Greek word for virtue) and the deontic or deontological approach (from *deon*, the Greek word for duty). For Kant and those who followed him, a truly good person was one who has internalized and follows the moral law, which like any legal code is formulated as a set of prescriptions, commands, or imperatives. Kant distinguished between two sorts of imperatives: hypothetical and categorical.

*Hypothetical:* As the term suggests, hypothetical imperatives, like hypothetical statements, have an "if-then" structure, linking an antecedent condition and a consequent action or action-mandate. The action that is the object of the command is considered good only because it is a means to achieve an ulterior end or proposition (the antecedent): "If you want *y,* do *x,*" or negatively, "Avoid *x* if you want *y.*" Thus seemingly moral injunctions such as "Keep your promises if you want people to trust you," and "Don't steal if you want to avoid problems with the police," are hypothetical in form and for that reason not part of the moral law.

*Categorical:* In contrast, a truly moral action has neither antecedent nor consequent components. Its rightness is simply unconditioned, that is, independent of considerations of external goals or circumstance. There are no "ifs, ands, or buts": the action is commanded simply because it is considered to be of value in itself. Thus, the general form of a moral imperative is "Do *x*" or "Do not do *y*"—as in "Keep your promises" and "Do not steal."

Of course, it is possible to issue obviously nonmoral commands that are categorical in the trivial sense that no antecedent is uttered, as when a parent says, "Wash your hands before coming to the table." What makes a truly moral imperative different from "Keep your promises" is, then, something over and above the simple absence of an antecedent term. This "special something" is, Kant believed, a formal quality of the maxim underlying the action in question. To examine this quality we need to understand Kant's notion of a maxim or, to use a phrase common in contemporary analytic philosophy, the relevant act description. Kant's own example is a person who normally tells the truth but is prepared to lie when doing so is to his or her advantage. Such a person has adopted the maxim "I will lie whenever doing so is to my advantage," and is acting on that maxim whenever he or she engages in lying behavior. Of course, many maxims have nothing to do with morality, since they are purely pragmatic policies such as straightening one's desk at the end of each workday or not picking up hitchhikers.

Now we can return to the "special something" that makes a maxim a moral maxim. For Kant it was the maxim's universalizability. (Note that universalizability is a fundamentally different concept than universality, which refers to the fact that some thing or concept not only should be found everywhere but actually is. However, the two concepts sometimes flow into each other: human rights are said to be universal not in the sense that they are actually conceptualized and respected in all cultures but rather in the sense that reason requires that they should be. And this is a moral "should.") However, in the course of developing this idea, Kant actually developed several formulations of the Categorical Imperative, all of which turn on the idea of universalizability. Commentators usually list the following five versions:

1. *Act only according to a maxim that at the same time you could will that it should become a universal law.* In other words, a moral maxim is one that any rationally consistent human being would want to adopt and have others adopt it. The above-mentioned maxim of lying when doing so is to one's advantage fails this test, since if there were a rule that everyone should lie under such circumstances no one would believe them—which, of course, is utterly incoherent. Such a maximum destroys the very point of lying.

2. *Act as if the maxim directing your action should be converted, by your will, into a universal law of nature.* The first version showed that immoral maxims are logically incoherent. The phrase "as if" in this second formulation shows that they are also untenable on empirical grounds. Quite simply, no one would ever want to live in a world that was by its very nature populated only by people living according to immoral maxims.

3. *Act in a way that treats all humanity, yourself and all others, always as an end, and never simply as a means.* The point here is that to be moral a maxim must be oriented toward the preservation, protection, and safeguarding of all human beings, simply because they are beings that are intrinsically valuable, that is to say ends in themselves. Of course, much cooperative activity involves "using" others in the weak sense of getting help from them, but moral cooperation always includes the recognition that those who help us are also persons like ourselves and not mere tools to be used to further our own ends.

4. *Act in a way that your will can regard itself at the same time as making universal law through its maxim.* This version is much like the first one, but it adds the important link between morality and personal autonomy: when we act morally, we are actually making the moral law that we follow.

5. *Act as if by means of your maxims, you are always acting as universal legislator, in a possible kingdom of ends.* Finally, the maxim must be acceptable as a norm or law in a possible kingdom of ends. This formulation brings together the ideas of legislative rationality, universalizability, and autonomy. What Kant had in mind can be illustrated by imagining a parliament of partisan but nonetheless civil senators or deputies who have, over and above their personal feelings, a deep-seated respect for each other as legislators, typically accompanied by courtly rhetoric such as "I would respectfully remind my esteemed colleague from the great state of ___ that..."

It is important to understand that for all its power, the Categorical Imperative functions as a negative criterion for evaluating moral maxims, in that it tells us directly which ones to avoid and only indirectly which ones we must adopt. It is also important to keep in mind that it is not itself a moral judgment but rather a second-order criterion according to which first order moral judgments or maxims can be evaluated and defended.

**Further Reading:** Beck, L. W. (1960). *A commentary on Kant's critique of practical reason.* Chicago: University of Chicago Press. Guyer, P. (Ed.). (1998). *Kant's groundwork of the metaphysics of morals: Critical essays.* Lantham, MD: Rowman and Littlefield. Originally published 1785. Kant, I. (1967). *Kant's critique of practical reason, and other works on the theory of ethics* (T.K. Abbott, Trans.). London: Longmans. Originally published 1789. Kant, I. (1998). *Groundwork of the metaphysics of morals* (M. Greg, Ed. & Trans.). Cambridge: Cambridge University Press. Paton, H.J. (1947). *The Categorical Imperative: A study in Kant's moral philosophy.* London: Hutchinson's University Library.

*Susana Patino Gonzalez and Thomas Wren*

## Catholic Church

The Catholic Church is a worldwide, Christian organization, believed to have been founded by Jesus Christ and his first followers in the early part of the first century.

Catholics, as members of the Catholic Church are called, comprise the single largest Christian denomination, numbering over 60 million in the United States and 1.3 billion worldwide. The Catholic Church is a Bible-believing church and adheres to the teachings of Jesus as found in the Christian Gospels as well as the books of the Hebrew Scriptures or Old Testament. For Catholics, Jesus Christ is the central figure of human history, and the institution of the church exists, according to his will, to proclaim the kingdom of God and share the good news of salvation won for all through the life, death, and resurrection of Jesus.

The church is organized hierarchically. The head of the Catholic Church on earth is the pope, who by custom resides at the Vatican, a nation-state in central Italy completely surrounded by the city of Rome. The pope is also the civic leader of the geopolitical nation-state that is coterminus with the Vatican.

The expansive organization of the church is most clearly seen in its division of the world into regional geographic districts known as dioceses. Each diocese has territorial boundaries and is further subdivided into smaller regional districts called parishes. Dioceses are led by administrators appointed by the pope. The head of an individual diocese is called a bishop. Bishops in turn appoint leaders to each of the parishes in their dioceses. These leaders are called pastors.

In addition to governance, the pope, bishops, and pastors also share a responsibility for teaching and especially for overseeing the accurate and appropriate articulation of the tenets of the Catholic religion as it has been passed down over the centuries from generation to generation. Throughout history, church leaders have taken strong moral positions on questions of importance ranging from slavery and usury to abortion and contraception. Official church teaching, while related to the Bible and to the examples and values of Jesus, is often an application or interpretation of biblical values. Modern-day moral questions, therefore, such as positive eugenics and embryonic stem cell research, are the subjects of official teachings of the Catholic Church, even though such concepts are absent in the Bible.

Moral behavior has been a focus of the Catholic Church since the time of Jesus. A Catholic moral code is best understood as a moral theology, a view of the human person as made in the image and likeness of God. This God-given dignity is the foundation of moral behavior for Catholics, dictating that persons be respected because of their inherent dignity. At various times in history, this theological approach to morality has served as the basis for church teaching against racism, war, poverty, unjust wages and working conditions, and abortion.

In 2002, the Catholic Church was beset by a sexual abuse scandal that lessened its moral authority. Bishops, in their discretion to assign pastors to parishes, had been routinely assigning and reassigning pastors who had sexually abused children of minority age. These reassignments, often done quickly and quietly, left many abusers with access to children and were often done without contacting legal authorities. While the legal and fiscal ramifications of the abuse crisis are far from settled, the Catholic Church and especially its leaders have experienced a decline in their moral integrity that is necessary for leadership.

Church leaders continue to speak out on pressing moral questions of the day, and often become involved in the animated political debate surrounding those issues. In 2006, Pope Benedict XV gave a provocative address at Regensberg in Germany that inflamed the Muslim world, in large part because of the use of a citation from a medieval source that associated Islam with violence. In the same year, and as an example of the breadth of the Catholic Church's moral interests, official church statements were released on homosexuality, global terrorism, the Israeli-Palestinian conflict, marriage, hunger, the environment, and health care.

The Catholic Church has a long history, extending over 2,000 years, addressing moral questions, and teaching about Jesus. It seems likely that given its organization, size, and reach, it will continue to exercise influence over moral debates and remain engaged in contemporary moral issues. The effectiveness of its impact will always be related to its ability to adapt and apply the teachings of Jesus to current situations as well as its own perceived integrity among its members and the wider society.

**Further Reading:** Häring, B. (1978). *Free and faithful in Christ: Moral theology for clergy and laity.* New York: Seabury Press. *The new Catholic encyclopedia* (2nd ed.). (2003). New York: Thomson Gale. *The official Catholic directory.* (2006). New York: P.J. Kenedy & Sons.

*Ronald J. Nuzzi*

## Character Counts!

Character Counts! (CC!) is an educational program dedicated to building moral character in America's youth. The Character Counts! approach to moral education originated from the results of a 1992 survey conducted by the Josephson Institute of Ethics. The survey included a sample of approximately 9,000 high school and college students and tapped ethical issues such as cheating, lying, stealing, and drunken driving. Character Counts!, a program developed and delivered by the Josephson Institute of Ethics, aims to create a unified approach to building character through a particular set of virtues known as the Six Pillars of Character by enlisting community stakeholder support in schools, youth-serving public agencies, and nonprofit organizations. The Six Pillars include trustworthiness, respect, responsibility, fairness, caring, and citizenship.

At the foundation of Character Counts! is the idea that character can be transmitted, taught, enforced, and modeled by parents, teachers, coaches, peers, and the surrounding community. Emphasis is placed on the authority of expert adults to present character knowledge (i.e., the Six Pillars), to the novice or young learner, which in turn leads to the development of habits and dispositions reflective of societal and community norms (Wynne, 1991). CC! is a directive traditional character education program that focuses on the inculcation of particular virtuous traits of character. It assumes the choices one makes in all realms of life influence and reflect one's character development; thus, individuals are held responsible for their own development and maintenance of good character (Narvaez, 2005).

Participating CC! schools and communities anecdotally and self-report a host of psychosocial and academic benefits from participation in Character Counts!, which include but are not limited to a drop in underage drinking, drug use, vandalism, cheating, and truancy, in addition to an increase in academic achievement. For example, a cross-sectional study in Florida schools that imposed the CC! program observed increased comprehensive test scores and decreased discipline referrals (Williams & Taylor, 2004). In addition, a five-year study involving South Dakota schools that implemented the Character Counts! program found that participating schools reported a decrease in crime and drug use from 1998 to 2000 (Josephson Institute of Ethics, 2006). The limited empirical research on Character Counts! appears to support the premise that the CC! program has a positive influence on children's behaviors and academic performance, but experimental program effectiveness warrants additional empirical examination. The CC! emphasizes the importance of content (the Six Pillars) and demonstrates the impact environment and social influences can have on individual character development.

Character Counts! Sports, the Pursuing Victory With Honor (PVWH) sportsmanship campaign, helps adults in sports contexts cultivate values in athletes. The PVWH campaign and the Arizona Sports Summit Accord (a set of principles that can be adopted and applied to develop and enhance the character of athletes) originated from a May 1999 meeting sponsored by the Josephson Institute of Ethics that brought together leaders and scholars interested in creating ethical change and character building in and through sports.

To highlight the importance and prevalence of CC! programs nationwide, President George W. Bush declared October 16–October 22, 2005, National Character Counts! week.

***Further Reading:*** Harms, K., & Fritz, S. (2001). Internalization of character traits by those who teach Character Counts! *Journal of Extension, 39,* 6. Josephson Institute of Ethics. (2006). *Character Counts!* Narvaez, D. (2006). Integrative ethical education. In M. Killen & J. Smetana (Eds.), *Handbook of moral development* (pp. 703–33). Mahwah, NJ: Erlbaum. Williams, R.D., & Taylor, R.T. (2004). *Leading with character to improve student achievement.* Character Counts! Retrieved on June 13, 2006, from www.charactercounts.com; Wynne, E.A. (1991). *Character and academics in the elementary school.* New York: Teachers College Press.

*Nicole M. LaVoi and Erin Becker*

## Character Education

Character education is the process of learning values that have implications for how life is lived and how decisions are made. Character is composed of good and bad traits that influence our intellectual, personal, and social development. Typically, the promotion of character is found in the K–12 school system but is encouraged in various informal ways through family, church participation, team activities, and other venues.

Good character centers on virtues that are considered timeless and require effort to practice on a daily basis. The virtues of character are traits such as honesty, integrity, compassion, self-discipline, perseverance, flexibility, and faith. Character education is often thought of as knowing the good, loving the good, and doing the good. Knowing the good is developing an awareness of good character and why it is important to practice. Loving the good is seeing value in having good character, and doing the good is simply practicing good character in one's daily involvements.

Formal character education in the schools began with the *McGuffey Readers* in 1836. The books were filled with fables, stories from the Bible, heroes, and universal truths and virtues that were meant to encourage schoolchildren to become good citizens. Although there were religious overtones in advocating these values, cleanliness, patriotism, hard work, and frugality were important middle class values to learn. Also, there was less of a concern about the use of religious materials in the public school system as there is today.

In the early 1900s there was concern for the moral decline of youth that contributed to a multitude of organizations that encouraged good character. Scouting groups and others sought to leverage friendships within the groups that would have peer influence on the character practice. During World War II there was much debate over what to call character education and how to logistically facilitate character education. Regardless of disagreements, there emerged individual and collective efforts that demonstrated character. Children and adults participated in conservation efforts, war bond and scrap metal drives, and morale building. In addition, there were many opportunities for children and young adults to take greater responsibility for household chores and farming duties. This was partly out of necessity because a large percentage of adult males were in the service away from home.

In the late 1960s what was known as citizenship education became values clarification and was coupled with Lawrence Kohlberg's (1966) moral development method. His method allowed students the freedom to use a seven-step assessment process to determine the values they want to use and practice. The teacher was effectively removed from directly teaching character. This movement had overtones of moral relativism in that there were no consistent guiding principles for decisions, but situational choices determined by the individual alone.

The 1990s have seen a renewed interest in character education within the school and community settings. Many reasons abound; however, most seem related to the perceived decline of the family, along with trends in hostile behavior of youth and a recommitment to shared ethical values.

In an attempt to reinvigorate the promotion of character in the schools Kevin Ryan and Karen Bohlin (1999) advocate a six-step model. Teachers need to recognize the power of modeling behavior and provide a positive example to the students they teach. Furthermore, teachers should explain the difference between good and bad character. Without fully understanding how character is defined in a practical way, students are left guessing how to implement the concepts. The third step is exhortation. Teachers need to be willing to advocate for what is good and what is bad as it relates to character. This approach is somewhat opposite to the early value clarifications movement. However, children are shown to benefit from behavior encouragement. The fourth step is to experience both success and failure in the context of learning. Achieving and not achieving goals are a part of life that everyone encounters. The challenge rests in how an individual handles success and failure that can shape the ideals of hard work, humility, and a resilient self-worth. The fifth step is ethos or an ethical environment. The school culture itself should embrace the practice of good character and ethics. Doing so provides a constant influence to the students and teachers throughout the school, not just in a particular classroom. The sixth step in the model is having expectations of excellence. Children have a tendency to rise to the occasion and are not inspired by mediocrity. Striving for excellence does not mean perfectionism. Excellence represents doing one's best, while perfectionism demands an all or nothing approach to goal achievement.

Part of character education is to have students critically reflect on the virtues and how they apply to their own lives. Also, by considering motivations for practicing good character, one begins to form the values for doing good. John Yeager (1998) found that practicing good character at an early age sets a foundation for consistent, positive behavior patterns over the life span. Furthermore, virtues are not isolated from one another in their contribution to well-being. Scott Hall (2006) suggested the use of a character identity inventory to help assess how the practice of both virtues and vices contribute to various degrees of well-being in life domains such as relationships, leisure, and work. Regardless of the character initiative, the interest in good character remains a visible and dynamic process for development over the life span.

**Further Reading:** Bennett, W.J. (1993). *The book of virtues.* New York: Simon and Schuster. Hall, S.E. (2006, March 22). Developing character identity: A new framework for counseling adults in transition. *Adultspan Journal.* Kohlberg, L.A. (1966). Cognitive-developmental analysis of children's sex-role concepts and attitudes. In E.E. Maccoby (Ed.), *The development of sex differences.* Stanford, CA: Stanford University Press. Ryan, K., & Bohlin, K. (1999). *Building character in schools.* San Francisco: Jossey-Bass. Yeager, J. (1998). *Character and health: Cultivating well-being through moral excellence.* New York: Pearson Custom Publishing.

*Scott E. Hall*

## Character Education Movement

During the first three or four decades of the twentieth century, character education became a "major preoccupation of schooling" (Leming, 1997) and a common topic of educational leaders, commentators, and researchers. This period of attention and concern has become known as the "Character Education Movement."

The causes of the Character Education Movement can be categorized as social, intellectual, and institutional (Cunningham, 2005). The social causes included immigration, urbanization, and the increasingly strong position of corporations in the economy. Intellectual causes included the naturalization of psychological explanations, the interest in the relationship between genetics and morality, and the rise of connectionism as an explanation of learning. Institutional causes included compulsory schooling, a National Morality Codes Competition announced in 1917, as well as attention paid to character education by the National Education Association, the Religious Education Association, and other prominent groups. In 1918, the National Education Association's Educational Policies Commission published its Seven Cardinal Principles of Secondary Education, which labeled the seventh principle, "Ethical Character," as of paramount concern.

The dramatic increase in attention to character education during this period does not suggest that any significant consensus emerged about what character is or how it is acquired. Disagreements can be identified between those who supported traditional values and those who wanted students to learn how to make their own decisions; those who believed character is based on religion and those who sought a secular form of character education; those who wanted a specialized curriculum in character education and those who wanted it to be the concern of the entire school; and those who believed that character traits are universally valued and those who emphasized the importance of particular cultures and beliefs. Strong disagreement also existed between connectionists such as Lewis Terman and Edward Thorndike and idealists such as William Chandler Bagley and Willerd W. Charters. Terman and Thorndike denied that morality could be learned in general or that there was any transfer from one situation to another of character traits such as courage and honesty, while Bagley and Charters emphasized the importance of teaching students to form generalized conceptions of good character to help integrate their personalities. The connectionists also tended to emphasis the inheritability of moral behavior, while the idealists were prone to see it more as a matter of individual experience and choice.

The debate about whether character traits had any empirical validity reached its head when Thorndike convinced the Rockefeller Foundation to fund a major study, called the Character Education Inquiry. The inquiry, conducted from 1925 through 1930 (and discussed in detail in the entry about Mark A. May), focused on the question of whether character education methods were effective not only in influencing student behavior but also in establishing consistency of behavior. The study found some effectiveness of some methods, but overall concluded that "fundamental changes in...school procedure" (May & Hartshorne, 1927, p. 715) and "radical changes are called for in our prevailing methods of character education" (Hartshorne & May, 1930, p. 762). More importantly, the study could find little evidence that improvements in character are transferred from one situation to the next, meaning that character education could be truly effective only if it trained each student to behave in particular ways in each possible morally charged circumstance he or she would face. This finding was taken by some observers to mean that the concept of "character" itself has no clear meaning, or at least that the widely used methods of character education were ineffective.

Certainly, the economic depression of the 1930s and the advent of World War II were distracting elements that may have contributed to the end of the Character Education Movement (see Leming, 2002). Increasingly, the concept of "character" was replaced in educational writings by terms such as personality, values, and moral reasoning. This remained the case until the 1980s, when renewed attention to character led to a new character education movement (see Cunningham, 2005).

*Further Reading:* Cunningham, C.A. (2005). A certain and reasoned art: The rise and fall of character education in America. In D.K. Lapsley & F. Clark Power (Eds.), *Character psychology and character education* (pp. 166–200). South Bend, IN: University of Notre Dame Press. Hartshorne, H., & May, M.A. (1930). A summary of the work of the Character Education Inquiry, Part II. *Religious Education, 25*(8), 754–62. Leming, J.S. (1997). *Teaching values in social studies education: Past practices and current trends.* Utah State Office of Education. Retrieved July 22, 2006, from http://www.uensd.org/USOE_pages/Char_ed/fed_proj/utah/hist/teaching.htm. Leming, J.S. (2002, November). *Hartshorne and May: A reappraisal.* Paper presented at the annual meeting of the Association for Moral Education, Northwestern University, Evanston, IL. May, M.A., & Hartshorne, H. (1927). Experimental studies in moral education. *Religious Education, 22,* 712–15.

*Craig A. Cunningham*

## Character Education Partnership

The Character Education Partnership (CEP) is a national advocate and leader for the character education movement. The organization is based in Washington, D.C. Their mission is helping to develop young people of good character who become responsible and caring citizens. They believe that character education is essential; that it must be comprehensive throughout the school; that it is very effective when done right; that it should be a core mission of all schools; and that it reinforces what is taught in homes, worship centers, and communities.

As a nonprofit, nonpartisan, nonsectarian, coalition of organizations and individuals, CEP is committed to fostering effective character education in K–12 schools across the United States and beyond. The organization functions as an umbrella for character education, serving as a leading resource for people and organizations that are integrating character education into their schools and communities. CEP's membership includes the nation's leading education organizations. Its board of directors is made up of corporate leaders and leading experts in the field of character education.

CEP focuses on defining and encouraging effective practices and approaches to quality character education and provides a forum for the exchange of ideas. CEP's *Eleven Principles of Effective Character Education* are the nationally regarded standard for planning quality character development initiatives, and they provide a framework for building comprehensive character education initiatives in schools and districts. CEP's *Quality Standards* represents a rating tool that schools may use to judge how well their efforts measure up to the standards set by the *Eleven Principles*.

## CEP Programs

The National Schools of Character (NSOC), CEP's annual awards program, recognizes exemplar K–12 schools and districts demonstrating outstanding character education initiatives that yield positive results in student behavior, citizenship, school climate, and academic performance. This program has a primary goal to disseminate model character education practices across the United States. It does this through its annual publication featuring the NSOC. A new program, State Schools of Character (SSOC), began with a pilot site in New Jersey in 2006 and has since spread to include around 15 total states. Each of the 10 National Schools of Character winning schools or districts receives a prize of $20,000. Half of the funds are used to strengthen their existing character programs, and the other half must be used for outreach activities that help other schools strive toward effective character education. Applications for the NSOC and SSOC awards are judged using the *Quality Standards*.

The annual National Forum on Character Education is the linchpin in CEP's training and networking activities and is a catalyst for encouraging schools, districts, businesses, and communities to join forces in a local and national call to character. The conference highlights the commonality of purpose among educators, researchers, and a wide range of organizations, all working to develop young people of good character who become caring and responsible citizens. The conference typically features presentations representing research and best practice, not only in the field of character education, but also from related fields of social and emotional learning (SEL), civic education, and service learning.

CEP provides professional development to schools and districts in the form of consultation, regional institutes, and seminars. The organization has developed a framework for providing multiyear support to initiatives that have multiple schools, including leadership development, baseline data collection and continued evaluation, development of local and school capacity by training coaches and school-based mentors, and skill-based training on culture change, SEL integration, and integration of character development and ethical understanding into the academic curriculum. A primary resource for this work is CEP's *Eleven Principles Sourcebook: How to Achieve Quality Character Education in K–12 Schools* (Beland, 2003).

## Organizational Structure

A volunteer leadership group of national experts in their fields participate in CEP's Board of Directors and serve as the Educational Advisory Committee to the executive director and senior staff. They ensure the organization stays focused on its fundamental mission, and review programs and services of CEP in order to keep them relevant and practical to teachers and administrative educators. The organization also has a National Leadership Council composed of a group of distinguished national-level leaders, also supporting CEP and its mission. The organization is led by an executive director and has a full-time staff and office in Washington, D.C. CEP is financially supported by corporate sponsorships, foundations, donations, grants, and revenue generated by its products and services.

*Further Reading:* Beland, K. (Ed.). (2003). *The Eleven Principles Sourcebook.* Washington, D.C.: Character Education Partnership.

*Merle J. Schwartz*

## Character, Development of

Developing character is a process and concern that affects not only the individual but also society. As social beings, humans must develop a basic competence for interpersonal relationships while at the same time come to know and practice self-respect. Having good character generally means to understand, value, and practice certain virtues that contribute to a positive view of self and relationships with others. Such virtues typically include love, honesty, courage, perseverance, responsibility, and compassion. Practicing the opposite vices of hate, dishonesty, cowardice, idleness, irresponsibility, and cruelty does not reflect the type of character that promotes constructive individual and community development.

The idea of developing one's character can be found in the early works of Plato and Aristotle and within major religious texts. Character development is not only timeless, but is life span oriented. In other words, one's character is evolving and is influenced by experiences from an early age to late life. A person's basic concept of right and wrong is initially influenced by parents, friends, siblings, the media, and school to name a few. Mixed signals are received on how one should act, think, and feel. This early modeling begins to shape the framework for what virtues are valued and have priority in how one makes decisions and experiences consequences.

The major institutions that influence character in adolescents—family, church, and schools—have changed over the years. Family structures have shifted away from that of moral educator to individualistic pursuits and constant change. The value of a nuclear family community and the desire to persevere in difficult times has weakened. The church has received much competition in the attention persons give to spiritual pursuits, if any. Historically, the church has strived to serve as a moral beacon and gathering place for spiritual communities. However, the rise of private quests, materialism, and independent self-guidance has lessened the role of church as center for moral and character development. Schools have also experienced shifts over the years in the role they play in advancing good character. The early *McGuffey Readers* with their moral undertones gave way to the values clarification movement and moral relativism. Recent character initiatives show strong momentum by schools to be facilitators of good character in students, which is a promising shift.

Probably one of the most controversial influences to adolescent character is the media. Television, film, music, the Internet, and video games depict varying degrees of character and moral flexibility. The lines between moral and immoral behavior become blurred, leaving questionable ideas of how to treat oneself or others. The level of public concern, though, would suggest that there at least should be a balance to the media's directions. The virtues and morality one follows are often found in the decisions that are made.

The basic pattern to character development and moral maturity requires one to know the good, love the good, and do the good. Knowing the good is being aware of virtues and vices and how they impact one's life. Loving the good simply means to value one's knowledge of the virtues and believe that practicing virtuous living is most desirable. Doing the good is taking actions on the virtues and ensuring that good character is practiced in everyday activities and relationships. Hall (2006) proposed a relationship between the virtues and vices that one practices—their character identity—and that person's successes and struggles.

The development of character within the individual and community is not mutually exclusive. A person and his or her community influence and are influenced by one another. This type of reciprocal growth suggests that individuals and their actions do not rest in isolation. To know this demands a level of respect and responsibility in the choices made with regard to relationships and everyday interactions.

There are many current initiatives and long-standing organizations dedicated to preserving and promoting character. Making a habit of good character practice is perceived to have long-term benefits to one's mental, emotional, physical, social, and moral development.

**Further Reading:** Bennett, W.J. (1993). *The book of virtues.* New York: Simon and Schuster. Hall, S.E. (2006). Developing character identity: A new framework or helping adults in transition. *Adultspan Journal, 5*(3), 15–24. Likona, T. (2004). *Character matters: How to help our children develop good judgment, integrity, and other essential virtues.* New York: Simon and Schuster. Ryan, K., & Likona, T. (1987). Character development: The challenge and the model. In K. Ryan & G. McLean (Eds.), *Character development in schools and beyond* (pp. 3–35). New York: Praeger.

*Scott E. Hall*

## Characteriological Research

Characteriological research (also known as "characteriology," "characterology," and "personology") is the attempt to categorize the inner qualities of a person from observations of the person's exterior physiology—body type, facial features, or shape of the head. Often based on the view that characters fit into a limited number of types or categories, characteriological research flourished between 1830 and 1930, but faded as twentieth-century empirical research failed to validate either the correlation between particular physiological measurements and particular character traits or types or even the usefulness of general character traits as causes or explanations for behavior.

Characteriological thinking probably has its roots as a natural human biological adaptation, since it is quite useful for humans to be able to quickly assess strangers' tendencies or size up their intentions (determining whether they are "friend" or "foe"), just by looking at them. The face and eyes, in particular, and a person's body posture, in general, have been seen as windows into the soul of a person, with most people believing that they can "see" someone's personality within a few moments of meeting. This capacity to assess others quickly has been formalized in many cultures as a kind of divination practiced by shamans, prophets, and, in the modern world, salesmen.

Formal characteriology in the Western world can be traced to the ancient Greeks, especially Aristotle, who discussed the relationship between facial or body characteristics and personal dispositions in several of his works including the *Prior Analytics*. The practice of reading the face to determine a person's future also thrived in ancient India. With the increasingly scientific/anatomical approach to health and medicine that developed in the eighteenth and nineteenth centuries, various theories emerged that connected particular aspects of the anatomy or physiology—such as humors, certain organs, or bodily secretions—with particular attributes of personality. We see this in the lingering tendency to speak of someone's "gall" or to describe their words as "bilious" or "heartfelt."

The Austrian physician Franz Josef Gall (1758–1828) is generally considered the father of characteriology for his work showing that different regions of the brain can be associated with various psychological phenomena such as sentiments, propensities, and moral and mental faculties. The view that the brain has specialized regions eventually led to the attempt to tie external observations of the head to predicted personality characteristics.

Characteriology is closely related to *phrenology* (which studies character through measurements of the head) and *physiognomy* (which studies the overall shape of the face or body). Two additional related practices are *palmistry*, which attempts to discern character traits or people's futures from lines on the palm, and *pathognomy*, which studies the expression of emotions. Charles Darwin (1809–1882) dabbled in physiognomy and pathognomy in his *The Expression of the Emotions in Man and Animals* (1872), which suggested that since emotional expression is similar in different species and individuals, inner emotional states and hence sensitivities and perhaps character could be read from the face. Central to all of these practices was the view that genetic or hereditary factors—which would be expressed in body type or skull shape—were the most important predictors of a person's character type.

The height of the popularization of characteriological research can be seen in an article in *Scientific American* from 1913, in which a series of portraits of men were used to illustrate character types. One very executive-looking man was claimed to be able to "win and hold the loyalty of all grades of working men." Another was "Determined. Liberty-loving. A natural pioneer. The motive type. (Note squareness of features with long lines.)" Yet another, who had a "convex upper and concave lower face," was "a man who is original, a keen observer, tenacious, courageous, and broadminded," while another was the "Russian motive type, of coarse texture; forceful, vigorous, and unrefined" (Newton, 1913). This article also demonstrates how judgments about character were very often suffused with racial or ethnic stereotypes.

From its inception, the field included both those who sought objectivity and acceptance within the scientific community and those who were more interested in exploiting an ignorant public eager for new insights into the relationships between observable phenomenon and ethical or moral dispositions. The nineteenth century was a time in which intellectuals and the general public sought surer means of perfecting the individual and society, and characteriology offered both diagnosis and the possible reform of various personal and social ills. If, it was reasoned, characteriology could provide an objective assessment of a person's moral or mental strengths and weaknesses, then an educational remedy might be created in turn. Similarly, characteriologists expended considerable energies trying to describe the physiological predictors of criminal behavior, both for the sake of prevention and rehabilitation.

The rise of psychology as an empirical, rather than speculative, field led inevitably to the erosion of scientific support for many of the claims of characteriologists.

Generalizations about correlations between the shape of the skull or body and character types broke down as controlled experiments (such as those performed by Cleeton and Knight, 1924) replaced the performance of individual practitioners, many of whom likely relied on intuition or even deception for their claims. A gradual shift from seeing heredity as the primary factor in character development to acknowledging the importance of experience and environment (as seen in the rise of psychoanalytic approaches to understanding personality) further eroded claims that the inner qualities of a person could be ascertained from relatively unchanging physical characteristics.

Belief in the relevance of physiological features for character and personality was further eroded by research showing that character cannot be satisfactorily understood in terms of a small set of character "types" nor as the combination of general character traits. The Character Education Inquiry (1925–1928) concluded that there is no such thing, statistically, as an "honest" or "tolerant" person; people's behavior varies with changes in situations. This severely undermined characteriological research because it questioned the very notion that generalizations could be made about a person's character on the basis of any observations, let alone the person's physical shape. Gordon Allport (1897–1967) helped move the focus of research from character to the somewhat-less-loaded term "personality" (see Nicholson, 1998).

The system of characteriology developed by L. Hamilton McCormick (heir to the McCormick reaper fortune) in the 1920s was a late attempt to construct a system that was compatible with scientific advancements. McCormick made broad claims for his system's usefulness to teachers, employers, salespeople, and prospective mates. McCormick's ideas are still studied by people who attend the University of Characterology.

The word "characteriological" continues to be used in psychological literature to imply the enduring features of a person's character (for example, their values) that may be considered as causally involved in the person's behavior. Some studies of the etiology of addiction or criminality continue to rely on character attributions, most likely because these aspects of personality remain unexplained by biochemical mechanisms. On this view, continued discussion of character as an explanatory factor represents the current limits of neurophysiological understanding; thus, the use of the term will probably continue to diminish, at least in scientific literature. As a folk technique, however, reading character from the face or body continues to flourish (see Oldham & Morris, 1995), as does the practice of adopting certain facial or bodily characteristics to imply character traits in the theater and movies.

*Further Reading:* Allport, G. (1960). *Becoming: Basic considerations for a psychology of personality.* New Haven: Yale University Press. Cleeton, G. U., & Knight, F. B. (1924). Validity of character judgments based on external criteria. *Journal of Applied Psychology, 8,* 215–31. Darwin, C., & Ekman, P. (2002/1872). *The expression of emotion in man and animals* (3rd ed.). Oxford: Oxford University Press. Kretschmer, E. (1925). *Physique and character: An investigation of the nature of the constitution and of the theory of the temperament* (W. J. H. Sprott, Trans.). New York: Harcourt, Brace & Co. Newton, H. (1913, July 26). The scientific employment of men: Standardizing human character. *Scientific American, 109,* 68–69, 75, 77. Nicholson, I. A. (1998, February). Gordon Allport, character, and the "culture of personality," 1897–1937. *History of Psychology, 1*(1), 52–68. Oldham, J. M., & Morris, L. B. (1995). *The new personality self-portrait: Why you think, work, love, and act the way you do.* New York: Bantam.

*Craig A. Cunningham*

## Cheating

Cheating is a form of academic dishonesty, a violation of accepted standards or rules intended by the student to gain an unfair advantage with respect to examinations, quizzes, course assignments, or any activity employed by instructors to gauge students' progress and/or knowledge. Cheating takes many forms. In the contained environment of the classroom or lecture hall, cheating may consist of copying another student's answers on quizzes and tests; providing answers to another; and using unauthorized sources for gaining test answers such as crib notes, cell phones, or advance information about the test. In an open environment, where students are unsupervised or work independently, cheating may consist of copying another's homework assignment, plagiarizing another's work, and gaining illicit assistance. Cheating reflects negatively on students' integrity and invalidates the assessment of their knowledge. Widespread cheating also undermines the integrity of educational systems, casting suspicion on the reliability of students' grades and certificates.

Though cheating has always been a significant problem in education, it has become more widespread in recent years. For example, in 1969, 33.8 percent of high school students confessed to using a cheat sheet on a test; by 1989, 67.8 percent had confessed to such use (Schab, 1991). McCabe (2001) found, in his survey of students in public and private high schools, 39 percent admitted to using crib notes in an exam, 63 percent had copied from another on an exam, and 77 percent had received answers from peers who had already taken the same test. Compounding the problem of increases in the incidence of cheating in schools are problems in the broader society. Daily students can hear and read about dishonest acts committed by well-known leaders in, for example, business, politics, and sports. Given these problems in the broader society, it is of little surprise that cheating happens in schools. Against this backdrop, however, schools are charged with helping students to value honesty over dishonesty and to see the merits of integrity.

To deal constructively with the problem of cheating, educators need to understand the causes and conditions that lead to the behavior. Such knowledge can help in determining proper sanctions and finding ways to stem the problem. The causes of cheating include technological, sociocultural, and individual factors. Certainly electronic devices and the spread of the Internet contribute to the ease with which students can commit acts of academic dishonesty. Students are almost limitless in the ways they can access information instantaneously and incorporate it, often without detection.

General cultural factors contributing to the rise in cheating include a growing cynicism about the integrity of adult role models in general and the competitive nature of U.S. society. If students see adults cheating in their work and home lives, they may more easily see cheating as commonplace and find admonitions against it hypocritical. Moreover, students are socialized to value competition and winning in a capitalist, meritocratic society. From almost nursery school onward, students compete for scarce positions in good schools, engage in high-stakes testing, and vie for admissions into top-rate high schools and colleges. Such a system often forces young people to be concerned with achieving at any cost. Well-intentioned parents with high expectations often impose serious pressure on their children to do well, not only in academics but also in extracurricular endeavors. Children growing up under such pressure may feel they have no alternative but to cheat. Furthermore, sometimes children are actually encouraged to cheat by misguided parents who may interfere with a school's disciplinary action if their child is accused of cheating or who may actually complete assignments for their children. For example, in McCabe's

(2001) survey, 20 percent of the respondents reported that they had turned in an assignment that had been done by their parent.

Besides competition and parental pressures, student responses on surveys and in focus groups shed light on some ways in which teachers contribute to the problem of cheating. For example, teachers may ignore the problem, or avoid confronting the problem, or attend to the problem differently for different students. When teachers behave in such a way, students may get the message that it is all right to cheat. Students may also cheat if teachers have not taught well or if their tests contain questions about information not covered in class. Teachers may be disinclined to deal with cheating because of burdensome bureaucratic procedures or because administrators may side with outraged parents rather than support the teachers. Overburdened teachers may also want to avoid the time-consuming process entailed in pursuing an alleged case or the time that it takes to teach students about what they did wrong and how to seek more honorable alternatives. In schools where cheating is not addressed, besides getting the message that cheating is tolerated, otherwise honorable students may feel compromised. That is, if there are some students earning good grades by cheating and this goes undetected or unaddressed, honest students may feel that they will be penalized by being honest and will choose then to cheat. Other reasons why individual students may choose to cheat include fear of failure and peer pressures in support of cheating.

To forestall the problem of cheating, teachers need to help children to understand what constitutes academic honesty and dishonesty and about the importance of honesty. They also need to provide guidelines for how students may share information, collaborate with peers, and work independently. Teachers should also consider the developmental level of the students. What students understand as dishonesty, the forms that dishonesty may take, and the ability of students to work independently change over time. Teachers, administrators, and parents need to consider the changing needs and capacities of students as they progress through all levels of education in order to offer meaningful assistance and input that will maintain academic honesty. At every level, students' honesty is most ensured through a system-wide set of policies on academic integrity that all parties (students, teachers, parents, and administrators) have discussed and ratified, and, most importantly, adhere to consistently (McCabe et al., 2001). Often referred to as an honor code, such a system requires coordination, communication, and sustained active commitment.

*Further Reading:* Calabrese, R.L., & Cochran, J.T. (1990). The relationship of alienation to cheating among a sample of American adolescents. *Journal of Research and Development in Education, 23,* 65–72. McCabe, D.L. (2001). Cheating: Why students do it and how we can help them stop. *American Educator, 25*(4), 38–43. McCabe, D.L., Trevino, L.K., and Butterfield, K.D. (2001). Cheating in academic institutions: A decade of research. *Ethics and behavior, 11*(3), 219–32. Schab, F. (1991). Schooling without learning: Thirty years of cheating in high school. *Adolescence, 26,* 839–47.

*Ann Marie R. Power*

## Child Development Project (CDP)

The Child Development Project (CDP) was initiated in the 1980s as a long-term, comprehensive, elementary school intervention project. The overall goal of CDP was to design, implement, and evaluate a program for promoting children's prosocial development that could be delivered primarily by classroom teachers with some parent involvement. At the time of its inception, CDP was unique in the comprehensiveness of its program and the extensiveness of its research and evaluation. The project was first implemented in three elementary schools in a suburban district in northern California (Watson, Solomon, Battistich, Schaps, & Solomon, 1989). In succeeding years it was implemented in urban, suburban, and rural schools across the country (Solomon, Battistich, Watson, Schaps, & Lewis, 2000).

The original CDP included a classroom program, a family involvement program, and a schoolwide program. Three approaches were at the heart of the classroom program:

- A values-rich literature-based approach to reading and language arts (Developmental Studies Center, 1998);
- An approach to cooperative learning (Developmental Studies Center, 1997); and
- Developmental Discipline, a relationship based, problem-solving approach to classroom management (Watson & Ecken, 2003).

The schoolwide program highlighted prosocial values and provided opportunities for students to engage in prosocial activities from raising money to help disaster victims to a buddies program (Developmental Studies Center, 1994, 1997a).

The family involvement program included both family events at school, such as family read-aloud nights, and *Homeside,* a set of values-related activities for students and caregivers to do together at home (Developmental Studies Center, 1995–1997).

With time and experience, the program developers came to see the creation of a "caring community of learners" as an essential goal, and the program components were seen both as vehicles for creating community and as dependent on community for their effectiveness (Solomon, Watson, Battistich, Schaps, & Delucchi, 1996).

For many teachers, CDP represented substantial changes in their beliefs about teaching and learning, and in their classroom practice. In particular, the project stressed the importance of building students' internal motivation to learn and act in prosocial ways. At the time the project was first implemented, the predominant approach to classroom motivation was through the promise of rewards or the threat of consequences.

CDP's approach to instruction was based on both the cognitive developmental constructivism of Jean Piaget and the social constructivism of Lev Vygotsky. Teachers were asked to take a scaffolding or guiding approach rather than a telling approach to both academic and moral instruction.

Because of the extensive changes teachers would have to make, the three major studies evaluating the program involved substantial professional development and careful assessment of the level of implementation students experienced. The findings from these studies are both encouraging and cautionary. As anticipated, there was considerable variation across classrooms in program implementation, and outcomes varied directly with the level of implementation. Teachers were able to successfully implement the original CDP program in all schools and settings; however, in some schools the number of teachers implementing the classroom program was too small to positively impact student outcomes.

When CDP was widely implemented, it had numerous and long-lasting effects. Students showed positive changes in a broad range of attitudes, inclinations, feelings, and behaviors—for example, greater commitment to democratic values, conflict resolution skills, concern for others, trust in and respect for teachers, prosocial motivation, altruistic and positive interpersonal behavior, and sense of efficacy, along with less loneliness, social anxiety, and drug use. Students also showed increased intrinsic academic motivation, class engagement, enjoyment of class, and liking for school (Solomon, Watson, Delucchi, Schaps, & Battistich, 1988; Battistich, Watson, Solomon, Schaps, & Solomon, 1991). Positive findings were also found in two follow-up studies. Middle school students from program schools were found to be more engaged in and committed to school, more prosocial, and engaged in fewer problem behaviors than comparison students. Program students also had higher academic performance, and associated with peers who were more prosocial and less antisocial than their matched comparison students during middle school (Battistich, Schaps, & Wilson, 2004).

One consistent finding that has had a significant effect on approaches to moral education relates to the importance of school and classroom community. In all three studies of the effects of CDP, students' sense of community was related to a broad range of positive student outcomes, among them social competence, intrinsic academic and prosocial motivation, democratic values, and concern for others (Battistich, Solomon, Watson, & Schaps, 1997).

Concerns for the difficulty of achieving good program implementation on a large scale, disappointment at the program's inability to consistently produce academic gains, and increased demand in schools for more rigorous reading instruction led Developmental Studies to drastically reshape the program. The current version of CDP consists of three separate programs—Caring School Community, a program involving class meetings, buddies, and schoolwide and family involvement activities; Making Meaning, a reading comprehension and social communication skills program; and SIPPS, a systematic decoding program.

*Further Reading:* Battistich, V., Schaps, E., & Wilson, N. (2004). Effects of an elementary school intervention on students' "connectedness" to school and social adjustment during middle school. *The Journal of Primary Prevention, 24*(3), 243–62. Battistich, V., Solomon, D., Watson, M., & Schaps, E. (1997). Caring school communities. *Educational Psychologist, 32*(3), 137–51. Solomon, D., Battistich, V., Watson, M., Schaps, E., & Lewis, C. (2000). A six-district study of educational change: Direct and mediated effects of the Child Development Project. *Social Psychology of Education, 4,* 3–51. Watson, M., Solomon, D., Battistich, V., Schaps, E., & Solomon, J. (1989). The Child Development Project: Combining traditional and developmental approaches to values education. In L. Nucci (Ed.), *Moral development and character education: A dialogue.* Berkeley: McCutchan. Watson, M., & Ecken, L. (2003). *Learning to trust: Transforming difficult elementary classrooms through Developmental Discipline.* San Francisco: Jossey-Bass.

*References:* Battistich, V., Watson, M., Solomon., D., Schaps, E., & Solomon, J. (1991). The child development project: A comprehensive program for the development of prosocial character. In W.M. Kurtines & J.L. Gewirtz (Eds.), *Handbook of moral behavior and development: Vol. f3 Application.* Hillsdale, NJ: Erlbaum. Developmental Studies Center. (1994). *At home in our schools: A guide to schoolwide activities that build community.* Oakland, CA: Author. Developmental Studies Center. (1997a). *Blueprints for a collaborative classroom.* Oakland, CA: Author. Developmental Studies Center. (1997b). *That's my buddy: Friendship and learning across the grades.* Oakland, CA: Author. Developmental Studies Center. (1998). *Reading, thinking, and caring.* Oakland, CA: Author. Developmental Studies Center. (1995–1997). *Homeside activities: Conversations and activities that bring parents into children's schoolside learning.* Oakland, CA: Author. Solomon, D., Watson, M., Battistich, V., Schaps, E., & Delucchi, K. (1996). Creating classrooms that students experience as communities. *American Journal of Community Psychology, 24*(6), 719–48. Solomon, D., Watson, M., Delucchi, K., Schaps, E., & Battistich, V. (1988). Enhancing children's prosocial behavior in the classroom. *American Educational Research Journal, 25*(3), 527–54.

*Marilyn Watson*

## Christian Ethical Teaching

Christian ethical teaching is a code of moral conduct used to guide behavior that is based on the teachings of Jesus Christ as found in the four Gospels of the New Testament. Christian ethics take Jesus Christ as their inspiration and norm, basing ethical principles and moral imperatives on his words, example, and teaching.

As a general field of inquiry, ethics involves the quality of relationships among and between a community of persons. It typically prescribes certain behaviors as a way to protect the rights of individuals and preserve the common good and proscribes other behaviors that are detrimental to individual well-being and the common good. Ethics is concerned with justice, the fair, equitable treatment of all persons. Ethical systems are useful to society and to social groups within a given society as a way to solve problems, settle disputes, balance conflicting goods, and promote a peaceful and orderly lifestyle.

Many ethical theories and precepts are designed to provide direction to people in the midst of a dilemma, requiring a difficult choice between alternatives. Utilitarian approaches tend to focus on the maximization of pleasure and the avoidance of pain. Utilitarian ethics prescribes choosing the course of action that provides the most utility in advancing happiness and avoiding suffering. Deontological approaches point to the requirement of doing one's duty as the highest ethical norm. Deontological ethics prescribes that even when it is difficult, one's duty is paramount, and therefore an ethical education is necessary so that in challenging situations, a clear discernment of duty is possible. Many other ethical theories provide a similar framework for making moral decisions.

Christian ethical teaching is distinct in terms of its content because its origins lay in the four Gospels found in the New Testament. The Gospels are biblical narratives of the life of Jesus, preserved and handed on from first-century Palestine. While the Gospels do not offer historical reporting of a modern sort, the Gospels are believed to hold essential and obligatory teachings based on the life of Jesus Christ as faithfully transmitted through his early followers and the church they established.

Jesus's example in the Gospel is provocative and challenging. He seems fond of social outcasts and those marginalized by society. He dines with tax collectors, embraces those with leprosy, and has bold exchanges with religious and political leaders. He pays attention to those who are sick, disabled, and hurting in any way. He uses his power miraculously to heal, to help others, even to bring the dead back to life. In dealing with difficult situations, he prescribes his followers to love their enemies and to pray for those who persecute them. When punished or injured, he counsels to turn the other cheek. While not wanting to establish a specific social order or government, he repeatedly proclaims the establishment of what he calls the "kingdom of God."

Jesus's harshest words are reserved for religious leaders, whom he often challenges for their manifest hypocrisy. Political leaders are acknowledged, but Jesus's clear focus is the primacy of God's reign, and not any earthly ruler. His clearest command of an ethical principle is the maxim, "love one another."

Christian ethical teaching looks to these examples and to other elements in the life of Jesus to help construct an approach to moral decision making. Christian ethics, therefore, refers to making moral decisions based on Jesus's example and teaching. A modern-day, reductionist view of this approach is well expressed in the question, "what would Jesus do?" While many contemporary ethical dilemmas are so modern and unique as to defy easy extrapolation to the life of Jesus several thousand years ago, the question reveals the rootedness that Christian ethics attempts to retain in the life and ministry of Jesus.

Based on this example, Christian ethics advocate for the poor and underprivileged. Jesus is often described as having had a preferential option for the poor, so his followers are obligated to do likewise. Peace studies often look to Christian ethical teaching for support, because Jesus resisted the use of force even in the legitimate defense of his own life. Given the miraculous power of God that he demonstrated in healing the sick and repeatedly responding to their manifest needs, he declined to use any of this power in self-defense or for his own self-aggrandizement. Advocates for peace see a radical pacifism in Jesus and challenge his followers to respond similarly.

Christian ethical teaching depends on Jesus and on how his words and actions are interpreted and explained. The growth and development of Christian ethics will involve the study of the Gospels as well as applying the results of such study to contemporary problems in the modern world.

*Further Reading:* Catholic Biblical Association of America. (1970). *The new American Bible.* New York: P.J. Kenedy. Keating, J. (Ed.). (2004). *Moral theology: New directions and fundamental issues: Festschrift for James P. Hanigan.* New York: Paulist Press. Pojman, L.P. (1998). *Moral philosophy: A reader* (2nd ed.; L.P. Pojman, Ed.). Indianapolis, IN: Hackett. Rachels, J. (2003). *The elements of moral philosophy* (4th ed.). Boston: McGraw-Hill.

*Ronald J. Nuzzi*

## Citizenship

The prevalent contemporary definition of citizen, and citizenship, is a status of full membership in a nation. In a context of the United States, full membership provides rights (the right to vote is cited often as the most fundamental) and responsibilities (e.g., obeying laws and serving on juries, when called and selected).

To trace the history of citizenship in the Western tradition, we can look to Athens. Aristotle defined citizenship as limited in terms of who was a citizen (women and slaves were excluded) and as a participatory activity; citizens were expected to be involved in the politics of the city-states. Those who did not participate in public political life were referred to as "idiots" (in the sense of idiosyncratic and self-centered rather than unintelligent).

For moral educators, the historical issues and struggles around issues of citizenship provide significant pedagogical opportunities. For example, in U.S. history, women were denied full citizenship until the ratification of the 19th Amendment to the Constitution in 1920. The framers of the Constitution denied citizenship to slaves but, in terms of allocating seats in the House of Representatives, each slave would count as a fraction of a person. The outcome of these issues—the abolition of slavery and women's suffrage—are generally accepted within the United States and the previous state of affairs as ethically objectionable. That many of the same issues remain matters of debate in other countries provide opportunities to reexamine the fundamental issues.

Another issue with many ethical dimensions is under what conditions, if any, can and should noncitizens become citizens. The United States is often called a "nation of immigrants," and, consequently, the concept of a noncitizen becoming a citizen (at least *some* noncitizens and under *some* conditions) is fairly well accepted within the United States, but the notion is rejected and/or the practice rare in many other nations. Which people get into the United States, how many, how they arrive (e.g., with or without documentation, by volition, or as a refugee), and what is and should be required for citizenship remain hotly debated topics.

Defining who is a citizen raises difficult issues. The same is true of what are the duties and expectations that accompany citizenship. Whether citizenship entails a positive obligation to get involved in the political life of the community is controversial. With the passage of the 26th Amendment in 1971, the age of majority and full citizenship—in terms of the right to vote—changed from the age of 21 to 18. However, it is the youngest voters, aged 18–26, who as a group have the lowest rates of casting ballots in elections. They are not unique; typically a minority of U.S. citizens who are eligible actually cast a ballot in elections. Other nations, such as Australia, mandate voting and sanction nonvoters with fines for failing in what the Australian law deems a positive obligation of citizenship.

Voting is an important measure of civic engagement but only one. Besides low engagement in the political process, most forms of involvement (also called social capital) have been in decline for four decades in all sectors of the society. Programs such as AmeriCorps, the Peace Corps, and Volunteers in Service to America (VISTA) provide voluntary opportunities for youth to engage in national service. A period debate is about the fairness and wisdom of requiring young citizens to engage in service (either in the military or as civilian volunteers).

Diversity within the citizenry is another issue that is disputed. One question is whether diversity is positive or negative in its consequences to the community. A related, but distinct, question is the degree to which immigrants should be forced or expected or encouraged to follow the customs of the dominant culture. While the issues play out in several different contexts, one that frequently recurs is whether the United States has (*de facto*) or ought to have (*de jure*) an official language. In recent history, several initiatives in several states have been placed on ballots, voted upon, and disputed in courts. In addition to the legal questions, ethical considerations are also present and are important opportunities for dialogue and deliberation in moral education settings.

The definition of citizen has shifted through centuries from being based on the city in which one resides. For example, in the early years of U.S. history, one's colonial or state affiliation was the political body by which one determined citizenship. Arguably, it was after the U.S. Civil War that the importance and identification for national citizen status eclipsed statehood.

That the definition of primary citizenship has shifted in concentric circles from city to colony/state to nation leads to some interesting speculation and debate about whether the national boundaries will, too, give way to other notions of citizenship. One example is the transition in Europe to a single currency and relaxed restrictions regarding travel between nations. Could this lead to a primary identification based on continent rather than nation? In another expansion of orientation and identification, some argue for a definition of world or global citizenship. The consequences, Constitution, and other elements of what this would entail are presently hypothetical. However, the desirability and ethical issues that arise are opportunities for moral education in classrooms, schools, and communities (small and large).

This description of citizenship and the concomitant issues that accompany the investigation is a short overview and certainly does not exhaust the topic. However, for a concluding question, consider ancient Athens again with the question of whether, in being questioning and critical of the leaders and their actions, Socrates was a good citizen. The answer given has great implication for the goals of moral education. The obvious importance for moral education is whether children should be encouraged to be patriotic and supporters of their nation or to be critical of their country or some combination of patriotic and critical. Many popular moral/character education programs emphasize only respect for authority. Because the current example is still a matter of controversy two millennia after the fact, perhaps the overarching goal for moral educators is to prepare children to become citizens prepared to engage in the ethical discourse.

**Further Reading:** Banks, J.A. (1997). *Educating citizens in a multicultural society.* New York: Teachers College Press. Callan, E. (1997). *Creating citizens: Political education and liberal democracy.* New York: Oxford University Press. Parker, W.C. (2003). *Teaching democracy: Unity and diversity in public life.* New York: Teachers College Press. Putnam, R.D. (2000). *Bowling alone: The collapse and revival of American community.* New York: Simon and Schuster. Soder, R., Goodlad, J.I., & McMannon, T.J. (Eds.). (2001). *Developing democratic character in the young.* San Francisco: Jossey Bass.

*Robert W. Howard*

## Civic Education

Civic education can be defined as the acquisition of knowledge, skills, and dispositions that are needed for effective and responsible citizenship in a democratic society. The primary goal of civic education is to facilitate informed participation in the democratic processes of responsible political life. Civic education is considered by many to be of critical importance as a means to transmit the fundamental values and principles of American constitutional democracy (Goodlad, Mantle-Bromley, & John, 2004). Historically, schools have assumed the responsibility for the development of civic competence. Schools fulfill that responsibility through informal curricula beginning in the elementary grades and continuing with formal curricula in the secondary grades.

Formal instruction in civics and government is intended to provide students with the basic understanding of American government and our political system. Civics educators recognize that students need to understand not only the workings of their own government but also other political systems as well, in addition to the relationship of American politics and government to global affairs (Bergerson, 1991). Formal instruction in civic education provides a basis for understanding the rights and responsibilities of citizens in American constitutional democracy and a framework for competent and responsible participation in the global political arena.

Formal civic education in the schools is augmented by informal instruction in many other institutions that have contributed to our civic character. For example, religious institutions, family, community organizations, and the mass media have all exerted influence on our general knowledge about American government and politics.

Additionally, the governance of the schools and the relationship between schools and their communities should reiterate the fundamental values and principles of American constitutional democracy. In other words, we should expect our schools to hold students accountable for behaving in accordance with fair and reasonable standards and for respecting the rights and dignity of others both in the schools and in their communities (Guarasci & Cornwell, 1997).

Education in civics and government should be focused on the development of such skills as are required for competent participation in the political process. These include such skills as (1) the capacity to influence policies and decisions by working collaboratively with others, (2) the ability to clearly express interests and concerns to key decision and policy makers, and (3) the ability to build coalitions and seek consensus with others in one's community. Such skills are defined by many civics educators as participatory skills, which are best developed when students are given opportunities to interact with local community members and government representatives (Guarasci & Cornwell, 1997). There are many examples of the sort of learning opportunities that promote these participatory skills. For example, students might be assigned to interview persons in the public and private sectors who are involved in the political process; they might also observe meetings and public hearings dealing with particular issues in their community. Students can also learn how to monitor the political process by tracking how issues are reported in the media, and comparing those reports with public documents and accounts gathered from various special interest groups and government agencies.

Students should also be encouraged to learn how to influence politics and government by taking part in the governance of their own schools and classrooms. They might work together with peers and teachers to learn how to resolve conflicts, reach consensus about school rules, advocate for changes in school policies, and assume leadership roles in their communities. The characteristics of students who possess civic virtues are those who demonstrate the following dispositions: civility toward others, acceptance of responsibility for the consequences of one's actions, self-discipline and respect for constitutional law, open-mindedness and tolerance for alternative values and belief systems, perseverance in working to further the public good, generosity of spirit and time in pursuit of helping others, and loyalty to the values and principles of democracy (Bergerson, 1991).

Lisman (1998) argues that education has a critical role to play in challenging the dominant views of politics and education, and that service-learning partnerships with community service organizations can facilitate this critical role. Academically based community service programs have been used with promising results across the country and have proven to be an efficacious educational pedagogy in helping students to acquire civic virtues. Since constitutional democracy itself is intended to advance such fundamental values as liberty, equality, justice, and the common good, students have an obligation as citizens in training to strive for governmental policies consistent with those values. Civic education lesson plans should be designed to teach students that responsible self-government requires citizens to anticipate the consequences of their actions and to justify them in terms of fundamental democratic values. This learning objective is clearly not an easy task to achieve, and considerable moral deliberation should be brought to bear when considering the design of such lesson plans. The process of assessing the extent to which proposed curricula support fundamental democratic values should occupy an important part of curriculum planning and design. In a democratic pluralist society, the responsible citizen is called upon to confront persistent problems with thoughtful and decisive action. The realities of our global community in the twenty-first century make these lessons essential in order to function as participatory agents of good citizenship.

***Further Reading:*** Bergerson, P. J. (1991). *Teaching public policy: Theory, research, and practice.* New York: Greenwood Press. Goodlad, J. I., Mantle-Bromley, C., & John, S. (2004). *Education for everyone: Agenda for education in a democracy.* San Francisco, CA: Jossey-Bass. Guarasci, R., & Cornwell, G. H. (1997). *Democratic education in an age of difference: Redefining citizenship in higher education.* San Francisco, CA: Jossey-Bass. Lisman, C. D. (1998). *Toward a civil society: Civic literacy and service learning.* Westport, CT: Bergin & Garvey. Soder, R., Goodlad, J. I., & McMannon, T. J. (Eds.). (2001). *Developing Democratic character in the young.* San Francisco, CA: Jossey-Bass.

*Monalisa M. Mullins*

## Civic Engagement

Civic engagement refers to activities like voting, membership in voluntary associations, working on a political campaign, and volunteering for a charitable group. Some scholars include paying attention to public affairs under civic engagement's umbrella. Since it can potentially encompass such a wide range of diverse activities, any discussion of civic engagement requires careful attention to what is meant by the term. The general category of civic engagement can be informatively subdivided into separate components. Empirical research both old and new reveals that civic engagement can be grouped into activities that are consensual in nature and those that are rooted in conflict. Consensual activities properly have the label of "civic" engagement, while conflictual forms of engagement are better described as "political." An example illuminates the distinction between the two. Imagine two people, each of whom wishes to help the homeless population. A civic form of engagement with that objective might consist of volunteering in a soup kitchen or homeless shelter. Political engagement would consist of lobbying for a change in laws affecting the homeless, or working on the campaign for a candidate with one's preferred policy positions regarding the homeless. The ends of each type of engagement are the same—helping the homeless—but the means differ. In drawing the distinction between civic and political engagement, one should keep in mind that these descriptions are "ideal types," and that some activities share a blend of civic and political motivations, although, empirically, most fall into one category or the other. Voting, for example, is widely considered to be *sui generis,* as it has both a civic and a political motivation.

Note that civic and political engagements are not mutually exclusive. One can engage in both. Indeed, people who engage in one type of activity are generally more likely to engage in the other.

Political engagement warrants our attention because it sits at the heart of representative democracy. Ample evidence shows that elected representatives do respond to the input of their constituents. Therefore, a fully representative democracy requires the represented to be politically engaged. Inequities in political engagement thus lead to democratic distortion. Groups that are underrepresented are less likely to have their voices heard and, thus, are less likely to have their preferences reflected in public policy.

The reason that civic engagement is worthy of our attention dates back at least to Alexis de Tocqueville. In his magnum opus, *Democracy in America,* this French aristocrat trenchantly observed that Americans learn the "art of association" through what we today call civic activity. Contemporary social science elaborates on de Tocqueville's fundamental insight, by conceptualizing civic activity as both a cause and a consequence of social capital—by which is meant the norms and social networks that develop through interpersonal association. Like physical and human capital, social capital is a morally neutral term. While some of its consequences are negative—gangs, for example, have a lot of social capital—many are also salutary. Communities with higher levels of social capital have better levels of health, lower rates of crime, better schools. Social capital-rich communities also have more responsive governments, suggesting an important link between civic and political engagement.

Much of the discussion about political and civic engagement has centered on their trends over time within the United States. Most famously, Robert D. Putnam has presented considerable evidence that, with a few telling exceptions, levels of both civic and political engagement have declined precipitously over roughly the past 30 years. The breadth of the decline is dramatic and is concentrated mostly among people born after 1960.

As noted, however, there has not been a decline in all forms of engagement. As one example, while the general trend in voter turnout over the past 50 years has been downward, participation has spiked in some presidential elections—1992 and 2004 in particular. In the former, third-party candidate Ross Perot brought many new voters to the polls, while the closeness of the 2004 contest stimulated massive efforts at voter mobilization.

A second countertrend is the considerable increase in volunteering, especially among people under 30—the group that has experienced the sharpest decline in other forms of engagement. A small component of this increase is driven by mandatory community service requirements tied to high school graduation, while a larger component results from students who perform community service to burnish a resume or college application. A sizable portion, though, consists of young people who wish to contribute to their local, national, and world communities, which, of course, is not inconsistent with more instrumental motivations for such service. One can do well by doing good. Whatever the motivation, surveys of young people show that they often learn of community service opportunities through their schools.

The exceptions to the general decline in political and civic engagement remind us that declension is not inevitable. Nor is it inexorable. Putnam and others have not only documented that recent decades have seen engagement levels drop; multiple sources of evidence demonstrate that engagement has risen and fallen during different periods of American history. The last great period of such civic and political reinvigoration was the late 1800s and early 1900s, when a plethora of new organizations were created as a response to a period of great social change—including tremendous technological transformation, rapid immigration, and marked income differences. Today, we live in a period of comparable change, complete with new technology, an influx of immigrants, and high levels of income disparity. Now, as then, Americans must find new ways to foster both political and civic engagement.

While there are no easy solutions to spurring greater levels of engagement, the two countertrends to the general decline suggest possible avenues of change. The example of voter turnout reminds us that political actors, especially America's parties, play a huge role in facilitating engagement in the nation's electoral process. Extensive evidence shows that voters are most likely to become engaged in a campaign when they are personally contacted—even a brief doorstep conversation has far more effect than a barrage of automated phone calls or televised campaign ads.

The rise of volunteerism, much of which is tied to students' experiences in school, reminds us of the role America's educational institutions can play in fostering both civic and political engagement. Indeed, the *raison d'etre* of the common, or public, school was to prepare citizens of a diverse nation for active and engaged citizenship—an objective, empirical evidence shows, that is met by the nation's private school sector as well. Given that the sharpest decline in engagement is among young people, it seems logical to look to reform the one institution through which virtually all youth pass—their school. At this point, the precise way in which the nation's schools can play a role in fostering civic and political engagement is yet to be determined. There are, however, hints in the existing research literature that can be pursued further. Specifically, schools with a participatory ethos—that is, with a high level of social capital—are incubators for students' engagement in their community.

Changes in both political and educational practices have been mentioned as illustrative examples only, as they are probably not enough to stem the decline in civic and political engagement. More needs to be done. Just as the turn of the last century was marked by a flurry of civic innovation, so must our era meet the same challenge.

*Further Reading:* Campbell, D.E. (2006). *Why we vote: How schools and communities shape our civic life.* Princeton, NJ: Princeton University Press. Putnam, R.D. (2000). *Bowling alone: The collapse and revival of American community.* New York: Simon and Schuster. Zukin, C., Keeter, S., Andolina, M., Jenkins, K., & Delli Carpini, M.X. (2006). *A new engagement? Political participation, civic life, and the changing American citizen.* London: Oxford University Press.

*David E. Campbell*

## Civic Virtue

Civic virtues are traits or values that are deemed essential for the functioning and the well-being for the community. That civic virtue is positive is true by definition. What is not tautological is whether it is civic virtue (singular) or virtues (plural) and, if manifold, what virtues to include in the list. Furthermore, if the virtues are plural, whether one or more virtues are primary (from which others can be derived) remains a debated question.

Recognizing that the good of the community may be in conflict with the narrower good of the individual, most conceptions of civic virtue in a democratic society include a balancing of individual and group well-being. That in the United States in 1835 citizens had a disposition to temper their own self-interest and consider their duties to the "species" was noted by Alexis de Tocqueville in the second volume of his *Democracy in America.* Without these habits, de Tocqueville did not believe the democracy could be sustained, that unbridled individualism would be destructive. Family life, religious communities, and local politics provided opportunities to foster and sustain the habits of the heart.

Promoting civic virtues—particularly in children and youth—in the form of active involvement in the community has traditionally been a responsibility of schools. Many states enumerate a list of virtues to be promoted and fostered in public schools. For example, California's Education Code mandates that students be taught principles of morality, truth, justice, patriotism, equality and human dignity, kindness, and good manners (among others). In addition, the California code requires that students should be taught to avoid idleness, profanity, and falsehood.

Besides schools, communities of faith, voluntary community associations such as fraternal orders play a role (albeit one that has diminished in recent history). For example, Boy and Girl Scout organizations explicitly attempt to foster civic virtue. Consider the descriptors in the Girl Scout Law (in its current form and in part): honest and fair, friendly and helpful, considerate and caring, courageous and strong, responsible, respect myself, others, and authority, and use resources wisely. The Law is an attempt to be specific about which traits should be included and supported by the scouting program.

No nationwide consensus exists for a specific definition or list of traits to be included in civic virtue; nor do most lists of traits address what to do in instances when the traits conflict or are mutually exclusive. To use the Girl Scout Law to illustrate, if one lives in a despotic regime *respecting authority* might be counterproductive to making *the world a better place.*

Civic virtue and the concomitant charge to balance individualism and the community interests inherently raises ethical issues. The major approaches to moral education can find common ground in supporting the concept of civic virtue—albeit in their own construction and with different definitions of what constitutes (or is primary among) the virtue(s). The explicit emphasis on a list of traits makes the concept of civic virtues resonate well with the *traditional character education* approach to moral education. Character educators tend to define virtues as specifically plural but with a claim that the virtues are universal. An example is the *Character Manifesto* from the Center for the Advancement of Ethics and Character at Boston University that lists integrity, courage, responsibility, diligence, service, and respect for the dignity of all persons. In contrast with the traditional character education approach, which endorses multiple virtues, sees moral education as transmitting the virtues to youth, and helps them discern which virtue is appropriate in a given context, the *caring* and *cognitive developmental* approaches to moral education identify a single—but different—primary virtue: caring and justice, respectively. The ethic of care emphasizes relationships among individuals and of individuals and their communities. At the core of the ethic of care is establishing positive relationships and enhancing the relationship—through interactions in the relationships to be their best ethical selves. The relationship is seen as a form of moral education, and caring is seen as the fundamental civic virtue. As noted, *justice* is the civic virtue that cognitive-developmental moral educators see as primary, and it was evident that early Kohlbergian moral education interventions used moral dilemma discussions. Lawrence Kohlberg's later moral education projects were broader and included real-world relationships and issues as sources of moral issues. Still the primary value was included in the term for the schools: Just Communities—small schools practicing direct democracy.

**Further Reading:** de Tocqueville, A. (2000). *Democracy in America* (H.C. Mansfield & D. Winthrop, Trans.). Chicago: University of Chicago Press. (Original work published in 1835.) Noddings, N. (2002). *Educating moral people: A caring alternative to character education.* New York: Teachers College Press. Oakes, J., Quartz, K.H., Ryan, S., & Lipton, M. (2001). *Becoming good American schools: The struggle for civic virtue in education reform.* San Francisco: Jossey-Bass. Power, F.C., Higgins, A., & Kohlberg, L. (1989). *Lawrence Kohlberg's approach to moral education.* New York: Columbia University Press. Ryan, K., & Bohlin, K. (1999). *Building character in schools: Practical ways to bring moral instruction to life.* San Francisco: Jossey-Bass.

*Robert W. Howard*

## Civil Disobedience

Civil disobedience can be described as the clear, open refusal to conform to a law or policy believed to be fundamentally unjust. The refusal is typically marked by nonviolence and is usually a means of forcing concessions from the government. Practitioners of civil disobedience not only risk punishment, they expect it. Practitioners of civil disobedience routinely offer themselves up as sacrificial arrestees to demonstrate the injustice of the law or policy.

Throughout history, acts of civil disobedience famously have helped to force a reassessment of society's moral parameters. The Boston Tea Party, the suffragette movement, the resistance to British rule in India led by Gandhi, the U.S. Civil Rights movement led by Martin Luther King Jr., student sit-ins against the Vietnam War, are all instances where civil disobedience served as an important mechanism for broad social change. The degree and style of activity utilized by the protesters in even the above listed historical events vary drastically as well—from the arguably riotous participants in the Boston Tea Party, to the classically passive resistance used in the sit-in protests against the Vietnam War, and Gandhi's opposition to the salt laws of Great Britain.

The philosophy behind civil disobedience can be traced to classical and biblical sources, but its modern incarnation can be found in Henry David Thoreau's *On the Duty of Civil Disobedience*. The term "civil disobedience" was coined by Henry David Thoreau in his 1848 essay. Thoreau used the term to describe his refusal to pay the state poll tax implemented by the American government to fund, among other things, a war in Mexico that Thoreau believed unjust. In his essay, Thoreau observes that only a very few people serve their society with conscience, thereby resisting society for the most part. The sobering fact, however, is that these persons are commonly treated by it as enemies instead of heroes. Thoreau himself spent time in jail for his protest—which supports the proposition that the person who opposes society is often initially no hero of that society.

In this work, Thoreau suggests that the individual member of a society, from whom the state derives its authority, must follow the dictates of conscience in opposing unjust laws. To Thoreau, individuals are sovereign, especially in a democracy, and the government only holds its power by delegation from free individuals. Any individual may, then, elect to stand apart from the domain of law. Indeed, history would later show that the Nuremberg Principles[1] require disobedience to national laws or orders that violate international law. The Nuremberg Principles arguably amount to a legal duty to commit civil disobedience in opposition to laws (that violate international law—which itself is an attempt to set global standards of morality). The modern citizen may be in an eternal no-win situation. The citizen cannot do certain acts and then use the defense that law or state demanded that he commit those acts (the Nuremberg Principles). However, to commit civil disobedience against laws believed to be unjust is to also welcome punishment. Have we required too much of our citizens?

Thoreau's work influenced Mohandas Gandhi, who incorporated these techniques to gain Indian rights in South Africa and later to secure independence for India. By choosing the salt law (which was a tax on a natural product from the sea water that was consumed by every person) to defy the British laws, Gandhi exposed the fundamental oppression attendant to this tax, which was then easily related to the masses. Gandhi was able to rally the people of India behind him by calling upon them to pick up salt from the earth or distil it from the sea as their natural right.

Gandhi was able to use the technique as an effective political tool and play a key role in bringing about the British decision to end colonial rule of his homeland. His was a rare but unqualified success in the history of civil disobedience.

Dr. Martin Luther King Jr. later incorporated civil disobedience into his protests against racial injustice. His views on civil disobedience are evidenced in his *Letter from Birmingham Jail* (1963). In it, King wrote:

> One who breaks an unjust law must do so openly, lovingly, and with a willingness to accept the penalty. I submit that an individual who breaks a law that conscience tells him is unjust and who willingly accepts the penalty of imprisonment in order to arouse the conscience of the community over its injustice, is in reality expressing the highest respect for law.

Through nonviolent civil disobedience, the civil rights movement was able to dramatically change the South. The Congress of Racial Equality initiated sit-ins and other organized nonviolent actions. The Montgomery bus boycott successfully promoted the Civil Rights movement's message nationwide.

Mass nonviolent action was a critical component of several other movements in the United States, including the Industrial Workers of the World free speech confrontations, the Congress of Industrial Organizations sit-down strikes from 1935–1937 in auto plants, and the United Farm Workers grape and lettuce boycotts.

Opponents of the Vietnam War employed draft card burnings, pouring blood on draft cards, draft file destruction, mass demonstrations, sit-ins, blocking induction centers, draft and tax resistance, and the historic 1971 May Day traffic blocking in Washington, D.C., during which 13,000 people were arrested.

> Philosophically, civil disobedience can be attacked as fundamentally unjustified in a democratic society. Indeed, if the people are the source of the laws and the procedure of creating these laws, is it not incumbent upon the people who oppose these laws to follow proper procedure in opposing them (such as voting, lobbying, etc.)? Both Thoreau and King have addressed these issues. Thoreau argues that the reality of the situation is that people opposing laws do not always have the time or the resources to explore the often glacial legislative method of changing an unjust law or policy. King similarly argues that the procedural route has not achieved justice for his people in 340 years; more direct action is therefore required.

In the modern world, civil disobedience seems to have given way to terrorism, rebellion, and more dramatic and extreme means of effecting social change. Whether an act may be morally justified as civil disobedience, or a more radical, unjustified act of violence, often depends today on the perspective of the actor.

Civil disobedience taken in support of concerns such as the environment or other modern social concerns may be indicative of a breakdown of citizen involvement in the legislative process. It may be the case that these breakdowns are ultimately a part of all real democracies. In this case, it could be argued that the civilly disobedient act out of respect for the democratic process itself. Whatever the purpose or means, civil disobedience remains today a part not only of liberal democracies but also in any society seeking to bring about broad policy change.

### Note

1. The Nuremberg Principles were a set of guidelines for determining what constitutes a war crime. The document was created by necessity during the Nuremberg Trials of Nazi party members following World War II.

*Further Reading:* Gandhi, M.K. (1928). *Satyagraha in South Africa* (V.G. Desai, Trans.). Ahmedabad: Navajivan Publishing House. King, M.L., Jr. (1964). Letter from Birmingham Jail. In *Why we can't wait* (pp. 76–95). New York: New American Library. Thoreau, H.D. (1980). *Walden and "Civil Disobedience."* New York: Signet Classics.

*Danny Cevallos*

### Cognitive Moral Development

Cognitive moral development refers to the psychological process of change that individuals experience in their thinking about consequences or final results of issues of morality, including how they think about justice, rights, duty, rules, and roles (deontic judgments) and how they think about what is good or of value (teleological judgments). Change is a process of transformation along a continuum of which there is a movement forward and a transformation from one form of thought to another, moving toward a better and improved way of thinking about morality. The process of development is not smooth and regular; it may have jumps and pauses although it proceeds along an invariant sequence.

Lawrence Kohlberg articulates a theory of moral psychology that describes six stages of thought and judgments about moral prescriptions. In other words, his theory articulates what ought to or should be done in a moral conflict, and people develop according to these stages. His theory of moral development through these stages shares psychological assumptions with Jean Piaget's theory of cognition called constructivism and builds on Piaget's theory to describe the stages and to explain moral transformation or development. Kohlberg extends Piaget's moral theory beyond childhood morality into a more comprehensive description of how individuals' moral reasoning changes over time and with experience.

To explain cognitive moral development, Kohlberg describes a universal sequence of stages development that every individual "goes through": Each individual actively constructs each stage in his/her own mind, due to maturation, social interaction, experience, and perspective-taking opportunities. A person constructs, or actively cognitively creates, reasons as to what is morally obligatory, or what one "should" do, in a situation where there is a conflict between what is the right or wrong choice of an action, or among two or more "right" courses of action. The reasoning is based on what is morally right and why. In this way, moral development is an active cognitive construction of morality by the individual and is not a process whereby conceptions of morality exist already intrinsic to the person, waiting to be drawn out from preexisting characteristics in the mind (a priori), nor is it inculcated by others, nor is it solely culturally transmitted. However, culture and social experiences play a role in cognitive moral development, because as members of society, social experiences influence individuals as they actively construct their moral reasoning, and thus influence and drive moral development. Each person strives to make sense of the moral world, and as such, all people are "moral philosophers," and the structure of the development of these "philosophies" follows a universal course of change or development. Not every person will develop through all six stages, but every person will develop according to Kohlberg's developmental stage sequence.

The cognitive moral developmental process follows the assumptions of organization and adaptation of cognitive structures or stages outlined by Piaget. Piaget describes two stages of moral development in childhood: Heteronomy and Autonomy. In these stages, considerations of rules, duty, and justice shift from being external to the self and authority-based, to internal, constructed, and egalitarian. These stages, like his cognitive constructivist stages, follow an invariant sequence where each successive stage is a hierarchical integration of the content and structures of previous stages, resulting in that next stage being qualitatively different from the previous stage or stages of development, and that each different stage is in itself a "structural whole" (*structures d'ensemble*) or system of thought operations.

Again following Piaget's cognitive constructivism, Kohlberg describes cognitive moral development as a process through which people develop increasingly complex and integrated systems of reasons, and more philosophically adequate or "better" reasons about what is moral. These reasons or moral judgments that people universally construct are grouped according to the operations of moral thought characteristics—a sequence of six stages of moral reasoning. Each stage is increasingly better or more elaborate than the previous stage and uses moral thought operations that are more reflective of increasingly equilibrated, reversible, and philosophically grounded (deontic and/or teleological) reasons and include increasingly differentiated and integrated social perspectives on moral issues. Kohlberg's six stages of cognitive moral development are grouped into three levels, with two stages comprising each level. Level I, Preconventional Morality, is characterized by cognitive moral reasoning that lacks the conventional norms of society and instead focuses on authority and individualism. Stages 1, Heteronomous Morality, and 2, Concrete Reciprocity and Mutual Exchange, reflect preconventional cognitive moral reasoning. Level II, Conventional Morality, is characterized by reasoning about the norms of social groups: individual groups and systems. Stages 3 and 4, respectively, reflect reasoning about mutuality and norms of interpersonal interaction, and about norms that govern and maintain the integrity of a social system. Level III, Postconventional Morality, is characterized by a perspective that transcends conventions and constructs and understands underlying principles for the establishment, continuation, and obligatory responsibility of upholding a philosophically grounded moral point of view. The process by which stage change, or moral development, takes place has been theoretically explained in several ways.

In equilibration theory, a person experiences cognitive conflict when he/she perceives his/her current way of reasoning about morality as not adequately addressing the moral situation at hand. Through discourse, reflective abstraction is stimulated in the cognitive conflicting situation, and the individual reconstructs his/her way of thinking, specifically the structure of his/her thinking, to be more adequate, inclusive, complex, and philosophically morally justified. This is often referred to as dilemma discussion or transactive discussion (Colby & Kohlberg, 1987; Lapsley, 1996). Another explanation of the process of cognitive moral development is through participation in increasingly complex and responsible role-taking opportunities. As individuals face greater demands on their own responsibility for decision making, experience more complex social arrangements and conflicting moral perspectives, and face climates that focus on moral concerns, their thinking about moral issues is challenged, and cognitive moral development is stimulated (Power, Higgins, & Kohlberg, 1989). A third explanation of moral development is through metacognitive and metaethical reflection. Through conscious awareness of and reflection on thought processes and strategies, including psychological theories and one's own current thinking about morality, people's moral cognitions develop (Oser & Schlafli, 1985; Schrader, 1988). These three explanations of cognitive moral development share the common theme that development takes place through active engagement with others, in morally salient environments and situations, where the reasoner actively reflects on his/her own and others' moral reasoning and actions. These situations create opportunities for cognitive reorganization, which is the mechanism of cognitive moral development.

***Further Reading:*** Colby, A., & Kohlberg, L. (1987). *The measurement of moral judgment, Volume I.* Cambridge: Cambridge University Press. Lapsley, D.K. (1996). *Moral psychology.* Boulder, CO: Westview Press. Piaget, J. (1932/1965). *The moral judgment of the child.* New York: Norton. Power, F.C., Higgins, A., & Kohlberg, L. (1989). *Lawrence Kohlberg's approach to moral education.* New York: Columbia University Press. Oser, F., & Schlafli, A. (1985). But does it move: Difficulty of moral change. In Berkowitz, M.W., & Oser, F. (Eds.). *Moral education: Theory and application.* Hillsdale, NJ: Lawrence Erlbaum Associates. Schrader, D.E. (1988). *Exploring metacognition: A* *description of levels of metacognition and their relationship to moral judgment.* Doctoral dissertation, Harvard University.

*Dawn E. Schrader*

## Cognitive Moral Education

Cognitive moral education involves the transformation of the system of cognitive operations, or structure, of students' thinking about moral issues. Cognitive moral education specifically targets the cognitions or thoughts about knowledge as well as the strategies involved in making moral judgments and decisions primarily through a constructive developmental point of view. Cognitive moral education might best be characterized by the premise that "human beings are above all reasoning beings" (Nussbaum, 1999). This approach includes emotional components naturally involved in thought and its construction. Cognitive approaches to moral education focus on how people construct meaning and understanding of the moral world, which is done through moral discussion, reflective and reflexive thought, and interactions and moral emotional climate within individuals' social contexts. Moral understanding is not gained solely through appropriation of cultural moral norms and values of adults and society, but is created, or cognitively constructed, by individuals through reflection on social experience. In contrast to cognitive moral education, moral education may, in its more general form, refer to education about virtues, character, and values (Wynne & Ryan, 1993).

Kohlberg and Mayer (1972) identified three ideological streams of moral education: romantic, cultural transmission, and progressivism. The first two streams embrace a philosophical perspective of virtue and character ethics such as those promoted by Wynne and Ryan (1993), and the last stream embraces a philosophical perspective of universalizable moral claims regarding justice and reasoning. The latter is the cognitive moral approach to education. Moral education programs typically fall into one of these three philosophical perspectives, although the perspectives are not mutually exclusive.

To elaborate, a romantic perspective focuses on the inner values and personal fulfillment of each person. In some ways, research emphasizing the moral self or moral personality may be considered within this approach. A cultural transmission perspective focuses on inculcating past generations' knowledge, skills, and values to the present generation. Combined, the romantic and cultural transmission streams exemplify the philosophical perspective of character education.

In contrast to both of these streams, cognitive moral education espouses progressive ideals drawn from John Dewey and elaborated by Lawrence Kohlberg, in which individuals interact cognitively, emotionally, and socially in a moral environment or context such as a classroom, school-community meeting, or small-group dialogue. The goal is to promote the students' development of moral judgment. Cognitive moral development is stimulated by actively engaging in thought and discourse about moral problems, leading to possibilities of cognitive conflict and the restructuring of thought. The various parts of a cognitive developmental approach to moral education thus include dilemma discussion, social interaction, and a moral climate or environment. While behavioral change is not the specific target of cognitive moral education—cognitive structural change is—behavioral changes often occur as cognitive changes take place. Cognitive developmental moral education brings about changes in cognition and, as such, the concept of *decalage,* or the breadth of application of cognitive structures to a range of activities may occur, and changes in social and emotional areas of development appear.

Discussion of moral dilemmas for cognitive moral education originated with Moshe Blatt who devised a program of cognitive moral education involving what he described as Socratic dialogue, and others (for example, Berkowitz, Gibbs, Lind) later elaborated into real-life dilemma and transactional discussions. Discussions involve either relevant real moral issues that are close to people's experiences or hypothetical ethical dilemmas. The educational process of cognitive moral education involves moral reasoning in which participants' moral judgments are within approximately one to two Kohlbergian stages of each other, but ideally creating a "plus one" situation where some of the reasoning in the discourse is one stage above each reasoner's level. Teachers or other adults serve as "moral advocates" to provide and stimulate such "plus one" reasoning through questions and modeling of higher stage moral considerations and judgments. Empirical analyses of results of numerous studies that use a cognitive developmental approach to moral education demonstrate what has come to be known as the "Blatt Effect" in which students' cognitive moral reasoning evolves during the process of an educational intervention of several months in higher proportions than those who do not participate in such dilemma discussions.

In addition to using dilemma discussion and dialogue to create cognitive conflicts that encourage cognitive restructuring and change, teachers and other adults can also utilize deliberately structured moral environments as another type of cognitive moral education that results in moral development. These environments promote democratic participation in the life of schools and classrooms. Kohlberg's Just Community Approach (JCA) to moral education exemplifies this form of cognitive moral education. The JCA encourages teachers and student peers to understand and live by ideals of fairness, justice, and community responsibility, thereby creating a moral climate that allows the potentiality for active social cognitive exploration of moral understanding and action, which in turn promotes moral development. In such moral climates, social interactions enhance role-taking opportunities, discussion, and rational reflection on moral problems. Teachers advocate and model more sophisticated moral judgments and moral behaviors to students and students develop moral responsibility for each other and the community while concomitantly developing more sophisticated and principled moral understanding and cognitive processes. Fundamentally, cognitive moral education is Piagetian in its cognitive developmental process, which is constructivist, social, integrative of affect and cognition, and directed toward creating "possibilities" for thought transformation. The Just Community Approach as cognitive moral education combines the cognitive and affective elements of moral development by creating cognitive conflict in a morally safe, just, caring environment. While not explicitly designed with Turiel's domain approach to moral development in mind, the JCA involves the understanding of moral norms and conventions and addresses moral versus nonmoral considerations as students live within the context of a Just Community School and tackle real-life moral issues as they vary from context to context. Experiences such as service learning also create opportunities for role taking and reflection that promote cognitive moral development (Killen & Horn, 2000).

Recently, an integrative approach to cognitive moral education has been proposed that combines components from both traditional and cognitive philosophical perspectives, recognizing that moral reasoning and behavior are complex and multidimensional, and the goal is to develop moral expertise (Narvaez, 2006). Foundational to integrative moral education is cognitive development, in its interactive, transformational, constructive developmental essence of moral thought, while simultaneously incorporating traditional character requirements for participation in communities and society.

*References:* Power, F.C., Higgins, A., & Kohlberg, L. (1989). *Lawrence Kohlberg's approach to moral education.* New York: Columbia University Press. Killen, M., & Horn, S. (2000). Facilitating children's development about morality, community and autonomy: A case for service-learning experiences. In W. van Haaften, T. Wren, & A. Tellings (Eds.), *Moral sensibilities and education II: The schoolchild* (pp. 89–115). Bemmel, The Netherlands: Concorde Publishing. Kohlberg, L., & Mayer, R. (1972). Development as the aim of education. *Harvard Educational Review, 42,* 449–96. Narvaez, D. (2006). Integrative ethical education. In M. Killen & J. Smetana (Eds.), *Handbook of moral development.* Mahwah, NJ: Lawrence Earlbaum Associates. Nussbaum, M. (1999). *Sex and social justice.* New York: Oxford University Press. Turiel, E. (2006). Thought, emotions, and social interactional processes in moral development. In M. Killen & J. Smetana (Eds.). *Handbook of moral development.* Mahwah, NJ: Lawrence Earlbaum Associates. Wynne, E., & Ryan, K. (1993). *Reclaiming our schools.* New York: Merrill.

*Dawn E. Schrader*

## Colby, Anne

Anne Colby is recognized for her contributions to the measurement of moral judgment, the study of moral commitment, and moral and civic development in higher education. She received her B.A. from McGill University and her Ph.D. from Columbia University, both in psychology.

Working with Lawrence Kohlberg at Harvard's Center for Moral Education in the 1970s, Colby led a team that conducted follow-up interviews of Kohlberg's long-term longitudinal sample and carried out careful analyses of that 20-year data set. The research, published in *SRCD Monographs,* demonstrated the sequentiality and "structured wholeness" of Kohlberg's stages.

While at the center, Colby also played an important role in the development of a revised system for stage-scoring responses to Lawrence Kohlberg's moral judgment interview and is the first author of the two volume *Measurement of Moral Judgment,* which includes instructions for conducting and scoring moral judgment interviews, along with data on reliability and validity of the instrument. Along with Kohlberg, Colby collaborated with John Gibbs, Clark Power, Daniel Candee, Betsy Speicher, and Alexandra Hewer to produce the new *Standard Issue Scoring Manual.* This work attempted to specify in very concrete terms Kohlberg's distinction between moral judgment content and structure at each developmental stage and emphasized the importance of the overall *level of perspective,* in which the coherence of thinking within a given stage was grounded. The Standard Issue Scoring System is rather cumbersome, so it has been largely supplanted in contemporary research by James Rest's Defining Issues Test. Even so, it remains the definitive representation of Kohlberg's stages of moral judgment.

One seemingly trivial change Colby introduced into the scoring system carries theoretical significance that may not be immediately apparent. She changed the name of the composite score (calculated from separate dilemma scores) from *Moral Maturity Score* to the more neutral term, *Weighted Average Score.* This signified her conviction that moral judgment, though an important component of moral maturity, is only one of many important factors that make up an individual's developmental profile in the broader domain of moral functioning.

In keeping with this broader conception of moral development, Colby went on to study moral commitment through case studies of individuals she and her co-author William Damon termed "moral exemplars." This work is published in the influential book, *Some Do Care: Contemporary Lives of Moral Commitment*. The book stresses the central place of moral values and commitments in the exemplars' sense of self, their sense of certainty about their convictions, and their positive, hopeful attitudes toward their work. The moral judgment stage scores of the exemplars ranged from stage 3 through stage 5, in part depending upon their field of contribution (e.g., direct service to the poor versus protection of civil liberties) as well as on the exemplars' educational attainment. *Some Do Care* has helped to alter the landscape of moral psychology and education by encouraging studies of exceptional moral commitment and contributing to recognition of the importance of moral personality and moral self, alongside the field's continuing emphasis on moral judgment. This work was conducted while Colby was director of the Henry Murray Research Center: A Center for the Study of Lives at Radcliffe College, Harvard University.

After leaving the Murray Center, Colby became a Senior Scholar at the Carnegie Foundation for the Advancement of Teaching. While at the Carnegie Foundation, Colby's work has centered on the contributions of higher education to students' moral, civic, and political development. She has written two books on undergraduate education, along with colleagues at the Foundation. *Educating Citizens: Preparing America's Undergraduates for Lives of Moral and Civic Responsibility* presents case studies of American colleges and universities that have made a strong commitment to their students' moral and civic development. *Educating for Democracy: Preparing Undergraduates for Responsible Political Engagement* outlines strategies for increasing students' political understanding, skill, and motivation for responsible participation in the democratic process. Two other books Colby has co-authored while at the Carnegie Foundation address professional education, including the question of how to prepare students for integrity and a sense of public purpose in their work as professionals. These books are *Educating Lawyers: Preparation for the Profession of Law* and *Educating Engineers: Theory, Practice, and Imagination*.

**Further Reading:** Colby, A., Ehrlich, T., Beaumont, E., & Stephens, J. (2003). *Educating citizens: Preparing America's undergraduates for lives of moral and civic responsibility*. San Francisco: Jossey-Bass. Colby, A., Beaumont, E., Ehrlich, T., & Corngold, J. (2007). *Educating for democracy: Preparing undergraduates for responsible political engagement*. San Francisco: Jossey-Bass. Colby, A., Gibbs, J.C., Lieberman, M., & Kohlberg, L. (1983). A longitudinal study of moral judgment. *Monographs of the Society for Research in Child Development, 48*,(1–2), 1–124. Colby, A., & Kohlberg, L. (1987). *The measurement of moral judgment*. New York: Cambridge University Press. Colby A., & Damon, W. (1992). *Some do care: Contemporary lives of moral commitment*. New York: Free Press.

*F. Clark Power*

## Commitment

While there are many ways in which to define commitment, we discuss this construct in the context of moral personality research. Recent research in the area of moral psychology has focused on extending the field beyond the traditional developmental cognitive emphasis as exemplified by the work of Kohlberg (1981), Rest (1979), and Turiel (1983). One approach taken has been to study moral character, with commitment toward a moral cause as being an important virtue. While demonstrating commitment does not apply to all moral causes, it certainly applies to many as evidenced by two emerging lines of research studying moral excellence (Walker, 2002).

In one line of research on moral excellence, researchers have studied people nominated as moral or care exemplars. Often in the participant recruitment process, researchers use commitment as a criterion. For instance, Colby and Damon (1992) formed a blue ribbon panel of experts (e.g., philosophers, religious leaders, and others) to generate criteria that could be used to identify moral exemplars at a national level. One of the five criteria generated included reference to showing "sustained commitment to moral ideals or principles." Similarly, Hart and Fegley (1995) relied on an advisory board of religious leaders, youth group leaders and psychologists to finalize a list of criteria to select care exemplars. Included in this list was the criterion "commitment to friends and family." Hence, in the study of moral and care exemplars, the experts seem to agree that demonstrating commitment to others or to a moral ideal is an important characteristic.

A second line of research on moral excellence has narrowed in on the layperson's conceptions of moral excellence. In a study by Walker, Pitts, Hennig, and Matsuba (1995), participants were asked to identify two people whom they consider to be highly moral and to provide justifications. The majority of people named either a family member or a friend. Moreover, in justifying their choices, many people used "dedicated," which is a similar term to "commitment," to describe their nominee. In Matsuba and Walker's (1999) study, executive directors of social agencies were asked to nominate people whom they considered to be morally exemplary and provide justification. These justification responses were analyzed, and it was revealed that characteristics such as committed and dedicated were traits used to describe their nominees. Finally, Walker and Hennig (2004) asked people to generate characteristics associated with a highly just, brave, or caring individual. For each "type" of moral excellence, words such as committed, persistent, determined, and/or dedicated were employed and rated high in terms of being prototypical of such morally excellent people. Thus, even when laypeople are asked to conceive of morally excellent people, commitment, or another similar characteristic, is associated with such individuals.

While commitment can be considered an important moral quality, it, as a quality, cannot stand alone. That is, saying someone is "committed" tells me nothing of significance about this person, nor does it guarantee that he or she ought to be considered a moral exemplar. For instance, Hitler was committed to exterminating the Jews. Certainly, no reasonable person would consider Hitler a moral exemplar. Rather, what makes commitment a moral virtue is based on its association with specific moral causes or principles. In Colby and Damon's (1992) study, many of their moral exemplars served people living in poverty. Part of what led to these participants being considered moral exemplars was the fact that their service to the poor had been long term. That is, they have shown a commitment toward their moral cause. Hence, with commitment, the cause and its context matters.

Moreover, sustained commitment to moral causes seems to be associated with other characteristics and conditions associated with moral exemplars. Because moral exemplars' work requires sustained commitment, this means that they often have to sacrifice resources such as time or money, which would otherwise be designated to themselves or their loved ones. This was the case for most of Colby and Damon's (1992) exemplars. Also, sustained commitment can involve potential risk to one's life. This was true of exemplars such as Martin Luther King Jr. and Dietrich Bonhoffer. There is nothing note-worthy about people who are committed to moral causes when there is no associated sac-rifice. What makes sustained commitment a moral virtue is the fact that it often entails personal hardship, danger, and self-sacrifice in order to sustain the commitment.

**Further Reading:** Colby, A., & Damon, W. (1992). The development of extraordinary moral commitment. In M. Killen & D. Hart (Eds.), *Morality in everyday life: Developmental perspectives* (pp. 342–70). New York: Cambridge University Press. Hart, D., Yates, M., Fegley, S., & Wilson, G. (1995). Moral commitment among inner-city adolescents. In M. Killen & D. Hart (Eds.), *Morality in everyday life: Developmental perspectives* (pp. 371–407). New York: Cambridge University Press. Walker, L.J., Pitts, R.C., Hennig, K.H., & Matsuba, M.K. (1995). Development of rea-soning about morality and real-life moral problems. In M. Killen & D. Hart (Eds.), *Morality in everyday life: Developmental perspectives* (pp. 371–407). New York: Cambridge University Press.

**References:** Colby, A., & Damon, W. (1992). *Some do care: Contemporary lives of moral commit-ment.* New York: Free Press. Hart, D., & Fegley, S. (1995). Prosocial behavior and caring in adoles-cence: Relations to self-understanding and social judgment. *Child Development, 66,* 1346–1359. Kohlberg, L. (1981). *Essays on moral development: Vol. 1. The philosophy of moral development.* San Francisco: Harper & Row. Matsuba, M.K., & Walker, L.J. (1999, April). *The traits of young moral exemplars.* Poster presented at the meeting of the Society for Research in Child Development, Albuquerque, NM. Rest, J.R. (1979). *Development in judging moral issues.* Minneapolis: University of Minnesota Press. Turiel, E. (1983). *The development of social knowledge: Morality and convention.* Cambridge, England: Cambridge University Press. Walker, L.J. (2002). Moral exemplarity. In W. Damon (Ed.), *Bringing in a new era in character education* (pp. 65–83). Stanford, CA: Hoover Institution Press. Walker, L.J., & Hennig, K.H. (2004). Differing conceptions of moral exemplar-ity: Just, brave, and caring. *Journal of Personality and Social Psychology, 86,* 629–47. Walker, L.J., Pitts, R.C., Hennig, K.H., & Matsuba., M.K. (1995). Development of reasoning about morality and real-life moral problems. In M. Killen & D. Hart (Eds.), *Morality in everyday life: Developmen-tal perspectives* (pp. 371–407). New York: Cambridge University Press.

*M. Kyle Matsuba*

## Conduct Disorders

According to the *Diagnostic and Statistical Manual of Mental Disorders* (American Psy-chiatric Association, 2000), the essential component of conduct disorder is a repetitive and persistent pattern in which age-appropriate societal norms or the basic rights of others are violated. Subtypes include childhood onset, adolescent onset, and unspecified onset. Behaviors fall into four main categories: aggressive conduct causing or threatening physi-cal harm to people or animals, nonaggressive conduct that causes property loss or damage, deceitfulness or theft, and serious violations of rules. It is estimated that 2 percent of girls and 7 percent of boys in elementary school meet a diagnosis for conduct disorder (Offord, Boyle, & Racine, 1991), and it is argued that conduct disorder is more prevalent in boys due to the gender differences in physical harm to others (Capaldi & Wu Shortt, 2003). There is also evidence that a disproportionate number of youth in urban areas (Graham, 1979) compared to rural areas (Rutter, Tizard, & Whitmore, 1970) are diagnosed with conduct disorder.

The term "conduct disorder" encompasses a large domain of behaviors (Dodge, 2000), and there is a long-standing belief that conduct problems may be related to developmental inadequacies (Piaget, 1932) and a deficiency in moral reasoning and judgment (Jurkovic, 1980). In a review of 35 studies examining the relationship between moral reasoning, conduct disorders, and delinquency, Smetana (1990) found that, controlling for intelligence, antisocial children reason at a lower level of moral maturity than their non-disturbed counterparts. While Smetana (1990) found evidence of a relationship, she argued that a theory explaining the moral development of conduct-disordered youth needs to be developed.

Dodge (2000) discussed a model of the information processing steps that takes place when a conduct-disordered youth responds to social cues. These cues are an important link because morality, social conventions, and psychological knowledge formulate from the differentiation of social experiences and interactions (Smetana & Turiel, 2003). For example, boys who attend to hostile features, or interpret cues in a hostile way, are more likely to respond in an aggressive manner (Dodge, Pettit, Bates, & Valente, 1995). Moreover, children who evaluate aggressive responses as less "morally bad" are also more likely to display chronic aggressive behavior (Deluty, 1983). While the above description highlights the cognitive processes for conduct disordered youth and the connection to moral development, there are also biological predispositions, family factors, and sociocultural contexts that are also correlated with the broad domain of conduct disorder.

Research suggests a strong behavior facilitation system with a cognitive emphasis on immediate gratification could lead to instrumental aggression (Quay, 1993) and a weak behavior inhibition system that inadequately regulates impulse control could lead to chronic aggression (Rogeness, Javors, & Pliszka, 1992). Other biological factors connected to conduct problems include low resting heart rate (Raine, 1993), low IQ (Farrington, 1998), low school attainment (Lipsy & Derzon, 1998), low verbal intelligence (Moffitt & Lynam, 1994), and low empathy (Ellis, 1982).

Family contextual factors such as low socioeconomic status, poor parenting (e.g., harsh discipline), and peer aggression and rejection are also associated with conduct problems in adolescence (Capaldi & Wu Shortt, 1993). Research also suggests environmental factors at the neighborhood and cultural level affect conduct disorder. Living in a crowded (Hammond & Yung, 1991), disadvantaged, high crime, high poverty, disorganized neighborhood increases the levels of crime and violence (Farrington, 1998; Shaw & McKay, 1969), but considerable debate exists on the direct and indirect effects of these factors on individuals and families (Gottfredson, McNeil, & Gottfredson, 1991); Sampson, Raudenbush, and Earls (1997) find the effects of neighborhood factors persist after individual predictors are controlled.

In sum, research suggests social-cognitive processes such as the interpretation of social cues is an important factor in understanding the relationship with moral development but also salient are the biological, individual, family, and sociocultural factors at work affecting both conduct problems and moral development.

*Further Reading:* American Psychiatric Association. (2000). *Diagnostic and statistical manual of mental disorders, fourth edition, text revision.* Washington, D.C.: Author. Capaldi, D.M., & Wu Shortt, J. (2003). Understanding conduct problems in adolescence from a lifespan perspective. In G.R. Adams & M.D. Berzonsky (Eds.), *Blackwell handbook of adolescence* (pp. 470–93). Malden, MA: Blackwell Publishing Ltd. Dodge, K.A. (2000). Conduct disorders. In A.J. Sameroff, M. Lewis, & S.M. Miller, *Handbook of developmental psychopathology* (2nd ed., pp. 447–63). New York: Kluwer Academic/Plenum Publishers. Lipsy, M.W., & Derzon, J.H. (1998). Predictors of violent or serious delinquency in adolescence and early adulthood: A synthesis of longitudinal research. In R. Loeber & D.P. Farrington (Eds.), *Serious and violent juvenile offenders: Risk factors and successful interventions* (pp. 86–105). Thousand Oaks, CA: Sage. Smetana, J.G. (1990). Morality and conduct disorders. In G.R. Adams & M.D. Berzonsky (Eds.), *Blackwell handbook of adolescence* (pp. 157–79). Malden, MA: Blackwell Publishing Ltd.

*References:* American Psychiatric Association. (2000). *Diagnostic and statistical manual of mental disorders, fourth edition, text revision.* Washington, D.C.: Author. Capaldi, D.M., & Wu Shortt, J. (2003). Understanding conduct problems in adolescence from a lifespan perspective. In G.R. Adams & M.D. Berzonsky, *Blackwell handbook of adolescence* (pp. 470–93). Malden, MA: Blackwell Publishing Ltd. Deluty, R.H. (1983). Children's evaluations of aggressive, assertive, and submissive responses. *Journal of Clinical Child Psychology, 12,* 124–29. Dodge, K.A. (2000). Conduct disorders. In A.J. Sameroff, M. Lewis, & S.M. Miller (Eds.), *Handbook of developmental psychopathology* (2nd ed., pp. 447–63). New York: Kluwer Academic/Plenum Publishers. Dodge, K.A., Pettit, G.S., Bates, J.E., & Valente, E. (1995). Social information processing patterns partially mediate the effect of early physical abuse on later conduct problems. *Journal of Abnormal Psychology, 104,* 632–43. Ellis, P.L. (1982). Empathy: A factor in antisocial behavior. *Journal of Abnormal Child Psychology, 10,* 123–34. Farrington, D.P. (1998). Predictors, causes, and correlates of youth violence. In M. Tonry & M.H. Moore (Eds.), *Violent children and adolescents: Asking the question why* (pp. 19–35). London: Whurr. Gottfredson, D.C., McNeil, R.J., & Gottfredson, G.D. (1991). Social area influences on delinquency: A multilevel analysis. *Journal of Research in Crime and Delinquency, 28,* 197–226. Graham, P. (1979). Epidemiological studies. In H.C. Quay and J.S. Werry (Eds.), *Psychopathological disorders of childhood* (2nd ed., pp. 185–209). New York: Wiley. Hammond, W.R., & Yung, B.R. (1991). Preventing violence in at risk African-American youth. *Journal of Health Care for the Poor and Underserved, 2,* 1–16. Jurkovic, G.J. (1980). The juvenile delinquent as a moral philosopher: A structural-developmental perspective. *Psychological Bulletin, 88,* 709–27. Lipsy, M.W., & Derzon, J.H. (1998). Predictors of violent or serious delinquency in adolescence and early adulthood: A synthesis of longitudinal research. In R. Loeber & D.P. Farrington (Eds.), *Serious and violent juvenile offenders: Risk factors and successful interventions* (pp. 86–105). Thousand Oaks, CA: Sage. Moffitt, T.E., & Lynam, D.R. (1994). The neuropsychology of conduct disorder and delinquency: Implications for understanding antisocial behavior. In D.C. Fowles, P. Sutker, & Sherryl H. Goodman, *Progress in experimental personality and psychopathology research* (pp. 233–62). New York: Springer-Verlag. Offord, D.R., Boyle, M.C., & Racine, Y.A. (1991). The epidemiology of antisocial behavior in childhood and adolescence. In D.J. Pepler & K.H. Rubin (Eds.), *The development and treatment of childhood aggression* (pp. 31–54). Hillsdale, NJ: Erlbaum. Piaget, J. (1932). *The moral judgment of the child.* Glencoe, IL: Free Press. Quay, H.C. (1993). The psychobiology of undersocialized aggressive conduct disorder: A theoretical perspective. *Development and Psychopathology, 5,* 165–80. Raine, A. (1993). *The psychopathology of crime: Criminal behavior as a clinical disorder.* San Diego, CA: Academic Press. Rogeness, G.A., Javors, M.A., & Pliszka, S.R. (1992). Neuro-chemistry and child and adolescent psychiatry. *Journal of the American Academy of Child and Adolescent Psychiatry, 31,* 765–81. Rutter, M., Tizard, J., & Whitmore, K. (1970). *Education, health, and behavior.* London: Longmans. Sampson, R.J., Raudenbush, S.W., & Earls, F. (1997). Neighborhoods and violent crime: A multilevel study of collective efficacy. *Science, 277,* 918–24. Shaw, C.R., & McKay, H.D. (1969). *Juvenile delinquency and urban areas* (rev. ed.). Chicago: University of Chicago Press. Smetana, J.G. (1990). Morality and conduct disorders. In G.R. Adams & M.D. Berzonsky (Eds.), *Blackwell handbook of adolescence* (pp. 157–79). Malden, MA: Blackwell Publishing Ltd. Smetana, J.G., & Turiel, E. (2003). Moral development during adolescence. In G.R. Adams & M.D. Berzonsky (Eds.), *Blackwell handbook of adolescence* (pp. 247–68). Malden, MA: Blackwell Publishing Ltd.

*Chris R. Stormann and Daniel J. Flannery*

## Conflict Resolution/Mediation

Conflicts are inevitable among people. Being able to resolve conflicts peacefully and constructively is imperative in maintaining harmony among individuals and groups, yet not all conflicts are resolved constructively. The three basic manners in which conflicts are resolved include the following: coercion, disengagement, and negotiation (Laursen, Finkelstein, & Betts, 2001). In using coercion, one party submits to the demands of the other. Coercion may involve one party making commands or employing physical or verbal aggression. Disengagement occurs when the parties withdraw from the conflict and do not reach a resolution. Negotiation involves both parties talking things out. Often, the parties discuss each other's desires, goals, and feelings and then create a solution that is acceptable to both parties. To facilitate positive negotiations among conflicted parties, the process of mediation may be used. Mediation involves a neutral and impartial third party assisting conflicted individuals in negotiating and creating a resolution that pleases all involved.

Of the three manners in which conflicts may be resolved, the most positive and constructive is negotiation. Thus, many educators have focused on teaching children and adolescents how to resolve conflicts peacefully through negotiation rather than resorting to violence or other destructive means. Before turning to how educators have addressed teaching conflict resolution, the ways in which children and adolescents *naturally* resolve interpersonal conflicts (i.e., resolving conflicts without explicit school-based conflict resolution) is discussed.

Developmental trends show that children frequently use coercion compared to adolescents, who tend to employ negotiation in resolving interpersonal conflicts (Laursen et al., 2001). However, two important contextual factors need to be considered. First, negotiation is more common among friends than among acquaintances or siblings for both children and adolescents. Second, negotiation is the more common strategy when children and adolescents are asked about how they resolve conflicts compared to when they are actually observed resolving conflicts (coercion tends to be more prevalent in the latter) (Laursen et al., 2001).

Given the prevalence of coercive strategies used by children and adolescents when observed resolving their own conflicts, explicit school-based education in conflict resolution appears valuable. Bodine and Crawford (1998) describe four different approaches for school-based education in conflict resolution. The first is the process curriculum approach, which is used to teach conflict resolution principles and skills in a time-limited course (e.g., workshops or daily/weekly lessons in a semester course period). Common practice in this approach is to adopt a conflict resolution curriculum as a separate entity in the total curricular offering to students. Program for Young Negotiators and Street Law, Inc. are examples of programs using this approach.

A second type of approach uses peer mediation programs, which are schoolwide or gradewide programs that have trained students to assist other students in constructively resolving conflicts through negotiation. Peer mediation programs can either have a small number of selected students to serve as peer mediators or have the entire student body trained to mediate peers' conflicts. Examples of peer mediation programs include the Community Board Program and Illinois Institute for Dispute Resolution.

The peaceable classroom approach, the third type of conflict resolution approach, is holistic in nature in that it integrates conflict resolution into the curriculum and classroom management as well as using cooperative learning methods. Curriculum integration involves conflict resolution training that is integrated into an existing curriculum (e.g., Social Studies or English). Teaching Students to Be Peacemakers program, Educators for Social Responsibility, and Children's Creative Response to Conflict are known for their holistic peaceable classroom approach.

The fourth approach is the peaceable school approach, which integrates conflict resolution into the total operation of the school. Every member of the school community learns and uses conflict resolution concepts and skills. This approach is comprehensive in that it incorporates each of the three previous approaches (curriculum, mediation, and peaceable classroom approaches) as well as systemic changes in the policies and practices in the operation of the school. The Resolving Conflict Creatively Program (RCCP, described more in detail on p. 370) and Creating the Peaceable School program are examples that use this approach.

Although conflict resolution programs have existed in schools since the early 1980s, they have dramatically increased in popularity, with as many as 8,000 programs existing in U.S. schools (Johnson & Johnson, 1996). Unfortunately, of the thousands of conflict resolution programs that are now in schools, evidence regarding their effectiveness is sparse (Johnson & Johnson, 1996). Academic literature in this area contains more descriptions of programs than formal research or published evaluations of their effectiveness. Of the published evaluations of their effectiveness, most of the research shows that the conflict resolution programs are effective and successfully teach students how to constructively resolve conflicts through using negotiation. However, reviewers of this research (e.g., Johnson & Johnson, 1996; Campbell, 2003) have criticized many of the studies for lacking methodological rigor and not having a strong theoretical foundation. Also, there have been few systematically organized projects that demonstrate long-term effectiveness. A few exceptions to this area of research include RCCP (see p. 370 for more information) and the Teaching Students to Be Peacemakers program, which shows that elementary through high school students can and do learn constructive conflict resolution strategies and that conflict resolution training leads to higher academic achievement.

*Further Reading:* Bodine, R. J., & Crawford, D. K. (1998). *The handbook of conflict resolution education: A guide to building quality programs in schools.* San Francisco: Jossey-Bass Publishers. Campbell, K. (2003). The efficacy of conflict-mediation training in elementary schools. *The Educational Forum, 67,* 148–55. Laursen, B., Finkelstein, B. D., & Betts, N. T. (2001). A developmental meta-analysis of peer conflict resolution. *Developmental Review, 21,* 423–49. Johnson, D. W., & Johnson, R. T. (1996). Conflict resolution and peer mediation programs in elementary and secondary schools: A review of the research. *Review of Educational Research, 66,* 459–506.

*Tonia Bock*

## Conscience

The conscience consists of moral emotions and of ideas about right and wrong that guide behavior. Conscience is also sometimes inferred from the rule-abiding conduct that it is held to cause. Research into early conscience development has yielded new insights that may help illuminate the nature and causes of conscience in older children and adults.

### Early Development

Current approaches to conscience development emphasize its early origins. A long-standing question is how and whether early child compliance relates to conscience development. Some scholars believe that moral development rests on a foundation of procedural learning about what to do and what not to do. Others disregard early compliance because it is derived from parental values rather than constructed by the self, so it is neither autonomous nor reflective of consciously understood moral values. Kochanska has recently suggested that early child motivation can be inferred from the quality of conduct, and has shown that, as early as the second year, compliance that is self-sustaining and emotionally positive predicts continued rule-abiding behavior outside adult supervision. This committed compliance is described as a precursor of conscience.

**Conduct.** Children begin to show signs of self-control during the toddler period, and by preschool age they have a surprising capacity to understand and follow simple rules even when there is no adult present. Many factors contribute to differences among children in the early development of internalized conduct, including child temperament, parenting, and their interaction. Children's emotion and regulation are both important. For example, dysregulated anger negatively predicts compliance, and anxiety positively predicts compliance. While parent discipline was once regarded as the central cause of conscience development, recent research suggests a more complicated picture, with a more qualified role for discipline. Parent discipline is not only a cause of but also a reaction to the child's behavior, and its impact depends on the child's temperament and on the overall relationship context. Furthermore, discipline tactics are not consistently trait-like, but vary as a result of the parent's mood, understanding, and goals in a given situation. With these qualifications in mind, maternal responsiveness remains an important predictor of child internalization.

**Emotion.** The development of guilt, the moral emotion about which we know the most, is similarly complex, involving many of the same factors as early moral conduct. Recent research has implicated anxiety-prone temperament, gentle parental discipline, child-committed compliance, and parent-child relationships characterized by mutual responsiveness and shared pleasure as precursors to the development of guilt during the preschool years. A recent study has also shown that infants' eagerness to learn from their mothers through imitation, as early as 14 months, predicts later guilt and internalized conduct. This suggests that the long understood basic social learning mechanism of imitation is still important to conscience development. In this body of research, early guilt is assumed to be a normative and functional emotion, promoting the development of moral conduct and moral understanding, though at older ages excessive guilt can be dysfunctional. It is important also to distinguish guilt from shame. While guilt functions to promote reparation, shame inhibits action and can lead to self-protective withdrawal in the face of adult disapproval. Developmentalists have only begun to seriously examine the origins of, and early differences in, shame.

**Moral self and moral understanding.** Children's developing moral understanding also begins early and has many influences. Moral understanding requires an understanding of psychological, as well as physical, harm. Early behavioral standards for right and wrong conduct also depend on understanding another person's approving and disapproving reactions to one's behavior. By preschool age children are not only aware of others' emotional responses to their actions, but can understand that other people have beliefs, intentions, desires, and emotional reactions that differ from the child's own. Parent verbal messages about other people's thoughts and feelings in general, and about the connections between child behavior and others' feelings in particular, serve as important sources of information for early moral understanding. The emotional tone with which these messages are delivered and the relationship context in which such conversations take place also influence the child's emerging self-understanding. An important issue here is how understanding another's feelings can become, or fail to become, connected to sympathy for the other. After all, sophisticated social understanding can also be used to inflict harm on another person. The specific contents of moral understanding depends on adult values that are communicated to the child, which vary by culture. With regard to early moral self-development, even three-year-old children can begin to reflect on their own actions and how they affect other people. From these reflections the child begins to develop a sense of the self as a moral person. However, we know very little about how these early beginnings, which include understanding of harm and help, of approval and disapproval, and of the self as acting well or acting badly, can contribute to more mature forms of moral understanding such as distributive justice, reasoning about moral dilemmas, and empathic reasoning.

### From Early Conscience to Later Morality

Surprisingly little longitudinal work follows up early rule abiding conduct, guilt, or moral understanding to later conscience. The relevance of early development can be inferred from the close parallel between causes of psychopathy, a condition characterized by the absence of conscience, and the developmental findings. In particular, historical and contemporary views of adult psychopathy emphasize deficiencies in the ability to learn through anxiety and impoverished social relationships. Two parallel causes, anxious temperament and close parent-child relationships, are among the strongest predictors of preschool conscience. Nevertheless, we have many more questions than answers about the path from early conscience to its mature forms. Some of these questions involve how the components of conscience become linked over time. From the third through fifth years, both guilt and moral cognitions appear to become progressively more connected to moral conduct, but we need to know more about when anxiety and guilt fail to inhibit behavior, and about how the newly developing understanding of others does or does not lead to feelings of personal responsibility.

*Further Reading:* Aksan, N., & Kochanska, G. (2005). Conscience in childhood: Old questions, new answers. *Developmental Psychology, 41,* 506–16. Emde, R.N., Biringen, Z., Clyman, R.B., & Oppenheim, D. (1991). The moral self of infancy: Affective core and procedural knowledge. *Developmental Review, 11,* 251–70. Forman, D.R., Aksan, N., & Kochanska, G. (2004). Toddlers' responsive imitation predicts preschool conscience. *Psychological Science, 15,* 699–704.

*David R. Forman*

## Conscientization

The concept of conscientization (Portuguese, *conscientização*) is largely attributed to the work of the Brazilian philosopher and educator Paulo Freire (1922–1997) most particularly in his *Education for Critical Consciousness* (1973) and the highly influential *Pedagogy of the Oppressed* (1970). In general, conscientization refers to the ongoing process by which the oppressed come to critically know the historical, political, economic, and social structures that bind them. Once this reality is understood, the oppressed are in a position to take action to transform rather than merely reform their existential situations. Two distinctions of action and focus characterize the differences between consciousness raising and conscientization. In the former, there is no requirement for either action or consideration of social structures. The focus is upon individual psychological awareness and improvement. In the latter, while understanding the dehumanizing nature of one's current circumstances is necessary, it is hardly sufficient. According to the logic of conscientization, it is only through action with corresponding attention paid to the social that a deeply human and just world can be actualized.

Within conscientization, there are assumed to be three levels of consciousness called by Freire the semi-intransitive (magical), the naïve (transitive), and the critical (transitive). Just as intransitive verbs do not take an object, an intransitive consciousness is one that does not act on the world as an object. A magical consciousness perceives the world in a very limited manner—individuals see the causes of oppression as existing in the nature of things, as God's will, as just the way things are supposed to be, as conforming to bounded systems impervious to change. Therefore challenge becomes a hopeless endeavor and action impossible. The second level, named naïve, represents a movement toward a somewhat more expansive understanding of the world, yet perceives problems as existing largely in individual psychological deficiencies and unquestioned role requirements as dictated by the system. Issues are not seen in their complexity, reality is often fanaticized, forced friendliness stifles inquiry, and an emphasis on the past becomes the norm. Change, if and when it happens, focuses on altering individual behavior rather than concentrating on systemic, structural, and normative obstacles as is the case with critical consciousness, the third level. From a societal point of view, the critical moves to integrate the past, the present, and the future. Its emphasis is upon deep examination of reality, problem posing rather than technocratic problem solving, continuous reflection, rejection of passivity, and testing assumptions. Further characteristics include openness to being confronted in the spirit of inquiry, dialogue rather than polemics, and action constituted by praxis (the symbiotic relationship between theory and praxis).

While not ignoring psychological benefits to the individual, the critical proclaims the power of a societal collaborative struggle as a transitive move to challenge oppression in all its forms within the objective world. For Freire, the task of conscientization, as movement from the magical through the naïve to the critical, is social, not individual. According to Elias (1976, p. 133), perhaps the best definition of conscientization is given by Freire as "the process in which men, not as recipients, but as knowing subjects, achieve a deepening awareness both of the sociocultural reality which shapes their lives, and of their capacity to transform that reality through actions upon it." It should be noted that after the early 1970s, Freire stopped using the term conscientization/conscientização because he believed it had been seriously misused, particularly in its use as individualistic and skill based "consciousness raising." However, he never rejected the pedagogical process to which it applied. *Education for Critical Consciousness* and *Pedagogy of the Oppressed* offer his expanding understanding of conscientization as the bedrock of his educational theory and associated pedagogical practice. In combination these two works provide not only the precise methodology of conscientization he employed first in Brazil and then in Chile after his exile from Brazil but also a justification for considering critical consciousness as a procedure compatible with progressive and democratic educational forms.

### *Measurement*

While mindful of Freire's caution against turning the pedagogy of consciousness into mere technique, a proscribed methodology, Smith (1976) drawing primarily from *Pedagogy of the Oppressed* developed a Conscientização Coding Categories (C-Code) matrix that attempts to make operational Freire's critical work to guide assessment procedures to assess the levels of conscious among the poor and marginalized. The C-Code uses

**Table 1.**  Conscientizacáo Coding Categories

| Pedagogy Questioning | Magical Conforming | Naïve Reforming | Critical Transforming |
|---|---|---|---|
| I. Naming: What is the problem? Should things be as they are? | Problem denial and avoidance, survival problems, God's will, fate | Oppressed deviates from ideal expectations | Rejection of oppressors, self and peer affirmation |
| II. Reflecting: Why are things as they are? Whoor what is to blame? | Facts attributed to superior power, simplistic casual relationships, bad luck | Plays host to oppressors' ideology, understands how oppressor violates norms | Rejects oppressors' ideology, understands how the system works |
| III. Acting: What can/ should be done to change things? What have you done? | Fatalism, nothing resignation, acceptance, dependence on the oppressor, wait for good luck | Models oppressors' behavior, meets oppressors' expectations | Boldness, risk taking behavior, self-actualization, comrade-ship, change norms |

verbal samples of individuals responding to self-identified protocols that are either written or visual. A legitimate protocol is one that (1) represents an honest response, (2) reflects in some way the answers to several questions: What problems do you have? Should things be as they are? Why are things as they are? What can be done to change things? and (3) represents individuals' responses to their own and/or their peer group's life problems and not those of another sociocultural group. Table 1 indicates the relationship between the levels of consciousness on the horizontal axis and the forms of questioning on the vertical.

Smith (1976) linked conscientization to Lawrence Kohlberg's theory of moral development. More recently, Mustakova-Possardt (2003), using critical consciousness as foundational, has expanded the meaning of moral development and education by incorporating ideas of love, spirituality, care, virtue, neurophysiology, and an "increasingly interconnected, justice-and-equity oriented view of life."

Criticisms of Freire's conscientization are numerous. A comprehensive compilation can be found in Ohliger (1995).

**Further Reading:** Elias, J. (1976). *Conscientization and schooling: Freire's and Illich's proposals for reshaping society.* Philadelphia, PA: The Westminster Press. Freire, P. (1970/2000). *Pedagogy of the oppressed.* New York: Continuum. Freire, P. (1973). *Education for critical consciousness.* New York: Continuum. Mustakova-Possardt, E. (2003). *Critical consciousness: A study of morality, in global, historical context.* Westport, CT: Praeger. Ohliger, J. (Compiler). (1995). *Critical views of Paulo Freire's work.* Iowa Community College Summer Seminar. Available at http://www.uow.edu.au/ arts/sts/bmartin/dissent/documents/Facundo/Ohliger1.html. Smith, W. (1976). *The meaning of conscientizaçao: The goal of Paulo Freire's pedagogy.* Amherst, MA: Center for International Education, University of Massachusetts.

*Tom Wilson*

## Consequentialism

We often say that it is the results that count. If someone was harmed, it does not matter much how or by whom or with what intention. What counts is that he or she suffered harm, and that harm hurts. Even if an action was well intentioned—even if it was performed by someone we care about, causing harm by accident—we are harmed in the end. An enemy might just as well have done that harm, for all it matters to how we are left when it is over.

It would not be very plausible to pose ethical views that failed to weigh the heavy consequences of actions. But views that merit the name consequentialist say something far bolder and more interesting. They hold that only the consequences count. Consider how odd this position is. Suppose we try to help someone, but they end up in ruin anyway. Does that mean all our trying counts for nothing? And what of our good intentions as well? Suppose Mother Teresa pitched in to help with even better intentions and more steadfast effort, exerted even while she was having a fatal heart attack. The help involved is no different from that of, let us say, a vicious killer trying to torture and kill our intended recipient but merely landing them, or allowing them, to fall into ruin.

Imagine that we do something good for someone in the hope that they will "pay it forward"—that they will see the value of being treated well and wish to treat others well in turn. In the end, they do not get the message. At least they do not act on it. Others then do the same thing for this person, but for crass purposes—in hope that they will get access to their possessions—sports equipment, a luxury car or boat, or some other "selfish" reward. These others have ulterior motives, but we have noble ones. However, since the results are the same, the moral value or quality of each instance is the same.

Worse yet, suppose the recipient is fooled by those hungrily eyeing his boat into thinking he has been done a truly good-hearted deed. He then offers the deceptive donor endless boating invitations in appreciative return. Yet he further misunderstands the aim of the pretend-good act as urging him, the recipient, to pay the pretend-good deed forward, thereby acquiring nobility. (This could not have been further from the donor's scheming mind.) And the recipient mistakenly follows that mistaken urging. As a result, this highly manipulative and misconceived state of affairs can be judged morally superior to the truly noble one. Why? Simply because more people benefit, replies the consequentialist. The outcomes form a bigger heap since the manipulator enjoys his boating fun, the recipient feels both grateful and noble, feelings greatly enjoyed, and others get to be recipients of further good deeds as he pays his good fortune forward.

This seems morally cockeyed. "The ends here do not justify the means" might be our reaction. At least the deceptions would strike us in this way. "And they do not validate the confusion or misunderstanding either." But whether or not they do, we typically distinguish strongly between ends and means in our actions, taking both seriously. This shows our recognition that ends or consequences are not all that count. In fact, not only the means of an action count for us, but the action's ends, meaning their intended purposes, not merely their actual results. Certainly if a result occurs by accident, unforeseen, it seems quite different in quality than an intended one. If we are harmed by our closest loved one as opposed to an enemy, that makes all the difference in the world to us. (Et tu Brute?)

Why consequentialism is interesting, then, is because it tries to show us why our eminently plausible, well-accepted views are false. Such a demonstration would be quite eye-opening. Seen as a moral-philosophical experiment, consequentialism tries to debunk obvious moral tenets and cherished beliefs. It challenges both the instrument (useful) and inherent (in-itself) value of good intentions, for example, also valuable traits, virtues, and their expression in honest or courage actions. Opponents of this position, in turn, try to expose the moral quality of these moral phenomena to disconfirm the consequentialist hypothesis. On both sides, this research goes forward by common observation of how we think and behave ethically, and of the opinions we hold credible. But mostly it proceeds through the marshaling of good reasons, making careful distinctions between considerations that may be confused with each other. Consequentialist views may grant moral relevance to intentions, virtues, efforts, and the like. But these have value only insofar as they are a component, accompaniment, or conduit to the moral consequences of actions.

Being harmed by a spouse as opposed to an enemy matters, but as a feature of the result, say the consequentialists. We experience unexpected harm from a friend as a distinct sort of harm. It is not experienced as enemy-harm. Hence the results are not the same. Being betrayed as opposed to defended against matters, but in the nature of the result—I was betrayed in fact: the betrayal was not just attempted or considered. Even when it is merely attempted, that itself can be seen as a result. It is the result of a deliberation and choice that is then acted on, but misses its target. Even as a conduit or means to ends, that is, these constitute kinds of consequence. They are partial results, interim results, subconsequences along the path to an ultimate result of an action.

Actions usually have many results, after all—intended, predictable, unexpected. They have what we call side effects of many sorts. Whether or not we were aiming at these hardly changes the fact that they happened. Our intended actions are really chains of intentions, efforts, and consequences that lead to the next intention, effort, and consequence. Eventually these lead to the ultimate aim or result of this means-end chain.

These are the sorts of observations that make the consequentialist case seem stretched and reductionistic trying to save the exclusive importance of consequences by building everything else into them. Common sense, by contrast, leans toward moderation and the integration of different viewpoints into a multifaceted whole. From this perspective, consequentialism merely lobbies for a stronger emphasis on consequences than is usual. It questions the degree to which we weight and credit other moral considerations. But when suffixes like "ism" or "ist" are attached to a viewpoint, we expect something more radical and ideologically stubborn than sensible balance of perspectives or open inquiry into a possibility. The point of an "ism" is to go too far, for effect. Only because consequentialism stretches beyond emphasis, generalizing its focus toward universality and exclusivity can it yield unexpected insights and correct a degree of taken-for-granted commonsense overgeneralization in the opposite direction.

A reductionist view of this sort poses a whole new extremist outlook in which the varied range of our moral concepts and rationales have a hidden and deep common essence. Conspiracy theory has the same function. This allows us to supplant myriad piecemeal principles like "Be honest," "Always try to do what's right," or even "Do unto others as you would have them do unto you," with a singular one: "Always act so as to produce the most beneficial consequences—to advance overall welfare, or happiness." To the extent it succeeds, we are left with only one sort of thing to remember—focus on results, get good overall results, or, perhaps, get the best results you can.

Expecting, commonsensically, that such radical reduction is preposterous from the outset, we should appreciate how far it gets, revealing the greater importance of consequences. But where such reductionism fails, we should also appreciate its partial reconfirmation of common sense and the enhanced explanation that it provides of it. Consequentialist research shows us why the means to ends have distinct value apart from this role, even when performing it. And by contrasting this status with an intention's or trait's status as a means or consequence, consequentialism helps outline the qualities that compose it.

Consequentialism's attempts to rally rival concepts to its cause also reveal how moral concepts perform double duty. Consider the principle, "Act so as to advance the greatest quality of moral character in society, or the greatest amount of good will and moral morale." Here what are often personal means to social ends are played up in their role as social ends. Instead of being virtuous and optimistic to the end of increased economic wealth or social welfare, we can seek social virtue as the highest wealth. Consequentialism can perform the same service for whole viewpoints. "Treat people the way you would wish to be treated because over time and overall this produces the most beneficial consequences for all." Put more radically, "Always and only do things for their own sake (Be honest because honesty has inherent worth) because doing so promotes the greatest overall good." That is, honesty promotes trust that promotes solid economic partnership and increased productivity. This sort of reduction may upset us: "The whole point of my developing good character or treating people well is because it is the right and good thing to do, period—not because it is useful for other things, especially material wealth." But this reduction also may reveal hidden motives to ourselves, providing surprisingly good additional reasons for acting morally. It also can provide important fallback rationales— "Well, even if all this work to be a better person does not seem inherently worth it in the end, it will make my part of the world a better place." And conceptually, consequentialist reductionism in particular helps provide a rationale for what is otherwise quite mysterious like doing something for its own sake, or for right's and morality's sake.

Like ethical egoism and utilitarianism, consequentialism challenges such "inherent motivation" or "inherent value talk" as either logically specious or motivationally chimerical. To be motivated by ideas or ideals in themselves is contrary to the psychological laws of human nature, promoting moral masochism and authoritarianism. We act for benefits, for beneficial goals and consequences. Reconsidering the peculiarity of such inherence-motivation rationales leads to liberating questions. Why not do things for our sake, for people's sake, not morality's sake? Is that so bad after all? Is not ethics our tool and should it not be our tool rather than our taskmaster? How else can following it be voluntary and meritorious—a matter of free will? Rather than sullying ethics, an alliance with interests and benefits, as represented by consequences, can make nobility a more inviting option motivationally. And is not this quite proper when the interest pursued is that of others generally, not simply our own?

In moral education, these sorts of questions, and the reductionist, consequentialist researches that spawn them, can provide a greatly underestimated service. It can keep morality this side of moralism, preventing its slippage into the perennial trap of scolding, restricting, and threatening to punish us for being as we are, not always as we might be.

*Further Reading:* Scheffler, S. (1988). *Consequentialism and its critics.* New York: Oxford Press. Slote, M.A. (1985). *Common-sense morality and consequentialism.* London: Routledge-Kegan Paul.

*Bill Puka*

## Constructivism

Constructivism is a theoretical framework that considers knowledge to be acquired through an active process in which learners construct new ideas and cognitive information based upon their current and past knowledge and experience. The constructivist approach to teaching and learning is based on the epistemological premise that an individual learner actively creates knowledge and skills through individual and social processes of interaction with the environment. Thus, knowledge is derived from a dynamic and reciprocal exchange of environmental stimuli (the external factor) and the individual's own cognitive processing mechanisms (the internal factor). John Dewey's philosophy of education is sometimes credited as an early theoretical framework for this approach, particularly with regard to his emphasis on experiential learning pedagogy at the University of Chicago's Laboratory School.

Constructivism provides a broad base for interpretation because it is also closely related to the theories of psychologists like Lev Vygotsky, Jean Piaget, Jerome Bruner, and Edward Thorndike, to mention but a few. Constructivism is often juxtaposed in contrast to the behaviorist model of learning, which many consider to have been the dominant paradigm in K–12 education for most of the past century (Derry, 1996). According to the behaviorist model, learning is conceived as a process of manipulating and conditioning observable behavior through selective reinforcement of an individual's response to events that occur in the environment. Thus, behaviorism as applied in the classroom setting would tend to focus on both the student's efforts to learn and on the teacher's efforts to transmit it. On this view, the primary role of the student is to be a passive receptor, and the primary role of the teacher is to be an active transmitter of information. This behaviorist model of learning theory is strongly committed to a teacher driven and teacher directed instructional approach. The emphasis on the role of the teacher is driven by the assumption that students are essentially tabula rasa, or blank slates waiting to be imprinted by external information and environmental stimuli.

Advocates of constructivist pedagogy tend to approach curriculum planning in reverse of the more traditional behaviorist models of curriculum development. Constructivist educators tend to seek opportunities to first learn about their students and the variety of experiences that they bring to the classroom, and then to develop curriculum that would build upon the knowledge these students already have. This model places significant value on the cultural context in which learning occurs, and assumes that not all students will have shared experiences and previous knowledge. By contrast, advocates of the behaviorist model prefer to design curriculum to meet predetermined skills sets and learning objectives that would typically target a particular age group (Winn, 1993). This pedagogical difference with respect to curriculum development is not trivial, especially in light of high stakes standardized testing that most school districts are now required to conduct.

Proponents of constructivism argue that knowledge does not have an objective or absolute value apart from our own interpretations of such. According to this epistemological framework, we build our view of what constitutes truth and reality based on our experiences and interactions with the environment. Because our past and current experiences figure so predominantly in the learning process, constructivist educators encourage the development of and appreciation for multiple learning perspectives that are culturally diverse. Students are expected to play an active role in all aspects of the learning process, including articulation of the goals and objectives for particular fields of study, as well as in the selection of criteria for evaluation and assessment of learning.

In the constructivist classroom, teachers view themselves as guides and facilitators in the educational process. They provide activities and create environments that are intended to encourage self-analysis and metacognition. The learning environment, curriculum, and tasks are expected to be relevant to the experiences students actually encounter in their daily experience, and to authentically represent the practical knowledge needed to successfully negotiate the world outside the classroom.

Constructivists rely on a process of guiding the learner through a level of skills that the learner can perform with help from a tutor or facilitator. This process is based on Vygotsky's concept of scaffolding, which allows students to perform tasks that would otherwise exceed their ability without that important assistance and guidance from the teacher (Hogan & Pressley, 1997). Scaffolding describes the appropriate level of teacher intervention and support that will best help students to reach their full level of potential with respect to the performance of particularized skills sets.

Constructivist frameworks in education value collaborative and cooperative learning as preferred tools for exposing students to a multiplicity of viewpoints. Such processing is understood to take place not only in individual contexts, but also through social negotiation and experience. In the classroom setting, affording students an opportunity to share their thoughts and feelings with their peers promotes an appreciation of the multiplicity of values and experiences (Winn, 1993). All students' previous knowledge, beliefs, and attitudes are considered to be reviewed as contributing in some meaningful way to the reevaluation and refinement of their problem solving and higher order thinking skills. This appreciation of prior knowledge and experience points to the fact that the constructivist paradigm in learning theory essentially emphasizes the process of learning rather than the product. This process orientation means that the acquisition of knowledge can no longer be assessed and evaluated in terms of objective end product answers on tests. In the constructivist classroom, learning is a process of helping students to construct their own meaningful representations of the world. Because of this tentative nature of knowledge acquisition, the constructivist perspective acknowledges a diversity of representations and multiple truths as having important implications for teaching and learning.

*Further Reading:* Bransford, J.D., Vye, N., Kinzer, C., & Risko, R. (1990). Teaching thinking and content knowledge: Toward an integrated approach. In B. Jones & L. Idol (Eds.), *Dimensions of thinking and cognitive instruction.* Hillsdale, NJ: Erlbaum. Derry, S. (1996). Cognitive schema theory in the constructivist debate. *Educational Psychologist, 31,* 3/4, 163–74. Doyle, J.K. (1997). The cognitive psychology of systems thinking. *System Dynamics Review, 13,* 3, 253–65. Hogan, K., & Pressley, M. (Eds.). (1997). *Scaffolding student learning: Instructional approaches and issues.* Boston, MA: Brookline Books. Winn, W. (1993). A constructivist critique of the assumptions of instructional design. In T.M. Duffy, J. Lowyck, & D.H. Jonassen (Eds.), *Designing environments for constructive learning.* Berlin: Springer-Verlag.

*Monalisa M. Mullins*

## Convention on the Rights of the Child (United Nations)

The United Nations Convention on the Rights of the Child (CRC) is an international treaty and the preeminent framework of children's rights standards for the world. It expresses the evolving universal positive ideology of the child, moving toward valuing the child as a unique person in addition to the benefits the child brings to society and other persons. The convention is values laden throughout.

The roots of the convention can be found in the history of children and the development of child-relevant human rights documents and standards. At the end of the twentieth century children's rights had come to be nearly universally acknowledged, in large part due to the Convention, after having been ignored for most of human history. In the nineteenth and twentieth centuries, the conceptualization of children advanced from being considered the property of parents, which provided them with little to no protection by society, through being viewed as present and potential societal resources, and eventually being recognized as having a personal identity and being the subjects of rights.

International rights standards and requirements are embodied in treaties, instruments that are legally binding and that hold ratifying or officially committed nations (usually referred to as states parties) accountable, and in nonbinding declarations, standards, and rules. The codification of child rights relevant standards has occurred in all these forms. The preamble of the Convention on the Rights of the Child recognizes the historical background supporting children's rights represented in the Geneva Declaration of the Rights of the Child of 1924 and the Declaration of the Rights of the Child (adopted by the UN General Assembly in 1959); and in the application to children's rights of the Universal Declaration of Human Rights (adopted by the UN General Assembly in 1948), the International Covenant on Civil and Political Rights, and the International Covenant on Economic, Social and Cultural Rights (adopted by the UN General Assembly in 1966).

The United Nations Convention on the Rights of the Child (United Nations General Assembly, 1989) is a comprehensive treaty on children's rights. The Polish government initiated its development through a proposal in 1979 to draft a treaty to give legally binding protection to the rights of children. Ten years of deliberations by national representatives to the United Nations ensued to produce the Convention (Detrick et al., 1992). The UN General Assembly adopted the Convention without dissent in 1989, and it entered into force in 1990. This history and the fact that the Convention accumulated ratification by 191 of the 193 acknowledged nations by 1997 make it the most successful human rights treaty in history.

The Convention has become the chief principles base and guiding framework for child advocacy work internationally and within most nations. This position has been achieved for numerous reasons. The Convention was developed through a highly participatory process involving most of the world's nations. It embodies a comprehensive range of minimum standards and aspirational goals. It arguably has risen to the level of universal standards since all but two recognized nations have ratified it. Accountability procedures applied to its implementation are relatively transparent and participatory. Nations report progress they have made periodically and publicly to the UN Committee on the Rights of the Child, the official monitoring mechanism for the Convention. The committee is elected by states parties to the convention and is to be made up of experts of high "moral" standing. The committee also accepts alternative reports from nongovernmental organizations on the status of national compliance, and the committee comments on and recommends publicly the status of implementation and the need for further improvements. Furthermore, progress in implementation is encouraged through guidance and moral persuasion by the committee and a wide range of international and national governmental and nongovernmental agencies.

The Convention is made up of three divisions: Part 1 includes 41 articles on substantive rights principles and standards; Parts 2 and 3, made up of 13 articles, cover implementation mechanisms and procedural matters such as states parties reports to the Committee on the Rights of the Child, ratification, entry into force, and amending procedures. The articles of the Convention on the Rights of the Child are frequently conceptualized as falling under themes of survival, protection, development, and participation.

As examples, the right to life, survival, and development is covered in Article 6; the right to protection from all forms of physical, mental, and sexual violence, abuse, neglect, and exploitation are covered in Article 19; the rights to education on the basis of equal opportunity and to education promoting the full development of personality, talents, and mental and physical abilities are covered in Articles 28 and 29; and civil rights, including the rights to express one's views and have them given due weight, access to and exchange of information, freedom of belief, and freedom of association are presented in Articles 12–15 and 17.

Moral and ethical values and principles, as well as concern for the education and evolving development of the child, pervade the Convention. Its preamble justifies the establishment of the Convention as a support to respect the inherent dignity of human beings, their inalienable rights, freedom, justice, peace, and social progress, as well as the special developmental immaturity of the child state, the full and harmonious development of the child, and preparation of the child to live in the spirit of peace, dignity, tolerance, freedom, and solidarity. The Convention makes it clear that the child's evolving capacities or maturity are to be respected by those providing guidance to the child (see Articles 5, 12, and 14) and that support is to be given to the child's ethical and moral development; see Article 29, which states that the aims of education should include development of respect for human rights, fundamental freedoms, for one's own parents and culture, for the cultures of others, and for the natural environment; and, consistent with the preamble, that the child should be prepared for a responsible life in a free society, in the spirit of understanding, peace, tolerance, equality of sexes, and friendship among all peoples. Specific encouragement for spiritual and/or moral development is found in Articles 17, 23, and 32 dealing, respectively, with access to information and media, children with disabilities, and protection from exploitative and dangerous work.

Children's rights as established in the Convention deal primarily with the legal, moral, and ethical responsibilities of governments. However, this does not usurp the rights and responsibilities of parents, which are specifically considered in 19 articles of the CRC; nor does it suggest that governments and laws alone can achieve the full spirit of the rights it embodies. The CRC explicitly and implicitly refers at numerous points to the responsibilities of private as well as public institutions and bodies, and it is generally recognized that human rights, including children's rights, must become a part of the fabric, moral imperatives, of everyday living if their intent is to be realized. The Convention, state party implementation reports to the Committee on the Rights of the Child, alternative nongovernmental reports, and the critiques, responses, and recommendations of the committee itself in their regard can be found on the Web site of the Office of the UN High Commissioner for Human Rights (http://www.ohchr.org/english/bodies/crc/index.htm).

***Further Reading:*** Detrick, S. (Ed.), with Doek, J., & Cantwell, N. (1992). *The United Nations Convention on the Rights of the Child: A guide to the "Travaux Preparatoires."* Dordrecht: Martinus Nijhoff. Hart, S.N., Cohen, C.P., Erickson, M.F., & Flekkoy, M. (Eds.). (2001). *Children's rights in education.* London: Jessica Kingsley. Hodgkin, R., & Newell, P. (1998). *Implementation handbook for the Convention on the Rights of the Child.* New York: UNICEF. United Nations (UN) General Assembly. (1989, November 20). *Adoption of a convention on the rights of the child.* New York: Author. Verhellen, E. (Eds.). (1996–2004, Series). *Understanding children's rights.* Ghent, Belgium: University of Ghent.

*Stuart N. Hart*

## Cooperative Learning

Cooperative learning is often construed as students simply working together in the classroom. However, cooperative learning is much more than this. A more informed, complete definition of cooperative learning is given: a family of instructional practices in which the teacher organizes students in a systematic manner to work in groups to learn and master material. According to Johnson and Johnson (1998), cooperative learning should involve the following elements: face-to-face promotive interaction by students, positive interdependence, individual and group accountability, appropriate use of social skills, and group processing. Each of these elements is briefly described below.

Face-to-face promotive interaction involves two key ideas. First, the students must be interacting with one another, not working independently in group-like clusters. Second, the interaction must be promotive in that students are encouraging and facilitating their group members' efforts to complete tasks and accomplish their joint goals.

Positive interdependence is another critical element in cooperative learning that entails group members knowing that they "sink or swim together." A group member must (a) see oneself as being linked to others in a way that he or she cannot succeed unless one's group members do as well and (b) coordinate one's own efforts with that of the group members' efforts to successfully complete the task. If positive interdependence does not exist, individuals would either work competitively against each other within the group so that the group's success is hindered or work individualistically so that there is no relation among participants' efforts or goal attainments.

Accountability should also occur in cooperative learning, for it creates a sense of responsibility in accomplishing specific goals. Accountability may be individual- and/or group-oriented. Individual accountability involves being responsible for completing one's own share of work and facilitating other group members' efforts. Group accountability involves the group members, as a whole, being responsible for completing a goal.

The appropriate use of social skills is important in cooperative learning. Having socially unskilled students working together will likely result in unsuccessful group work due to unresolved conflicts, competition, or disengagement from the group. Important social skills needed for successful cooperative learning include trusting other group members, communicating accurately and precisely, accepting and supporting each other, and resolving conflicts constructively.

Group processing, the last element in cooperative learning, involves group members reflecting on their time together to describe which actions were conducive and hindering to accomplishing group goals and to make decisions about which actions should be continued or changed in future group work. This process is important because it can lead to improving group members' effectiveness in contributing to the group's successful goal completion.

What does cooperative learning look like in the classroom? Educators have used several different kinds of cooperative learning methods. A few of the more widely used, researched methods are briefly described below. See Slavin (1990) for more details on each of these methods.

In Student-Teams-Achievement-Division (STAD), the teacher first presents the lesson, followed by students being assigned to four-member learning teams. Within their teams, students work to make sure that all team members have mastered the lesson. In the last step, all students are individually assessed on the lesson. Team members cannot help one another at this time. Team members' assessment scores are then averaged to form team scores. This method is most useful when teaching material with single right answers.

The Jigsaw method takes on a different approach, wherein students are assigned different materials to master and then teach their assigned material to peers. A Jigsaw involves three steps. (1) Students are assigned material to master. (2) Students meet in groups made up of students who were all assigned the same material. At this point, students discuss the material in depth and decide what and how to teach their material to their peers. (3) Students meet in groups made up of individuals who each have differently assigned materials. Students then take turns teaching their assigned material to their team members.

Group Investigation involves groups of students choosing topics from a unit that is being studied by the entire class. Once the group of students has chosen their topic, they must break the topic into individual tasks and perform their respective tasks that lead to the preparation of a group report on their topic. Group Investigation is most appropriate for larger-scale projects that require the acquisition, analysis, and synthesis of information in order to solve complex problems.

Structured Controversy engages students in academic conflicts. First, a controversial issue is chosen by the teacher. Students are then assigned to one side of the issue. Once students have studied their positions, they form small groups consisting of members who represent each side and then discuss both sides of the controversial issue, following a structured method of argumentation. In the structured process, students are required to take the other side's perspective, think critically on both sides of the issue, and integrate their analysis and information to come to a consensus.

Teams-Games-Tournaments involves groups of students competing with other groups. After the teacher presents the lesson, students study and master it in their groups. Students then engage in tournaments in which groups compete with other groups. As with STAD, this method is most appropriate for material with single right answers.

Cooperative learning methods have become quite popular among educators: recent surveys have shown that 62 to 93 percent of teachers use cooperative learning in their classrooms (Slavin, Hurley, & Chamberlain, 2003). Given its popularity, it is important to ascertain whether cooperative learning methods are actually effective in increasing student academic performance. A substantial body of research has shown that cooperative learning methods are, in fact, effective. However, an important discovery within the body of research is that cooperative learning tends to be most effective when used with (1) structured group interactions (rather than unstructured) and (2) individual and/or group assessment (with the exception of the Structured Controversy method; Slavin et al., 2003). In addition to positively influencing academic performance, cooperative learning has also been found to increase students' intrinsic motivation, positive attitudes toward schooling, positive cross-group relations (e.g., ethnicity, ability), and psychological health (Johnson & Johnson, 1998; Slavin et al., 2003). Thus, cooperative learning, when used and implemented successfully, is a valuable tool for classroom teachers and enhances not only students' academic learning but many other classroom behaviors as well.

*Further Reading:* Johnson, D.W., & Johnson, R.T. (1989). *Cooperation and competition: Theory and research.* Edina, MN: Interaction Book Company. Johnson, D.W., Johnson, R., & Holubec, E.J. (1994). *Cooperative learning in the classroom.* Alexandria, VA: Association for Supervision and Curriculum Development. Johnson, D.W., & Johnson, R.T. (1998). Cooperative learning and social interdependence theory. In R.S. Tindale (Ed.), *Theory and research on small groups* (pp. 9–35). New York: Plenum Press. Slavin, R.E. (1990). *Cooperative learning: Theory, research, and practice*. Englewood Cliffs, NJ: Prentice-Hall. Slavin, R., Hurley, E.A., & Chamberlain, A. (2003). Cooperative learning and achievement: Theory and research. In I.B. Weiner, D.K. Freedheim, J.A. Schinka, & W.F. Velicer, *Handbook of psychology: Educational psychology* (Vol. 7, pp. 177–98). New York: Wiley.

*Tonia Bock*

## Counseling

Counseling is a profession and process that is typically referred to as talk therapy. It is a process of dialogue between a trained professional and a person or persons who are struggling with various life issues. The counseling professional applies psychological, mental health, and human development concepts to address wellness, personal growth, career development, or pathological matters. Interventions used may include cognitive, affective, behavioral, or systemic methods to explore client concerns. The practice of counseling is theory-based and allows for specialization in areas such as depression, anxiety, grief, and transitions, with diverse populations and developmental ranges.

The process of counseling is similar to guidance and psychotherapy in that the intent is to help others. However, there remain distinct differences. Guidance typically occurs in the school setting and assists individuals in identifying what they most value. Counseling takes it a step further and helps individuals make changes in the way they think, feel, and behave with responsibility for those changes. By tradition, psychotherapy is focused on serious intrapsychic or relational issues and conflicts. Additionally, psychotherapy typically involves a long-term relationship with a therapist with an emphasis on reconstructive change. Counseling, however, seeks to help resolve situational or developmental concerns and often does not exceed 12 sessions within six months.

Unfortunately there is often a stigma associated with mental health assistance. Partly responsible is the influence of Western culture on being independent and self-sufficient. Struggles that people experience are diverse and may be difficult for them to resolve alone. Talking with a friend or reading a relevant book may be helpful as alternatives to counseling. Participating in counseling requires a level of commitment from the client and counselor. Part of the therapeutic process is for the counselor to gain awareness of the client's problems by listening to his or her story and perceiving the dilemma. At the same time, the client risks sharing his/her story in a way that will be useful to the process. As the issues are clarified and client goals are determined, there are often activities or "homework" for the client to do outside of the counseling sessions. The intent of the homework is for the client to implement his/her awareness into his/her daily functioning. For instance, a client who feels lonely and states that he/she has no friends might be encouraged to join an organization or explore opportunities to meet others with similar interests.

Historically, counseling as a profession is fairly new with the majority of theories and interventions having been developed from the mid-1900s to the present. A theory is a reason and framework used by counselors to better understand a client's problems with ways to help alleviate those problems. There are five basic requirements that constitute a good theory: (1) it is clear, easy to understand, and communicable, (2) it is comprehensive and provides explanations for a variety of occurrences, (3) it is explicit and heuristic, (4) it includes a way to achieve a desired end, and (5) it is useful to counselors and provides guidelines for practice and research (Hansen, Stevic, & Warner, 1986).

Counseling theories can best be grouped into four major areas, or forces. The first force, behaviorism, focused on the understanding of human behavior through direct observation. B. F. Skinner was a popular behaviorist and used the principles of physical science in his work with humans. Psychoanalysis followed as the second force and sought to integrate the unconscious and conscious struggles of the mind. Depth psychologists such as Sigmund Freud and Carl Jung believed the unconscious had a direct influence on behavior and personality. Dream work was introduced with these theories. The third force was the Humanistic movement with Carl Rogers, Rollo May, and Abraham Maslow leading the way. The hope was to develop a therapeutic approach that more fully explored what it meant to be human. Themes associated with humanism include self-actualization, life meaning, individuality, and love and belonging. The fourth force to emerge was coined Transpersonal Psychology, which integrates the notion of a divine relationship that moves beyond the human limits of the previous forces.

Practicing from a theoretical orientation is beneficial to both the counselor and the client. Theory gives reason to the process of counseling to avoid haphazard practice that could be harmful if misused. Theory also influences what the counselor hears, observes, and focuses upon in therapy. Over the past decade counseling theory has been streamlined to meet the demands of insurance companies and the general fast-paced lifestyle of clients. Brief therapy approaches have gained popularity, which focus on change through cognitive restructuring and behavior modification.

Legal and ethical considerations are also paramount in the counseling relationship because the profession is based on values. Codes of ethics define boundaries to practice and limits to confidentiality with clients and hold counselors accountable and protect the client.

New trends on the horizon consider the technological advances of client/counselor access. Internet counseling, electronic record keeping, and distance education hold many implications to consider in the twenty-first century.

**Further Reading:** Gladding, S. T. (2004). *Counseling: A comprehensive profession* (5th ed.). Columbus, OH: Prentice-Hall. Hansen, J. C., Stevic, R. R., & Warner, R. W. (1986). *Counseling: Theory and process* (4th ed.). Boston: Allyn & Bacon.

*Scott E. Hall*

## Courage

Courage is the disposition to dare appropriate risks, in the face of dangers, in order to accomplish good ends. It involves good judgment about which risks it is appropriate to dare relative to the purposes at stake, about which one must also have good judgment. Courage has two synonyms that have different connotations and suggest different ways of being courageous. With "bravery," the paradigm or prototypical situation is one in which a person faces immediate danger to himself/herself and/or others, on the battlefield or in an emergency such as a natural disaster, and takes action in order to protect innocent life. There is little time to think, and actions may seem automatic, proceeding apparently without deliberation about risks. In the case of "fortitude," the paradigm or prototypical situation is one in which a person holds steady, enduring physical or psychological pain, maintaining his honor while accomplishing some worthy end, as when one endures torture as part of withholding information from a malefactor or when one endures verbal and physical assaults as part of participating in court ordered racial desegregation. In this sort of case, action is obviously deliberate and more a matter of steadfastness than of quickness.

Because courage is a disposition to act in a certain way rather than an individual act, a courageous person might sometimes be rash or cowardly, acting out of character and making a mistake, not thereby ceasing to be a person genuinely in the habit of being courageous. The same holds for cowardly people who act courageously and so out of character on specific occasions. One cowardly act does not make one a coward, nor one courageous act a courageous person.

On Aristotle's account of courage, the disposition involves two feelings: fear and confidence. The courageous person experiences a proper amount of fear and also has the appropriate amount of confidence in the circumstances. Excessively fearless and fearful persons did not have names, according to Aristotle. The person who has too much confidence and dares too much risk, relative to the good to be served, is rash or reckless, and the person who dares too little is cowardly. Today we might say that a person with a so-called thrill-seeking personality may be more likely to err on the side of rashness, whereas a person who is risk-averse may be more likely to err on the side of cowardice.

The contrast between the Aristotelian and Kantian accounts of courage should be observed. On a Kantian account of virtue, virtue is strength of will in doing one's duty. As such, it enables a generalized continence, where one does the right thing in spite of one's contrary inclinations, desires, and/or feelings. The more effort one has to exert to defy these, the more admirable he is for doing so—with his character reflected not in the appropriateness of his desires and inclinations but in how valiantly he is able to work to overcome them. This continence requires courage in the sense of fortitude. One resolves to do his duty and does it, come what may. The more he is afraid, and the less confident he is, the more courage he needs. Strength of will and hence virtue may vary independently of strength of feeling, desire, or inclination.

So a Kantian account of courage contrasts with an Aristotelian account in rendering courage a strength that enables one to overcome one's feelings rather than a disposition to experience the feelings of fear and confidence in the right manner and amount, and on the appropriate occasions. Also, the Kantian account puts the emphasis on steadfastness and resolve to hold to decisions deliberately made, leaving out the apparent automaticity with which some courageous people act in emergencies.

People's feelings, desires, and inclinations, and also the quickness with which they make decisions, are affected by their experiences and training. With training and experience come confidence, and one feels fear in more discerning ways. A person seeking to locate people stranded in a burning building who has had extensive training and adequate previous experience may be able to make split-second decisions with more confidence and may feel fear only in specific scenarios that he/she has learned pose special dangers to which he/she must be alert. A person who has grown up arguing politics and religion with relatives and who has also endured taunts and discrimination because of some stigma he/she carries relative to the majority may have a finer discernment about the pitfalls of certain argument situations and the advantages of certain argument strategies—and hence a quicker uptake and more steady resolve—when defending controversial ideals or unpopular opinions as an adult in the face of strong pressures to be conventional.

Experience and training enable one to make good practical decisions, some of which even seem to be automatic. They need not thereby be nondeliberate. Through experience in many contexts within a domain, one develops a sense of what sorts of circumstances arise in a given context and develops action routines arising out of reflection on the advisability of her choices in previous cases. The good practical judgment exhibited by a courageous person in taking action in emergencies may seem nondeliberate but may actually proceed from routines and habits developed though much reflection.

*Further Reading:* Aquinas, St. Thomas. (2006). *Summa theologiae. Blackfriar's edition* (Vol. 42, IIa IIae, see especially Q 123). Cambridge: Cambridge University Press. Irwin, T. (Trans.). (2000). *Aristotle's Nicomachean ethics* (2nd ed., see III.vi–ix). Indianapolis, IN: Hackett. Lapsley, D. K., & Narvaez, D. (2006). Character education. In W. Damon & R. Lerner (Series Eds.) & A. Renninger & I. Siegel (Vol. Eds.), *Handbook of child psychology* (Vol. 4, pp. 248–96). New York: Wiley. Walker, L. J., & Hennig, K. H. (2004). Differing conceptions of moral exemplarity: Just, brave, and caring. *Journal of Personality and Social Psychology, 86,* 629–47.

*Don Collins Reed*

## Cultural Transmission

California, like most states, spends approximately 50 percent of its annual budget on education. Although literacy and computational skills are an important rationale for such funding, the foundational sentiment is that without those skills the perpetuation of democracy would be impossible. Thus, the prime motivation for governmental support for education is to pass on to succeeding generations the culturally relevant knowledge, skills, and attitudes that shape our social, political, and moral orientations.

### Variations in and Origins of Cultural Differences

Recent research has found that intercultural variations are common. Not all groups see the same thing in the same way. For example, Chinese and American subjects were found to have different viewing patterns, divergent views of everyday social events, and even differences in eye movements when looking at the same pictures. According to Richard Nisbett of the University of Michigan, "If people are literally looking at the world differently, we think it would be natural for them to explain the world in different ways" (Roach, 2005; Nisbett & Norenzayan, 2002).

Philosophic differences between cultures are distinct as well. Bertrand Russell (1959), asked why he did not include the wisdom of the East in his classic text on Western philosophy, responded,

> in some vital respects, the philosophic tradition of the West differs from the speculations of the Eastern mind. There is no civilization but the Greek in which a philosophic movement goes hand in hand with a scientific tradition. (Russell, p. 310)

Culture is transmitted through interactions. The socialization process between parents and children, and likewise between social institutions and citizens, is influenced by the routines and specific expectations that are designed to establish a moral order to which the child (or the citizen) is expected to adapt (Shonkoff & Phillips, 2000). In this way, differentiated cultural and societal values are reinforced. It is now accepted that one's culture has a very significant influence on early childhood development (e.g., Bronfenbrenner, 1979; Vygotsky, 1978; Rogoff & Chavajay, 1995).

## Is Western Culture Distinctly Different?

The United States is the oldest continuing democracy in the world. Underlying democracy are concepts relating to the natural rights of its citizens (e.g., life, liberty, and the pursuit of happiness; the consent of the governed). That such a government should invoke esteem was expressed by Thomas Jefferson in a letter dated June 24, 1826:

> May it (democracy) be to the world what I believe it will be..., the signal of arousing men to burst the chains under which monkish ignorance and superstition had persuaded them to bind themselves, and to assume the blessings and security of self-government.

In the words of Christopher Hitchens (2005), because of its ideals, "every major system of tyranny in the world has had to run at least the risk of a confrontation with the United States."

The struggle to maintain democratic principles has resurfaced in the twenty-first century. The facts of September 11, 2001, have changed the political landscape not only in the United States, but in Europe as well. Italian political interviewer and author Oriana Fallaci argues that the people of the West (i.e., Europeans) have surrendered to non-Western influences (Varadarajan, 2005). Warns Fallaci,

> You cannot survive if you do not know the past. We know why all the other civilizations have collapsed—from an excess...of richness, and from lack of morality, of spirituality. The moment you give up your principles, and your values...you are *dead*. (Varadarajan, 2005)

## Transmitting Culture

In a small booklet distributed nationally in 1984, a distinguished group of scholars, educators, and policy makers called on Americans to ensure "the continuity of our country" by focusing attention on youth character (Thanksgiving Statement Group, 1984). "What children become is largely the result of what adults expect—and the examples they set. A proper education transmits not only cognitive skills and knowledge but also sound character and values" (p. 3). The modern character education movement in the United States was substantially revitalized in the second half of the twentieth century by the dissemination of this document.

In the ensuing decades, much has been written about the responsibility of the schools to transmit ideas related to Western culture and democratic ideals. On the one hand, there are calls for more intense study of "courses and textbooks incorporating the various strands that have forged the American culture" (Ravitch, 1985, p. 315), and, on the other hand, there are calls for action projects, including civic participation and service learning (e.g., Westheimer & Kahne, 2004). A compromise position has been forged by the Center for Information and Research on Civic Learning and Engagement (CIRCLE). Its publication, *The Civic Mission of Schools,* identifies approaches to civic education determined to be effective. These approaches include a sound formal instruction in government, history, law, and democracy as well as opportunities to apply those concepts.

Charles Quigley (2005) of the Center for Civic Education summed up the need for continued transmission of democratic ideals:

> Each generation must work to preserve the fundamental values and principles of its heritage, to work diligently to narrow the gap between ideals of this nation and the reality of the daily

lives of its people, [and] to more fully realize the potential of our constitutional democratic republic.

***Further Reading:*** Bennett, W.J. (Ed.). (1993). *The book of virtues: A treasury of great moral stories.* New York: Simon & Schuster. James, E. T. (Ed.). (1964). *The American Plutarch: Eighteen lives selected from the Dictionary of American Biography.* New York: Charles Scribner's Sons. Kennedy, C. (Ed.). (2002). *Profiles in courage for our time.* New York: Hyperion.

***References:*** Bronfenbrenner, U. (1979). *The ecology of human development.* Cambridge: Harvard University Press. Center for Information and Research on Civic Learning and Engagement. (2002). *The civic mission of schools.* Retrieved November 24, 2005, from http://www.civicyouth.org/research/areas/civicmissionofschools.htm Hitchens, C. (2005, July 12). The export of democracy. *Wall Street Journal,* p. A16. Nisbett, R.E., & Norenzayan, A. (2002). Culture and cognition. In D.L. Medin and H. Pashler (Eds.), *Stevens' handbook of experimental psychology, Volume II: Memory and Cognitive Processes* (3rd ed.). New York: John Wiley & Sons. Quigley, C. (2005). *The civic mission of schools: What constitutes an effective civic education?* Retrieved November 24, 2005, from http://www.civiced.org. Roach, J. (2005). *Chinese, Americans truly see differently, study says.* Retrieved August 23, 2005, from http://news.nationalgeographic.com/news/2005/08/0822_050822_chinese_2.html. Ravitch, D. (1985). *The schools we deserve: Reflections on the educational crises of our time.* New York: Basic Books. Rogoff, B., & Chavajay, P. (1995). What's become of research on the cultural basis of cognitive development? *American Psychologist, 50,* 10, 859–77. Russell, B. (1959). *Wisdom of the West.* London: Crescent Books. Shonkoff, J.P., & Phillips, D.A. (Eds.). (2000). *From neurons to neighborhoods: The science of early childhood development.* Washington: National Academy Press. Thanksgiving Statement Group. (1984). *Developing character: Transmitting knowledge.* Posen, IL: ARL. Varadarajan, T. (2005, June 23). Prophet of decline. *Wall Street Journal,* p. A12. Vygotsky, L.S. (1978). *Mind in society: The development of higher psychological processes.* Cambridge: Harvard University Press. Westheimer, J., & Kahne, J. (2004, Summer). What kind of citizen? The politics of educating for democracy. *American Educational Research Journal, 41,* 2.

*Jacques S. Benninga*

# D

## Damon, William

William (Bill) Damon is a noted scholar who has made wide-ranging contributions to educational and developmental psychology, with particular emphasis on the areas of intellectual and moral development. His attention to and study of the enhancements of the character and competence of young people, and the guidance he provides parents and educators in a variety of settings, have made his writings appealing far beyond a traditional academic readership. His impact is felt in a number of professional fields as well, including journalism, law, and business. The founding editor of *New Directions for Child and Adolescent Development,* the editor-in-chief of *The Handbook of Child Psychology* (1998 and 2006 editions), and the author of several books and numerous articles, Damon is currently the Director of the Stanford Center on Adolescence, Professor in the School of Education at Stanford University, a member of the National Academy of Education, and a Senior Fellow at the Hoover Institution on War, Revolution, and Peace. Born in Brockton, Massachusetts, in 1944, Damon is married and the father of three grown children.

Damon's scholarly interests and writing have ranged from the development and articulation of innovative educational methods to the promotion of good work and the study of purpose and thriving in adolescence and emerging adulthood. His methodological contributions have included peer collaboration, project-based learning, and the youth charter movement. The youth charter is a model for engaging the many and varied constituents of a community in attending to the moral development of their youth. The approach delineates an ideal, thoughtful, and systematic process by which community standards are discussed and agreed upon.

In addition to these endeavors, Damon has taken up the study of moral exemplars and their contributions to society. Damon's work in this regard promotes a moral identity theory that maintains that committed moral behavior is directly related to the importance of morality to the person's sense of self. A further study, the Good Work Project, with Howard Gardner and Mihaly Csikszentmihalyi, focuses on exemplary leaders and practitioners known for both their success and their high ethical standards in the world of work.

The project attempts to understand both the approaches and the pressures that these moral exemplars face within their respective professional settings. Related to this work, Damon worked with the Committee of Concerned Journalists to create a series of workshops to promote excellence and ethical standards in news reporting. This effective mid-career training program for journalists has been used in hundreds of newsrooms throughout the country. In another outgrowth of the Good Work Project, in a recent book Damon examines the evolving nature of philanthropy and the innovative practices that are currently challenging the field and influencing its general direction.

Damon is a strong proponent of the positive youth development movement that seeks to assist young people in achieving their full potential. The movement has grown out of a dissatisfaction among many developmentalists with the historical overemphasis on the deficits encountered in youth rather than on the true capacities of young people and their developmental potential. He has written about the transformative impact of the positive youth approach on various areas of research, including the nature of the child, the interaction between the child and community, and moral development.

As Director of the Stanford Center on Adolescence, Damon oversees, among other projects, a research team conducting a comprehensive longitudinal study examining the development of purpose among adolescents and emerging adults. Purpose, in this research context, is defined as a stable and generalized intention to accomplish something that is at once meaningful to the self and of consequence to the world beyond the self. The center, in conjunction with the Thrive Foundation for Youth, is also currently studying adolescent thriving and the means by which thriving in youth might better be understood and nurtured. Thriving in this context is not to be measured by the typical standards, such as academic success or athletic prowess, but rather, by the direction and meaning of a young person's efforts in pursuit of a worthwhile goal. A young person's thriving in a particular area or activity is related to that person's sense of purpose and whether there exists the appropriate social support to sustain the effort toward that goal.

Damon's earlier work, and the topic of a number of his early scholarly books, examined the moral conduct of children and adolescents in social situations. Damon espoused and articulated the notion that moral thinking and behavior develop in the social interplay of family, peers, educators, and others; and that moral character will either be nurtured or not within these settings and relationships. These earlier studies gave way eventually to what has become Damon's strongest contribution to educational psychology, his ability to survey and synthesize the large canon of research in the areas of human, particularly moral, development, and to make it available to a readership within and beyond the academy. Damon asserts that building character and competence in children requires less emphasis on promoting self-esteem and child-centered practices, and a return to higher moral standards and expectations.

*Further Reading:* Damon, W., & Verducci, S. (2006). *Taking philanthropy seriously: Beyond noble intentions to responsible giving.* Bloomington, IN: Indiana University Press. Damon, W. (2004). *The moral advantage.* San Francisco: Berrett-Koehler. Gardner, H., Csikszentmihalyi, M., & Damon, W. (2001). *Good work: When excellence and ethics meet.* New York: Basic Books. (German, Spanish, Chinese, Portuguese, Romanian translations, 2001–2005). Damon, W. (1997). *The youth charter: How communities can work together to raise standards for all our children.* New York: The Free Press. Damon, W. (1995). *Greater expectations: Overcoming the culture of indulgence in our homes and schools.* New York: The Free Press. (Italian, Japanese translations, 1997–1999.) Colby, A., & Damon, W. (1992). *Some do care: Contemporary lives of moral commitment.* New York: The Free Press. Damon, W. (1990). *The moral child: Nurturing children's natural moral growth.*

New York: The Free Press. (Italian, Japanese, German, Chinese, Polish, Korean, Danish translations, 1995–2004).

*James M. Lies*

## Declaration of Human Rights (Universal)

The Universal Declaration of Human Rights was adopted by the United Nations General Assembly on December 10, 1948. Support for human rights had been a major priority of the United Nations since its founding in 1945, in part to ensure that the atrocities and devastation of the Second World War would not be repeated. The Charter of the United Nations states that it has determined "to reaffirm faith in fundamental human rights, in the dignity and worth of the human person, in the equal rights of men and women and of nations large and small." Article 1 of the Charter identifies that among its purposes is "promoting and encouraging respect for human rights and for fundamental freedoms for all without distinction as to race, sex, language, or religion."

The Universal Declaration of Human Rights falls within the United Nations programs to establish international standards to protect peoples' human rights against violations by individuals, groups, and nations. Though it is not legally binding, it has become the primary international statement of human rights moral imperatives and, in some cases, these imperatives have been incorporated in national laws. The Declaration is distinct from international covenants and conventions (i.e., treaties) that have the force of law for nations that ratify them; see, for example, the United Nations Convention on the Rights of the Child. When the Declaration was adopted by the United Nations, its General Assembly called upon all its member countries to make it public and "to cause it to be disseminated, displayed, read, and expounded principally in schools and other educational institutions, without distinction based on the political status of countries or territories." The prominence of the educational and moral dimensions of the Declaration is evident in this background history and an analysis of the Declaration.

The Declaration is composed of a preamble and 30 Articles. The preamble notes that the foundation of freedom, justice, and peace in the world is dependent on respect for the "inherent dignity" and "equal and inalienable rights of all members of the human family," whereas "contempt" for these rights has resulted in "barbarous acts which have outraged the conscience of mankind." Teaching and education are recognized to be required to promote rights and freedoms. Articles 1 and 2 present human dignity as foundational, indicating all human beings "are born free and equal in dignity and rights," "are endowed with conscience," and "should act in the spirit of brotherhood" without discrimination or distinction. Articles 13–19 address civil liberties and other liberal rights. As examples, rights are proclaimed to life, liberty, and security (Article 3); freedom from slavery (Article 4) and torture or cruel, inhuman, and degrading treatment (Article 5); recognition as a person before the law (Article 6) and equal protection of the law (Article 7); protection of privacy (Article 12); freedom of movement (Article 13) and to seek asylum (Article 14); freedom to marry and found a family (Article 16) and to own property (Article 17). Articles 18 and 19 are relevant to moral development and expression in that they establish the rights to freedom of thought, conscience, and religion and their manifestations privately and publicly (Article 18) and to the right to freedom of opinion and expression (Article 19). Articles 20–26 articulate political, social, and economic rights,

including rights to freedom of peaceful assembly and association (Article 20); to participate in government and public service (Article 21); to social security (Article 22); to work,
to have free choice in employment, to receive fair remuneration, and to form and join
trade unions (Article 23); to rest and leisure (Article 24); and to an adequate standard of
living and special care and assistance for motherhood and childhood (Article 25).
Article 26 establishes the right to free and compulsory elementary education and availability of secondary education directed toward the full development of the human personality,
strengthening of respect for human rights and fundamental freedoms, promoting understanding, tolerance, and friendship among all nations and peoples, and furthering peace.
Articles 27 and 28 promote the rights to cultural life, including enjoying the arts and scientific advances, and to protection of moral and material interests resulting from one's scientific, literary, and artistic production. The last set of articles, 28–30, establishes the
rights to conditions that are necessary if the other rights of the Declaration are to be realized, including social and international order, assumption by everyone of duties to the
community, necessary limitations on the exercise of rights as determined by law to secure
the rights and freedoms of others, including the "just requirements" of morality, and that
rights and freedoms not be exercised contrary to the purposes and principles of the United
Nations.

The Declaration was intended to set forth the rights of all members of the human family, but mentions children only in Article 25, regarding issues of special care, and
Article 26, regarding parental rights to choose the kind of education given their children.
Otherwise, its application to children is unclear. It is, however, relevant to the evolving
recognition of the rights of children. Its child specific predecessor is the much shorter,
more limited Geneva Declaration of the Rights of the Child, adopted by the International
Save the Children Alliance in 1923 and adopted by the General Assembly of the League
of Nations in 1924. Its child specific successors are the Declaration of the Rights of the
Child proclaimed by the General Assembly of the United Nations in 1959 and the much
more comprehensive, detailed, and legally binding treaty, the Convention on the Rights
of the Child, adopted by the United Nations General Assembly in 1989.

*Further Reading:* Glendon, M.A. (2002). *The world made new: Eleanor Roosevelt and the Universal Declaration of Human Rights.* New York: Random House. Ishay, M.R. (2004). *The history of
human rights from ancient times to the globalization era.* Berkeley: University of California. Morsink,
J. (2000). *The Universal Declaration of Human Rights: Origins, drafting and intent.* Philadelphia:
University of Pennsylvania Press. United Nations General Assembly. (1948, December). *The Universal Declaration of Human Rights.* New York: Author.

*Stuart N. Hart*

## Defining Issues Test

The Defining Issues Test (DIT) is a widely used measure of moral judgment development created by James Rest, a student of Lawrence Kohlberg. Building off his dissertation
work on moral comprehension, Rest wondered whether items written to represent Kohlberg's stages could form the basis of an objective measure of moral judgment development. After various attempts, Rest settled on what is now known as the DIT.
Depending on the version, the DIT has five or six stories, each of which are followed by
12 items. The majority of these items are written to reflect the critical features of each
dilemma as defined by different Kohlberg stage constructions. The non-stage-based items

were written as reliability checks and are used to identify participants who attend to the complexity of the statements rather than their meaning.

Participants taking the DIT are first asked to consider the protagonist's role in the story and to consider the most appropriate course of action on a three-point scale (pro, con, or cannot decide). Following the action choice, participants are then asked to consider and rate each of the 12 items in terms of the item's importance in deciding what the protagonist ought to do. Finally, the participant is asked to consider the 12 items as a set and rank the top four items in terms of their overall importance.

Scoring of the DIT focuses on the ranking task and summarizes the importance given to various stage conceptions. Early in the assessment of the DIT it was found that the best developmental index attends to the importance of the postconventional items (i.e., Kohlberg's stages 5 and 6). This index became known as the P-score and represents the weighted sum of the postconventional items. This value is presented as a percentage of total possible ranked items. A newer score, the N2, improves on the P score by adding information from other non-postconventional items.

As an objective measure, the DIT is limited to those age ranges that can reliably read the dilemmas and items and follow the multiple subtasks (i.e., selecting an action choice, then completing the ratings and rankings). For this reason, the DIT is typically used in populations where the researcher can assume at least an eighth to ninth grade reading level. The DIT, therefore, should be viewed as a measure of adolescent and adult moral judgment development and is most sensitive to the shift from a conventional view of morality to a postconventional view.

Since its inception in the early 1970s, there have been nearly a thousand studies that use one or another version of the DIT. These data have created a large and varied research base upon which to judge the measure. To that end, DIT researchers point to six primary validity criterion including: (1) sensitivity to educational interventions; (2) differentiation of known groups; (3) links to moral action; (4) correlations with measures of moral comprehension; (5) longitudinal trends; and (6) links to political attitudes and choices. These criteria blend the more traditional validity concerns such as discriminate and convergent validity, with specific considerations associated with a developmental measure. In addition, internal consistency reliability estimates of the DIT are typically in the high 70s to low 80s in age heterogeneous samples. In comparison to other measures in the field, the DIT is one of the most well-established and reliable measures of moral judgment development available to researchers.

It should be clearly noted that the DIT is not simply a paper and pencil measure of Kohlberg's stages and theory. Early in the development of the measure, DIT researchers began a process that moved the theoretical underpinnings of the measure away from the theoretical model assumed by Kohlberg. These modifications have been significant and range from a different model of development (the DIT assumes a continuous model), different assumptions about the distinction between content and structure (the DIT assumes a clear distinction is unwarranted), different descriptions of the developmental markers (the DIT assumes ordered moral schema versus stages), and different views about the privileged position awarded to spontaneous production in defining and measuring development (the DIT assumes a tacit sentence fragment approach that is more consistent with the moral schema view). Overall, therefore, the DIT assumes a theoretical model that is informed by, but is quite different from, Kohlberg's theory. To highlight both this legacy and the significant differences from Kohlberg's theory, the DIT is claimed to measure a neo-Kohlbergian model of moral judgment development.

*Further Reading:* Rest, J. (1979). *Development in judging moral issues.* Minneapolis, MN: University of Minnesota Press. Rest, J.R. (1986). *Moral development: Advances in research and theory.* New York: Praeger. Rest, J., & Narvaez, D. (1994). *Moral development in the professions.* Hillsdale, NJ: Lawrence Erlbaum Associates. Rest, J., Narvaez, D., Bebeau, M., & Thoma, S. (1999). *Postconventional moral thinking: A neo-Kohlbergian approach.* Mahwah, NJ: Lawrence Erlbaum Associates. Thoma, S.J. (2006). Research using the Defining Issues Test. In M. Killen and J. Smetana (Eds.), *Handbook of Moral Development.* Mahwah, NJ: L. Earlbaum.

*Stephen J. Thoma*

## Deliberate Psychological Education

Deliberate Psychological Education is a tradition of developmental psychology and education committed to fostering psychological maturity via social interactions, as part of school curriculum. Supported by modern psychological theories, deliberate psychological education applies the notion that development occurs in a sequence of age-related stages. Stages develop in sequences oriented toward ending goals. Final stages are more adaptive for humans in social contexts, as well as self-fulfilling or self-actualizing. Thus, education can be guided by a progression of learning toward ideal ending states that, when practiced in schools, help students to achieve maturity with complex and better-organized thinking and social, emotional, and moral skills.

Programs applied Jean Piaget's cognitive development theory, Lawrence Kohlberg's moral reasoning development theory, Robert Selman's theory of social perspective taking, Erik Erikson's theory of identity formation, Jane Loevinger's theory of ego development, and Carl Rogers's counseling and communication skills. However, Rogers's theory is an exception, as his is not a stage theory of human development but provides counseling strategies toward better organization of people's feelings, thoughts, and attitudes. Therefore, counseling psychology was applied to programs of deliberate psychological education in facilitating development as self-actualization.

Deliberate psychological education was initially applied to programs of moral education. Jean Piaget and Lawrence Kohlberg advocated that psychological research can be translated into *active* education. For example, Kohlberg's (1989) theory of moral reasoning development indicated that individual growth and social renewal were possible via interventions and reformulation of whole school curriculums. According to Kohlberg, education should allow students to participate democratically in schools as members of a community. Working with real-life conflict situations in schools, students would develop a deeper understanding of their own moral thinking, would deepen their abilities to take the perspective of others, and would become autonomous citizens in their societal views.

Moshe Blatt (1975) initiated what became known as the Blatt Effect in moral education. He showed that students would experience a progression of stage changes if instructors would challenge students with a +1 stage of reasoning and motivate students in role-playing. Blatt's moral education interventions took the scientific method into schools. To explain, researchers applied quasi-experimental methodology to compare experimental interventions for moral development with traditional moral education.

Following Blatt, Kohlberg and several of his students provided sound empirical findings of interventions demonstrating a stage progression in moral reasoning development in schools that promoted opportunities for growth through active participation in the democratic sharing regarding decisions about rules and policies and in organized moral discussions in classrooms.

Norman Sprinthall also defended deliberate psychological education in practice by arguing that education should not allow the social, cognitive, moral, and emotional development of a child to be left to the mercy of random forces in diverse social contexts. Children and adolescents are vulnerable and can be at risk for not maturing psychologically. In this way, Sprinthall expanded deliberate moral education to programs that promoted development in the areas of cognition, personality, socialization, interpersonal skills, and, of course, moral functioning, among other areas. One example of such an integrative program developed by Sprinthall was *Learning Psychology by Doing Psychology*. In this program, Sprinthall focused on the passage from childhood to adolescence that is marked by the event of formal operations, which opens the door to a young adolescent's new quality of thinking about sociomoral issues. Cognitive and sociomoral development creates emotional conflicts for a young person, and, therefore, it is necessary that education support cognitive development, interpersonal skills moral development, and ego development using the theories of Piaget, Selman, Kohlberg, and Loevinger, respectively. From Rogers, teachers and counselors would find help with communication strategies to prevent adolescents from derailing from the cognitive, sociomoral, and ego developmental tracks. Examples of a curriculum in this program include a class on the psychology of counseling, a class on teaching and the practice of active listening skills and learning to use an active listening scale, and social moral discussions about real-life issues.

Questions for educators in deliberate education programs:

1. To what degree is this particular area developing in relation to one's experience?
2. What are individual differences and promises to have every student reach the end point in each theory?
3. Are students integrating their cognitive, emotional, personality, and social and moral development?

Deliberate education programs lost power when psychology moved away from large stage-like theories. However, the cycle of science shows that each one of the authors mentioned above is far from being forgotten. Thus, their ideas endure the test of time, as the programs prepare to come back in an even more powerful way.

***Further Reading:*** Blatt, M., & Kohlberg, L. (1975). The effects of classroom moral discussions upon children's moral judgment. *Journal of Moral Education, 4,* 129–161. Power, F.C., Higgins, A., & Kohlberg, L. (1989). *Lawrence Kohlberg's approach to moral education.* New York: Columbia University. Sprinthall, N.A. (1976). Learning psychology by doing psychology. A high-school curriculum in the psychology of counseling. *Social Education, 40*(4), 52–84.

*Júlio Rique*

## Delinquency

Internalized moral beliefs and higher levels of moral development have long been attributed to adolescents' ability to refrain from delinquent behavior. Conversely, youth who have retarded moral development are believed to be more prone to antisocial behavior and delinquency. Durkheim (as cited in Hirschi, 2004, p. 18) wrote, "We are moral beings to the extent that we are social beings." In other words, moral development may be understood as the extent to which we have internalized the norms of the society in which we are living (Hirschi, 2004, p. 18). Hirschi (2004) refers to moral "beliefs" as a key component of his well-established social control theory. Moral beliefs—along with meaningful attachments to intimate others and legitimate aspirations—are the primary bonds that tie most youths to society and prevent them from engaging in delinquent acts.

Children, however, are not born with an innate sense of morality. Rather, their understanding of "right" and "wrong" evolves as they age and mature. In an early study of moral judgment and its effect on beliefs about rule breaking, Piaget (1932) presented children with moral dilemmas to gain insights into their thinking. He found that children under the age of 10 or 11 see rules as inflexible and handed down from parents or even a higher power, whereas older children begin to see rules as man-made constructs that are subject to change if all are in agreement that it would be in the best interest of society. As a result, younger children are likely to make moral judgments based upon the consequences that questionable behavior may bring (e.g., parental disapproval, punishment). Older, morally developed children, however, are able to see acts for their motives rather than simply their consequences (Crain, 1985). As an illustration, when faced with the moral dilemma of stealing food to feed a hungry child, morally undeveloped children will see the behavior as always wrong because it is against the rules and will result in some punishment. Morally developed children, however, understand that laws are relative to society's need for order and, in fact, the misdeed of stealing the food is far outweighed by the need to feed the child.

Following in the tradition of Piaget, Lawrence Kohlberg developed perhaps the best-known description of the stages of moral development. Unlike Piaget, however, Kohlberg (1963) believed that moral development takes place as a result of individuals becoming socialized as they face moral choices throughout their lives, rather than simply as a result of aging. According to Kohlberg, moral development may progress through six possible levels, ranging from the lowest level in which morality is based solely on obedience to authority for fear of punishment (stage 1) through the highest level of moral development where morality is defined as that which makes for a principled and just society (stage 6). Empirical evidence suggests that juvenile delinquents operate at lower levels of moral development (stages 1 and 2 where rules are imposed on the youth rather than having been internalized) as measured by Kohlberg's six stages (Crain, 1985).

More generally, immature moral reasoning skills have been consistently found in delinquent youth (Nelson, Smith, & Dodd, 1990), and conduct disordered youths have been found to have significantly less guilt and fear associated with delinquent acts because they have not internalized social norms (Cimbora & McIntosh, 2003).

Given the established link between moral development and delinquency, it is not surprising that some delinquency treatment programs have a moral development component. For example, the *Aggression Replacement Training* (ART) curriculum combines social skill training, or structured learning, with anger management training, and moral education (Goldstein & Glick, 1987). ART has been used in schools as well as detention facilities. Therapist modeling and group role-playing are used to observe and practice the development of social skills such as identifying problems, stating complaints, and resisting group pressure. Anger control training involves using self-talk to decrease aggressive and impulsive behaviors. Three randomized controlled studies found that youth improved social skills (Goldstein & Glick, 1987); however, behavioral improvement was mixed (Coleman, Pfeiffer, & Oakland, 1992). A more recent model, *Equipping Youth to Help One Another Program,* combines ART with Positive Peer Culture. In one randomized controlled study detention youth showed significant improvements in social skills and conduct and were less likely to recidivate within 12 months compared to controls (Leeman, Gibbs, & Fuller, 1993).

*Further Reading:* Goldstein, A. (1999). Teaching prosocial behavior to antisocial youth. In D. Flannery & C.R. Huff (Eds.), *Youth violence: Prevention, intervention, and social policy.* Washington, D.C.: American Psychiatric Press. Goldstein, A.P., & Glick, B. (1987). *Aggression replacement training.* Champaign, IL: Research Press. Nelson, J.R, Smith, D.J., & Dodd, J. (1990). The moral reasoning of juvenile delinquents: A meta-analysis. *Journal of Abnormal Child Psychology, 18*(3), 231–39.

*References:* Cimbora, D.M., & McIntosh, D.N. (2003). Emotional responses to antisocial acts in adolescent males with conduct disorders: A link to affective morality. *Journal of Clinical Child and Adolescent Psychology, 32*(2), 296–301. Coleman, M., Pfeiffer, S., & Oakland, T. (1992). Aggression replacement training with behaviorally disordered adolescents. *Behavioral Disorders, 18*(1), 54–66. Crain, W.C. (1985). *Theories of development.* Saddle River, NJ: Prentice-Hall. Durkheim, E. (1961). *Moral education* (Everett K. Wilson and Herman Schnurer, Trans.). New York: The Free Press. Goldstein, A.P., & Glick, B. (1987). *Aggression replacement training.* Champaign, IL: Research Press. Hirschi, T. (2004). *Causes of delinquency.* New Brunswick: Transaction Publishers. Leeman, L.W., Gibbs, J.C., & Fuller, D. (1993). Evaluation of a multi-component group treatment program for juvenile delinquents. *Aggressive Behavior, 19,* 281–92. Nelson, J.R, Smith, D.J., & Dodd, J. (1990). The moral reasoning of juvenile delinquents: A meta-analysis. *Journal of Abnormal Child Psychology, 18*(3), 231–39. Piaget, J. (1932). *The moral judgment of the child.* New York: Free Press.

*Eric Jefferis and Daniel J. Flannery*

## Democratic Classrooms

Democratic classrooms include students as decision makers in establishing and enforcing rules for the classroom. These classrooms allow students to learn democracy and morality through *doing* democracy and morality. Life in classrooms inevitably raises moral issues, minimally in (1) how students are treated and treat each other and (2) issues of fairness in teaching, assessment, and grading. One purpose of schooling has been and remains helping children make the transition from the primary group of the family, and introducing them to secondary groups where the relational ties are diminished and the ability to live in a world of peers is fostered and developed. As is true with any social structure in which individuals spend a significant amount of time, this will pose questions of how the people in the environment treat each other, how resources—great or small, tangible or not—are distributed, how differences of opinions will exist, conflicts will be created, and, ideally, how they will be resolved in a fair manner.

The essential element of such environments is the classroom meeting. The classroom meeting serves a range of functions in moral education and is endorsed by moral educators, independent of orientation—caring, character, or cognitive-development.

No student is too young to address issues of fairness. For example, Vivian Paley's kindergarten class provides a powerful and well-documented example. Concerned that their more popular peers in play and other activities were excluding some students, Paley suggested to the students that they consider a rule for the classroom, "You can't say, 'You can't play.'" In the book by the same name as the suggested rule, Paley describes the well-established process of classroom meetings and how, before any rule was discussed or adopted, it would be proposed for a time of reflection. Paley describes the immediate reaction of both the kindergarten students as well as the older students in the school. When the rule is adopted and implemented, the effect is powerful and positive.

One purpose and benefit of classroom meetings is to create a safe and caring environment. Another is to discuss current events in the classroom, school, immediate community, country, and world—introducing students to the knowledge and developing the skills and dispositions required of democratic citizens in the school and the world beyond. A third purpose is classroom management. As a result of the several goals, most democratic classrooms conduct meetings daily, share information, have discussions, and deliberate about issues and events. In addition, typically, a major meeting and a more formal meeting are held once a week to address governance issues.

Because of the size and nature of the classroom, direct democracy is the norm. As is true with any democratic group, the scope of the decisions is constrained by other governmental bodies. In democratic classrooms, students serve in the role as legislators; the teacher typically serves the role of administrator and plays a strong role in enforcing the classroom rules. In this structure, the students can experience a laboratory for democracy and morality in a safe environment.

Many democratic classrooms, by discussing and reflecting on current issues, are motivated to involve themselves and make a positive difference. Service learning is a teaching strategy ideally suited to this goal. Service learning is a combination of community service and learning. Participating in community service is one of the dispositions of democratic citizenship to be fostered and encouraged, but to be service learning the service must be explicitly linked to curriculum content. For example, students in an eighth grade American history or civics class might tutor refugees on the knowledge required to pass the test required for the refugees to become citizens of the United States. In doing so, students are likely to encounter ethical issues related to how the people they are helping became refugees.

Several moral education programs place an emphasis on the role of classroom meetings. Democratic classrooms can sensitize and educate both adults and students to moral issues. One purpose of the weekly formal meeting in a democratic classroom is to assess how well the members of the class are living up to the expectations that they have created for themselves. Adults in school environments frequently underestimate the degree to which students experience bullying behaviors—ranging from teasing and harassment to extortion to physical intimidation and violence. One example of the power of democratic classrooms, documented by recording a classroom meeting, occurred in a school implementing the Child Development Program of the Developmental Studies Center. It shows a teacher coming to recognize that a significant problem of teasing/bullying exists in the classroom and that, unwittingly, she might have been contributing to it. The Community of Caring is another moral education program that emphasizes the power of student voice using Teen Forums, which provide a formal opportunity for secondary students to raise concerns and suggest solutions to policy makers on the school, community, and national levels.

*Further Reading:* Child Development Project. (1996). *Ways we want our class to be: Class meetings that build commitment to kindness and learning.* Oakland, CA: Developmental Studies Center. Developmental Studies Center (Producer). (1994). *Teasing* [Video recording]. Oakland, CA:

Developmental Studies Center. Paley, V. (1992). *You can't say "You can't play."* Cambridge, MA: Harvard University Press. Wade, R.C. (Ed.). (2000). *Building bridges: Connecting classroom and community through service-learning in social studies.* Washington, D.C.: National Council for the Social Studies. Watson, M. (2003). Learning to trust: Transforming elementary classrooms through developmental discipline. San Francisco: Jossey-Bass.

*Robert W. Howard*

## Democratic Schools

Democratic schools empower and involve stakeholders in the school community in creating and enforcing school policies and rules. A broad consensus exists between both moral educators (from the range of approaches—cognitive developmental, character, and caring) and educators in general that one purpose of schooling is the preparation of citizens prepared to engage in a democratic society. In the United States and the United Kingdom (among other nations), a descriptive and conservative argument can be advanced: that because democratic participation is a current feature of those societies that citizen preparation ought to be one of the aims of schools. However, one could argue based on ethical principles that independent of the type of society that does exist, education should prepare individuals with the requisite knowledge, skills, and dispositions for democratic participation and governance.

Because schools are social institutions, conflicts and ethical issues of fairness (among others) are inevitable. Through creating and enforcing school rules, grading policies, and distributing resources—called by some a hidden curriculum—schools are engaged in a moral education. The question is not whether schools will engage in moral education, but how and whether what is taught implicitly is actually ethical.

Many educators see the governance of classrooms and schools as an opportunity to create, in effect, laboratories for democracy and moral education by involving students—with teachers and administrators (and in some schools with support staff, parents, and community members)—in making and enforcing school rules and norms. By being engaged in democracy, students learn knowledge, skills, and dispositions of autonomous citizenship.

Democratic schools differ among themselves by (a) whether the school is part of a public school system or is an independent school, (b) whether decisions are made by all members of the community in a direct democracy or by representative democracy, (c) which range decisions are within the purview of the legislative body, and (d) whether enforcement includes a judicial body made up of members of the democratic school (e.g., a fairness committee) to settle disputes, or the school administration, or both. In the United States, education is a responsibility of state governments that have (except Hawaii) delegated most decisions and local school districts. The federal government has a presence in most school districts and schools (e.g., the No Child Left Behind Act of 2001) as a consequence of providing funding for programs and the schools' agreement to be bound by federal policies and regulations. As a result, any school—democratic or traditional—is limited in the range of decisions that can legitimately be made. For example, most states dictate through law the minimum number of days school must be in session and the method for assessment of academic achievement, and a democratic school in this environment could not unilaterally change the school calendar or substitute a different measure of student learning for the one determined by the state. Finally, most school systems have entered into collective bargaining agreements with professional associations or unions that limit the range of democratic decisions at the school level. Within these parameters, democratic schools can and do make decisions about important issues such as free speech (whether a student's T-shirt message constitutes offensive and disruptive speech), school rules (whether the school should participate in a speech competition in which only U.S. citizens are allow to enter), organization (e.g., whether advisory groups should be arranged heterogeneously to permit another opportunity to mainstream special education students), and normative expectations for community members.

Among moral educators and the public school context in the United States, several democratic high schools have a high profile, including small alternative schools that practice direct democracy and schools with representative democratic governance. The first category includes Brookline (Massachusetts) High School's School-Within-a-School; Cluster School in Cambridge, Massachusetts; Just Community Schools in New York City; and Scarsdale (New York) Alternative School. In the second category are Brookline (Massachusetts) High School, Hanover (New Hampshire) High School, and Hudson (Massachusetts) High School. Democratic schools are not limited to older students; among democratic elementary schools are Heath Elementary in Brookline (Massachusetts) and the MicroSociety School network that includes approximately 200 schools in 40 states in the United States.

In contrast with public schools, independent schools can have greater flexibility. One of the most famous democratic schools is Summerhill, established in 1921 in England by A. S. Neill. Summerhill is independent of the government-controlled system in Britain and provides a comprehensive example of democratic governance of a school. At Summerhill, meetings—similar to town meetings common in New England in the United States—are held frequently, and the range of decisions includes the curriculum. Freedom is a norm for both the community as a system and individuals within it. Students can choose what to learn as well as how, when, and how often to study. That means that, unlike students and schools in much of the United Kingdom and the United States, students are not placed in classes by age, led by a teacher, and taught a predetermined curriculum in reading, for example, in a highly structured manner. Instead of sitting in a desk in a classroom, a Summerhill student might spend hours painting alone or in an informal group.

In the United States, the Sudbury Valley School in Framingham, Massachusetts, operates with both a similar philosophy and a libertarian structure as does Summerhill. Created in 1972, Sudbury Valley is the catalyst for an international network of similar schools including about 14 in the United States. At Sudbury Valley the range of democratic decision making is broad and includes making decisions about the school's budget, hiring personnel, and determining if teachers or other employees will stay with the school for another year.

***Further Reading:*** Apple, M.W., & Beane, J.A. (1995). *Democratic schools.* Alexandria, VA: Association for Supervision and Curriculum Development. Greenberg, D., Sadofsky, M., & Lempka, J. (2004). *The pursuit of happiness: The lives of Sudbury Valley alumni.* Framingham, MA: Sudbury Valley School Press. Carnegie Corporation of New York & CIRCLE: The Center for Information and Research on Civic Learning and Engagement. (2003). *Civic mission of schools.* New York: Carnegie Corporation. Mosher, R.L., Kenny, R.A., & Garrod, A.C. (1996). *Preparing for citizenship: Teaching youth to live democratically.* Westport, CT: Praeger Publishers. Power, F.C., Higgins, A., & Kohlberg, L. (1989). *Lawrence Kohlberg's approach to moral education.* New York: Columbia University Press.

*Robert W. Howard*

## Democratic Values

Consider the following amalgam culled from several lists (and representative of the group) of democratic values: justice, equality, responsibility, freedom, diversity, privacy, and the rule of law. While some citizens may argue for another value to be included or perhaps one removed, the more fundamental challenge is to understand the values as they exist and sometimes come into conflict in the daily life of democracy—both political and social. Here moral educators can promote moral reasoning and actions in their students. One option is in the analysis of current events. For example, how does one make choices about the relative importance of privacy and freedom in an era when the rule of law places restrictions on both with the goal of promoting security? Is equality supported or eroded by affirmative action policies? Should sexual orientation be a type of diversity that is treated differently—in terms of law—when two people want to marry?

Democracy can be defended on ethical grounds in that the process and outcome: (1) is more likely than other systems to treat citizens with respect and dignity, (2) supports equality, and (3) includes fundamental notions of freedom (including the freedom to choose one's representatives and to pursue one's own notion of the good). No single and universal set of democratic values exists. It might be that one recognizes democratic values when one sees them (as pornography was defined by Supreme Court Justice Potter Stewart) or as one experiences democratic values and the conflicting interpretation of what behaviors and policies are conforming and which are incompatible.

Democracy, and the values that undergird it, include political democracy and social democracy. The political is what first comes to most individuals' minds upon hearing the term. The political dimension includes the governmental structures and the constitutional processes of the state, including voting, paying taxes, serving on juries when called, and so on. Social democracy involves the daily life of citizens and how they treat each other in walking on the street, conversing in coffee shops or libraries, engaging in commercial exchange, behaving while driving automobiles, and so on. The common points between the two types of democracy are many. Perhaps the most fundamental is that both require engagement. Democracy is as much a verb as a noun—an ongoing series of participatory events, not a spectator amusement. What values—and what is valued—bring to both types of democracy is a set of expectations and, in effect, rules for the game. The goals for moral educators are to introduce students to democracy and its conventions, to highlight the ethical dimensions, and to frame unresolved issues.

Among the other characteristics of democracy is the dual nature of democracy as an ideal and democracy in daily life. The ideal of democracy has historically been a motivator to individuals even when the daily reality is far from the ideal. Two of the most eloquent examples of the democratic idea as a beacon are the Declaration of Sentiments from the 1848 Women's Rights Convention held in Seneca Falls and the argument for justice articulated by the Reverend Martin Luther King Jr. in his *Letter from Birmingham Jail*. In making both cases for equality, Elizabeth Cady Stanton (and her colleagues) in New York and King over a century later in Alabama focused not on revolution but on the ideals and promises of the founding and fundamental documents of the United States.

Perhaps the most important of the responsibilities of all educators—and particularly those who identify as moral educator—is to address the declining engagement in the United States in both political and social democracy. The data for both are collected by social scientists and are readily available. For example, the majority of eligible voters in the country frequently do not exercise this right/obligation. In addition, the involvement in the civil society—through joining organizations and informal socialization—has been declining for four decades.

At the end of the Constitutional Convention in Philadelphia, a woman is reported to have asked Benjamin Franklin as he was leaving whether the convention had established a monarchy for a republican form of democracy. The reported answer, "A republic madam, if you can keep it." The challenge Franklin issued of 1787 remains one today.

*Further Reading:* Baker, J.H. (2005). *Sisters: The lives of America's suffragists.* New York: Hill and Wang. Branch, T. (1999). *Parting the waters: America in the King years 1954–63.* New York: Simon and Schuster. Ellis, J.J. (2001). *Founding brothers: The revolutionary generation.* New York: Vintage. Putnam, R.D. (2000) *Bowling alone: The collapse and revival of American community.* New York: Simon and Schuster. Zinn, H. (2005). *People's history of the United States: 1492 to present.* New York: HarperCollins.

*Robert W. Howard*

## Deontology

If you believe that "the ends justify the means" when taking an action, you are not thinking deontologically. If you think, by contrast, that certain actions are inherently right, and others wrong (with rare exception), deontology is your guide. The motto here is to do things simply because we should, because it is right—to act for duty's sake, morality's sake, even if no further advantage accrues from one's act ("deon" means "duty" in Greek). And, for the deontologist, virtually nothing is more important when deciding how to act than doing the right thing. Deontology typically views "ends-justify-means" thinking as a root of immorality, along with the tendency to mix moral considerations with interested and practical ones.

Putting these points philosophically, deontological thinking is autonomous, essentialist, and supremacist. That is, it views morality as a separate and distinct area of concern, defined by its intrinsic qualities, and of highest comparative importance among standards for action. Morality trumps the range of nonmoral considerations—material (economic), legal, political, familial, cultural, or personal.

Thinking deontologically makes decisions simpler, though often more difficult to carry through. No calculation of consequences is involved. Should I lie to avoid embarrassment, or to get out of being sanctioned, or to avoid losing a golden opportunity? "No" is the answer in each case. One should not lie period. Exceptions are allowed, but only where a more weighty duty in itself conflicts with the present one. The duty never to kill is an example. In extreme instances, the scale of bad consequences can be so extensive for a particular action as to change the nature of choice. For example, preventing genocide or a massacre may fall in a different category from simply weighing the welfare of more people against the welfare of others or (more to the deontological point) against the rights of others. Allowing certain events to occur may simply be unconscionable or indecent (in themselves) when they can be prevented. A duty of necessary intervention or strict benevolence may be said to apply. And it could override a weaker inherent duty such as that "not to lie."

Acting deontologically is often more difficult because considering the consequences and goals of actions also means gathering additional motivations for action. Often interested motivations are more psychologically powerful than moral ones, which tend to be conceptual or intellectual. Deontological strictures compensate for this problem demanding only proper action, not proper motives, which it merely prefers and credits. We are to act as if only moral considerations were moving us when we cannot actually muster such pure motives.

Many moral exemplars achieve their moral status by aligning their personal interest and desires with their duties. They no longer need to act out of a sense of duty from then on. This is seen as the goal of moral development and education in some traditions. We recognize that doing things "because one has to" is not as admirable as doing them, say, out of love for people one is affecting. To act out of duty fails to fully identify with morality and embody it, always remaining instead its seemingly oppressed servant. (As early as Confucius, making Li Yi—making outer conformance to moral ritual one's heartfelt path—was the ultimate moral goal.) Ultimately what we wish is for children to love goodness and love other people, or at least respect and show concern for them. In their training we wish to recruit all the positive reasons and desires we can for doing so.

Seemingly the deontologist does not see things this way. Why give credit to someone who does the right thing because he/she likes to? Where is the effort in that? Where is his/her sense of duty or morality, as opposed to hedonism? Without pain—an eternal struggle to do the right thing, in opposition to temptation—there is no (moral) gain. And the pain of self-sacrifice for the right is the best sign that no pleasures are lurking behind an act, luring it to good ends.

Perhaps this is a misunderstanding of mature deontological thinking and its implications for moral education or development. It is one thing to have personal likes that happen on moral actions as a kind of hobby. It is another thing to purposely transform one's motivations and oneself so that one's appreciation of doing right and fighting for justice inspires your every deed. This turns desires into values, not values into tastes and preferences. The desired "struggle" to be good is in one's many choices and efforts to become a better person and stick with one's elevating efforts. Once being so becomes second nature, the effort and choice to express oneself as moral duty bids is "already in there," showing itself implicitly in all one does.

Deontology is a category from metaethics, the study of ethical theories or views. It is usually contrasted with teleology, moral thinking that aims at good consequences or goals. ("Telos" means "target" in Greek.) A remarkable thing happened when scholars reflected on the similarities and differences of the great ethical traditions and their theoretical forms. Most of them could be defined by just two of their general concepts, it turned out—right and good. Two simple logics distinguished how they defined right, moreover, and related it to good. One (teleology) saw what is right as promoting good, as aiming at or striving toward the good, and as producing as much good as possible. The other (deontology) defined what is right within the striving itself, within the means to an end. Being honest or telling the truth is right in itself. It should be done for its own (or right's) sake, even when the results are unpleasant.

In ethics circles, concepts like "ought to" and "should," "duty" and "obligation," have been essentially bifurcated ever since, meaning either doing what is right or doing what is beneficial. Deontology and teleology turn out to be very crude categories. Arguably there is much of ethics that falls outside them or violates their great divide. Virtue ethics, for example, since they seem good in themselves, seem to be pursued as ends in themselves. And they are not chosen actions, to be judged right and wrong, but traits or states of being. When they move, it is in self-expression, not pursuit. Their main "should" is to maintain or be preserved as in our "having integrity." What some call "moral values" also seem inherently valuable and should be pursued as ends for their own sake. When ethical theories of virtues or values are devised, they normally take an intuitionist or pluralist form, which cannot be reduced to a deontological or teleological logic.

Still, these crude logical categories can prove extremely useful in even commonsense ethical thought. By simply determining whether someone's viewpoint conforms to one of these simple logics, in relating right to good, we can predict its major strengths and weaknesses. We can pinpoint where its weak links lie and foresee how to build on its strengths. This is very useful in moral education. And while these logics conflict, it is possible to make them complement each other—even to compensate for each other's weaknesses in combination. Students can be reminded to look both at the intrinsic reasons for doing something right and also for the benefits accruing from doing so when making a decision. They can be reminded that violating basic and strict responsibilities represents precisely those means that cannot be justified by good ends, while making other tradeoffs between costs and benefits may be justifiable. (A good side lesson to teach here is why justifying certain questionable actions by their good consequences is not saying they are right or just—merely that they are not as objectionable as the relevant alternative.)

The main weaknesses of deontology are found in dogmatism and arbitrariness since we often cannot identify the intrinsic reason to doing something right, beyond conventional upbringing and indoctrination. Deontological thinking simply can credit the importance of goods, values, virtues, and the consequences of actions. It treats them as if they were amoral, not simply of somewhat limited moral relevance at times. Teleological thinking seems to miss what is most notable and special about morality, a certain desirable purity or integrity. Morality does not bend to ulterior motives or compromise its soul. It does not look for excuses to get out of doing what it should, but rather stands upright and tall where it feasibly can.

We should not step on people or run roughshod over them to get what we want. We should not use them, manipulate them, or push them unduly toward even the best of ends. If we are going to get along, and do so voluntarily, there must be some ground rules we agree to and make sure not to betray. And we need assurance that we can count on each other to play by these basic rules. These are the insights of deontology.

*Further Reading:* Kymlicka, W. (1988). Rawls on teleology and deontology. *Philosophy and Public Affairs, 17*(3), 173–190. MacDonald, J.E., & Beck-Dudley, C.L. (1994). Are deontology and teleology mutually exclusive. *Journal of Business Ethics, 13,* 615–623.

*Bill Puka*

## Developmental Assets (Search Institute)

The Developmental Assets approach to youth development involves attending to a set of 40 assets trademarked by the Search Institute, an applied social science research center that focuses on positive youth development, located in Minneapolis, Minnesota. The assets represent a distillation of research and theory on youth development and provide a framework for communities, schools, youth programs, and other concerned individuals wanting to proactively facilitate healthy youth development and moral education.

The 40 Developmental Assets include four categories of external assets and four categories of internal assets. The external assets are factors that young people receive from others. The categories are support (such as "family support" and a "caring school climate"), empowerment (such as "safety" and living where the "community values youth"), boundaries and expectations (such as "school boundaries" providing clear rules and "positive peer influence"), and constructive use of time (such as "creative activities" and a "religious community"). The internal assets are personal qualities of youth that guide positive developmental choices and experiences. The categories are commitment to learning (such as "achievement motivation" and "reading for pleasure"), positive values (such as "caring" and "integrity"), social competencies (such as "interpersonal competence" and the ability to engage in "peaceful conflict resolution"), and positive identity (such as a "sense of purpose" and a "positive view of personal future").

The Search Institute first introduced the Developmental Assets in the 1990s, building off several research traditions in social science and education. These traditions include research investigating resilience, a process whereby people adapt in reasonably healthy ways to high levels of risk and adversity, and research investigating the protective factors that predict healthy developmental outcomes. Resilience researchers have consistently found that a surprising number of at-risk youth persevere and succeed when they have internal and external assets that allow them to manage most of the challenges they confront. Thus, rather than focusing exclusively on identifying risks and reducing problem behaviors, much recent attention has been devoted to identifying strengths and focusing on building the assets that youth can use toward healthy development.

This positive approach to youth development is a point of emphasis within the Developmental Assets approach. In fact, the Developmental Assets have become closely associated with "positive youth development"—a field of study that assumes that healthy development depends as much on building strengths as it does on eliminating weaknesses. Scholars of positive youth development are particularly interested in using research findings in applied settings, and the accessible nature of the Developmental Assets fits well with this purpose.

Research specifically addressing the Developmental Assets mostly derives from scholars affiliated with the Search Institute. In surveys investigating assets and outcomes among youth in the United States and Canada, the Search Institute finds clear associations between greater quantities of assets and positive developmental outcomes such as maintaining good health, succeeding in school, helping others, avoiding drugs and alcohol, and better mental health. This research recommends having more than 31 of the 40 assets as ideal for facilitating optimal outcomes, although on average North American youth have the benefit of less than 20 assets. The Search Institute has also reviewed large bodies of other research addressing general concepts underlying the Developmental Assets, although more research is necessary to clarify the applicability of the assets with diverse groups of youth in distinct community contexts.

Ultimately, the Developmental Assets concept provides one way to link research, practice, and policy related to positive youth development. The assets translate findings about resilience and protective factors in ways that provide a tangible framework for working toward healthy communities for youth. The Search Institute contends that no one developmental asset is most important—healthy development depends upon individuals, communities, families, and programs that work together to ensure all youth have the opportunity to thrive. Moral education shares with the Developmental Assets approach a concern with the values and competencies that contribute to the development of meaningful moral standards and belief systems.

*Further Reading:* Benson, P. L. (2006). *All kids are our kids: What communities must do to raise caring and responsible children and adolescents.* San Francisco: Jossey-Bass. Lerner, R. M., & Benson, P. L. (Eds.). (2003). *Developmental assets and asset-building communities: Implications for research, policy, and practice.* New York: Kluwer Academic/Plenum Publishers. Lerner, R. M., Taylor, C. S.,

& von Eye, A. (Eds.). (2002). *Pathways to positive development among diverse youth: New directions for youth development, No. 95*. San Francisco: Jossey-Bass. Scales, P.C., & Leffert, N. (2004). *Developmental assets: A synthesis of the scientific research on adolescent development*. Minneapolis, MN: Search Institute.

*Andrew M. Guest and James M. Lies*

## Developmental Education

Developmental education is the application of human development theory to varied educational contexts from early childhood through adulthood. It has as its overall objective the design of educational experiences that will promote healthy psychological development in the cognitive, interpersonal, ego, and moral domains across the life span. The approach posits that human development results from interactions between organismic (biological) and environmental (contextual) levels of organization.

Developmental education draws on a number of central theoretical assumptions including the following: (a) meaning is constructed; (b) an emphasis on understanding how individuals are making meaning from their experiences; (c) development occurs as people interact with their environments; (d) development is described as becoming more complex, integrated, and complete over time; (e) development does not occur automatically, rather it depends on interactions within an environment that offers both support and challenge; (f) skills are needed for developmental growth, and these skills reflect a developmental range that individuals can access depending on the degree of contextual support provided; and (g) construction and reconstruction of meaning occurs through assimilation and accommodation and affective dissonance, leading to greater integration and differentiation of the psychological self. Thus, developmental education creates deliberate experiences that engage the organizing principles, reasons, and affect people use for interpreting their experiences. For example, Robert Selman (2003) has investigated how educational experiences promote social awareness and the growth of interpersonal understanding in children, adolescents, and adults. The overarching goal is for persons to become more complex, allocentric, integrated, and principled over time.

Multiple educational design components are engaged in developmental educational programming. Norman Sprinthall and Lois Thies-Sprinthall (1983) summarized key design conditions for developmental education in general and teacher education in particular. First, developmental education experiences must be contextualized. Educational programming must account for prior knowledge, experiences, and performance of learners. In addition to understanding personal, social, and cultural history, this condition emphasizes building trust within the designed educational experience.

A second key condition is complex new "human-helping" experiences. When adolescents or adults engage in complex new human-helping roles in schools and classrooms, the experience (action) can cause "knowledge disturbances" as one encounters information or concepts that differ from one's prior knowledge. Analysis and reflection (inquiry) spur the Piagetian interacting processes of assimilation and accommodation in relation to the immediate new experiences. An example of a complex new "human-helping" experience might be sustained service learning where an adolescent spends time each week tutoring elementary students.

The complex new experience is a necessary but not sufficient condition for constructive-developmental change. The person must reflect on the new experience. This condition of guided reflection (co-reflecting on meaning of experience) or guided inquiry (reflecting and analyzing experience) includes both self-assessment and reflection through carefully planned activities, ongoing discussions, and dialogue journals. These assessment and reflection activities are typically guided by a "more capable other" with the goal of optimal meaning making.

Support (encouragement) and challenge (prompting the learner to accommodate to new learning) represent the fourth condition, and both are necessary for learning and development. This is the most complex pedagogical requirement of developmental education. Consider a situation in your own experience when your method of problem solving and understanding no longer fits and then think of the feelings aroused. Such an experience gives us a clearer sense of the effects of disequilibrium during new learning and the connected roles of support and challenge. Without question, learning how to manage support and challenge as an educator is the most difficult of the developmental education conditions. Beyond the need to balance support and challenge, there is a second need for differentiation of instruction because each individual differs in his/her need for support and challenge.

Balance represents the fifth condition of developmental education. Neither action (e.g., complex new human-helping experience) nor reflection alone is enough to promote development. It is important that there is a balance between the new human-helping experience (action) and reflection. In researched programs this means that the practice-based experiences are sequenced with guided inquiry each week. Too great a time lag between action and reflection appears to halt the growth process.

The final condition is continuity. The complex goal of fostering changes in ego, conceptual/epistemological understanding, or moral reasoning and behavior requires a continuous interplay between experience and reflection. Research suggests that one- or two-week workshops do not prompt changes in psychological development. Typically, at least four-to-six months are needed for significant learning and development to occur, and all the conditions just described must be present.

***Further Reading:*** Selman, R. (2003). *The promotion of social awareness.* New York: Russell Sage Foundation. Sprinthall, N., & Thies-Sprinthall, L. (1983). The teacher as an adult learner: A cognitive-developmental view. In G. Griffin (Ed.), *Staff development: Eighty-second yearbook of the National Society for the Study of Education* (pp. 13–35). Chicago: University of Chicago Press.

*Alan Reiman*

## Dewey, John

In the first half of the twentieth century, John Dewey reigned as the most eminent American philosopher of education. John Dewey was born on October 20, 1859, the third of four sons born to Archibald and Lucinda Dewey of Burlington, Vermont. He attended public schools in Burlington and entered the University of Vermont in 1875. After obtaining his doctorate in 1884, Dewey accepted a teaching post at the University of Michigan, where he stayed for ten years. While at Michigan, Dewey collaborated with James H. Tufts, with whom he would later write *Ethics* in 1908. In 1894, Dewey left Michigan to teach at the University of Chicago. It was during his years at Chicago that Dewey's Hegelian idealism yielded to an experiential based theory of education, which would soon come to be most closely associated with pragmatism. While at the University of Chicago, Dewey was greatly influenced by his association with Jane Addams, who created Hull House as an outreach for Chicago's marginalized immigrants. Dewey served on the Hull House Board of Trustees for many years and met regularly with Addams to discuss pedagogical issues.

The experience in the laboratory school provided the material for his first major work on education, *The School and Society,* which was published in 1899. In 1904 Dewey left the University of Chicago to accept a post at Columbia University, where he would spend the rest of his professional life. His interest in moral education did not diminish at Columbia, and he quickly became involved with work at the Teachers College. During his first decade at Columbia, Dewey published what would become two of his most famous works: *How We Think* (1910), which articulated his theory of knowledge and its application to education, and *Democracy and Education* (1916).

Dewey's approach to moral education reaffirms his belief that as moral thinkers we are involved participants rather than passive spectators of the world we come to judge. Dewey's ethical theory recognized that students learn through a variety of educational environments, and that their unique and individual perspectives can contribute greatly to the learning and teaching environment in the classroom. It was one of Dewey's complaints that traditional models of education made the student an entity separate from the lessons, thus erecting barriers between subject and object that could not easily be overcome. By setting educational objectives firmly within the natural world, Dewey's theory of naturalistic moral education attempted to avoid many of the traditional problems of both empirical and rational epistemology. In presenting such an argument, it is important to recognize the epistemological framework that drove Dewey's propositions, that is, the understanding that all practical knowledge is (in some way) the product of social construction.

The importance of Dewey's theories of naturalistic epistemology and experiential education is critical in helping us understand the justification for moral education curriculum. He understood that education is ultimately social, communal, interactive, and reciprocal. This means that attention must be given to the interaction between the students and teacher in each educational experience, as well as the temporal connections between past and present experiences. Dewey strongly believed that any plausible conceptualization of moral education would necessarily need to call for additional development of a model in which the dimensions of theory and practice, and of individual and society, are joined in curriculum development. For these reasons, Dewey was critical of both rationalism and empiricism as those two philosophical frameworks were strictly understood. The implications of those conceptual frameworks created an unpalatable dichotomy for understanding moral agency: either human experience is not a part of the world of nature at all (as in Descartes' rationalism) or else a Humean arch-empiricism must reign.

Like William James, Dewey believed that pragmatism is a valuable middle ground between the extremes of empiricism and rationalism, incorporating what is best in both. The main problem with these traditional rival epistemological views, he believes, is that each operates with an impoverished notion of what experience is. Dewey's point here seems to be that experience and knowledge are a matter of interactions between knower and the known, and neither is left at the end exactly as it was at the beginning. According to Dewey, what counts as intelligent intervention is any method of learning that succeeds in transforming confused situations into clear ones.

Dewey thought that intelligence can be as effective in the realm of morality as it is in science. Because the basic cognitive situation is the problem situation, and because hypotheses are created to resolve such situations satisfactorily, the concepts involved in hypotheses are necessarily related to our moral concerns and interests. Ideas, concepts, and terms, then, are intellectual tools we use as long as they serve our purposes and discard when they no longer accomplish that task. They are to be construed as instruments for solving problems.

Today, Dewey would probably advise that in order for our students to cope with and be able to manage their futures, they must develop the skills and processes of social inquiry gained through experience, and they must be able to ask really tough questions. But none of this will be achieved unless the educational leaders of today accept their responsibility to encourage and support the development of critical and reflective thinking. For many educators, nurturing citizens who will be full participants in the democratic process is a primary impetus for their commitment to a moral education curriculum. His approach to moral education in *Democracy and Education* emphasized an eclectic synthesis of Jean-Jacques Rousseau and Plato's educational philosophies. He criticized Rousseau's idealization of the individual, but also challenged Plato's view as exclusively favoring the interests of society. This eclecticism points to Dewey's perception of the individual as one who is essentially situated within a social context. He believed that moral education must reflect the individual's purpose of gaining full citizenship within the community, while still maintaining the individual rights associated with democracy.

Dewey frequently contributed to popular magazines such as *The New Republic* and *Nation,* and he became increasingly more involved in a variety of political causes, including women's suffrage and the unionization of teachers. He was often invited to speak on behalf of these political causes, and his retirement in 1930 from teaching did not diminish his interest in active citizenry. He continued to remain a vital force, working throughout his retirement, until his death in 1952, at the age of 92. Dewey was the most influential advocate of the progressive movement in education, which was quite popular and broadly integrated into the practices of American public schools.

***Further Reading:*** Boisvert, R.D. (1998). *John Dewey: Rethinking our time.* Albany, NY: State University of New York Press. Campbell, J. (1995). Understanding John Dewey. *Nature and cooperative Intelligence.* Chicago, IL: Open Court. Haskins, C., & Seiple, D.I. (1999). *Dewey reconfigured: Essays on Deweyan pragmatism.* Albany, New York: State University of New York Press. Hickman, L.A. (1998). *Reading Dewey: Interpretations for a Postmodern generation.* Bloomington, IN: Indiana University Press. Ryan, A. (1995). *John Dewey and the high tide of American Liberalism.* New York: W.W. Norton.

*Monalisa M. Mullins*

## Discipline

Discipline is one of the most basic methods of character formation. The word "discipline" comes from the Latin *disciplulus,* which means disciple, and the derivative, *disciplina,* refers explicitly to the process of teaching. Often, discipline is regarded as a response to misbehavior and, therefore, as having to do with various techniques for correction and punishment. Considerable attention has been given to whether corporal punishment is an appropriate means of discipline. Although corporal punishment was prevalent in the past, most countries in the world now outlaw the practice, and it is now in violation of the UN Convention on the Rights of the Child.

Assumptions about children's nature influence the approaches that parents, teachers, and other adults take to discipline. For example, if children are seen to be good by nature, practices are likely to be more permissive and oriented to children's development. If, on the other hand, children are seen as essentially impulsive and selfish, practices are likely to be more authoritarian and oriented to control. In her well-known research on parenting styles, Diana Baumrind (1967) identifies the authoritative approach, which combines clear expectations with open communication and warmth, as the best way to foster children's psychological health and sense of responsibility. A large body of parenting research (see Hoffman, 1970) indicates that disciplinary practices are most effective when caregivers practice induction by communicating expectations for behavior with reasons for why a behavior is right or wrong.

Many contemporary approaches to discipline recognize children are not blank slates or formless clay. Developing character requires more than simply telling children what to do or "shaping" their behavior through rewards and punishments. Discipline practices educate for moral development when they recognize that children are active learners by making children partners in their own education. This does not mean burdening children with decisions and responsibilities that are inappropriate for their level of maturity. It does mean, however, respecting and nurturing children's moral understanding and sense of agency to prepare them to become autonomous adults.

Discipline in school settings is typically referred to as classroom management. Classroom management approaches focus on efficient ways of establishing order in the classroom but generally include little if any guidance on how to foster moral or character development. Emile Durkheim, the great sociologist of education, criticized such approaches as "superficial" because they do not appreciate discipline as the "morality of the classroom." In Durkheim's view, teachers should use classroom rules and punishments to prepare students to be good citizens of society by teaching them how to become good citizens of the classroom community. The just community approach applies Durkheim's principles within a democratic framework in which students and teachers make and enforce rules together. In discussing rules and punishments, students are taught to deliberate about the moral values at stake, base their decisions upon a consideration of the common good, and take responsibility for themselves and the community as a whole.

Most approaches to discipline and classroom management do not involve democratic rule setting or the collectivism found in Durkheim and the just community approach but focus on the teacher-student interaction. For example, one of the most widely used approaches, Lee and Marlene Canter's Assertive Discipline, attempts to empower teachers by giving them a well-structured system of techniques for presenting and enforcing their expectations confidently, clearly, consistently, and forcefully. Thomas Gordan's Effectiveness Training focuses on helping caregivers to foster self-reliance by communicating their emotional responses to children's behavior in a more straightforward and educational manner. Although contemporary disciplinary approaches note the importance of protecting and building children's self-esteem, the Positive Discipline approach is especially sensitive to the debilitating effects of punitive discipline and, instead, provides techniques for affirming children and encouraging good behavior.

Most approaches to discipline do not engage moral development and education research in any systematic way. George Bear's *Developing Self-Discipline,* written primarily for school psychologists, and Marilyn Watson's *Learning to Trust,* written primarily for elementary teachers, are notable exceptions. Bear and Watson illustrate how properly administered discipline can foster moral development, self-control, and social skills.

**Further Reading:** Baumrind, D. (1967). Child care practices anteceding three patterns of preschool behavior. *Genetic Psychology Monographs, 75*(1), 43–88. Bear, G. (2004). *Developing self-discipline and preventing and correcting misbehavior.* Boston, MA: Pearson Allyn & Bacon. Canter, L., & Canter, M. (2001). *Assertive discipline: Positive behavior management for today's classroom* (3rd ed.). Bloomington, IN: Solution Tree. Gordon, T. (1991). *Discipline that works; Promoting self-discipline in children.* New York: Plume. Hoffman, M.L. (1970). Conscience, personality, and socialization techniques. *Human Development, 13,* 90–126. Jones, F.H. (1987). *Positive classroom discipline.* New York: McGraw-Hill. Watson, M. (2003). *Learning to trust: Transforming difficult elementary classrooms through developmental discipline.* San Francisco: Jossey-Bass.

*Ann Marie R. Power*


## Dissonance

Dissonance is a form of cognitive tension that occurs when there is a difference in what people know or believe and their behavior. For example, choosing to follow the group despite it being the wrong choice creates dissonance. Cognitive dissonance is a distressing mental state based on attitude. Avoiding cognitive dissonance is considered a basic human need that reflects one's need for consistency and predictability in life. Over the years, dissonance theory has made substantial contributions to the field of attitude change.

Dissonance becomes greater as the difference between beliefs and behavior widens and the issue becomes more important. However, dissonance naturally seeks resolution. As such, individuals attempt to reduce the dissonance by changing their beliefs or their behavior. This type of change is often referred to as cognitive restructuring and behavior modification. Festinger (1957) suggested that individuals use three types of approaches to avoid dissonance:

1. Selective exposure prevents dissonance. People try to remain in their comfort zone with regards to like-minded others, activities, or beliefs. By sticking with what one knows and is familiar with, there is little need for anxiety over real or perceived differences. The old cliché "birds of a feather flock together" may be as much related to reducing cognitive dissonance as sharing interests. A negative implication can be a lack of desire or willingness to consider different viewpoints or experiences. There is often a reluctance to do so because current attitudes would be challenged. Furthermore, one may hold the belief that to take into account other opinions means to agree with them. The challenge would be for an individual to first seek understanding rather than agreement without the confusion that they mean the same thing. Viewing diversity of thought and activities as an opportunity to learn through understanding can enhance life experience while also building community.
2. Postdecision dissonance creates a need for reassurance. People like to believe they make good decisions. However, for some, dissonance may increase after a decision is made. The likelihood of that happening is raised based on three criteria. The importance of the issue, the longer an individual procrastinates in choosing between equally acceptable choices, and the less opportunity to reverse his/her decision once it has been made. The act of choosing an option means to reject other choices. Stated differently, with a gain there is a loss. People have a need to know that they chose correctly. Examples range from answering correctly on a test to choosing a spouse. Although the content is different, the process is similar.

3. Minimal justification for behavior creates a shift in attitude. People need only a small amount of reward or punishment as incentive to change their behavior, resulting in a change of attitude about that behavior. Rationalizing behavior can emerge from one's inner desire to avoid guilt from one's actions. However, the justifications for behavior can also come from external sources as a way to motivate a certain behavior.

Aronson (1973) suggested that attitude comes from the amount of effort we put into a behavior. If it is difficult to become a member of a team, for instance, then our attitude of selectivity or elitism is greater. Furthermore, the higher the chance of letting the team down or looking foolish creates the dissonance.

Wicklund and Brehm (1976) concluded that being personally responsible for unwanted outcomes was the decisive cause of dissonance. This was especially true if there were at least two options in the decision and the individual realized the wrong choice was made yet continued with the decision. Consequently, if an individual did not have any choice in his/her decision then there would be less or possibly no dissonance. This concept is fundamental to fear of failure and further illustrates the human need for predictable and determined outcomes to one's decisions.

Fear of failure can lead to procrastination in decisions and participation in daily activities or major life events. The dissonance from not wanting to make the wrong decision or having outcomes not meet one's expectations can be overwhelming. This is especially true if a person ties his or her self-worth to the outcomes. If a person has a pattern of "failing" in his/her decisions and involvements, then he/she may try to reduce the dissonance by not participating or delaying decision making. However, a more appropriate way of reducing cognitive dissonance is for a person to redefine what it means to fail and to succeed. Viewing failure as less disastrous and success as less necessary can increase participation because dissonance is minimal.

Cognitive dissonance is part of the human experience that creates pause in how persons relate to others and make decisions. Furthermore, dissonance can serve as a moral compass and reason to reflect on the choices that are made.

**Further Reading:** Aronson, E. (1973, May). The rationalizing animal. *Psychology Today*, pp. 46–51. Festinger, L. (1957). *A theory of cognitive dissonance*. Stanford, CA: Stanford University Press. Wicklund, R., & Brehm, J. (1976). *Perspectives on cognitive dissonance*. Hillsdale, NJ: Lawrence Erlbaum Associates.

*Scott E. Hall*

## Distributive Justice

There is retributive justice, which pertains to restoring perceived social imbalance caused by a harmful act. There is social justice, which concerns receiving fair treatment in society and a fair share of the benefits of social life. Legal justice is fair treatment at the hands of the law, and divine justice is a religious belief in a deity's perfectly just will. Distributive justice, for its part, raises the question of how to fairly allocate finite resources.

In principle, the problem of distributive justice touches on any benefits and burdens susceptible of being transferred among human beings. Accordingly, it could embrace respect, power, recognition, social responsibility, as well as property, services, and opportunities. Questions may arise, too, concerning who is entitled to the benefits or who carries the burdens of distributive justice. For example, considerations of distributive justice are commonly appealed to in order to justify the social benefits that only citizens of a particular state—and no noncitizen—are eligible to receive. Treatment of distributive justice in contemporary political philosophy, however, tends to be universalist—that is, it assumes that all human beings are the proper subjects of distribution—and to focus on the question of fairness in allotting limited material goods and the means by which material goods are acquired.

In attempts to identify a legitimate basis for fair distribution three principles of distributive justice recur: the principle of equality, the welfare principle, and the principle of dessert.

According to the principle of equality, since no person is of greater or lesser worth than any other, all have a right to an equal share of available resources. In the simplest problems of distributive justice, such as that of how to fairly divide up a pie among a family, has much practical appeal. As the needs and desires of the set of subjects of distribution become more diverse and as the array of resources to be distributed becomes larger and more complex, serious problems begin to emerge. If the principle of equality is interpreted to mean that people have a right to the same quality or level of goods, then it runs up against the problem of how to construct a noncontroversial measure or "index" of the relative qualities of different shares. Are two desserts worth one main course? Or three? Surely, it depends on what is on the menu and people's subjective preferences. If the principle of equality is interpreted to mean that they receive exactly the same package or bundle of goods, as in the familiar cooperative organic box schemes where members receive a weekly allocation of the same selection of vegetables according to what is available (e.g., one cabbage, a squash, a pound each of runner beans and onions) the principle runs up against the objection that, because of people's arbitrary preferences, it would almost certainly lead to a situation where people are overall worse off than they would be under some other arrangement. If I love squash but hate cabbage and you love cabbage but cannot stand squash, would not our overall satisfaction be greater if I got the squash and you got the cabbage? The intuition that needs and preferences are relevant in the calculation of fair distribution suggests the welfare principle.

Simply put, the welfare principle says that goods should be distributed in such a way as to maximize overall well-being. The meat from a hunter's kill is to be divided up among the hunter's family consisting of her elderly mother, a baby, a grossly obese teenager, and her brother, a famous idler. Strictly equal distribution in this situation, as in the example of the organic box scheme above, would likely lead to more dissatisfaction and waste than if distribution were graded according to dietary need. However, the obese teenager and the indolent brother raise two distinct problems for the welfare principle. On account of his corpulence, the obese teenager needs more meat than, say, the hunter does in order to satisfy his hunger. But how legitimate is this need? Overall well-being might be best served by giving the teenager less meat (assuming losing weight is in his and possibly the group's best long-term interest) even though this allocation would be inconsistent with his preferences, decrease his short-term satisfaction, and, in so doing, possibly fail to achieve the greatest overall short-term well-being. The difficulty of prioritizing and predicting these two incompatible forms of well-being is another instance of the index problem. The hunter was the one who killed the animal. Surely, on these grounds, if she wants more of it, then she has a legitimate claim to a larger share of it than her lazy brother does despite their equal dietary needs. Neither the welfare principle nor the principle of equality can account for the intuition that dessert can also be a factor in problems of distributive justice.

In one sense, the "principle of dessert" is infelicitous as a term to refer to the idea that people have a claim to economic goods in some proportion to their role in producing them. After all, the very problem of distributive justice is that of ensuring that people get what they justly deserve. Be that as it may, the primary category in dessert-based appeals to depart from the principles of equality and welfare is contribution: the productivity, skill, talent, or knowledge that an individual brings to the production of economic output. Other categories are effort expended in work activity and compensation for costs and risks incurred in work. Appeals to dessert-based distributive principles are a staple of justifications of the wide income disparities characteristic of capitalist economies. Short order cooks make less money than miners do because mining is more physically demanding (effort) and risky (compensation) than working in a restaurant. A CEO makes far more money than his secretary does because his work is that much more decisive to the success or failure of the company (contribution). It is worth noting that, unlike the principles of equality and the welfare principle, the principle of dessert is "incomplete" as an overarching principle of resource allocation. That is, it applies only to productive adults, necessarily transferring the work of justifying resource allocation to nonproductive members of society—the elderly, children, the sick and infirm, the unemployed, and so on—to other principles.

The elaboration and defense of competing theories of distributive justice is a central preoccupation of contemporary political philosophy. A theory of distributive justice advances a proposal for how to achieve distributive justice in society by articulating and prioritizing basic principles of distributive justice in light of salient empirical and economic facts and in consideration of the demands of individual rights. The most important theory of distributive justice in recent decades is John Rawls's theory of justice (1971). The centerpiece of his theory is the "difference principle," which states that social inequalities are acceptable insofar as they benefit society's least-advantaged members. In moral psychology, William Damon's (1975) theory of the development of "positive justice reasoning" traces a series of stages that reflect children's growing conceptions of distributive justice. It features the principles of equality, welfare, and dessert, and at the highest stages children are able to coordinate such principles with an appreciation of context and the purpose of social arrangements.

*Further Reading:* Damon, W. (1975). Early conceptions of positive justice as related to the development of logical operations. *Child Development, 46*(2), 301–12. Kymlicka, W. (2001). *Contemporary political philosophy* (2nd ed.). Oxford: Oxford University Press. Lamont, J. (1994). The concept of desert in distributive justice. *Philosophical Quarterly, 44,* 45–64. Rawls, J. (1971). *A theory of justice.* Cambridge: Harvard University Press.

*Bruce Maxwell*

## Domain Theory

Domain theory holds that children construct social concepts within discrete developmental frameworks, or domains, that are generated out of qualitatively differing aspects of their social interactions. Three basic conceptual frameworks of social knowledge are posited by domain theory: morality, societal convention, and personal issues. Concepts of morality address the nonarbitrary and therefore universal aspects of social relations pertaining to issues of human welfare, rights, and fairness (Turiel, 2002). Children as young as three years of age have been found to treat moral transgressions such as the unprovoked hitting and hurting of another child as wrong even in the absence of a governing rule, because of the intrinsic effects (pain and injury) that the act of hitting has upon the victim (Turiel, 2002). Children's moral development entails progressive transformations in their conceptions of justice and human welfare (Turiel, 2002).

Morality can be distinguished from concepts of social conventions, which are the consensually determined standards of conduct particular to a given social group. Conventions established by social systems such as norms or standards of dress, how people should address one another, table manners, and so forth derive their status as correct forms of conduct from their embeddedness within a particular shared system of meaning and social interaction. The particular acts in and of themselves have no prescriptive force in that different or even opposite norms (e.g., dresses for men, pants for women) could be established to achieve the same symbolic or regulatory function (e.g., distinguishing men from women). Thus, children and adults view the wrongness of violations of conventions, such as addressing teachers by their first names, as contingent upon the presence of a rule or norm governing the action (Turiel, 2002). The importance of conventions lies in the function they serve to coordinate social interaction and discourse within social systems. Concepts of social convention have been found to be structured by underlying conceptions of social organization (Turiel, 2002).

While morality and convention deal with aspects of interpersonal regulation, concepts of personal issues refer to actions that comprise the private aspects of one's life, such as the contents of a diary, and issues that are matters of preference and choice (e.g., friends, music, hairstyle) rather than right or wrong. The establishment of control over the personal domain emerges from the need to establish boundaries between the self and others, and is critical to the establishment of personal autonomy and individual identity (Nucci, 2001).

The distinctions drawn among moral, conventional, and personal concepts have been sustained by findings from more than 70 studies published over the past 30 years. This work includes observations of naturally occurring peer and adult-child interactions, developmental interviews of children and adults, and cross-cultural studies conducted in a number of countries.

These domains correspond to what Jean Piaget referred to as partial systems with respect to the mind as a totality. Each partial system forms an internally equilibrated structure that may operate on its own as in the case of moral judgments about unprovoked harm, or may interact with other systems requiring interdomain coordination as in the case of judgments regarding the right or wrong of social conventions privileging men over women within traditional societies (Turiel, 2002).

Applications of domain theory to moral education, like the approaches based on Piaget and Lawrence Kohlberg, assume that children's moral growth and social growth result from the student's efforts to make sense of the social world rather than from the direct acquisition of rules and standards set by adults. Unlike the approaches based on Piaget and Kohlberg, however, domain theory based moral education does not assume that morality of young children is dominated by convention, or heteronomous obedience to authority. Instead, this approach to moral education views morality and convention as forming different conceptual systems from early childhood, which may be stimulated by domain consistent educational practices (Nucci, 2001). Moral development is fostered by classroom interactions involving justice and fairness, and stimulated by moral discourse focusing on what is the fairest or most caring resolution to social conflicts or moral situations. Education for development in the area of social convention involves social experiences and classroom discourse around the purposes of such norms for social order. Finally, rather than subordinate complex issues to moral concerns for rights, or the cultural conventions of a particular era, domain analysis affords the teacher a basis from which to engage students in reflection on both conventional and moral aspects of issues, and relating these different values dimensions to one another.

*Further Reading:* Nucci, L. (2001). *Education in the moral domain*. Cambridge, UK: Cambridge University Press. Smetana, J.G. (2002). Culture, autonomy, and personal jurisdiction in adolescent-parent relationships. In H.W. Reese & R. Kail (Eds.), *Advances in child development and behavior* (Vol. 29, pp. 51–87). New York: Academic Press. Turiel, E. (2002). *The culture of morality: Social development, context, and conflict*. Cambridge, UK: Cambridge University Press.

*Larry Nucci*

## Domain Theory, Social Convention

Social convention refers to social rules or norms that are established within a particular social group or social system. Examples of social conventions are norms for greeting people, titles or forms of address to use when speaking to someone, norms defining what clothes to wear to a social gathering, and so forth. Schools have many social conventions particular to educational institutions. Illustrative examples of school conventions are norms about raising your hand in order to speak in class, lining up before entering a classroom, and wearing a school uniform. Social conventions are arbitrary in the sense that there is nothing prescriptive about the actions that they regulate. Western dress conventions, for example, could just as easily have established that dresses are for men and pants for women as a way to differentiate between the sexes.

Although conventions are arbitrary, they serve an important social function. John Searle (1969) describes social conventions as constituent elements of social systems. Conventions provide the shared norms that allow members of a social system to interact with one another in predictable ways. For example, conventions about how to run a meeting define the time at which people gather, the procedures for establishing an agenda and arriving at decisions, the process by which members participate, and the manner in which the meeting is terminated. Without social conventions, a meeting could not take place. Each social system and culture relies upon conventions to define shared everyday ways of acting. It is in this sense that Searle describes conventions as constituent of social systems.

Children learn the content of their society's conventions beginning at very young ages. However, the arbitrary nature of conventions makes it difficult for children to grasp their larger function. It is not until middle adolescence that a majority of Western children achieve an understanding of social convention in terms of social systems. The process of development of concepts of social convention follows an oscillating pattern between periods affirming the importance of convention and phases negating it. This oscillation indicates the difficulty children have in accounting for the function of arbitrary social norms. Seven levels of reasoning about social convention have been defined (Turiel, 1983). Five of these levels correspond to school age. Children ages 6 to 8 years tend to be in a period of affirmation in which conventions are thought to define the social world as it should be. Instances of contradictions to general conventions, such as a neighbor adult who allows children to refer to him by his first name, are viewed as anomalies rather than as evidence that conventions are highly variable and unstable. Slightly older children (ages 8 to 10 years), however, view these same anomalies as evidence that conventions are so variable that conventions do not matter. At roughly ages 10 to 11 years, children in the United States reaffirm conventions on the grounds that they stem from authorities who establish conventions in order to reduce chaos (no running in the hallways). In middle school (ages 12 to 14), however, this basis for affirming convention gets turned on its head, as conventions are now viewed as simply the arbitrary dictates of authority. Finally, in middle adolescence (ages 14 to 16) conventions are viewed as establishing order within a social system. Thus, they are viewed as binding upon members participating within a social system. Evidence for these levels of development has been obtained with children and adolescents within the United States (Nucci & Becker, 2004).

In domain theory, social conventions are distinguished from moral issues of fairness and human welfare (Turiel, 1983). Interactions may occur between convention and morality when conventional norms address behaviors in the service of fairness, or establish forms of social organization that unfairly privilege one group relative to another. An example of the first form of moral-convention interaction would be norms for lining up to buy movie tickets. This is a convention that establishes a procedure (first come, first served) for fairly distributing a limited resource (tickets). An example of the second form of domain interaction would be gender norms that provide males privileges not shared by females (e.g., inheritance conventions that give all of the property to the eldest son). Reasoning about such multifaceted issues, according to domain theory would draw from the person's level of understanding about convention as well as their concepts about morality (Turiel, 2002).

**Further Reading:** Nucci, L., & Becker, K. (2004, October). *Toward a computer based assessment of adolescent concepts of convention.* Paper presented at the annual meeting of the Association for Moral Education, Dana Point, CA. Searle, J. R. (1969). *Speech acts.* London: Cambridge University Press. Turiel, E. (1983). *The development of social knowledge: Morality and convention.* Cambridge, UK: Cambridge University Press. Turiel, E. (2002). *The culture of morality: Social development, context, and conflict.* Cambridge, UK: Cambridge University Press.

*Larry Nucci*

## Durkheim, Emile

Emile Durkheim (1858–1917) is one of the founders of sociology. Born in Epinal, France, he began teaching philosophy in 1882 in Bordeaux. In 1913, he became a professor of the Science of Education and Sociology at the Sorbonne. His major works include *The Division of Labor in Society* (1893); *The Rules of Sociological Method* (1895); *Suicide: A Study in Sociology* (1897); and *The Elementary Forms of the Religious Life* (1912). He also lectured on moral education at the Sorbonne (1902–1903). After his death, these lectures were collected into the book, *Moral Education: A Study in the Theory and Application of the Sociology of Education* (1925).

Durkheim began writing about society around the time of the industrial revolution. The increasing urbanization, rapid social change, and social pluralism brought about by industrialization prompted Durkheim's concern for how societies would maintain social order and achieve social solidarity. In simple homogeneous societies, religion was the common force for maintaining order. In complex heterogeneous societies, religion's hold was weakening. For Durkheim, society, embodied in the nation state was a compelling substitute for the transcendent in maintaining social order. Schools, he offered, could develop moral capacities in children. Durkheim (1925/1961) elaborates his theory in a series of lectures on moral education, positing three "elements" of morality: the spirit of discipline, attachment to the group, and autonomy.

The spirit of discipline includes rules, regularity, and authority. Rules are customary or regular; they are the same regardless of the day or time. Following a rule is a matter of obligation, regardless of personal taste or inclination. Within the rules themselves resides a notion of authority, an "influence which imposes upon us all the moral power that we acknowledge as superior to us" (Durkheim, p. 29). Rules are like commandments; they have moral force. Discipline then consists of regularity and authority. The "spirit" of discipline is the "fundamental element of morality" (Durkheim, p. 31). For Durkheim, discipline is not a means to an end, but an end in itself. For him it is natural that humans have a sense of discipline, that they possess a degree of self-mastery, that they know their limits, and that they constrain themselves. Discipline serves a social good because it helps keep society organized. Just as a biological organism follows rules, so also do humans, for the safe conduct of social life. To do otherwise is to court catastrophe: "all living organization presupposes determinate rules, and to neglect them is to invite disaster" (Durkheim, p. 37).

The second element of morality is attachment to social groups, based in the natural order of things: humans seek harmony in their physical world as well as in their social world. Furthermore, people need society to be moral. Humans follow rules not for personal ends but for impersonal ends, namely, the good of society: "to act morally is to act in terms of the collective interest" (Durkheim, p. 59). For Durkheim, society anchors human beings, gives them meaning, brings them out of their own self-absorption, and nourishes personality. Though he admits to some antagonism between self and society, Durkheim feels strongly that humans prefer society to being by themselves. Society has different spheres, from the personal ties of family to the remote ties to one's country. Durkheim believed that schools were the suitable agencies to help children attach to the state: "the school is the only moral agent through which the child is able systematically to learn to know and love his country" (Durkheim, p. 79).

The third element of morality is autonomy. Durkheim's notion of autonomy hinges on the dual nature of morality. On the one hand, one obeys out of duty; on the other hand, one obeys out of desire. Both of these aspects are embodied in society, which resides in the mind as well as in reality. Society both constrains and compels humans, yet to be moral, an act must be autonomous. For Durkheim, true autonomy entails being aware of the order of things and understanding the reasons for that order. One obeys a law not just out of fear of sanctions but because one understands its reason and utility and deems it good or without better alternatives. In Durkheim's rational morality the liberating force of understanding is science: "Science is the wellspring of our autonomy" (p. 116). Given morality's dependence on understanding, Durkheim advises, "to teach morality is neither to preach nor to indoctrinate; it is to explain" (p. 120).

Durkheim's moral education did not seek to teach one virtue after another, but rather to develop capacities prerequisite to conducting oneself morally: "to develop and even to constitute completely...those general dispositions that, once created, adapt themselves readily to the particular circumstances of human life" (p. 21). Teachers were to function as the "priests of society" by using the processes of the classroom group as a means of moral and civic education. Durkheim rejected the idea that moral education could be confined to discrete lessons. Because morality pervades the collective, moral education should permeate the entire school day. For Durkheim, the classroom should be a cherished group to which children feel obliged and attached, paralleling the sentiments they should have for society in general. Durkheim warned against teachers dominating students and advises that they gain student support for the rules. Though he overlooks the democratic process, he believes rules are based on the authority of the group as a whole and not the teacher's will. His theory addresses shared responsibility among students and the meaning of punishment and rewards. Though largely overlooked, his theory has much to offer contemporary moral and character education.

*Further Reading:* Boote, D.N. (2002). Durkheim's naturalistic moral education: Pluralism, social change, and autonomy. *Philosophy of Education Yearbook,* 319–27. Durkheim, E. (1925/1961). *Moral education: A study in the theory and application of the sociology of education.* New York: Free Press. Piaget, J. (1965). *The moral judgment of the child.* New York: Free Press. (Original work published 1932.) Power, F.C., Higgins, A., & Kohlberg, L. (1989). *Lawrence Kohlberg's approach to moral education.* New York: Columbia University Press.

*Ann Marie R. Power*

# E

## Early Childhood Education

The starting point for work with children's morality is often found in everyday conflicts. These situations are important for children's moral discoveries (Johansson, 2007). Conflicts of rights as well as acts that threaten one's own and others' well-being hold potential for children's moral learning.

The instructional strategies of teachers are influenced by their ideas about how children learn morality, by their own understanding of moral questions, and by what constitutes the moral child. A common idea is that children's understanding of others' emotions should be the basis for the development of morality. From a cognitive perspective, children are presumed to have few possibilities to understand moral problems because their ability to think and express themselves verbally is limited. Often teachers emphasize children's inability to be moral, and the necessity to change the child. Punishment and rewards are the essential tools to effect change, at least from a behavioristic perspective.

According to these views, morality is a property of the child, and rarely is the context, or the role of the adult, deemed important considerations. Another approach, however, emphasizes the importance of clarifying children's perspectives about moral conflict. These perspectives can vary within the situation, among the children involved, and by how the teachers are interpreting the situation.

The moral values important to children often seem to be overlooked by teachers despite the fact that teachers try to help children express their own feelings and to understand the perspective of others. Oftentimes adults substitute their own judgment about fairness and consideration as a point of departure. They use encouragement and praise, but also sanctions and blame, to support the moral values esteemed by adults.

However, the notion that children can develop their own moral values, or that children are important to each other in their learning of morality, seems less common (Corsaro, 2003). Indeed, even young toddlers can experience and express moral values and the experience of concrete relationships in preschool is one context where moral values are learned:

> Björn, almost two years old, is sitting on the floor of a large bright playroom. Björn is examining a garage, looking at it and putting his fingers in the elevator. Malin, a little over two

years old, sits down beside Björn and starts to play with the garage. Now Björn stops his playing. He looks first at Malin and then straight ahead. Quiet. After a while Malin takes Björn's hand and pulls, while at the same time getting up. Björn, however, does not rise but leans ahead and bites Malin's hand. Standing beside Björn, she looks down at her hand and she screams. Then she becomes quiet, holds up her arm and looks round the room. Björn looks at her but soon goes back to playing with the garage. A teacher comes over to the children. "What's wrong Malin?" Did he wipe his nose on you?" says the teacher, drying Malin's hand with a paper towel. "He didn't bite you did he?" "Yes," Malin says emphatically. The teacher turns to Björn who's humming and playing with the garage. "Björn," she says in a clearing questioning tone. "Böön!" answers Björn in the same tone. "You aren't allowed to bite!" says the adult. "There," he says in a matter-of-fact voice, pointing at Malin's arm. "Bad, bad, you mustn't do that," says the adult.

The values involved in this situation concern rights and others' well-being. The children, however, seem to have different interpretations of the values of importance. Conflicts like this can be used and structured to help children's moral discoveries by encouraging responsiveness. This means to be sensitive to the other person's situation and to be willing to act in order to support the other. A child can learn about morality under certain important conditions; these include the other's reactions, what the implications and consequences of the acts might be, personal closeness to the other, and whether or not the child is the recipient or "victim" of the acts. Unfortunately, many teachers use this information to deal with prevention and to solve conflicts, not to utilize these situations in order to give children opportunities to discover values. The suggested strategy is a matter of encouraging communication and exchanging perspectives between children rather than working through sanctions and blaming.

Consequently, when interpreting children's actions, it is important to take the wholeness of the bodily child into account, to consider the entire situation, where other children, as well as the teachers, are parts, and to be open to the complexity of the life-world of preschool. It is essential for teachers to be reflective about the way their educational strategies influence children's moral discovery. Effective early childhood moral education actively involves children in the care of others in the context of everyday life and respects children's ways of understanding and experiencing moral values (Johansson, 2002).

***Further Reading:*** Corsaro, W. (2003). *We are friends right? Inside kid's culture.* Washington, D.C.: Joseph Henry Press. Johansson, E. (2002). Morality in preschool interaction: Teachers' strategies for working with children's morality. *Early Child Development and Care, 172,* 203–21. Johansson, E. (2005). Children's integrity—A marginalised right? *International Journal of Early Childhood, 37*(3), 109–24. Johansson, E. (2006). Children's morality—Perspectives and research. In B. Spodek & O.N. Saracho (Eds.), *Handbook of research on the education of young children* (pp. 55–83). Mahwah, NJ, London: Lawrence Erlbaum Associates. Johansson, E. (2007). *Etiska överenskommelser i förskolebarns världar* [*Moral contracts in preschool children's worlds*]. Göteborg: Acta Universitatis Gothoburgensis. Johansson, E. (in press). Morality and gender—Preschool children's moral contracts. In O. Saracho & B. Spodek (Eds.), *Contemporary perspectives on research in socialization and social development in early childhood education.* Charlotte, NC: Information Age Publishing. Killen, M., & Smetana, J.S. (Eds.) (2006). *Handbook of moral development.* Mahwah, NJ, London: Lawrence Erlbaum Associates.

*Eva Johansson*

## Eisenberg, Nancy

Nancy Eisenberg is a prominent developmental psychologist who has made significant contributions to the study of positive social development (Eisenberg, 1992). Her theories and research have highlighted the critical role of moral thinking, moral emotions, temperament, and parenting in prosocial behaviors (i.e., actions that benefit others). She is a prolific writer and her research has innovated the methods used to understand those processes. Furthermore, as editor of several major research journals and through various other services to the profession, Eisenberg has impacted the broader discipline of developmental and social psychology.

Eisenberg's contributions to the field of developmental psychology began during her graduate training at the University of California–Berkeley (Ph.D., 1976) where she studied under Paul Mussen, a pioneer researcher on early childhood socioemotional and personality development. It was during her graduate training that her interests in the origins and development of other-oriented cognitions, emotions, and behaviors began.

In her master's and doctoral dissertations, she explored the development of prosocial reasoning among children. Prosocial reasoning is the thinking process in situations when one's own needs are in conflict with those of another's. Through a series of studies, Eisenberg developed her theory of prosocial moral reasoning. One of her significant early contributions is her ongoing longitudinal study of prosocial moral reasoning and behaviors, which is now over 25 years old (Eisenberg, Guthrie, Cumberland, Murphy, Shepard, Zhou, & Carlo, 2002). This was the first study devoted to understanding prosocial behaviors in children, adolescents, and young adults.

Eisenberg extended the predominant theory of morality developed by Lawrence Kohlberg (Eisenberg & Fabes, 1998). Eisenberg proposed that Kohlberg's stages of moral reasoning were too narrowly focused on issues of harm and punishment rather than issues of care and compassion. She also noted that Kohlberg's theory ignored the emotional component of moral behaviors and the importance of social and cultural contexts. Like Kohlberg, Eisenberg suggested that people become more sophisticated in their reasoning about dilemmas. Unlike Kohlberg, however, she noted that moral reasoning is only one component of moral functioning. Moreover, while a person might be capable of and predominantly use a particular type of prosocial reasoning, that person might sometimes use a less sophisticated type of prosocial reasoning under certain circumstances.

Following the development of her theory on prosocial reasoning, Eisenberg expanded her research to examine the role of emotions in moral behaviors (Eisenberg, 2005). This work made significant contributions in three ways. First, this research provided strong evidence for the role of emotions in people's decisions to help others at a cost to themselves. Second, the role of different kinds of empathic-related emotions were explored—for instance, differentiating the impact of distress toward oneself versus distress for others. In carefully controlled laboratory studies, Eisenberg showed that when individuals experienced pity or sympathy (sorrow or concern for others), they were more likely to help than when they felt distress for themselves (Eisenberg, Fabes, Miller, Fultz, Shell, Mathy, & Reno, 1989). And third, Eisenberg and her colleagues conducted a series of studies that tested the reliability and validity of psychophysiological and behavioral measures of emotions. These measures included observing facial expressions, measuring changes in heart rate, and measuring galvanic skin responses (i.e., measuring sweat).

Eisenberg followed this creative and significant line of work by exploring the role of parents and socialization in the development of empathic responding (Eisenberg, Fabes,

Schaller, Carlo, & Miller, 1991). Through a series of studies that included interviews, parent reports, and laboratory observations, her work showed that children's emotional responsiveness often matched that of their parents. For instance, children who displayed empathy to others in distress also had parents who displayed empathy to the same situations, while parents who displayed personal distress had children who displayed the same emotions. Moreover, she showed that parenting practices had a significant impact on children's empathy, particularly in the ways that parents reacted to the emotional expressions of their children.

Eisenberg's innumerable contributions to the study of children's social development have been acknowledged in many ways. She has earned a number of honors and distinctions for her work. For example, she was awarded a Regents Professorship distinction from Arizona State University. Eisenberg is also a Fellow of the American Psychological Association, and she has been awarded numerous Career Development Awards from the National Institutes of Health. Furthermore, in 1995, she was among five social scientists invited to a personal dialogue with the Dalai Lama (the religious leader of Tibetan Buddhism) on the topics of prosocial behaviors, compassion, and everyday morality (Eisenberg, 2002).

In recent years, Eisenberg has extended her work to examine the role of temperament on empathic responding and its implications for prosocial behaviors, and she continues to teach courses and train students in research.

*Further Reading:* Eisenberg, N. (1992). *The caring child*. Cambridge, MA: Harvard University Press. Eisenberg, N. (2002). Empathy-related emotional responses, altruism, and their socialization. In R.J. Davidson & A. Harrington (Eds.), *Visions of compassion: Western scientists and Tibetan Buddhists examine human nature* (pp. 131–64). New York: Oxford University Press. Eisenberg, N. (2005). The development of empathy-related responding. In G. Carlo & C. Pope-Edwards (Eds.), *Moral motivation through the life span* (pp. 73–117). Lincoln, NE: University of Nebraska Press. Eisenberg, N., & Fabes, R.A. (1998). Prosocial development. In W. Damon & N. Eisenberg (Eds.), *Handbook of child psychology, 5th ed.: Vol 3. Social, emotional, and personality development* (pp. 701–78). Hoboken, NJ: John Wiley & Sons. Eisenberg, N., Fabes, R.A., Miller, P.A., Fultz, J., Shell, R., Mathy, R.M., & Reno, R.R. (1989). Relation of sympathy and personal distress to prosocial behavior: A multimethod study. *Journal of Personality and Social Psychology, 57,* 55–66. Eisenberg, N., Fabes, R.A., Schaller, M., Carlo, G., & Miller, P.A. (1991). The relations of parental characteristics and practices to children's vicarious emotional responding. *Child Development, 62,* 1393–1408. Eisenberg, N., Guthrie, I.K., Cumberland, A., Murphy, B.C., Shepard, S.A., Zhou, Q., & Carlo, G. (2002). Prosocial development in early adulthood: A longitudinal study. *Journal of Personality and Social Psychology, 82,* 993–1006. Merrens, M.R., & Brannigan, G.G. (1996). *In search of the good heart: Nancy Eisenberg*. New York: McGraw-Hill.

*Gustavo Carlo and Maria Rosario T. de Guzman*


## Eleven Principles of Character Education

The Character Education Partnership (CEP) has eleven principles (Lickona, Schaps, & Lewis, 2002; 2003) of effective character education. These principles were written by national experts in the field and represent a framework that schools can use for developing and/or sustaining comprehensive character education initiatives. The principles of effective character education are as follows.

1. *Promotes core ethical values as the basis of good character.*

Character education holds that widely shared, pivotally important, core ethical values (such as honesty, fairness, caring, and respect for self and others) form the basis of good character, as well as supportive performance values (such as diligence, a strong work ethic, and perseverance). A school committed to character development stands for these values (sometimes referred to as "virtues" or "character traits"), defines them in terms of behaviors that can be observed in the life of the school, models these values, studies and discusses them, uses them as the basis of human relations in the school, celebrates their manifestations in the school and community, and holds all school members accountable to standards of conduct consistent with the core values.

In a school committed to developing character, these core values are treated as a matter of obligation, as having a claim on the conscience of the individual and community. Character education asserts that the validity of these values, and our responsibility to uphold them, derive from the fact that such values affirm our human dignity, promote the development and welfare of the individual person, serve the common good, meet the classical tests of reversibility (that is, Would you want to be treated this way?) and universality (that is, Would you want all persons to act this way in a similar situation?), and inform our rights and responsibilities in a democratic society. The school makes clear that these basic human values transcend religious and cultural differences, and express our common humanity.

2. *Defines "character" comprehensively to include thinking, feeling, and behavior.*

Good character involves understanding, caring about, and acting upon core ethical values. A holistic approach to character development therefore seeks to develop the cognitive, emotional, and behavioral aspects of moral life. Students grow to understand core values by studying and discussing them, observing behavioral models, and resolving problems involving the values. Students learn to care about core values by developing empathy skills, forming caring relationships, helping to create community, hearing illustrative and inspirational stories, and reflecting on life experiences. And they learn to act upon core values by developing prosocial behaviors (for example, communicating feelings, active listening, and helping skills) and by repeatedly practicing these behaviors, especially in the context of relationships (for example, through cross-age tutoring, mediating conflicts, community service). As children grow in character, they develop an increasingly refined understanding of the core values, a deeper commitment to living according to those values, and a stronger capacity and tendency to behave in accordance with them.

3. *Uses a comprehensive, intentional, proactive, and effective approach to character development.*

Schools committed to character development look at themselves through a moral lens to assess how virtually everything that goes on in school affects the character of students. A comprehensive approach uses all aspects of schooling as opportunities for character development. This includes what is sometimes called the hidden curriculum (for example, school ceremonies and procedures; the teachers' example; students' relationships with teachers, other school staff, and each other; the instructional process; how student diversity is addressed; the assessment of learning; the management of the school environment; the discipline policy); the academic curriculum (that is, core subjects, including the health curriculum); and extracurricular programs (that is, sports teams, clubs, service projects, after-school care). "Stand alone" character education programs can be useful first steps or helpful elements of an ongoing effort but are not an adequate substitute for a holistic approach that integrates character development into every aspect of school life. Finally, rather than simply waiting for opportunities to arise, with an intentional and proactive approach, the school staff takes deliberate steps for developing character, drawing wherever possible on practices shown by research to be effective.

### 4. *Creates a caring school community.*

A school committed to character strives to become a microcosm of a civil, caring, and just society. It does this by creating a community that helps all its members form caring attachments to one another. This involves developing caring relationships among students (within and across grade levels), among staff, between students and staff, and between staff and families. These caring relationships foster both the desire to learn and the desire to be a good person. All children and adolescents have needs for safety, belonging, and the experience of contributing, and they are more likely to internalize the values and expectations of groups that meet these needs. Likewise, if staff members and parents experience mutual respect, fairness, and cooperation in their relationships with each other, they are more likely to develop the capacity to promote those values in students. In a caring school community, the daily life of classrooms and all other parts of the school environment (e.g., the hallways, cafeteria, playground, school bus, front office, and teachers' lounge) is imbued with a climate of concern and respect for others.

### 5. *Provides students with opportunities for moral action.*

In the ethical as in the intellectual domain, students are constructive learners; they learn best by doing. To develop good character, they need many and varied opportunities to apply values such as compassion, responsibility, and fairness in everyday interactions and discussions as well as through community service. By grappling with real-life challenges (for example, how to divide the labor in a cooperative learning group, how to reach consensus in a class meeting, how to reduce fights on the playground, how to carry out a service learning project) and reflecting on these experiences, students develop practical understanding of the requirements of cooperating with others and giving of oneself. Through repeated moral experiences, students develop and practice the skills and behavioral habits that make up the action side of character.

### 6. *Includes a meaningful and challenging academic curriculum that respects all learners, develops their character, and helps them to succeed.*

When students succeed at the work in school and feel a sense of competence and autonomy, they are more likely to feel valued and cared about as persons. Because students come to school with diverse skills, interests, and needs, an academic program that helps all students succeed is one in which the content and pedagogy are sophisticated enough to engage all learners. This means providing a curriculum that is inherently interesting and meaningful to students. A meaningful curriculum includes active teaching and learning methods such as cooperative learning, problem-solving approaches, and experience-based projects. These approaches increase student autonomy by appealing to students' interests, providing them with opportunities to think creatively and test their ideas, and fostering a sense of "voice and choice"—having a say in decisions and plans that affect them.

In addition, effective character educators look for the natural intersections between the academic content they wish to teach and the character qualities they wish to develop. These "character connections" can take many forms, such as addressing current ethical issues in science, debating historical practices and decisions, and discussing character traits and ethical dilemmas in literature. When teachers bring to the fore the character dimension of the curriculum, they enhance the relevance of subject matter to students' natural interests and questions, and, in the process, increase student engagement and achievement.

7. *Strives to foster students' self-motivation.*

Character is often defined as "doing the right thing when no one is looking." The best underlying ethical reason for following rules, for example, is respect for the rights and needs of others—not fear of punishment or desire for a reward. Similarly, we want students to be kind to others because of an inner belief that kindness is good, and a desire to be a kind person. Growing in self-motivation is a developmental process that schools of character are careful not to undermine by excessive emphasis on extrinsic incentives. When such schools give appropriate social recognition for students' prosocial actions (for example, "Thank you for holding the door—that was a thoughtful thing to do") or celebrate character through special awards (for example, for outstanding school or community service), they keep the focus on character. Schools of character work with students to develop their understanding of rules, their awareness of how their behavior affects others, and the character strengths—such as self-control, perspective taking, and conflict resolution skills—needed to act responsibly in the future. Rather than settle for mere compliance, these schools seek to help students benefit from their mistakes by providing meaningful opportunities for reflection, problem solving, and restitution.

8. *Engages the school staff as a learning and moral community that shares responsibility for character education and attempts to adhere to the same core values that guide the education of students.*

All school staff—teachers, administrators, counselors, school psychologists, coaches, secretaries, cafeteria workers, playground aides, bus drivers—need to be involved in learning about, discussing, and taking ownership of the character education effort. First and foremost, staff members assume this responsibility by modeling the core values in their own behavior and taking advantage of other opportunities to influence the students with whom they interact.

Second, the same values and norms that govern the life of students serve to govern the collective life of adult members in the school community. Like students, adults grow in character by working collaboratively with each other and participating in decision making that improves classrooms and the school. They also benefit from extended staff development and opportunities to observe colleagues and then apply character development strategies in their own work with students.

Third, a school that devotes time to staff reflection on moral matters helps to ensure that it operates with integrity. Through faculty meetings and smaller support groups, a reflective staff regularly asks questions such as: What character building experiences is the school already providing for its students? What negative moral experiences (for example, peer cruelty, student cheating, adult disrespect of students, littering of the grounds) is the school currently failing to address? And what important moral experiences (for example, cooperative learning, school and community service, opportunities to learn about and interact with people from different racial, ethnic, and socioeconomic backgrounds) is the school now omitting? What school practices are at odds with its professed core values and desire to develop a caring school community? Reflection of this nature is an indispensable condition for developing the moral life of a school.

9. *Fosters shared moral leadership and long-range support of the character education initiative.*

Schools that are engaged in effective character education have leaders (for example, the principal, a lead teacher or counselor, a district administrator, or, preferably, a small group of such individuals) who champion the effort. At least initially, many schools and districts establish a character education committee—often composed of staff, students, parents, and possibly community members—that takes responsibility for planning, implementation, and support. Over time, the regular governing bodies of the school or district may take on the functions of this committee. The leadership also takes steps to provide for the long-range support (for example, adequate staff development, time to plan) of the character education initiative, including, ideally, support at the district and state levels. In addition, within the school students assume developmentally appropriate roles in leading the character education effort through class meetings, student government, peer mediation, cross-age tutoring, service clubs, task forces, and student-led initiatives.

10. *Engages families and community members as partners in the character-building effort.*

Schools that reach out to families and include them in character-building efforts greatly enhance their chances for success with students. They take pains at every stage to communicate with families—via newsletters, emails, family nights, and parent conferences—about goals and activities regarding character education. To build greater trust between home and school, parents are represented on the character education committee. These schools also make a special effort to reach out to subgroups of parents who may not feel part of the school community. Finally, schools and families enhance the effectiveness of their partnership by recruiting the help of the wider community (i.e., businesses, youth organizations, religious institutions, the government, and the media) in promoting character development.

11. *Evaluates the character of the school, the school staff's functioning as character educators, and the extent to which students manifest good character.*

Effective character education must include an effort to assess progress. Three broad kinds of outcomes merit attention:

a. The character of the school: To what extent is the school becoming a more caring community? This can be assessed, for example, with surveys that ask students to indicate the extent to which they agree with statements such as, "Students in this school (classroom) respect and care about each other," and "This school (classroom) is like a family."

b. The school staff's growth as character educators: To what extent have adult staff—teaching faculty, administrators, and support personnel—developed understandings of what they can do to foster character development? Personal commitment to doing so? Skills to carry it out? Consistent habits of acting upon their developing capacities as character educators?

c. Student character: To what extent do students manifest understanding of, commitment to, and action upon the core ethical values? Schools can, for example, gather data on various character-related behaviors: Has student attendance gone up? Fights and suspensions gone down? Vandalism declined? Drug incidents diminished? Schools can also assess the three domains of character (knowing, feeling, and behaving) through anonymous questionnaires that measure student moral judgment (for example, "Is it wrong to cheat on a test?"), moral commitment ("Would you cheat if you were sure you would not get caught?"), and self-reported moral behavior ("How many times have you cheated on a test or major assignment in the past year?"). Such questionnaires can be administered at the beginning of a school's character initiative to get a baseline and again at later points to assess progress (Lickona et al., 2002; 2003).

***Further Reading:*** Lickona, T., Schaps, E., & Lewis, C. (2002). *The eleven principles of effective character education.* Washington, D.C.: Character Education Partnership. Lickona, T., Schaps, E., & Lewis, C. (2003). *The eleven principles of effective character education.* Washington, D.C.: Character Education Partnership. Lickona, T., Schaps, E., & Lewis, C. (2007). *The eleven principles of effective character education.* Washington, D.C.: Character Education Partnership.

*Merle J. Schwartz*

## Elliott, Jane

Jane Elliott is the former schoolteacher from Riceville, Iowa, who conducted the famous "Blue Eyes/Brown Eyes" exercise more than 37 years ago in her third grade class. Today Elliot conducts diversity-training workshops across the country and is a recipient of the National Mental Health Association Award for Excellence in Education. In 1968, just two days after the assassination of Martin Luther King Jr., Elliott devised a classroom activity that she hoped would demonstrate to her third graders the experience of unfair discrimination and prejudice. She asked the students to separate into two groups based on the color of their eyes, blue or brown. Elliott remembered reading that the Nazis had also used eye color as one criterion for separating prisoners in concentration camps. Those with blue eyes were more often spared from being sent to their death in the gas chambers or the ovens because they possessed this physical trait associated with the Aryan race. Elliott wondered if such examples of discrimination still existed in her society.

After asking the students to divide themselves into the blue-eyed and brown-eyed categories, she proceeded to explain to the class why one group was superior to the other, based on supposed "scientific" evidence regarding the levels of melanin in one's body. Elliott suggested that the inferior group (the blue-eyed students) were lazy and incompetent, and could not be trusted. Drawing again from the example set by the Nazis of pinning yellow Stars of David on Jewish citizens, she made students in the blue-eyed group wear arm bands made of green construction paper that identified them as members of this inferior group (Hecker, 1992). The blue-eyed students were also segregated in the cafeteria, standing in lines, and even had designated water fountains from which they were permitted to drink.

At the conclusion of this exercise, she reminded her students what the purpose of the lesson had been, namely, to understand what racism must feel like to the person experiencing discrimination. She asked her students to write an essay about what they had learned from the exercise, and she was amazed by their responses. Elliott shared some of the students' essays with her mother, who passed them on to the editor of this small rural farm town's only newspaper. Some of those students' essays were published with the story titled "How Discrimination Feels." The story was picked up by the Associated Press, and Jane Elliott suddenly found herself in the national spotlight for having conducted a hypothetical thought experiment about discrimination with a class of eight year olds. Johnny Carson invited her as a guest on his nationally televised program, and after her appearance she was bombarded with hate mail and harsh criticisms of her pedagogical tactics. Some of those letters suggested that White children are not used to such mistreatment, and it would cause them lifelong psychological harm (Hecker, 1992).

While her appearance on the Johnny Carson show had catapulted Jane Elliott into the limelight, it had also taken a heavy toll on her family's life in Riceville, Iowa. Her children were bullied, beaten, and harassed because of their mother's small attempt to demonstrate what discrimination feels like. Her husband's business was also negatively impacted by the notoriety that Jane Elliott had brought upon the good people of Riceville. She was ostracized and strongly criticized even by her fellow teachers for conducting this classroom activity, and her family suffered irrevocably at the hands of a few of the citizens in her small hometown. Despite these hardships for the Elliott family, she continued to teach in the Riceville school system for the next 17 years. During those years, she continued to conduct the blue-eyes/brown-eyes exercise with each new group of students who came into her class. Finally, in 1985, she asked for an unpaid leave of absence in order to begin corporate workshops on diversity training, but her request was denied. Elliott eventually moved her family away from Riceville, Iowa, and went on to become an internationally recognized lecturer on racism and a diversity training consultant.

Today, Elliott reports that she is still shocked by the ease with which her third grade students had adapted to and internalized these labels of inferior and superior status, and the blue-eyes/brown-eyes exercise has strengthened her conviction that racism is a learned behavior. She claims that the climate of racial prejudice has not diminished in today's society, as demonstrated by the fact that participants in her diversity training workshops still harbor feelings of prejudice and hatred against racial and ethnic groups different from their own. While she continues to promote appreciation for ethnic and racial diversity, she concedes that the war against prejudice is not over. Elliott is often invited to lecture on college campuses, and conducts diversity-training workshops for corporations internationally. The power of her blue-eyes/brown-eyes thought experiment has been strong enough to warrant coverage by national news media and public broadcasting (PBS). A 30-minute documentary program was produced by ABC news in 1970, and *Frontline* followed with a one-hour documentary that also demonstrated how Elliott's experiment had been used as a diversity training exercise by correctional facility employees (Cose, 1993). She continues to use the exercise as a springboard for discussions about racism and discrimination both in this country and around the world.

**Further Reading:** Cose, E. (1993). *The rage of a privileged class.* New York: Harper Collins. Hecker, A. (1992). *Two nations: Black and White. Separate, hostile, and unequal.* New York: Ballantine. Kane, P.R., & Orsini, A.J. (2003). *The color of excellence.* New York: Teachers College Press. Lincoln, C.E. (1999). *Race, religions and the continuing American dilemma.* New York: Hill & Wang. Williams, J. (1987). *Eyes on the prize.* New York: Viking Press.

*Monalisa M. Mullins*

## Emotional Development

Emotions are organized reactions to events that are relevant to the needs, goals, and interests of the individual and are characterized by physiological, experiential, and overt behavioral change (Garaigordobil, 2004). Relationships with caregivers and peers are necessary for emotional development because they provide differing experiences and serve distinct functions. Caregiver-child relationships provide children with comfort, protection, and security during infancy. Relationships with peers are contexts in which children elaborate on the skills acquired in the caregiver-child relationship, and emotions play a role in whether a child's peer relationships are successful or not (Holodynski, 2004). In essence, the caregiver-child relationship is a training ground for emotional skills, as the skills acquired in it are transferred into peer relationships. Emotional development is therefore linked with advances in social development, because emotions are not only expressed in a social context but also within the caregiving interactions (Sroufe, 1997).

An important part of emotional development is the ability to control one's emotions. In infancy and early childhood, regulation of emotions shifts gradually from external sources (for example, parents) to self-initiated, internal resources. Caregivers soothe young children, manage their emotions by choosing the contexts in which they behave, and provide children with information (for example, facial cues) to help them interpret events. With age and advances in cognitive ability, children are better equipped to manage emotions themselves (Sroufe, 1997). The way children express their emotions is related to the evaluations of their social competence by people in their social world. Thus, in the process of learning to get along with peers the child is constrained toward regulating emotional expressiveness (Dunn & Hughes, 1998). There are individual variations in children's ability to regulate their emotions. Older children and adolescents with developmental problems often have difficulty controlling their emotions (Holodynski, 2004).

Another dimension of emotional development receiving attention is emotional intelligence. Emotional intelligence refers to the ability to monitor one's own and others' feelings, to discriminate among them, and to use this information to guide one's behavior (Garaigordobil, 2004). Emotional intelligence influences emotional regulation.

Emotions take a developmental course across the human life span. Infants' emotional experiences can be determined through their facial expressions. Interest, distress, and disgust are present at birth; a social smile appears at about three weeks to three months; anger, surprise, and sadness emerge at about three to four months; fear is displayed at about five to seven months; shame and shyness emerge at six to eight months; and contempt and guilt appear at two years of age (Sroufe, 1997). Children use crying to communicate with their world. There is a controversy about whether parents should respond to an infant's cries. Developmentalists suggest that parents should soothe a crying infant because soothed infants will develop a sense of trust and secure attachment to their caregiver in the first year of life (Dunn & Hughes, 1998). Smiling is another important mechanism infants use to communicate with their world. Infants' smiling is strongly correlated with attachment to their caregiver. Infants show fear of and wariness toward strangers, referred to as stranger anxiety, usually in the second half of the first year of life (Holodynski, 2004). They show less stranger anxiety when they are in familiar settings and the stranger is friendly.

In early childhood, children begin to experience many emotions. There is an increase in the use of emotion language and in the understanding of emotions (Sroufe, 1997). They become more adept at talking about their own and others emotions. They are learning about the causes and consequences of feelings (Dunn & Hughes, 1998). Preschoolers show an increased ability to reflect on emotions and begin to understand that the same event can elicit different feelings in different people. They also show a growing awareness about controlling and managing emotions to meet social standards (Dunn & Hughes, 1998). The ability for children to appropriately express their emotions is paramount for social interactions (Sroufe, 1997).

During elementary school years, there is an increased ability to understand complex emotions such as pride and shame. There is an increased understanding that more than one emotion can be experienced in a particular situation. Children at this time have the tendency to take into account the events leading to emotional reactions, they have a marked improvement in the ability to suppress or conceal negative emotional reactions and the use of self-initiated strategies for redirecting feelings (Shipman, Zeman, & Stegall, 2001). During early adolescence, there is an increase in the emotional highs and lows. Young adolescents may be on top of the world one moment and down in the dumps the next (Garaigordobil, 2004). This is partly due to the pubertal changes at this time. It is important for adults to recognize that moodiness is a normal aspect of adolescence. There is little research on the developmental changes in emotions during adulthood. Developmentalists agree that knowledge-related and emotion-related goals change across the life span, with emotion-related goals being important when individuals get older. The emotional lives of older adults are more positive than previously envisioned. Older adults selectively spend more time in emotionally rewarding moments with friends and family (Holodynski, 2004).

It is important that individuals understand the emotions of their social partners because it enables them to perceive the communicative function of emotions they or another person is feeling. The understanding of emotions serves a survival function.

**Further Reading:** Dunn, J., & Hughes, C. (1998). Young children's understanding of emotions within close relationships. *Cognition and Emotion, 12*(2), 171–90. Garaigordobil, M. (2004). Effects of a psychological intervention on factors of emotional development during adolescence. *European Journal of Psychological Assessment, 20*(1), 66–80. Holodynski, M. (2004). The miniaturization of expression in the development of emotional self-regulation. *Developmental Psychology, 40* (1), 16–28. Shipman, K.L., Zeman, J.L., & Stegall, S. (2001). Regulating emotionally expressive behavior: Implications of goals and social partner from middle childhood to adolescence. *Child Study Journal, 31*(4), 249–68. Sroufe, A.L. (1997). *Emotional development: The organization of emotional life in the early years*. Cambridge, UK: Cambridge University Press.

*Winnie Mucherah*

## Emotional Intelligence

Emotional Intelligence (EQ) is a psychological construct that describes the capacity to perceive, organize, and manage the variety of emotional responses experienced by an individual and to assess and evaluate the emotional responses in others. The term "emotional intelligence" was popularized by Daniel Goleman in 1995, although other learning theorists and developmental psychologists have also formulated similar concepts to describe the special set of skills required to successfully negotiate social environments and to be self-reflective. For example, what Goleman referred to as emotional intelligence is very similar to Howard Gardner's 1975 articulation of interpersonal and intrapersonal forms of multiple intelligence.

These various explanations of alternative "intelligences" point to the fact that many psychologists believe that traditional measures of intelligence, such as the IQ test, are simply not adequate to give a full account of our cognitive abilities. It is interesting to note that emotional intelligence has proven a better predictor of future success than traditional methods like the grade point average, IQ, and standardized test scores (Bradberry & Greaves, 2005). There has been an increased interest in EQ, particularly regarding the implications of emotional intelligence for academic success. Researchers in cognitive psychology have concluded that people who score high on tests for EQ are more likely to self-report higher levels of personal satisfaction and feelings of happiness (Sitarenios, 2001).

Despite the wide variance in definitions of emotional intelligence, most cognitive psychologists recognize the following five characteristics (Goleman, 1995): (1) Self-awareness, which is defined as knowing your emotions, recognizing feelings as they occur, and being able to discriminate between them; (2) Mood management, defined as the ability to handle feelings relevant to the current situation and to react appropriately; (3) Self-motivation, which is described as the ability to direct yourself toward end goals despite feelings of self-doubt and inertia that may also be present; (4) Empathy, which is the ability to recognize feelings in others and to be sensitive to body language cues; and (5) Managing relationships, which is the ability to handle interpersonal interaction and resolve conflicts.

There is some disagreement among theorists as to whether emotional intelligence is stable or dynamic. Bradberry and Greaves (2005) suggest that EQ can be learned, and therefore capable of being increased over time and accumulation of experience. Mayer (2005) believes that EQ is stable, and therefore not capable of being increased. However, Mayer also distinguishes between emotional intelligence, which remains stable in his view, and emotional knowledge, which he concedes can be increased. Goleman's popularized view of emotional intelligence leaves some room for an individual's cognitive adaptation, but is otherwise closely aligned with Mayer's view that EQ remains stable. Although the definition of emotional intelligence is still debated, many cognitive psychologists now believe that this construct has both dynamic and stable components, based on research in neurophysiology that has identified the part of the brain where emotional responses are processed.

Human emotional responses are processed in a part of the brain called the amygdala, which plays a key role in directing our responses to both fear and pleasure. Most of the responses initiated by the amygdala are automatic, as when the perception of a life-threatening event or critical danger gives rise to the release of adrenalin in the bloodstream. The "fight or flight" response is another example of an automatic reflex triggered by the brain's perception of a critical situation. In such cases, the brain reacts to sensor information automatically, without waiting to be consciously selected through a logical sequence of analysis. These findings support the view that emotional intelligence is largely a stable construct; however, the amygdala is also controlled (in part) by the neocortex, a region of the brain that is capable of exerting some influence over automatic responses elsewhere in the brain. In light of the potential for control by the neocortex, the view that emotional intelligence can be increased is also supported by the research findings in neurophysiology.

***Further Reading:*** Bradberry, T., & Greaves, J. (2005). *The emotional intelligence quick book: How to put your EQ to work.* New York: Simon and Schuster. Eysenck, H. (2000). *Intelligence: A new look.* New York: Transaction. Gardner, H. (1975). *The shattered mind.* New York: Knopf. Goleman, D. (1995). *Emotional intelligence: Why it can matter more than IQ.* New York: Bantam Books. Mayer, J.D. (2005). A tale of two visions: Can a new view of personality help integrate psychology? *American Psychologist, 60*(4), 294–307. Mayer, J., Salovey, P., Caruso, D.R., & Sitarenios,

G. (2001). Emotional intelligence as a standard intelligence. *Emotion, 1,* 232–42. Sitarenios, G. (2001). Emotional intelligence as a standard intelligence. *Emotion, 1*(1), 232–42.

*Monalisa M. Mullins*

## Empathy

The word "empathy," which in ordinary language connotes the experience of being touched by another's suffering, is relatively new to the English language. Its first recorded use is in Edward Titchener's *Elementary Psychology of the Thought Processes,* published in 1912, as a direct translation of the German *Einfühlung.* This latter term, which means literally "feeling in," was coined in the field of aesthetics in the nineteenth century to express the idea that evaluative judgments involve the projection of the viewer's own feelings onto the object of judgment. Titchener derived empathy from the ancient Greek word *empatheia,* meaning simply profoundly emotionally affected. The systematic treatment of empathy has remained largely within contemporary psychology and closely related fields where it has, first, a cognitive sense that contrasts with a second affective sense.

In the cognitive sense, "empathy" is the ability to become aware of others' inner states: their beliefs, desires, intentions, and feelings (e.g., "Judith is delighted about her pregnancy"; "Bob is devastated by the news"). Because of psychoanalysis and counseling psychology's concern with understanding people's private experiences, it is no surprise that these fields embraced the term. Starting in the 1950s, Heinz Kohut and other like-minded psychoanalysts began to argue that empathy was the core competency of the psychoanalyst. Carl Rogers, the founder of client-centered therapy, considered empathy as an integral part of the "growth promoting climate," which, in this conception of therapy, is the main task of the therapist to provide for the client. The experience of being empathized with is inherently therapeutic, in Rogers's view. More recently in social cognition theory, a research area in contemporary psychology, empathy is an umbrella term that refers to all the range of psychological processes, faculties, and competencies involved in forming beliefs about others' inner experiences. In Lawrence Kohlberg's theory of cognitive moral development the ability to understand others' points of view is a cognitive competency basic to the process of "decentration," a key developmental process underlying cognitive moral development. As the child's capacity for moral reasoning matures, the considerations he/she appeals to in justifying moral judgments gradually shift from those that fit only with his/her own perspective, such as the prospect of punishment, to those that recognize that others have needs as well, as in the principle that one good turn deserves another, to the eventual ability to coordinate all relevant perspectives characteristic of the highest stages. In the context of cognitive developmentalism, however, this competency is almost invariably referred to as "perspective-taking," following Robert Selman, or "role-taking," following George Mead.

In its affective sense empathy refers to emotional solidarity between sentient beings: feelings *for* or *with* others in light of their feelings, experiences, or circumstances. Many commentators maintain a technical distinction between "positive" empathy, pleasant feelings at another's well-being (for example, "I am so happy for Milla that she got the job she wanted"), and "negative" empathy, unpleasant feelings for another in serious adversity (for example, "I feel your pain"). All agree, however, that taken in its affective sense empathy typically implies negative empathy.

Negative affective empathy, sometimes referred to as "empathic distress," is in developmental and social psychology associated with the study of prosocial and helping behaviors. Going back at least 30 years, this research agenda has sought to accumulate empirical evidence in support of the common assumption that empathizing amplifies motivation to perform prosocial, helping, and altruistic acts. It also explores related issues of whether empathic responding is innate or learned and the circumstantial factors that strengthen correlations between empathy and helping behaviors. Across the board, empathy has been found to correlate positively to indices of prosocial behavior.

Negative affective empathy poses particular definitional problems because it is not easily distinguishable from empathy in the cognitive sense and other related concepts and psychological phenomena. First, there is some semantic overlap between the cognitive and affective senses of empathy in that emotional solidarity frequently draws on beliefs about another's inner states. However, cognitive empathizing is at most a necessary condition of negative affective empathizing. Emotions like *schadenfreude* (taking pleasure in others' misfortunes) and the military technique of psychological warfare confirm that it is possible to be aware of another's distress yet not find their distress troubling. Psychopaths and cons are reputed to have exceptional cognitive-empathic abilities and to use this insight to harm rather than help others. Second, a feeling of distress in response to another's adversity is not in and of itself negative affective empathy. For example, repulsion at the sight of an injured driver at an accident scene is only empathic where the viewer interprets her feelings as feelings for the driver. Similarly, Hoffman (2000) and others observe a distinction between "empathic distress" and "personal distress." Personal distress occurs when awareness of another's serious distress evokes disturbing thoughts and feelings connected to one's own well-being rather than a victim's. A woman who, while listening to a stalking victim's emotional account of her trauma, dwells on her own security or a disturbing memory of a similar personal experience is said to be experiencing personal distress rather than empathy. Because personal distress often starts out as feelings of empathic distress for a victim before the object of concern shifts toward the observer himself, Hoffman (2000) speaks of "egoistic drift" and considers personal distress a kind of empathic overarousal. The existence of multiple synonyms is a third factor contributing to the difficulty of getting the meaning of "empathy" straight. Cognitive empathy, as indicated above, is referred to as "perspective-taking," "role-taking" in social psychology, but in cognitive theory it sometimes goes under the names of "mental simulation" and "empathic accuracy." For its part, negative affective empathy in ordinary English and in the philosophical literature is arguably indistinguishable from the emotions of "sympathy," "compassion," and possibly "pity."

**Further Reading:** Davis, M.H. (1994). *Empathy: A social psychological approach*. Madison: Brown & Benchmark. Eisenberg, N., Fabes, R.A., & Spinrad, T.L. (2006). Prosocial development. In *Handbook of child psychology. Vol. 3, Social, emotional, and personality development* (pp. 646–718). Hoboken: John Wiley & Sons. Hoffman, M. (2000). *Empathy and moral development: Implications for justice and caring*. Cambridge: Cambridge University Press. Ickes, W. (Ed.). (1997). *Empathic accuracy*. New York: Guilford. Wispé, L. (1987). History of the concept of empathy. In N. Eisenberg & J. Strayer, *Empathy and its development* (pp. 17–37). Cambridge: Cambridge University Press.

*Bruce Maxwell*

## Enright, Robert D.

Robert D. Enright, Ph.D., received his B.A. in Psychology from Westfield State College, Westfield, Massachusetts. He concluded graduate studies in 1976 under the advising of Norman A. Sprinthall, Ph.D., at the University of Minnesota at Minneapolis. Enright was introduced to the area of moral development and education during his graduate program at the University of Minnesota at Minneapolis. The University of Minnesota provided a strong influence, as well as mentors, because it housed the Center for Ethical Studies, a well-regarded research center for moral development in the United States, and Norman Sprinthall was pioneering a movement called Deliberate Psychology Education.

During his Ph.D. program, Enright became a consultant for Minneapolis Public Schools under the Deliberate Psychological Education Program. After receiving his Ph.D., he became a research fellow and research associate for the University of Minnesota and, later, spent a year as a visiting assistant professor at the University of New Orleans. In 1978, Enright established a successful career at the University of Wisconsin at Madison where he has been a full professor of Educational Psychology since 1984. Enright has been a licensed clinical psychologist for the State of Wisconsin since 1990.

Enright initially became well known for his scientific studies on distributive justice in the area of moral development and education. In 1980, Enright authored and published in developmental psychology the first and only available scale of distributive justice for children. During the 1980s, the area of moral development was very focused on justice issues. At that same time, Enright was innovative in the field, with the original theory that is the Moral Development of Forgiveness. Since then, the area of studies on forgiveness has flourished, and Enright has pioneered many accomplishments. In 1994, the *Handbook of Moral Behavior and Development* published Enright's theory on the moral development of forgiveness. Following this, he continued publishing several articles refining his original view of forgiveness, including a multidisciplinary book titled *Exploring Forgiveness,* co-authored with a contemporary British philosopher Joanna North, whose views have influenced Enright's psychology of forgiveness.

Enright defined forgiveness as being distinct from yet related to justice. His definition of interpersonal forgiveness in psychology has become a major reference in the field. Forgiveness occurs when

> people, upon rationally determining that they have been unfairly treated, forgive when they have willfully abandoned resentment and related responses (to which they have a right), and endeavor to respond to the wrongdoer based on the moral principle of beneficence, which may include compassion, unconditional worth, generosity, and moral love (to which the wrongdoer, by nature of the hurtful act, has no right). (Enright & Fitzgibbons, 2000, p. 29)

Enright's theory of forgiveness returns to Jean Piaget's (1932) initial work on justice reasoning. However, Piaget mentioned forgiveness as the end point of the development of justice by retribution, indicating that a person can move beyond justice claims to resolve justice issues. Enright expanded forgiveness, picking up where Piaget left off, and formulated a whole new area of research in what is now established as a field of studies on forgiveness in psychology. Enright developed a social-cognitive developmental model of forgiveness reasoning (or stages of forgiveness), a counseling model for interpersonal forgiveness, and, most important, the first measure of interpersonal forgiveness in psychology—the Enright Forgiveness Inventory (EFI), which is valid and reliable for use in seven cultures. Enright also hosted the first National Conference on Forgiveness held at the University of Wisconsin–Madison in March/April 1995. This was the first conference on the topic of forgiveness to be held on a university campus in the United States. In 1994, encouraging young scholars to study forgiveness, Enright founded the International Forgiveness Institute (IFI), also dedicated to disseminating knowledge on forgiveness. In 1999, Roy Lloyd, member of the International Forgiveness Institute, presented issues of forgiveness at the conference between Jesse Jackson and Slobodan Milošević, then the president of the Federal Republic of Yugoslavia, when three U.S. soldiers were being held hostage. The soldiers were freed in Kosovo after issues of forgiveness presented were accepted by Milošević.

Enright's academic accomplishments include four major books on the topic of forgiveness in psychology and 18 book chapters, 12 of which are about the topic of forgiveness in psychology. In his most recent book publication, Enright remains committed to bringing developmental and counseling psychology into education, particularly as it relates to forgiveness among children and adolescents. Enright's endeavors in this area have gone beyond entire books and book chapters. A new publication applies his theory of forgiveness to a longitudinal educational program on forgiveness in Northern Ireland. The goal of the program is to help children from sixth grade on, thus adolescents, forgo resentment via forgiveness for social harmony.

Enright can count among his work 64 scientific journal articles, published in the most respected journals in psychology and education. In addition, he has authored six monographs, four manuals for education and counseling in the areas of distributive justice and forgiveness, one manual for the Enright Forgiveness Inventory, and 12 minor publications that also are in several important newsletters in the United States and abroad. His record yet includes hundreds of presentations and lectures in several research institutions, schools, and the media by invitation.

Enright has received several honors and awards for his accomplishments on interpersonal forgiveness in psychology, among others: Aaron T. Beck Institute's national award, Assumption College, 1997–1998, for forgiveness research; participant in the documentary film on forgiveness for Today's Life Choices, Golden Dome Media, University of Notre Dame, which won an award at the New York Film Festivals, Fall 2000; and Paul Harris Fellow, Rotary International, for work in the peace movement in 2006. Still, anyone who knows Enright can attest to the recognition that he holds closest to his heart as being his recognition as an outstanding teacher for the thousands of adolescents, young undergraduates, and approximately 140 graduate students from several nations of the world.

*Further Reading:* Enright, R.D., Franklin, C.C., & Manheim, L.A. (1980). Children's distributive justice reasoning: A standardized and objective scale. *Developmental Psychology, 16,* 193–202. Enright, R.D., & North, J. (Eds.). (1998). *Exploring forgiveness.* Madison: University of Wisconsin. Enright, R.D., & Fitzgibbons, R. (2000). *Helping clients forgive: An empirical guide for resolving anger and restoring hope.* Washington, D.C.: APA Books. Enright, R.D. (2001). *Forgiveness is a choice.* Washington, D.C.: APA Books. Enright, R.D. (2004). *Enright Forgiveness Inventory.* Redwood City, CA: Mind Garden. Enright, R.D. (2007). *Rising above the storm clouds.* Washington, D.C.: Magination.

*Júlio Rique*

## Environmental Education

The goal of environmental education can be established most easily from a human-centered moral perspective. We depend on clean air to breath and clean water to drink. Healthy soils nurture plants that in turn nurture us. Toxic wastes cause innumerable diseases and sometimes death. Thus, children need to learn the knowledge and the skills to engage in behavior that sustains the natural world so as to sustain human life.

Yet that goal by itself can be read as a truism. It is like saying "we should seek to end poverty." Most people would say, "sure that is a good idea." But often at stake is how such goals are both achieved and coordinated with competing interests.

In his classic essay on the conservation ethic, Aldo Leopold (1949/1970) writes of his disappointment with traditional environmental education insofar as it fails to help people develop a "love, respect, and admiration for land, and a high regard for its value" (p. 261). "No important change in ethics," Leopold writes, "was ever accomplished without an internal change in our intellectual emphasis, loyalties, affections, and convictions" (p. 246). Thus, many environmental education programs engage children not only intellectually but also experientially, seeking to nurture children's loyalties and affections with the natural world.

To achieve these goals, one need not step far from one's home. Even in the inner cities there is nature at hand and under foot that can be used as the basis for environmental education. For example, a study that investigated the environmental views and values of African American children in Houston, Texas, found that these children were fascinated with the animals and vegetation within their reach: butterflies, ants, trees, worms, spiders, leaves, and flowers. As one parent said:

> My kindergarten daughter, she might see something that looks injured or, um, she saw a worm. She doesn't pick up these black ones or brown ones because they sting. So this one was a yellow one and she said he was hungry. So she picked him up and took him over to a leaf and put him on it. You know, they do those type things. (Kahn, 1999, pp. 223–24)

Other educators go further and argue that a goal of environmental education is to help children recognize not only their interconnection with natural entities and systems, but that nature itself has moral standing independent of human well-being. This orientation is sometimes referred to as biocentric (nature focused) as opposed to anthropocentric (human focused). Psychological evidence suggests that children are able, at times, to articulate two forms of a biocentric orientation. One form focuses on the intrinsic value of nature, for example, that nature has its own telos, or end point, or ideal way of functioning (for example, "without any animals the world is, like, incomplete, it's like a paper that's not finished" [Kahn, 1999, p. 137]). A second form focuses on the rights of nature (for example, "I think that the animals have as much right to live and to have good conditions of life as we do, and the pollution that affects us will affect them also" [Kahn, 1999, p. 177]).

While educating for a biocentric worldview may be desirable, it is clearly contentious. Thus, another framework, which has the potential to garner wide buy-in, builds from E. O. Wilson's evolutionary account of biophilia: what he calls an innate affiliation with life and life-like processes. In this account, the human mind came of age hundreds of thousands of years ago through daily interactions with a vibrant and diverse natural landscape and that still today we depend on such interactions not only for our physical health but also for our psychological well-being. Hundreds of empirical studies have, in turn, supported the biophilia hypothesis, showing that contact with nearby nature leads to increased enjoyment, fewer feelings of isolation, higher satisfaction with one's home and job, lower stress, and better health.

Regardless of one's goals vis-à-vis anthropocentric or biocentric values—or whether an account of biophilia straddles both orientations in a nuanced manner—environmental education depends on engaging children intellectually, experientially, and morally as they gain scientific understandings of how human activity affects larger ecological systems.

*Further Reading:* Kahn, P.H., Jr. (1999). *The human relationship with nature: Development and culture.* Cambridge, MA: MIT Press. Leopold, A. (1970). *A Sand County almanac.* New York: Ballantine Books. (Original work published 1949.) Orr, D.W. (1992). *Ecological literacy: Education and the transition to a postmodern world.* Albany, NY: State University of New York Press. Smith, G.A., & Williams, D.R. (Eds.). (1999). *Ecological education in action: On weaving education, culture, and the environment.* Albany, NY: State University of New York Press. Wilson, E.O. (1984). *Biophilia.* Cambridge, MA: Harvard University Press.

*Peter H. Kahn Jr. and Rachel L. Severson*

## Erikson, Erik

American psychoanalyst Erik Erikson was born near Frankfurt, Germany, in 1902. His parents were both Danish, and they encouraged Erik to study art and languages during his early school years. Although Erikson received no formal university schooling, he trained as a psychoanalyst in Vienna under the tutelage of Anna Freud from 1927 to 1933. Erikson immigrated to the United States in 1933, where he taught at Harvard University from 1933 to 1936 (and again from 1960 to 1970). His major contribution to the psychoanalytic tradition is his theory of eight psychosocial stages of development. First published in 1950, Erikson's *Childhood and Society* has continued to exert far-reaching influence in the field of child psychology.

Erikson's research included a wide variety of studies, such as post-traumatic stress disorder in returning veterans of World War II and child-rearing traditions among the Native American Sioux and Yurok tribes. He was also interested in studying the social behavior patterns of troubled adolescents and disturbed children. Erikson wrote extensively on what he considered to be the impact of rapid social changes in America, for example, the generation gap, juvenile delinquency, and racial and gender divides. As the preeminent psychoanalyst in America, Erikson was in agreement with most of the tenets of Freudian theory. However, there were some important differences between these two strong theorists. Freud believed that human personality is mostly developed in the first five years of life, while Erikson thought that our personality continues to develop throughout our lifetime. According to Erikson, we are influenced by the experiences at each of eight progressive stages of psychosocial development over the course of our life. These stages are Trust vs. Mistrust, Autonomy vs. Shame & Doubt, Initiative vs. Guilt, Industry vs. Inferiority, Identity vs. Role Confusion, Intimacy vs. Isolation, Generativity vs. Stagnation, and Integrity vs. Despair.

The first psychosocial stage of Trust vs. Mistrust occurs during the first year of life. Erikson defined trust as entailing both an essential trustfulness of others and also a sense of one's own trustworthiness. During this first year of life, according to Erikson, an infant will develop trust if his most basic needs for food and comfort are regularly met. He also said that some mistrust is necessary to learn to discriminate between honest and dishonest persons. However, if mistrust is more dominant than trust in this first stage of development, the child will become easily frustrated, suspicious, and withdrawn through later stages of development. The child that does not develop a sense of trust during this first year of life will also lack self-confidence later.

The second stage, Autonomy vs. Shame & Doubt, occurs during the second and third years of life. In this stage of development, Erikson emphasized the importance for parents to create a supportive atmosphere in which the child can experience some sense of self-esteem while also learning some self-control. The child is more likely to experience shame and doubt at this stage if basic trust was insufficiently developed during the first stage. However, autonomy can be gained if the child is given clear sets of rules and expectations that are not too overbearing or controlling on the part of the parents.

The third stage, Initiative vs. Guilt, occurs between the ages of four and five years. This is the stage in which the child must develop a sense of responsibility for his/her own actions. As the child develops an increased sense of responsibility, more initiative for actions is taken during this period. If the child is made to feel irresponsible and is overly anxious to act, then he/she will develop feelings of guilt and will hesitate to act upon future feelings of initiation. Erikson believed that most guilt feeling acquired at this stage could later be compensated for by a sense of accomplishment for some task.

Erikson's fourth stage, Industry vs. Inferiority, occurs between the ages of six years and puberty. During this stage of development, the child wants to become a full participant in what he/she perceives as the real world of work. The greatest single event during this stage is considered to be the child's entry into school. However, school is not the only classroom, and, according to Erikson, the learning process continues during this stage in every environment that the child encounters. Accumulated experiences that the child feels are successful will lead to a sense of industry, which he defines as competence and mastery. Lack of success at this stage leads to feelings of inadequacy and incompetence.

Each of these psychosocial stages serves as a progressive indicator of one's personality. In the fifth stage, Identity vs. Identity Confusion, the impact of the first four stages is brought to bear on our concept of self during the adolescent years. According to Erikson, adolescence is the critical period for identity formation, although later life-changing events may also subsequently alter one's perception of self-identity in significant ways. The sixth stage is Intimacy vs. Isolation, which occurs during young adulthood. At this stage, we are able to form lasting relationships with others (both as friends and as intimate partners) only if the identity formation was achieved during adolescence. According to Erikson, if we are confused about our own concept of self, then our ability to feel genuine intimacy with others will be severely compromised.

In the seventh stage, Generativity vs. Stagnation, young adults should begin to perceive themselves as leading successful lives that will contribute to society. Failure at this stage leads young adults to perceive themselves as slackers who cannot make any significant contribution to society. According to Erikson, when an individual feels that she has nothing of importance to contribute to the next generation, she will experience a sense of stagnation and inertia related to her life goals. One's sense of generativity (or stagnation) will also strongly impact the final stage of personality development.

The final stage, Integrity vs. Despair, occurs late in adulthood. It represents the period of reflection about one's life, and an assessment of the culmination of life experiences. At this last stage, adults will develop a sense of well-being associated with integrity if the previous stages of their psychosocial development have been successfully negotiated. However, feelings of despair can occur during this final stage of development if one's self-concept did not ultimately receive some positive reconciliation in the previous seven stages. After a lifetime devoted to the study of human personality development, Eric Erikson died in 1994.

*Further Reading:* Cole, M., & Cole, S.R. (1989). *The development of children.* New York: W.H. Freeman & Co. Friedman. L.J. (1999). *Identity's architect: A biography of Erik H. Erikson.* New York: Scribner & Sons. Hoare, C.H. (2001). *Erikson on development in adulthood: New insights from the unpublished papers.* New York: Oxford University Press U.S. Homburger, E. (1994). *Identity and the life cycle.* New York: W.W. Norton & Co. Santrock, J. (1996). *Child development.* Dubuque, IA: Brown & Benchmark.

*Monalisa M. Mullins*

## Ethics, Teaching of

"Ethics teaching" brings to mind two distinct but overlapping educational activities. One is instruction in ethical theory (or moral philosophy). This is an area of academic study that is itself divisible into normative ethics, first-order questioning into the reasons why some acts are morally better than others (because they are conducive to more overall good, cohere with fundamental moral principles, or represent virtuous conduct?), and metaethics, the second-order investigation into a clutch of highly abstract questions regarding the fundamental nature of moral experience and moral justification (What is moral goodness? How do we know the difference between right and wrong? Are there objective moral truths? What is the origin of moral value? Why be moral?). The other is instruction in practical (or applied) ethics. Practical ethics pertains to the ground-floor moral questions that are the stock and trade of ethicists and that preoccupy almost everyone from time to time. Among these problems are, of course, the contemporary moral issues widely debated in the mass media—abortion, capital punishment, physician assisted suicide, the treatment of animals, and so on—but practical ethics encompasses professional ethics as well and more personal concerns over such things as the value of friendship, honesty, marital fidelity, political participation, and even that of particular leisure activities.

Until the twentieth century, the study of ethics was the very summit of higher education, an idea that reaches all the way back to Antiquity. Descartes, for instance, described ethics as the fruit borne by the tree of human knowledge and the whole point of Hellenistic philosophy was to answer the question, "what kind of life is the best life for creatures like us to live?" In the nineteenth-century version of this thesis, the study of ethics was seen as indispensable to the aims of a traditional liberal education: the development of capacities of rational reflection, the acquisition of a broad understanding of the world and one's place in it, and the nurturance of democratic and humanistic values. Indeed, in the early American colleges ethics held pride of place as the most important subject. Tellingly, the teaching of the course was normally reserved for the college president himself, and its express purpose was to channel graduates' newly acquired knowledge and skills to the service of a broader social and personal good. For several decades in the early to mid-twentieth century, ethics teaching suffered a period of significant decline in an intellectual climate where, for a combination of philosophical and ideological reasons, ethics was no longer regarded as a serious academic subject. Ethics has resurfaced in the past 30 years but has lost most of its former preeminence. A specialized subject among others, ethics is now taught almost exclusively inside philosophy departments for the sake of propagating and advancing ethics as an academic discipline or as a component in programs of professional formation.

While contemporary moral philosophy aspires to the status of a purely theoretical enterprise and tends to spurn its erstwhile role as a guide to the good life, practical ethics teaching retains a link to the past insofar as many teachers of ethics continue to regard their work as contributing to pragmatic ends. Annis's (1992) summary of the goals of a secular ethics course is representative. Ethics teaching should: (1) introduce the standard theories of normative ethics (that is, duty theory, consequentialism, and virtue theory) and the basic concepts and principles involved in practical reasoning; (2) illustrate how these theories and concepts apply to particular moral problems; (3) promote clear thinking and communication about ethics and ethical problems; (4) encourage students to be self-critical as regards their own moral values and commitments and to become more open-minded, tolerant, and differentiated in their responses to ethical controversies; and (5) stimulate moral sensitivity and moral imagination by engaging students with moral problems in nonintellectual ways. Professional ethics teaching embraces all these goals but should additionally: (6) raise awareness of the profession's established ethical norms (as expressed, for instance, in a code of ethics) and expose the conceptual connections between these norms and the profession's social purpose and the realities and requirements of professional practice and judgment.

Although the methods used to teach ethics tend to be flexible and subject to considerable variation from instructor to instructor, it is nevertheless possible to identify three principal approaches: the academic method, the plug-and-play method, and the casebook method.

The academic method analyzes and critiques moral arguments as they appear in published philosophical essays authored by ethicists. A course's base texts are typically grouped according to themes such as biomedical ethics, environmental ethics, or information technology ethics or they offer a representative sampling of rival perspectives on one specific moral problem (for example, informed consent, pornography, or peer-to-peer file sharing). This approach to teaching ethics is sometimes referred to as "theory-based teaching" because it focuses on moral problems understood in relatively abstract and general terms. The theory-based teaching of the academic method contrasts with so-called "case-based teaching," which focuses instead on cases: more-or-less detailed narrative descriptions of a moral agent faced with a concrete moral problem in a particular set of circumstances. The plug-and-play method and the casebook method are case-based in this sense.

The plug-and-play method studies cases by applying to them the standard theories of normative ethics. So, for instance, in approaching a case where a terminally ill patient requests assisted suicide one would begin by either attempting to identify the applicable higher-order moral principles (in the manner of duty theory), estimating the good and bad consequences for all those affected by the act (as in consequentialism) or questioning which virtues would be instantiated in the adoption of one action alternative or another (virtue theory). The educational value of this approach is that it illustrates the utility of philosophical theories in solving a moral problem, strengthens students' comprehension of the theories themselves, and gives them hands-on practice using them as a justificatory framework. The plug-and-play method is also sometimes recruited to serve theoretical ends because it can be used to draw attention to the practical limitations of the theories of normative ethics (as when their application to a particular case shows they can justify egregiously immoral acts) and to suggest their incommensurability as justificatory procedures (as when the application of two different theories justifies incompatible actions).

The casebook method studies cases by deriving moral principles from one's intuitive responses to the case. Here, one is meant, first, to articulate moral principles that could justify one's belief regarding the correct solution to the moral problem the case presents and, second, to test these moral principles for their adequacy either by attempting to apply them in other situations, verifying their consistency with other more fundamental moral principles or by some other means. The aim of such exercises is for students to achieve "reflective equilibrium" (Rawls, 1971) or a state where commitments to basic moral principles have come to cohere with particular moral judgments through a process of deliberation and reasoned adjustment. This method of teaching ethics is closely akin to the well-known casebook method of teaching law where students learn legal principles by deriving them from judges' rulings in legal cases.

*Further Reading:* Annis, D.B. (1992). Teaching ethics in higher education: Goals and the implications of the empirical research on moral development. *Metaphilosophy, 23*(1 & 2), 187–202. Bowie, N.E. (2003). The role of ethics in professional education. In R. Curren (Ed.), *Companion to the philosophy of education* (pp. 617–26). Oxford: Blackwell. Callahan, D., & Bok, S. (Eds.). (1980). *Ethics teaching in higher education.* New York: Plenum Press. Rawls, J. (1971). *A theory of justice.* Cambridge: Harvard University Press. Scholz, S., & Groarke, L. (1996). Seven principles for better practical ethics. *Teaching Philosophy, 19*(4), 337–55.

*Bruce Maxwell*

## Existentialism

Existentialism is a philosophy of human existence grounded in specific themes such as meaning, isolation, freedom, and death. Human beings are believed to be understood from their own subjective frame of reference and not from scientific theories of human nature and development. Also, any meaning derived from one's existence is self-generated without influence by God or the natural order of life. The world itself is thought of as an indifferent and confusing place, thereby placing further responsibility on each person for his/her own understanding and life direction. The need to make rational decisions in an irrational world adds to the challenge of knowing our existence.

Although the philosophy of existentialism as a movement emerged during the nineteenth and twentieth centuries, the concepts of existentialism can be found in the early writers of Socrates and the Bible among others. Blaise Pascal, the seventeenth century French philosopher, viewed human life as being composed of paradoxes and contradictions. Unlike existentialists of later years, he believed that having a god in one's life provided for ultimate meaning beyond the daily obstacles created and overcome as a way to escape boredom.

Søren Kierkegaard is viewed as the founder of modern existentialism who advocated that the human condition was one of uncertainty and irrationality. It was therefore believed that each individual should be deeply committed to determining and living a personally meaningful life. Following one's own path over societal norms would take risk and resilience. In opposition to the atheistic existentialists, Kierkegaard believed that the only way to truly save an individual from despair was to commit to God and the Christian way of life.

Friedrich Nietzsche was much more of a pessimistic philosopher in ideas about humanity. His fundamental belief rested with the individual will in creating life meaning. As such, he rejected any encouragement of moral conformity of the majority and rejected the concept of a higher power. Furthermore, he believed that individuals will never fully understand their existence, and, therefore, the best course of action is to set goals and pursue with passion with the awareness of eventual death and meaninglessness.

Martin Heidegger was a German philosopher who was not much different from Nietzsche in his basic belief in a confusing, indifferent world. Heidegger, too, thought that each person is responsible for choosing life goals and pursuing them with passion. In spite of such conviction, each person must realize that death is certain and life in the end holds no meaning.

Jean-Paul Sartre was the theorist who coined the term "existentialism" as a label for his own philosophical movement in France. Sartre's pessimistic and atheistic approach is that human life is futile in persons' needs and attempts to find a rational reason for existence. Nevertheless, he believed that people accept the freedom of choice and responsibility that is the process of living.

Although there are varying thoughts as to the exact nature of existential theory, several common themes have emerged over the years. The idea of moral individualism implies that there are no universal, objective, moral standards to serve as guiding principles. Each individual must decide his/her own method of making moral decisions. This subjective approach to decision making is stressed by all existentialists, and only by acting on one's beliefs and reflecting on personal experiences can truth be understood. Existentialists suggest that, although rational clarity is useful to have, reason does not predicate life's most important questions.

A second common theme among existentialists is the anxiety of living, also known as the anguish or dread over human existence. Believing in the tragedy of existence, that there is an underlying nothingness filled with guilt and suffering, adds to the anxiety of one's daily experience. Furthermore, existential dread, as opposed to fear, is related to nothing in particular. Persons who fear a "something" can begin to challenge the fear because it can be identified and, hence, worked through. Dread, however, is about nothing and, as a result, cannot be identified or confronted.

A third theme is the absurdity of one's existence. This is realized when one considers one's short time of existence in relation to the vast amount of time prior to birth and following death. Although persons are believed to be responsible for their own meaning and decisions, their participation in life may seem futile and confusing.

The idea of nothingness follows a conscious rejection of any structure designed to help define and make meaning of life and how decisions and relationships are shaped. Moral guidelines and various ideologies promote order and understanding. Without assimilating such structures, a person can feel lost with little purpose or direction. This awareness is tied to the existential theme of death. Death can occur both literally and figuratively. Being aware of one's own mortality can be a strong motivator to begin making decisions with meaning. Common events that influence death awareness may be a life-threatening experience or the death of one's parents. Death of a figurative nature can be experienced through such life events as graduating from college (death, or the ending, as a student) or marriage (ending old roles and beginning new ones). Heidegger believed that as one acknowledges the inevitability of death then the anxiety of death becomes less, thereby freeing one from life's trivial matters.

Isolation or, as philosopher Paul Tillich described it, estrangement is another existential theme. To be isolated is be separate from ourselves, others, and the world. As social beings we have an innate need to connect to others, and through this connection meaning is partly developed. Persons may contribute to their own isolation depending on the decisions they make. For instance, if individuals say that they have no friends (isolation from others), then a question would be how do they participate in their own isolation? It might be that they never try to initiate contact with others, but simply wait to respond when called upon. The opposite of isolation is to be connected. Therefore, as relationships develop and knowledge of self is expanded, anxiety is reduced. However, existentialists believe that we are ultimately alone at our point of death and that we remain alone in the responsibility of our choices in life.

The freedom to create meaning and our responsibility to do so are fundamental to the existentialist's paradigm and therefore a major theme. With freedom of choice comes the anxiety of choosing. Herein lays the paradox of freedom. People value the opportunity to make choices in relationships, careers, and daily decisions, yet are anxious if the outcomes of their choices do not meet expectations. Existential psychotherapist Viktor Frankl, who wrote *Man's Search for Meaning*, based on his experience in a Nazi concentration camp during World War II, used existential concepts in his struggles as a prisoner. Frankl discovered that through the freedom of choosing how we view a situation we create our own meaning.

Existentialism is essentially a philosophy for living and a way to contemplate human existence. The major concepts of existentialism raise questions that all humans face and struggle with personally and in relationship to others.

**Further Reading:** Frankl, V. (1985). *Man's search for meaning.* Boston: Washington Square Press. Kaufman, W. (Ed.). (1975). *Existentialism: From Dostoevsky to Sartre.* New York: Penguin Group. Marino, G. (Ed.). (2004). *Basic writings of existentialism.* New York: Random House.

*Scott E. Hall*

# F

## Fact-Value Distinction

Although interest in the fact-value distinction as such is probably of fairly recent (at any rate post-Cartesian) vintage, it is likely that the concerns at the heart of this issue are of some antiquity. Thus, for example, many of Plato's dialogues appear to be exercised by the difficulty of basing moral judgments on more than mere subjective opinion or social conformity, when it is seems—for one thing—that such judgments are not verifiable (or falsifiable) statements of empirical fact (although in Plato's case, matters are complicated by the fact that he does not believe that knowledge of any kind can be grounded empirically). Still, in its more modern form, the problem of the real or alleged gap between normative or moral and empirical or theoretical scientific claims or propositions seems to receive its clearest statement in the writings of the eighteenth-century Scottish empiricist philosopher David Hume.

There are, in fact, two main points at which difficulties regarding the nonempirical nature of moral judgments are raised by Hume. First, in his *Treatise of Human Nature,* Hume proposes an austere theory of knowledge according to which all that we can be said to know comes down to what he calls "matters of fact" (reports on experience) or "relations of ideas" (definitions, or rules for the uses of words). On the basis of this, Hume concludes that value judgments cannot be regarded as genuine sources of (objective) knowledge, and he proposes a fundamentally "projectivist" reduction of nonempirical (moral, aesthetic, religious) claims to expressions of feeling and emotion. Second, in a notorious passage of the *Enquiries,* Hume seems to argue that there can be no logical transition or valid inference from premises or statements purporting to describe what *is* or how things are, to (prescriptive) statements concerning how things *ought* to be. In the light of these assumptions, Hume effectively concludes that there are no purely rational grounds for moral value and agency, and that "reason is and only ought to be the slave of the passions." On this basis, Hume raises an issue for modern ethics that has continued to haunt subsequent moral theory and divide moral philosophers.

Such ethical division is perhaps most clearly apparent in the contrast between the two most influential of post-Humean modern moral perspectives. First, despite the fact that

Immanuel Kant rejects Hume's moral expressivism or emotivism, arguing that moral claims and judgments are rationally grounded in a distinctive kind of normative reasoning, his insistence that such moral deliberation is nevertheless independent of empirical evidence readily embraces the fact-value and is-ought dichotomies. In view of this, it is usual to trace the roots of modern so-called "noncognitivism"—views (such as emotivism, prescriptivism, and error theory) to the effect that there can be no value-independent "evidence" for moral judgments—to either or both of Hume and Kant. However, standing in much the same empiricist tradition as Hume, such nineteenth-century moral and political theorists as Jeremy Bentham, J.S. Mill, and Henry Sidgwick developed—partly in opposition to Kant's moral philosophy—a new form of naturalist ethics going by the name of "utilitarianism," which insisted that moral prescription or decisions about what to do could and should be based on the "teleological" grounds of what might or might not conduce to the promotion of human happiness or flourishing. In addition to the enduring impact of ultilitarianism, the second half of the twentieth century also saw the revival of an Aristotelian naturalism—in opposition to then currently fashionable forms of noncognitivism—which also held that moral prescriptions and values may be grounded in or informed by considerations relating human welfare to the "facts" of human nature.

However, the apparent impasse or deadlock to which opposition between naturalism and noncognitivism seems to have led, has drawn many to ask whether what should be questioned is what both these positions assume—namely, that the attempt to distinguish facts from values is any way intelligible. In fact, under the influence of various neo-idealist, nonrealist, and postempiricist philosophical views, distinctions between fact and value or theory and observation have been questioned in mainstream epistemology and philosophy of science at least since the nineteenth century. On many such essentially post-Kantian views of knowledge acquisition, we have been encouraged to regard human (scientific or other) forms of understanding as social or cultural constructs that dispose epistemic agents to see the world in ways shaped by specific—and perhaps merely local —interests and values. On such perspectives, no observation of the world is to be considered absolutely objective, if this means entirely innocent of theoretical or normative assumptions: hence, if the term "fact" is meant to refer to some value-free observation, there cannot be any such thing. Such views would seem to have influenced mainstream moral theory in two principal ways. On the one hand, many latter day moral theorists have focused on the social constructivist aspects of such epistemic perspectives, urging that moral values and virtues have local cultural origins that condition rival—if not incommensurable—moral visions. Such theorists have ranged from those who would still countenance the possibility of some rational (perhaps absolute idealist) resolution of moral differences between rival perspectives, to those who embrace outright moral relativism. On the other hand, however, modern scepticism regarding the fact-value distinction has also inspired the revival of a new moral realism, which holds that there are moral truths concerning the world (since reality admits of description or characterization in moral as well as other terms), and that individual moral growth turns crucially on the cultivation of a capacity to perceive (in a strong cognitive sense of perception) the world in morally correct (or at least more truthful) ways.

*David Carr*

## Faith

Faith, as a concept and practice, has been used for centuries to shape thought, emotions, and behavior. There are three common uses for the word "faith" that reflect three different definitions. Faith, as a noun, is used to depict one's religious views or a group of beliefs. Having faith can refer to our belief in something that does not have rational proof or material evidence. It can also mean having confidence in something or someone based on past experience or evidence. Faith can also be demonstrated by one's loyalty to a person, thing, or idea and further shapes the decisions one makes and one's life commitments.

Faith is often confused with belief, which is different in several ways. Beliefs are more related to existing ideas that one follows based on knowledge and understanding. Faith is focused toward the future, or what has yet to occur, and is based on hope and trust. Faith is also more aligned with being certain than is a belief. For instance, a person can believe something to be true, but might not be certain because of a limited knowledge. Faith, however, because it is grounded in hope and charged with emotion, does not require definitive knowledge.

Faith can also be considered the foundation for things we hope for, such as dreams and goals. Stated differently, faith provides an optimistic support that can help motivate one in the pursuit of one's ambitions. For example, if the outcomes of one's efforts do not match expectations, one can still maintain the faith that everything will turn out okay. Such a mind-set can help reduce the anxiety of perfectionism and the need to have a guarantee on our efforts.

Having faith as defined by one's religious orientation or spiritual relationship has received much focus by theologians, psychologists, and scholars. In his seminal book *Stages of Faith* (1981), James Fowler proposed a six-stage framework for understanding faith development as related to a person's struggle to find and build a relationship with the divine. The stages are hierarchical and require more complex thinking and maturity as one proceeds to each new stage.

The first stage, called Intuitive-Projective faith, occurs between the ages of three and seven, and is characterized by active imagination without logic. A child's psyche is exposed to the unconscious and taboos of his/her culture. Fear often accompanies this stage as the unconscious encourages thoughts and images of destruction and dread. There is also no real understanding of how to get beyond such thoughts.

The second stage, called Mythic-Literal faith, centers on the child's ability to integrate rituals and symbols while beginning to control his/her imagination toward more normative thinking. The child in this stage views the world subjectively along with a strict belief in justice and reciprocity. The risk of this worldview is to approach one's salvation or behavior in a "black and white" or either/or thinking fashion, resulting in perfectionistic tendencies.

Synthetic-Conventional faith is the third stage that represents the majority of the population. Adolescence is the beginning of this stage when a person's emerging identity is often sought through conformity in friendships, beliefs, and practices. Unfortunately, this stage of development is less about finding commonality and more about noticing differences that encourage good/bad, us/other relationships. Authority is centralized and goes to the majority of opinion, making it challenging for one to stand alone in one's convictions.

Stage four is Individuative-Reflective faith and is typically experienced by persons in their mid-thirties to early forties. Effort and angst characterize one's attempt to be separate from the group that helped shape one's identity. Personal responsibility for one's beliefs is heightened as is the courage and desire to question authority. Being disillusioned is part of the existential awareness of one's own existence that accompanies this stage. The complexity of the world is realized, and persons who remain in this stage can become cynical toward others by not trusting.

Stage five is known as Conjunctive faith and is represented by one's move from a rationalistic view of life to one of paradox and transcendence. The unconscious is looked upon with awe yet trepidation as symbolism and metaphor is explored within one's own culture and other cultures. The divisions that existed between an individual and others begin to wear away, and an emerging interest in universal connections occurs. Although there is a curiosity to new information, there remains hesitation to embrace other beliefs or ideas for fear of being disloyal to past allegiances.

Stage six is labeled Universalizing faith and builds on the universal interest in stage five, but without the trepidation to fully explore and consider differing views. A person's actions match his/her desire for a unified vision, and he/she may feel a sense of enlightenment to a new perspective of the world and relationships.

Fowler's model is similar to Lawrence Kohlberg's theory on the Stages of Moral Development in that movement is through stages and is progressively advanced. An issue between the theorists is whether faith development precedes moral development or vice versa. Furthermore, there remains the question of link between faith and moral development in terms of how decisions are made and relationships are fostered.

Fowler's notion of faith-knowing is desired by all humans with or without a specific religious orientation. It is ultimately about finding meaning about themselves, others, and the world. It is in this search that he suggests moral development is embedded.

Loder (1989) also focuses on faith development as transformations based on life changing events. Such events are typically unexpected and leave one with a different way of thinking, feeling, and behaving. Transformation is therefore more of an experiential nature than a path of deliberate study and contemplation.

The common theme among theorists is that faith development does not stand in isolation. As a construct it is multidimensional, involves personal and interpersonal development, and holds a close relationship with our understanding and practice of morality.

*Further Reading:* Buber, M. (1958). *I and thou.* New York: Collier Books, Macmillan Publishing Co. Fowler, J. W. (1995). *Stages of faith: The psychology of human development and the quest for meaning.* San Francisco: Harper. Loder, J. (1989). *The transforming moment.* Colorado Springs, CO: Helmers & Howard Publishing. Munsey, B. (Ed.). (1980). *Moral development, moral education, and Kohlberg.* Birmingham, AL: Religious Education Press.

*Scott E. Hall*

## Faith Development

From a theological perspective, faith can refer to God's gracious self-communication and to the human response to that gift. From a psychological perspective, faith refers to the latter, to the ways in which human beings orient their lives in the presence of God. Theories of faith development share an understanding that faith is more than an emotion or an irrational belief based on immaturity and dependence. A faith that is capable of development is a faith that becomes more differentiated and integrated with experience. It has a cognitive dimension but is much more than a system of beliefs. Faith is profoundly relational. It involves trust in God as the source and end of all being.

James Fowler, the leading faith development theorist, points out that faith involves not only knowing but also valuing and meaning-making. Faith directs as well as expresses our commitments and deepest convictions about the world, ourselves, and our possibilities and fulfillment. Faith is expressed in narratives as well as propositions. It is emotional as well as conceptual.

Although from a cognitive perspective faith may be regarded as a distinctive domain in contrast with the moral domain or the logical mathematical domain, faith is by definition at the very heart of human self-understanding and meaning-making. Faith is at the core of the human quest for happiness and transcendence.

Typically, theories of faith development presuppose the existence of God or of an ultimate being. Yet Fowler, among other theorists, recognizes that an individual's faith must include an explicit acknowledgement of God or an ultimate being. Belief in God or the ultimate may be tacit or implicit. Individuals may express their faith as their outlook on life or worldview. In this sense, faith development should be distinguished from religious or spiritual development, which involves particular conceptions of God or transcendence.

Theories of faith development use psychological constructs to investigate and describe the ways in which faith matures throughout the life cycle. The cognitive developmental theories of Piaget and Kohlberg have proved to be particularly helpful. They focus on the cognitive dimension of faith insofar as they illumine ways in which the articulations of faith become more rationally organized and coherent. As children develop the capacity for logical thinking and for taking the perspective of others, they are empowered with new and more penetrating ways of probing the meaning and worth of their lives. The life span developmental approach of Erik Erikson has also proven very useful for some faith developmental theorists, particularly Fowler. Erikson's psychosocial stages develop as a result of individual physical maturation and the age-related demands of society on the individual. Advance through Erikson's stages occurs simply as a result of age, whereas advance through the cognitive stages depends on the quality of the individual's interactions with the environment, which means that development occurs at different rates and often terminates at the intermediate stages.

Because Fowler's stage theory is the most widely used faith development approach, a brief sketch of his stages is provided below with the addition of a "Stage 0" derived principally from Erikson's theory.

### Stage 0: Primal Faith (Infancy)

Faith begins in early infancy at what Erikson calls the "Oral Sensory Stage." The infant's earliest experiences with parents and caretakers, who must be counted on to provide both psychological and physical nourishment, provide a foundation for experiencing on a level of feeling not yet capable of articulation of a basic trust or mistrust in the environment.

### Stage 1: Intuitive-Projective Faith (Early Childhood)

As children develop the capacity for language and symbolic thought, they use images to give sense and coherence to their experience. These images give expression to children's "terrors" as well as sources of strength and protection. Fowler describes children's understanding at this stage as "episodic" and lacking the linear quality of narrative at the next stage.

### Stage 2: Mythic-Literal Faith (Elementary-School Years through Early Adolescence)

At this stage, children check their powerful imaginations with concrete operational logic to sort out the real from the imaginary and to categorize and order their experiences. Children begin to appropriate the stories, symbols, and beliefs of their communities in a literal and often naïve way. Fowler describes children at this stage as being "trapped" in their narratives. They do not yet stand back from and reflect on their stories and symbols. Their notions of God and the supernatural tend to be highly anthropomorphic and dominated by a morality of concrete reciprocity. This morality, Fowler observes, can lead to the extremes of self-justification and perfectionism or of self-abasement.

### Stage 3: Synthetic-Conventional Faith (Adolescence)

As adolescents move to Stage 3, they are faced with the task of making sense of a world that has become more complex and demanding. The stories that provided meaning at the previous stage need to be reexamined and reconciled in the light of new and conflicting information. Formal operational thinking provides a new way of grasping the meanings behind the symbols and stories that they regard as authoritative. As adolescents develop mutual perspective taking, they begin to value relationships for themselves and to frame their perspective on others and God in interpersonal ways. Because of the importance attached to the maintenance of relationships, individuals at this stage tend to defer to trusted authorities and conform to conventional expectations.

### Stage 4: Individuative-Reflective Faith (Young Adulthood)

Fowler notes that late adolescents and young adults make the transition to Stage 4 as they adopt a more critical stance toward received beliefs and values about themselves, their world, and God. Through sustained reflection they attempt to construct a systematic worldview that is both inclusive and internally coherent. As they seek greater clarity about the world about them, they also seek to define an identity that comes from within and expresses their deepest convictions. Accepting responsibility for themselves and their commitments, they struggle to maintain a proper balance between conscience and the claims of authority.

### Stage 5: Conjunctive Faith (Mid-Life or Beyond)

This stage involves integrating elements of life experience and perspectives that may have been neglected or even dismissed at the previous stage. Fowler speaks of this as a stage in which one's past is "reclaimed" and "reworked" in an effort to come to terms with symbols, myths, and unconscious stirrings that can give one's life greater depth and complexity when faced with conflicting and even paradoxical polarities.

### Stage 6: Universalizing Faith

The faith divided at Stage 5 between the world as it is and the world as it is yet to become is unified at Stage 6 in a communion with the ultimate environment and "all being." Those at Stage 6 experience a oneness with God and a participation in the transformative power of God.

*Further Reading:* Fowler, J. (1981). *Stages of faith: The psychology of human development and the quest for meaning.* New York: Harper and Collins. Fowler, J. (1999). *Becoming adult, becoming Christian: Adult development and Christian faith.* San Francisco: Jossey-Bass. Fowler, J. W., Nipkow, K. E., & Schweitzer, F. (1991). *Stages of faith and religious development: Implications for church, education, and society.* New York: Crossroad.

F. Clark Power

## Family Life Education

Family Life Education (FLE) programs prepare individuals and families for the roles and responsibilities of everyday family life. The focus is on dealing with problems, preventing problems, and developing healthy relationships. The ultimate goal of FLE is the development of stable families making a positive contribution to the social fabric of the world in which they live. While the objectives of FLE programs may be diverse, for example, from understanding self and others to sexuality education to managing work and family life, the topics are more interrelated than first appears. The overarching premise of enhancing family life through application of research integrates the concepts.

There is considerable agreement about the content or subject matter of FLE. Most programs include education for one or all of the following areas of study: interpersonal relationships, self-awareness, child and adult growth and development, preparation for partnership and parenthood, decision making, sexuality, management of time, energy, and money, personal and family health, the impact of culture and community on family life, and the understanding of moral issues and actions.

Over time—the history of family life education begins with the establishment of the Land Grant Colleges and Universities—guiding principles have been generally agreed upon to describe not only how FLE is carried out but also what FLE should do as the programs educate for family living (Arcus et al., 1993). These principles are in no particular order.

1. *FLE has life-span relevance.* The Framework for Life-Span Family Life Education was developed by the National Council on Family Relations in 1987. That document gave broad age categories to guide FLE content at different grade levels in schools and universities as well as in community programs. There is some concern about this principle, since families may not proceed through developmental stages.
2. *FLE should be based on immediate needs of individuals and families.* The participants of FLE programs are asked to determine the nature of a particular program. Their needs are assessed by various means. The difficulty here is that expectations may be raised so that all needs can be met.
3. *FLE is interdisciplinary and involves many professions in its practice.* Among the fields from which important FLE concepts are drawn are the following: anthropology, biology, economics, education, home economics, law, medicine, philosophy, psychology, social work, and sociology. Although all have relevance, sociology and psychology are most heavily used with educational concepts being foundational. There has sometimes been competition among disciplines for FLE programs.

4. *FLE programs may be found in different settings.* Generally FLE is found in educational institutions, but it may also be offered by faith communities, workplaces, and governmental and private agencies.

5. *FLE focuses on an educational approach.* The distinctions between education and therapy or counseling may not be clear, but FLE programs declare that their purpose is to educate or equip, rather than to repair. Attitudes and emotions, as well as learning in order to change behavior, are a part of FLE. Generally, FLE educators are not prepared to be therapists.

6. *FLE programs present and show respect for differing family values.* FLE educators are to be as scrupulous as possible to present values and value-laden topics in ways that present both sides of issues and show respect for differing positions.

7. *FLE educators must be well-qualified.* The success of FLE programs is dependent on well-prepared and certified educators. The role of FLE educators is large. They must have knowledge of many content areas and skills in the process of teaching. The National Council on Family Relations has established a certification program standardizing practice as a Family Life Educator.

The future of FLE is dependent upon clarification of several issues facing the field. The name of the field is not clear. In secondary schools, the programs are called Family and Consumer Science, while in colleges and universities FLE may be Human Ecology, Human Development, Family Education, or Family Social Science. The methods and studies to evaluate outcomes of FLE need attention. The tension between education and therapy needs to be addressed. These issues need to be addressed in order for FLE's important goals to be achieved.

***Further Reading:*** Arcus, M.E., Schvaneveldt, J.D., & Moss, J.J. (1993). The nature of family life education. In M.E. Arcus, J.D. Schvaneveldt, & J.J. Moss (Eds.), *Handbook of family life education*. Newbury Park, CA: SAGE Publications. National Council on Family Relations. (1987). A framework for life-span family life education. *Family Relations, 36,* 5–10.

*Marilyn Martin Rossmann*

## Fenton, Edwin

Edwin Fenton is widely recognized for his leadership role in what—in the 1960s and 1970s—was a major initiative called, *The New Social Studies.* In moral education, Fenton made many contributions to curriculum and, arguably most importantly, to preparing teachers to conduct classroom discussions about moral dilemmas and issues.

Fenton's career is closely associated with Carnegie Mellon University where he began his professorial career in 1954 (the name at the time was Carnegie Technical Institute). Fenton's publications number over 200. The range of his knowledge and interests is evident in his two most recent books: *Carnegie Mellon 1900–2000: A Centennial History* and *Laugh the Blues Away: A Bluefish Cookbook.*

The New Social Studies was a movement that arose out of a concern about the poor state of knowledge of history among K–12 students, a concern about training teachers in the social studies to teach by using the "discovery method," and as part of a national response to the Soviet Union's launch of the Sputnik satellite. The underlying belief, in both the "hard" sciences and the social sciences was that students could best learn disciplines by using the methods used by scientists and academics.

The *Structure of Disciplines* approach, in the New Social Studies integrated the social science disciplines, but emphasized history and put a focus on teaching using primary sources and documents (perhaps the result of Fenton's training as an academic historian). The New Social Studies was both influential and sometimes controversial. Fenton's *The Americans: A History of the United States* was banned in 1972 by the Georgia State Board of Education because of its treatment of racial issues, its coverage of Vietnam, and its promotion of critical inquiry.

Arguably, the range of social transformations in U.S. politics and culture had by the late 1970s and 1980s created a condition where, in response, social studies began to focus less on the inquiry approach of individual disciplines and more on law-related and citizenship education. While the profile of the New Social Studies was waning, Kohlbergian moral education was growing in its influence in schools, particularly in the power of discussion of moral dilemmas.

Fenton found a natural match between his own interests and expertise and the early Kohlberg educational interventions that focused on discussion of moral dilemmas as a means for promoting development. In 1976, the National Council for the Social Studies—in the organization's publication *Social Education*—highlighted the controversies and issues of moral education. Fenton argued for Kohlbergian approaches, but emphasized that moral dilemma discussions alone would not be a sufficiently comprehensive approach to social studies or other disciplines. Lawrence Kohlberg saw promoting a student's development from one stage to a higher one as the primary aim of moral education, an aim he saw as consistent with and facilitated by Fenton's pedagogical prescriptions for the knowledge, skills, and dispositions of citizenship or civics education.

Fenton developed teacher-training workshops to help teachers successfully use moral discussion in classrooms. With his colleagues, Fenton developed a summer institute for educators in Pittsburgh. For the training, the Carnegie Mellon team developed a manual of valuable and concrete suggestions for teachers. The educators who were trained and others who knew of the materials benefited from the manual and keep it on their bookshelves to this day; regrettably, it was never published for general distribution.

Fenton and Kohlberg collaborated on several projects. One was a study of the impact of moral dilemma discussions in classrooms in high schools in Boston and Pittsburgh and subsequently in a second study of high school students in Cambridge, Brookline, and Pittsburgh. The project demonstrated the ability of moral dilemma discussions to promote moral reasoning, but the intervention did not survive after the funding. A year later Fenton and Kohlberg found that many teachers had abandoned the teaching strategy. This experience led Kohlberg to expand his moral education beyond the discussion of dilemmas in all disciplines to a focus on actual moral issues in classrooms and schools and to develop democratic communities at Cambridge Cluster School and Scarsdale Alternative School, and what were called Just Community Schools in New York City. The shift from discipline-based dilemma discussion to a broader view is a shift to the view of moral education being a component of civics/citizenship education advocated by Fenton. Among his contributions at Cluster was assisting in creating the school's Fairness Committee, which played a judicial function in the school's direct democracy.

Fenton was an exemplary teacher; in 1964 he received Carnegie Mellon's highest honor in teaching, the William H. and Francis S. Ryan Teaching Award, and in 1998 Fenton received the Robert Doherty Prize for his contribution to education at the university. Fenton was recognized by the Association for Moral Education in 1987 with the Kuhmerker Award, given to individuals who have made outstanding contributions to the organization and to moral education.

***Further Reading:*** Bruner, J. (1960). *Process of education.* Cambridge: Harvard University Press. Fenton, E. (1967). *The new social studies.* New York: Holt, Rinehart, and Winston. Fenton, E. (1976). Moral education: The research findings. *Social Education, 40,* 188–93. Fenton, E. (2000). *Carnegie Mellon 1900–2000: A centennial history.* Pittsburgh: Carnegie Mellon University Press. Fenton, E. (2001). *Laugh the blues away: A bluefish cookbook.* Pittsburgh: Ring Road Press.

*Robert W. Howard*

## Forgiveness, Stages of

The stages of forgiveness are an ethical and psychological framework of reasoning about the conditions that can make interpersonal forgiveness more likely to be offered to offenders. Enright, Santos, and Al-Mabuk (1989), working with a theory for interpersonal forgiveness in the moral development and social cognitive areas in psychology, identified six stages of forgiveness reasoning from the viewpoint of victims of injustices. The stages are related to age, religion, and practice of faith; quality of justice reasoning; and social contexts of hurt (for example, self-hurt, interpersonal hurt, or social conflicts). Enright explains that the terminology of stages in social cognitive frameworks (for example, Jean Piaget's cognitive developmental stages; Lawrence Kohlberg's stages of justice reasoning development) has been very much associated with the idea of rigid developmental schemas. However, the stages of forgiveness are soft reasons; a progression in the sequence of stages might include stage regressions, and people may think in terms of different stages at the same time. Enright also considers that it is appropriate to change the terminology of stages of forgiveness reasoning to styles of forgiveness reasoning.

The stages/styles of forgiveness reasoning are as follows:

*Stage 1—Forgiveness as Revenge:* This kind of thinking connects forgiveness with vengeance or expiatory punishment toward the person who offended. Victims relieve resentment or anger only after the other person is punished more severely than he or she deserves to pay for his or her fault.

*Stage 2—Forgiveness as Restitution or Compensation:* This kind of thinking connects forgiveness with benefiting from the release of resentment and anger after restitution (receiving back what was lost or stolen) or compensation (receiving something of value that would make one better for the loss).

*Stage 3—Social Expectations for Forgiveness:* This kind of thinking connects forgiveness to the desire to be a "good person" to fulfill social expectations of family and friends. Victims benefit socially from forgiveness because they appear to be good or generous toward someone else.

*Stage 4—Religious Orientation for Forgiveness:* This kind of thinking connects forgiveness to religious obligation (conventional forgiveness). Victims forgive to attend to the demands of his or her religious rules. It is important to notice differences between this stage and the previous stages. If a person forgives on account of social pressures, benefiting from God's generosity, or fear of being punished for breaking religious demands, this kind of thinking would be within the stage 3, stage 2, or stage 1 category because the person shows a utilitarian viewpoint of religion. Yet, a person with a religious orientation for forgiving might consider religious rules as a way to conduct his or her thinking toward genuine forgiveness. Religious people tend to offer forgiveness equally toward family members, friends, and strangers. Nonreligious people usually show their willingness to forgive family and friends more than strangers. Therefore, genuine religious thinking at this stage indicates that victims are following their spiritual beliefs as orientation for decentration of thoughts toward humanity.

*Stage 5—Forgiveness as Social Harmony:* This kind of thinking considers forgiveness genuinely for social equality or social justice. A person understands ideal reciprocity as "giving good to society after injustices will bring good to society." This is reciprocal thinking applied to social systems for conflict resolution. Victims think that one should forgive others as one wants others to forgive him or her. This is also a strategy to control society via promotion of peaceful relations between people or groups.

*Stage 6—Ethics Orientation for Forgiveness:* This is forgiveness given out of love for humanity. Victims articulate justice and benevolence for others, that is, mercy for the human condition. Forgiveness is not dependent on interpersonal or societal relationships but is grounded in love.

The stages or styles of forgiveness reasoning are relevant in basic psychological research for human development, the implementation of restorative justice programs, education for justice and benevolence, and therapy for helping clients to release anger and resentment via forgiveness.

**Further Reading:** Enright, R.D., & Fitzgibbons, R.P. (2000). *Helping clients forgive: An empirical guide for resolving anger and restoring hope.* Washington, D.C.: APA. Enright, R.D., Santos, M.J.D., & Al-Mabuk, R. (1989). The adolescent as forgiver. *Journal of Adolescence, 12,* 95–110. Enright, R.D., and the Human Development Study Group. (1994). Piaget on the moral development of forgiveness: Reciprocity or identity? *Human Development, 37,* 63–80.

*Júlio Rique*

## The Four Component Model

The Four Component model (FCM) was derived by James Rest (1941–1999) from an empirical literature review of research related to moral behavior (Rest, 1983). Rest created the model when it became clear that moral judgment, the primary area of research in moral development, could not account for all of moral development and behavior, contrary to the claims of Lawrence Kohlberg.

The FCM provides a situation-based, functional view of the necessary psychological components or processes for a particular moral behavior to ensue. Although the components may sound purely intellectual, each component is a combination of emotional and cognitive processes. The four components in the model are described in a logical order but may take place nearly simultaneously or in a different order: moral sensitivity, moral judgment, moral motivation, and moral action. Interactively each component can impinge on another, increasing, decreasing, or thwarting application and execution. In moving toward completing a moral action, an individual may fail at any point if one or more components are not executed. Although the FCM is used primarily to describe behavior *in situ,* an individual may develop expertise in one or more components. For example, he/she may be particularly sensitive but a poor judge; he/she may make excellent judgments but fail to follow through on action.

The first component, moral sensitivity, involves not only noticing and being receptive to a morally relevant problem but imagining possibilities for action, and their trajectories in time in terms of outcomes and reactions from others. Individuals vary in their sensitivity to moral problems, some noticing minimal slights while others require spilled blood. The Kitty Genovese incident, foundational to the field of social psychology, was instrumental in alerting psychologists to sensitivity factors in moral behavior. Genovese was a young woman who was murdered outside her apartment building over several hours despite the fact that over 30 neighbors saw and heard the entire incident; no one called for help until it was too late. The bystanders were not only confused about what was happening but they thought one of the other neighbors they saw watching would call for help. Thus moral sensitivity is influenced by comprehension of situation cues and other situational variables. Expert moral sensitivity engages empathy and generates multiple possible courses of action. It is the work of the second component to decide among options.

The second component, moral judgment, refers to reasoning about which action of those identified is the most moral and right in the circumstance. There are two traditions for viewing how people make judgments about morality. The first is from social psychology and older traditions, social norm theory. The person takes into account the particular features of a situation and selects from a catalogue of internalized norms the one that matches the situation. Although this may describe some decisions, Lawrence Kohlberg found another source for decision making. He outlined six stages of justice reasoning through which individuals develop. Each stage represents a formulation that the individual has constructed from social experience about what is most fair. Individuals move from a preconventional level that is self-concerned (stages 1 and 2), to a conventional level that is group oriented (stages 3 and 4), to a postconventional level concerned with process and principles (stages 5 and 6). Although a person may reason at a highly sophisticated level, there is no guarantee that he/she will act on the reasoning. Because of the gap between judgment and action, the next component, moral motivation, has become more important in moral psychology in recent years.

The third component, moral motivation, involves prioritizing the moral action that component two has identified. Moral motivation has to do with setting aside other priorities, goals, and needs in order to take on the moral action. Personal codes of ethics and social pressure may help individuals prioritize the moral action. However, according to ancient philosophers, moral failure often occurs here through "weakness of the will." Blasi has suggested that moral personality, an aspect of motivation, reflects the centrality of moral concerns to oneself.

The fourth component, implementation and character, requires the ability to work around impediments and avoid temptations to do otherwise, the final factors required for completion of the moral behavior. Implementation refers to the skills required to get the job done. Character refers to the ego strength and perseverance necessary to complete the action. Individuals can fail here also because they do not have the required skills or they do not know how to keep themselves on task in the face of obstacles and distractions.

The FCM has had its greatest impact in the field of education, particularly professional education. Several professional schools use the model to frame their ethics training (see Rest & Narvaez, 1994). A more recent iteration of the Four Component Model can be found in the Integrative Ethical Education model, designed for K–12 character education. In this model the four components are specified as sets of ethical skills that can be taught and honed to higher levels of expertise. Experts in sensitivity more easily empathize with others and see what needs to be done. Experts in judgment have multiple tools for reasoning. Experts in motivation are able to "keep their eye on the prize," while experts in moral implementation and character use a set of skills to complete the action, no matter what the obstacles.

Although the FCM is particularly useful in explaining completed moral behavior and in delineating what might be taught, it is not suited for indicating the "right answer" for any of the components. Since it is situation-based, what is "right" changes with the circumstance, a perspective that corresponds to ancient notions of virtue. Virtuous individuals know what to do and spontaneously do it in the right way at the right time.

The FCM was expanded to five components by Ann Higgins who included reflection and to 12 components by B.L. Bredemeier and D.L. Shields for sports. The FCM is similar to Ken Dodge's Social Information Processing model, created about the same time, which is used to identify social processing deficits in aggressive children.

***Further Reading:*** Narvaez, D., & Rest, J.R. (1995). The four components of moral behavior. In W. Kurtines & J. Gewirtz (Eds.), *Moral behavior and moral development: An introduction* (pp. 385–400). New York: McGraw-Hill. Rest, J.R. (1983). Morality. In J. Flavell & E. Markham (Eds.), *Cognitive development,* from P. Mussen (Ed.), *Manual of child psychology, Vol. 3* (pp. 556–629). New York: Wiley. Rest, J.R. & Narvaez, D. (Eds.). (1994). *Moral development in the professions: Psychology and applied ethics.* Hillsdale, NJ: Lawrence Erlbaum.

*Darcia Narvaez*

## Fowler, James

James Fowler is one of the foremost psychologists of religion in his generation. Bringing together a wide array of insights from the social sciences as well as theology, he is also one of the most outstanding "practical theologians." He is best known for his Stage Theory of Faith Development, which achieved a bold and daring synthesis of theological and psychological insights. Drawing on the cognitive developmental research of Jean Piaget and Lawrence Kohlberg and the life span developmental insights of Erik Erikson, Fowler describes the contours of the journey of faith from infancy to old age. Fowler's works have attracted wide attention across the scholarly community, particularly of those working in the psychology of religion, the development of the self, and religious and pastoral education.

Growing up in North Carolina and as the son of a Methodist minister, Fowler was attracted to issues of religious belief and social justice at an early age. He did his undergraduate study at Duke and his Masters of Divinity study at Drew. Enrolling in the Religion and Society Program at the Divinity School, he received his doctoral degree at Harvard in theological ethics. In the midst of his doctoral studies, he worked for a year as an assistant to Carlyle Marney at the Interpreter's House, a retreat center in North Carolina. There he learned how individuals revealed their faith through telling their life stories. Fowler's Interpreter's House experience led him to take an applied turn to theology and directly influenced the method he would later take in his Faith Development interviews. Returning to Harvard, Fowler completed his dissertation on H. Richard Niebuhr's theological ethics.

After receiving his doctoral degree, Fowler taught at Harvard where he laid the foundations for his faith development approach. With enthusiastic support and encouragement from Lawrence Kohlberg, Fowler began an innovative research program to describe how faith developed throughout the life span. Forming a team of graduate students from the fields of theology and psychology, Fowler transformed the life story approach into the semiclinical faith development interview. The interview asks participants to describe their life journeys and to address broad issues related to their ethical views, self-understanding, and sense of mystery and the ultimate. Out of a sample of 359 interviews, Fowler described his as a sequence of faith stages, which became the basis for his celebrated theory of faith development.

With support from the Joseph P. Kennedy Foundation, Fowler continued his work on faith development at Boston College. He then went to Emory University where he became the Candler Professor of Theology and Human Development and established the Center for Research on Faith and Moral Development. Later he directed Emory's Center for Ethics in Public Policy and the Professions until he retired in 2005. In recognition of his outstanding scholarly achievements, Fowler received an honorary Doctor of Divinity degree from Franklin College in 1993 and from the University of Edinburgh in 1999. His contributions to the area of psychology and religion were also honored by the Oscar Pfister Award from the American Psychiatric Association and by the American Psychological Association's William James Award.

Throughout his publications, Fowler emphasized that faith is best understood as a verb, not a noun. When faith is thought of as a verb, faith is a constructive activity of meaning-making. Deeply respective of religious traditions, Fowler, nevertheless, maintained that individuals had to assimilate their traditions according to their developmental stage and place in life. Influenced by Paul Tillich's view of faith as ultimate concern, Fowler held that faith involves a relationship with God or what he called "ultimate reality." Although many individuals may not explicitly acknowledge the "ultimate reality" that gives meaning and purpose to their lives, that reality, nevertheless, impinges upon the everyday reality that all acknowledge.

Fowler's research transformed the psychological study of religious experience. Prior to Fowler, the psychology of religion had been dominated by an interest in cults and aberrant behavior. Sigmund Freud's psychoanalytical understanding of faith as a sign of childish dependence was widely influential. Fowler demonstrated that faith was not only compatible with but contributed to psychological maturity and a responsible engagement with society. In his later work, Fowler provided a rich theological and ethical framework for integrating faith within a vocation to public ministry.

*Further Reading:* Fowler, J. W. (1981). *Stages of faith: The psychology of human development and the quest for meaning.* San Francisco: Harper and Row. Fowler, J. W. (1984). *Becoming adult, becoming Christian: Adult development and Christian faith.* San Francisco: Harper and Row. Fowler, J. W. (1985). *To see the kingdom: The theological vision of H. Richard Niebuhr.* Lanham, MD: University Press of America. Fowler, J. W. (1987). *Faith development and pastoral care.* Philadelphia: Fortress Press. Fowler, J. W. (1991). *Weaving the new creation: Stages of faith and the public church.* San Francisco: Harper San Francisco. Fowler, J. W. (2001). *Faithful change: The personal and public challenges of postmodern life.* Nashville, TN: Abington Press. Osmer, R. R., & Schweitzer, F. L. (Eds.). (2003). *Developing a public faith: New directions in practical theology: Essays in honor of James W. Fowler.* St. Louis, MO: Chalice Press.

*F. Clark Power*

## Free Will

It is commonly thought that the basic philosophical issue of free will is the question of whether we are really free to do what we want to do or whether this belief is a self-flattering illusion. This formulation of the problem assumes that the concept called human freedom is simply the opposite of the concept of naturalistic determinism. However, this exclusive either/or polarity is itself questionable for at least two reasons. One is that a third alternative is at least logically possible, namely that human behavior is neither free nor determined but rather a constellation of utterly random microevents. A second, more important reason is that many classical and contemporary philosophers have argued for an intermediate position, usually called compatibilism. According to this view, there is an important, logically consistent, and factually correct sense in which (1) everything including human actions and mental events has a set of jointly sufficient antecedent causes, but (2) the fact that everything has a cause does not render illusory our experience of ourselves as free agents, since one of these antecedent conditions is the agent's desire to do the action in question. In contrast, many contemporary philosophers, some of whom do believe in human freedom (philosophical libertarians) and some of whom do not (anti-libertarians), deny that freedom and determinism are compatible concepts. Thus the simple contrast of freedom and determinism has become part of a larger contrast between *compatibilism* and *incompatibilism.*

These debates have taken place in various contexts: theological (does God determine human fate?), biological (are we programmed by our instincts, genes, or neurological structures?), sociological (can one transcend one's environment?), psychiatric (is personality fixed in the first few years of libidinal struggle?), morality (should people be praised or blamed for their characters or deeds?), and so on. In what follows we focus on the moral dimension of the question of human freedom.

To begin, we should recognize that many scholars who have rejected philosophical libertarianism have not rejected morality itself. For instance, although Arthur Schopenhauer (1788–1860) repudiated the usual notion of individual freedom as the absence of necessity and used the term "will" to denote what might be called cosmic dynamism, he employed decidedly moralistic language to draw out the implications of his basic thesis that our inner essence is, in fact, none other than the transcendental will. Thus he condemned egoism as embodying a false understanding of oneself as having a self-contained will, and praised the virtues of generosity and justice, since they enable us to see beyond our individual desires and to appreciate the equally real presence of will in other persons and indeed in all of our fellow creatures. In similarly moralistic veins, Albert Einstein (1879–1955) made the famous statement that his avowed determinism "protects me from losing my good humor and taking much too seriously myself and my fellow humans as acting and judging individuals," and the legal philosopher H. L. A. Hart (1907–1992) argued that the general ascription of human freedom and moral responsibility was fundamental to the good order of society. Such views seem to suppose that morality and moral responsibility consist not so much in making the right choices as in being the right sort of person. This implicit reconciliation of (psychological) determinism and (moral) responsibility has been explicated in recent philosophical literature by means of "character examples" (Schatz, 1997; Kane, 2002). When he broke with Rome, Martin Luther (1483–1556) famously declared, "Here I take my stand. I cannot do otherwise —*Ich kann nicht anders.*" In saying this, Luther was not renouncing his freedom but rather accepting full responsibility for his action. The argument here is that his break with Rome was "determined" in a sense fully compatible with metaphysical libertarianism: over the course of many years Luther had made numerous free decisions, the upshot of which was a character comprising a set of standing motives and dispositions that made it literally unthinkable for him to continue his life as a Roman Catholic monk. (Of course, this interpretation of moral responsibility assumes that truly moral character traits acquired cognitively by repeated free choices are fundamentally different from nonmoral habits or action tendencies acquired by uncritical rule following brainwashing, indoctrination, or other sorts of noncognitive processes.)

Character examples seem to show that actions such as Luther's nailing his 95 Theses to the Wittenberg church door can be free even in the absence of alternative possibilities (*Ich kann nicht anders*). However, the presence of alternative possibilities is normally an important part of morally responsible choice. This point was developed in a classic article by the philosopher Harry Frankfurt (1971; see also Taylor, 1976), in which an agent takes a metaperspective on his or her "first-order desires" and affirms or denies them at a higher, executive level. This is what happens when, say, I take responsibility for my first-order affections and desires to be with a person I love. I identify myself with these desires and affections by declaring my love, plighting my troth, and so forth. In short, I "make them my will" and in the absence of external constraints I act accordingly. This hierarchical account is reminiscent of earlier accounts of moral struggle such as St. Augustine's self-description of wanting to be chaste but also not wanting it, or Aristotle's distinction between the virtuous person and the "incontinent" (*akratic*) person who may act rightly but lacks the commitment and character by which truly virtuous persons fully identify themselves with the right action.

However, moral traditions that focus on rules rather than character also lay great stress on the linkage between morality and freedom, which is to say on the importance of moral responsibility and, by extension, the evaluative judgments made by others (as well as by oneself) when moral rules are knowingly observed or violated. Moral responsibility includes the idea of causal efficacy but goes far beyond it, since the moral agent not only produces certain effects in the world (as does an exploding volcano or a raging bull) but does so in a specifically human way that includes foreknowledge and freedom of will. The most prominent representative of the juridical approach is Immanuel Kant (1724–1804), who compared moral judgments to legal prescriptions or imperatives that by their very nature evoke praise or blame as well as other sorts of evaluative response. However, since it is a forum for judging intentions as well as actions, even Kant's juridical model allows for degrees of moral responsibility and hence different evaluative shadings. The repertoire of evaluative responses is rich and complex: praise and blame, repentance and regret, honor and respect, guilt and shame, and so on. And each of these evaluations can be more or less strong, since responsibility in all its forms admits of degrees.

*Further Reading:* Dennett, D. (2003). *Freedom evolves.* New York: Viking Books. Fischer, J.M., & Ravizza, M. (1998). *Responsibility and control: An essay on moral responsibility.* Cambridge: Cambridge University Press. Frankfurt, H. (1971). Freedom of the will and the concept of the person. *Journal of Philosophy, 68,* 5–20. Kane, R. (2002). *The Oxford handbook to free will.* Oxford: Oxford University Press. Schatz, D. (1997). Irresistible goodness and alternative possibilities. In C.H. Manekin & M. Kellner (Eds.), *Freedom and moral responsibility: General and Jewish perspectives.* College Park, MD: University of Maryland Press. Schopenhauer, A. (1999). *On the freedom of the will.* Cambridge: Cambridge University Press. (Originally published 1841.) Taylor, C. (1977). What is human agency? In T. Mischel (Ed.), *The self: Psychological and philosophical issues.* Totowa, NJ: Rowman and Littlefield. Van Inwagen, P. (1986). *An essay on free will.* New York: Oxford University Press. Watson, D. (1982). *Free will.* New York: Oxford University Press.

*Thomas Wren*

## Freire, Paulo

Paulo Freire, born in 1921, was a Brazilian philosopher and progressive educator who is best known for his work in solidarity with the poor. Freire was exiled from Brazil in 1964 because of his efforts to educate peasants; he then moved to Chile, where he helped to established literacy programs that significantly reduced the rate of illiteracy. In 1969 he was invited to Harvard University as a visiting professor, and he remained there for 10 years. His most famous work is *Pedagogy of the Oppressed,* which was first published in 1970 while he was teaching at Harvard. Freire returned to Brazil in 1979, and he died in 1997 at the age of 76.

His influence has remained strong, particularly among progressive educators who are deeply concerned about escalating global poverty and its dehumanizing effects. In *Pedagogy of the Oppressed,* he promotes a philosophy of education that emphatically asserts our potential as human agents in the process of social change. Freire's philosophy of education is based on his belief in the possibility of personal and political transformation that can be reached through a process of critical consciousness. He defends a model of progressive education that is not separated from reflections about morality and emotions. Indeed, he embraces these as necessary conceptual frameworks for a truly liberatory model of education. Freire was strongly committed to his faith in Christianity, and he prioritized the values of love, humility, faith, trust, and hope throughout his writings.

Freire argues that there are two polemic models of education; the first is an authoritarian system that he calls the banking theory, and the second is the problem-posing theory. In the banking model, education is the practice of domination, and in the problem-posing model, education is the practice of freedom. For example, the banking model supports the notion of educators as the possessors of knowledge, the teachers who are almost omniscient in their wisdom, who reside in ivory towers, and who occasionally descend to impart wisdom to a chosen few students, who, of course, possess no knowledge of their own. In this banking metaphor of education, teachers "make deposits" of empirical data, for example, into the otherwise empty minds of their students, who may be said to have learned their lessons based on their ability to regurgitate the empirical data on a test. This model is a practice of domination insofar as the teacher aggressively pours in whatever facts she may choose, and the students passively receive those facts in a completely docile and submissive manner.

Contrast this view with the problem-posing model, which views education as the practice of freedom. In this model, the teacher does not merely pour the facts into the minds of her students, instead she poses problems as hypothetical or real scenarios for which they will together attempt to find some resolution. This model is therefore the practice of freedom insofar as it frees the student from passive submission, allows for some control over the objects of knowledge, and gives the student an opportunity to choose how to be actively engaged in his own learning process. The role of the liberated teacher is to create a learning environment that moves the students' knowledge beyond the level of merely storing and retrieving data to the level of critical consciousness. In his view, the banking model is essentially characterized by oppression, and the problem-posing model is essentially characterized by liberation.

Freire argues that the relationship between oppressed people and their oppressors is a relationship of codependency. He suggests that we must move toward some balance between the extremes of having too much and having too little of the basic material needs for human flourishing. Only through an intentional move toward balance can we become more fully human and break the codependency between the oppressors and the oppressed. Freire believed that our society's preoccupation with a consumer market has caused some (the oppressors) to be focused on a consciousness of possessions. This possessive consciousness serves to make the world a place of consumer ownership and, wrongfully, promotes an understanding of ourselves that is defined by our possessions. This negative transformation of the world causes us to define our self-worth as human beings in terms of how much material wealth we have. As Freire puts it, to be (to exist) is to have (to own). He believed that we are diminished as human beings when we are caught in this cycle of possessive consciousness.

In order to transform this unjust social order of the two extremes of wealth and poverty, we must be sincere about trying to honestly evaluate our feelings about material possessions as well as our feelings toward others. According to Freire, achieving true solidarity with all our brothers and sisters would require each of us to experience a "profound rebirth" that represents an alternative way of living. This new way of life would balance the extremes of either having too much or too little material wealth. Such a balance represents a commitment to become more fully human and to engage in critical consciousness. Thus, Freire has provided a conceptual road map for us to follow in the pursuit of what he calls our ontological vocation. What is the primary objective of liberation praxis? To be more fully human—that is our *raison d'etre,* our true reason for being. How do we fulfill that purpose? Primarily through the process of dialogic conversations, those dialogues in which all voices are heard and all experiences are valued.

Freire understood that knowledge about the political process is not enough to influence political decision; knowledge must also be connected to practical skills such as reading and writing beyond the minimum levels of social competency. For example, citizens must be able to write compelling, persuasive letters to newspapers and elected officials, and they must also develop skills in public speaking. The skills that individual citizens and advocacy groups should possess in order to better influence the political process are many, ranging from basic literacy and mathematics necessary to comprehend legal documents and complex statistics to critical analytical skills needed to understand social issues.

Freire did not overlook the impact of psychological traits that influence and sustain the participation of individuals and groups in the political process. These include traits such as self-esteem, motivation, persistence, patience, and ultimately, a willingness to participate in the political process despite its previous failures. It also includes the belief in one's capacity to influence the system. This belief in political efficacy is important because one's confidence in influencing public policy often depends on the individual citizen's perception of personal capacity to impact real political change.

Freire's concept of conscientization can be transformative for educators interested in emancipatory citizenship education. His pedagogical vision for civic education goes well beyond the traditional focus on legal knowledge and how government branches operate. In this sense, the concept of conscientization brings the tradition of popular education into the citizenship education debate. Freire understood that although the process of engaging in critical consciousness does help oppressed people to critically examine the causes of their oppression, it does not necessarily equip them with the tools and resources to influence the political process. Nevertheless, it can assist to further a democratic culture and to equalize political opportunities for all citizens.

***Further Reading:*** Freire, P. (1970). *Pedagogy of the oppressed.* New York: Continuum. Gronholm, C., & Katus, J. (Eds). (1999). *Issues of education and civil society.* Helsinki: Fonda. Nie, H., Junn, J., & Stehlik-Barry, K. (1996). *Education and democratic citizenship in America.* Chicago, IL: University of Chicago Press. Schugurensky, D. (2006). This is our School of Citizenship. In

Z. Bekerman, N. Burbules, & D. Silberman (Eds.), *Learning in hidden places: The informal education reader*. New York: Peter Lang.

*Monalisa M. Mullins*

## Friendship

Friendship is a mutually supportive, cooperative, and engaging interpersonal relationship between two individuals. In friendship, one is manifestly concerned for the welfare of another. The mutual caring, concern, and outward affection inherent among close friends are what set friendships qualitatively apart from acquaintances and other collegial associations. Friendship is central to an individual's social development, for one both shapes and is shaped through the distinctively personal experience of intimate friendship. Friendships are especially noteworthy in the context of moral development since it is within friendships that children learn to embrace the perspective of another person. Friendship becomes the first training ground for developing the skills of empathy. As the moral self emerges throughout adolescence, so too does the potential depth of complexity of one's friendships that are other-centered.

In the field of psychology, scholarly work on the nature and quality of friendship dates back to Harry Stack Sullivan's (1953) discussion of "chums," and his postulation that friendships represent a critical step toward social maturity, wherein the friend's well-being becomes essential to a child's sense of well-being. The initiation and maintenance of dyadic friendships in childhood and adolescence are important components of an individual's developmental trajectory. One key developmental milestone fostered by friendships is the emergence of reciprocal relations, in which participants attempt to understand one another's point of view and submit their points of view for mutual discussion. Reciprocity then fosters a mutual respect that is conducive to an intimate sharing of ideas, problems, and experiences wherein each adolescent receives critical feedback from the other. Friendships among the young have other developmental implications as well. Participation in and quality of children's friendship contribute to social adjustment and well-being over and above general acceptance by their peers. The developmental significance of friendship has also emerged in that positive friendships have been found to ameliorate loneliness and correlate with elevated levels of self-esteem and school adaptation (Bukowski, Newcomb, & Hartup, 1996).

While in childhood, friendships revolve more around shared activities and interests, by adolescence—and the concomitant emergence of one's perspective-taking ability—friendships begin to center more on mutual support, trust, and self-disclosure. Moreover, beyond shared interests, friends are attracted by jointly held attitudes, beliefs, and values. Two important characteristics of friendships are intimacy and similarity. Intimacy in friendship is described as the sharing of private thoughts, feelings, and problems through consistent and repeated self-disclosure. Girls, in particular, often cite the high levels of intimacy and faithfulness that they may share among a small number of close friends. Boys, while endorsing friendship loyalty, face more gender constraints about expressing private feelings or demonstrating vulnerability. The other prominent characteristic of adolescent friendships is similarity. Similarity often pervades friendships—in terms of sex, age, race, ethnicity, and personality characteristics. Friends typically share common educational aspirations, attitudes toward family closeness, orientations to school engagement, and tastes in fashion, music, and recreational activities.

Gottman and Parker (1987) outlined six functions of adolescent friendships: companionship, stimulation, physical support, ego support, social comparison, and intimacy/affection. Friends provide companionship by engaging in activities together and simply spending time in joint interests. Friendships are stimulating in that friends provide one another with new information, amusement, or provocative discussion. Physical support is another function of friendships in that friends often support one another through the sharing of resources, time, and aid. Friends provide ego support: a consistent expectation of encouragement and feedback that helps to provide an external view of oneself as competent and well functioning. Friendships create a means for social comparison—a lens through which individuals can compare, contrast, and situate themselves in the broader social world. Last, through self-disclosure and reciprocal sharing, friendships provide opportunities for intimacy and affection in the context of a warm, caring relationship.

Friendships—developmentally established and refined in youth—are important into adulthood and throughout the life span. Young adults, through education, work opportunities, and geographic mobility, often leave family and established social networks and must redevelop close contacts. Same sex and cross-gender friendships continue throughout middle adulthood and, although variable, are sustained through marriage, parenthood, and career development. Gerontologists confirm the salutary effects of friendships and social relationships in late adulthood, noting the increased health and longevity of the socially engaged versus the socially isolated.

***Further Reading:*** Bukowski, W.M., Newcomb, A.F., & Hartup, W.W. (Vol. Eds.). (1996). *The company they keep: Friendship in childhood and adolescence.* New York: Cambridge University Press. Gottman, J.M., & J.G. Parker (Eds.). (1987). *Conversations with friends.* New York: Cambridge University Press. Sullivan, H.S. (1953). *The interpersonal theory of psychiatry.* New York: W.W. Norton.

*James M. Frabutt*

# G

## Gender Issues

Gender issues is a broad sweeping concept that engages moral educators in critical discussion about competing ideologies among social theorists and the practical implications of these differences for men's and women's lives. Some feminist scholars focus primarily on gender inequality as a patriarchal tool to oppress women, while others argue that gender differences are primarily social constructs that function as mediators of social relations between men and women (Robinson, 1998). However, there is general agreement regarding the importance of several themes that have emerged in the context of gender issues, including, but not limited to, questions about reproductive rights, sexual discrimination, sexual objectification, patriarchy, pornography, and gender stereotyping.

In consideration of the implications for moral education, a conceptual framework of "gender issues" represents a diverse collection of concerns that are largely motivated by, but not limited to, the experiences of women. Examples of some of these concerns are related to the division of labor between men and women, the social stigmas attached to women's bodies, the perception of political inequality in power structures, and the perception of inequalities in legal representation, particularly in instances of domestic violence and sexual harassment.

There are also debates between theorists such as Carol Gilligan, on the one hand, who believe that there are important gender differences between the sexes that should not be discounted, and those like Nadine Strossen who believe that there are no essential gender differences between the sexes and that the roles observed in society are due to social conditioning. Furthermore, there is still considerable debate among natural scientists and social scientists as to whether psychological gender differences between men and women are fundamentally rooted in biology. Some scientists attribute many observed gender differences in men's and women's behavior to biological differences between the sexes, while others argue for a stronger focus on the effects of socialization in discerning the meaningfulness of masculine and feminine gender roles.

Many scholars argue that gender issues are essentially connected to the social constructs of race, sexuality, and social class (Conboy, Medina, & Stanbury, 1998). For example, the prevalence of violence against homosexual men in Western society and the practice of female genital cutting in Africa are often pointed to as expressions of cultural bias that oppress both men and women because of their gendered roles as masculine or feminine persons. Other theorists have suggested that the oppression of persons based on their gender identification is rooted more in economic terms than in race or sex. *A Vindication of the Rights of Woman,* written by Mary Wollstonecraft in 1792, remains one of the earliest works in Western philosophy to fully explore gender issues. Some 80 years later, John Stuart Mill wrote *The Subjection of Women* (1869) in which he claimed that the subordination of one sex to the other is "one of the chief hindrances of human improvement." Nonetheless, it would take several more decades before women received the right to vote in political elections.

When addressing gender issues, some theorists question not only the relationship between men and women, but the very meaning of the labels of male/masculine and female/feminine as used in our society (Conboy, Medina, & Stanbury, 1998). Some argue that gender roles and gender identity are themselves social constructs promoted by heteronormativity (Ayim, 1998; Wajcman, 1998). For these theorists, our concern with gender issues should primarily address the means to the liberation of both men and women from the oppressions of racism and divisions in social class.

A more recent gender issue for English speaking theorists has surrounded the use of gender-neutral language. Proponents of gender inclusive language seek to replace the traditional male pronoun with gender-neutral pronouns and to replace words such as "mankind" with "humanity." The need for gender neutrality in language is felt most strongly by those theorists who believe that the English language is imbued with sexism. They argue that the traditional use of the male pronoun as a placeholder for both men and women has prejudicially impacted the perceptions of reality. Thus, for example, "the student must place his exam on the desk" may sound only trivially biased; however, when children (both male and female) are constantly exposed to only the use of the male pronoun in every instance, then the continuous repetitions have the potential to alter the child's perception of reality with respect to his or her own gender identity.

Whatever focus scholars choose to further clarify the role of gender in the twenty-first century, there are some alarming statistics regarding gender inequalities that still remain in place globally. For example, according to the *United Nations Human Development Report 2004: Section 28, Gender, Work, Burden, and Time Allocation,* women work much longer on average than men; as much as 80 percent more when both paid employment and unpaid household tasks are accounted for as work hours. Even though women made up 49.5 percent of the world's population in 2004, they owned only one percent of the world's wealth, and earned only 10 percent of the world's wage income. The 2004 United Nations report also confirmed that women are grossly underrepresented in all of the world's major legislative bodies, with the 2004 average being just under 9 percent among both elected and appointed legislative officials. While proponents of gender equality have made tremendous gains in the past century, it is clear that social and economic issues related to gender remain important topics for critical discussion.

***Further Reading:*** Ayim, M.N. (1998). *The moral parameters of good talk: A feminist analysis.* Ontario, Canada: Wilfrid Laurier University Press. Addelson, K.P. (1991). *Impure thoughts: Essays on philosophy, feminism, and ethics.* Philadelphia, PA: Temple University Press. Conboy, K., Medina, N., & Stanbury, S. (Eds.). (1998). *Writing on the body: Female embodiment and feminist theory.* New York: Columbia University Press. Robinson, F. (1998). *Globalizing care: Feminist theory, ethics and international relations.* Boulder, CO: Westview Press. Wajcman, J. (1998).

*Managing like a man: Women and men in corporate management.* University Park, PA: Penn State University Press.

*Monalisa M. Mullins*

## Gilligan, Carol

Carol Gilligan was born on November 28, 1936, in New York City. She graduated with highest honors from Swarthmore College in 1958, and earned her doctorate in social psychology from Harvard in 1964. Gilligan remained at Harvard and worked with renowned psychologist Erik Erikson until 1970, when she became a research assistant for Lawrence Kohlberg. She was a founding member of the collaborative Harvard Project on Women's Psychology, a project that unites the psychological study of women with the study of young girl's development. She was awarded tenure as a full professor at the Harvard Graduate School of Education in 1986, where she taught courses in human development and educational psychology. In 1992 Gilligan was invited to teach at the University of Cambridge in England as a Pitt Professor of American History and Institutions, and in 1997 she was appointed as the first Patricia Albjerg Graham Chair in Gender Studies at the Harvard Graduate School of Education. After more than 30 years at Harvard, she is currently a professor at New York University. The recipient of numerous awards, in 1992 Gilligan was given the prestigious Grawemeyer Award in Education. She was named one of *Time* Magazine's 25 most influential people in 1996, and in 1997 she received the Heinz Award for knowledge of the human condition and for her challenges to earlier assumptions in social and cognitive psychology regarding what it means to be a human.

Gilligan's most influential work remains *In a Different Voice* (1982) in which she criticized Kohlberg's theory of moral development, which was based on Jean Piaget's groundbreaking work in child psychology. Gilligan's criticism specifically targeted the ways in which Kohlberg's theory seemed to discredit the responses of young girls who had been interviewed in his research studies at Harvard. She suggested that Kohlberg's interpretations of the female subjects' responses pointed to inadequacies in his theory of moral development (Belenky et al., 1996), and she pioneered a new psychology for women by rethinking the meaning of self, selfishness, and caring for others. In her research she asked four questions about women's voices: who is speaking, in what body, telling what story, and in what cultural framework is the story presented? Gilligan suggested that Kohlberg's standards for measuring moral development were not appropriate measures for women because women reason about morality in ways that are significantly different from that of men (Hekman, 1995).

Kohlberg's studies had demonstrated that female solutions to hypothetical moral dilemmas were "weak" when compared to the solutions offered by the male subjects in the studies. Gilligan rejected this conclusion and suggested that women reason about moral issues from a different conceptual framework, namely, an ethic of care framework. Her theory about this alternative way of thinking about morality has had far-reaching consequences for character education curricula in K–12 programs of study (Hill & Rothblum, 1998). The central claim that Gilligan makes is that men and women view relationships differently, and that the differences are significant with respect to moral reasoning.

Gilligan produces her own stage theory of moral development for women. Like Kohlberg's, it has three major divisions: Kohlberg's theory of moral development was primarily based on Piaget's cognitive developmental model. Gilligan's theory is based instead on an adaptation of Freud's model for ego development. Her nod to psychoanalysis was influenced by her understanding of Nancy Chodorow's work in Neo-Freudian psychology. Gilligan retained the three stages of moral development that Kohlberg had also elucidated: preconventional, conventional, and postconventional. But for Gilligan, the movement from one stage to the next was the result of changes in one's sense of self rather than in changes in cognitive capability (as was the case for both Kohlberg and Piaget's theories).

On her view, women are not inferior to men in their capacity to reason about moral issues; rather, they reason differently than men. According to Gilligan, women focus more on connections with others and building relationships among people. This alternative moral reasoning model is what she means by "an ethic of care," which she contrasted with an ethic of justice (as associated with Kohlberg's model). Gilligan's ethic of care moral theory is contrasted with moral theory based on an abstract theory of rights, justice, and impartiality, and she reasoned that the latter model is more often identified with the experiences of men than with women. Because Kohlberg's studies were grounded in assumptions based on this deontological justice and rights perspective, the interview responses of the male research subjects had appeared to be "stronger" than the responses of the females. By contrast, Gilligan's alternative perspective stressed a moral framework based on nurturance and concern for others. This ethic of care model emphasized the priority for relationships and connections between people.

There has been criticism of Gilligan's work, particularly from feminist theorist Christina Hoff Sommers (2001) who disagrees with Gilligan's argument that women and men have different moral voices. Sommers views Gilligan's work as "an anti-male agenda" that only serves to widen the gap in understanding between men and women in our society. In Gilligan's defense, she has stated unequivocally that the differences she notes in her work were not grounded in judgments of inferiority or superiority of either view. Gilligan's ethic of care moral framework suggested that nurturance and responsibility for others is just as valuable as an ethic of justice and rights. But for Gilligan, the justice and the care perspectives of morality are both necessary for human survival, and neither is superior to the other nor more or less mature.

However, many psychologists now disagree with the claim that men and women differ in their moral reasoning to the extent that Gilligan outlines. Several studies have found that both men and women use both an ethic of care perspective in their moral reasoning and an ethic of rights and justice. Some have also questioned the validity of some of Gilligan's findings based on her interview method of research (Sommers, 2001). Nonetheless, her book *In a Different Voice* has had a tremendous impact on subsequent research in the fields of gender studies, moral theory, and developmental psychology.

*Further Reading:* Belenky, M., Clinchy, B., Goldberger, N., & Tarule, J. (1996). *Women's ways of knowing: The development of self, voice, and mind.* New York: HarperCollins. Gilligan, C. (1982). *In a different voice: Psychological theory and women's development.* Cambridge, MA: Harvard University Press. Hekman, S.J. (1995). *Moral voices, moral selves: Carol Gilligan and feminist moral theory.* University Park, PA: Penn State University Press. Hill, M., & Rothblum, E.D. (Eds.). (1998). *Learning from our mistakes: Difficulties and failure in feminist therapy.* Ontario, Canada: Haworth Press. Sommers, C.H. (2001). *The war against boys: How misguided feminism is harming our young men.* New York: Simon and Schuster.

*Monalisa M. Mullins*

## Golden Rule

There may be no more prominent rule of thumb for being ethical than "do unto others as you would have them do unto you." Many have been suckled on this moral formula at home and in school across centuries and cultures. It is the first principle of fair-mindedness that undergirds mutual respect. Coincidentally, the major untraditional approach to American moral education for several decades stands on the same rationale. This "cognitive-developmental" approach recommends stimulating moral problem-solving abilities in children through moral-dilemma discussions in class. It urges the creation of democratic "just communities" in schools, and even prisons, where mutual respect is standard practice. Here the golden rule is seen as the foundation of democratic process—a recognition of the equal inherent dignity of each individual with fair co-operation and mutual aid as its chief implications.

In Western culture, the golden rule not only has marked the essence of fair play, but of love. Agape, the Christian notion of unconditional love, derives its commonsense source from this rule. Jesus's apparent statement of the rule merely echoes passages in Leviticus, the second book of the Hebrew Torah. Though its gold never shined through in Jewish Law as brightly as the later Decalogue or Ten Commandments did, no less a Jewish scholar than Hillel declared, "That which is hurtful to thee, do not to thy neighbor. This is the whole [Jewish] doctrine. The rest is commentary."

Notice Hillel's emphasis on the negative or restraint cast of this rule—Do *not* do unto others as one would *not* do unto oneself" is its generalized form. Harm or hurtfulness is its defining content. Both this "Do not" and the more modern "Do unto" version of the golden rule mark the central teaching of Confucianism. It is explicitly stated in the only writing of Confucius, the *Analects* (notes). And it was elaborated by later Confucians as Chung-Shu, "The Measuring Square." This principle had a righteous component (li)—involving adherence to conventional duties and practices, and a love component (Yi), which is often translated as "human-heartedness" or compassion.

The latter component suggests that ethics is based in empathy, not just proper behavior. To treat people well involves first putting oneself in their mental perspective. Here one feels how others treat them with the feelings or reactions the other has. Then one expresses the concern felt oneself when moved to embrace or avoid these reactions of the other.

None of these emotional or imaginative operations are explicitly stated in the golden rule itself. The focus is on how to treat people and one's desire or preference for certain treatment. Research shows that as children first develop moral sensibilities, they actually interpret the rule literally, in a largely egocentric, hedonic way (Kohlberg, 1971). To wit: if I like a certain way of being treated, I can treat others that way. This leads to crucial misinterpretations. If I do not mind getting into fights, I can pick fights with others. If I do not mind waiting around for someone, I need not show up on time for them.

But mature interpretations of the principle, in every tradition, stresses other-directedess —not putting oneself literally in the other's place but occupying their perspective as they experience it. "As you would have them do" is interpreted, "as it is sensible for someone in that situation to feel, transcending personal likes or dislikes." The gold in the golden rule is not personal tastes and preferences, nor using oneself as a model for how others feel or should feel. The aspiration is toward the universal, a rule of the human heart and mind that recognizes our equality to each other, both in our commonalities and differences from each other.

In key respects, the golden rule bids us to treat each other the way people would choose to be treated and should choose to be treated given the merited treatment coming to them as a person of worth and dignity with certain basic needs and interests common to all people. This is how the philosopher Immanuel Kant rendered the rule. Paraphrasing Kant's Categorical Imperative, "Act always so that you treat humanity or personhood—whether in oneself or in others—as an end in/to itself, possessing the dignity of self-determination." Always treat others, that is, in a way respectful of their legitimate will and reasonable choices in a community of mutual respect for individual choice. Put in the more typical "universalizability" form, "Act so that anyone interacting with you or among themselves could choose the rationale of your action as a sensible and shared basis for mutual interaction." Despite the structural insight of this logic, the method of cognitive role taking and process of empathy with which Confucius and others bid us apply it is left out of Kant. It is left out of the democratic, social-contract thinking that rose from Kant as well, against focusing on how to act toward people, not how to express one's heartfelt understanding of their experience and perspective.

The likelihood that the gold in the golden rule is about universalizing empathy is of first importance to moral education. It defines an educational target that does not involve rules at all—not internalizing them or learning to apply them. It foregoes anything like a code of conduct or outer conformance to it in one's behavior. One cannot successfully simulate the expressive reactions to empathic feelings by plying one's understanding of equal treatment. Much could such simulations show the genuineness needed for moral action. They would not express respect, but mimic its symptoms. And it is the expression of respect that makes for actual respect—ethical respect.

If the golden rule is about empathy and perspective-taking, students must learn these complex emotional and cognitive skills to catch its spirit. It bids us to promote interpersonal sensitivity and social skills above all, along with emotional and imaginative intelligence perhaps. Distinctly moral education, as typically conceived, is less germane. We must focus students on integrating these two complex capacities of empathy and perspective taking, a significant but overlooked challenge. The challenge is comparable to integrating the great plurality of moral virtues within one's personal character, then expressing them in proper selective combinations when taking any particular action. (Character education, like virtue ethics, has yet to face that challenge seriously.)

Great imagination is for both capacities, emotional imagination most of all. After all, empathy does not really mean feeling other's feelings, spontaneously or otherwise, but identifying with them. And that means fabricating or recreating them in one's heart and mind—raising a serious problem of accuracy. (This is why we can have empathy with fictional characters or people long dead, and debate over who really understands how they might have felt.) Learning to truly adopt someone's cognitive perspective, outlook, or viewpoint is key to "getting the feel" here. Learning to tailor empathic feelings to context is another difficult skill to teach and master, requiring a great deal of experience, self-observation, and monitoring. We must also learn to read others' reactions to our empathic attempts, gaining needed feedback on whether we captured their experience just right, or instead read our own feeling and outlook into their situation. This sort of projection is a typical shortfall in exercising the needed moral skills and compassionate abilities.

Perspective taking often includes role taking, and vice versa. Again conceptual and imaginative skills are required to master them, along with long practice in varied contexts. A perspective is not just a system of beliefs that can be learned like information. A host of subtle attitudes intermix with the beliefs involved, including prejudices, worries, and implicit expectations. There is a "feel" to be gotten when trying to understand and occupy someone's "mental space" and "orientation," when trying to "get in their head." Consider how difficult it is even to imagine how matters look from a certain role that someone is occupying, especially if we have never occupied a similar one. If he/she is a different type of person from us, views certain roles very differently due to upbringing or peculiarities of personal experience, he/she might as well be occupying a different role than seems the case, given the problem of identifying with him/her.

The upshot here is that heeding the golden rule may not involve "Doing unto" anyone at all, primarily. It may be about "walking a mile in their moccasins" then expressing how that makes us feel and react.

**Further Reading:**

Allen, C. (1996). What is wrong with the golden rule? *Information Society, 12,* 175–187.

Hare, R.M. (1975). Abortion and the golden rule. *Philosophy and Public Affairs, 4*(3), 201–222.

*Bill Puka*

## Good Life

"The Good Life" is the phrase commonly used to characterize or describe a human life that is full, satisfying, and happy. However, these three terms are not exact synonyms. A *full* life is, presumably, a busy one, or at least one that is rich, deep, and varied. A *satisfying* life, on the other hand, could be very quiet and simple, if those are the features that make a person living such a life contented. The same point holds for a *happy* life, except that happiness seems to be a stronger notion than simply contentment as well as more emotionally charged. Still other notions are associated with the phrase "Good Life," such as being worthwhile ("a life worth living"), sublime or holy or noble ("beatitude"), or at the other extreme, just very enjoyable ("fun"). In what follows, the term "happiness" serves as the umbrella concept for all these notions, since it provides the most general answer to questions such as "What life should I live?" and "How can life be developed in the fullest sense?"

Taken in this general sense, the idea of happiness has always played a significant role in the Western philosophical tradition. The ancient Greek and Roman philosophers recognized happiness as the supreme and final end of man and claimed that it could be attained through reason (Socrates, Plato, and Aristotle), through pleasure (epicureans and hedonists), and also through dominion over pain and the passions (the Stoics). Centuries later classical modern philosophers proposed ideas of happiness that were even more paradoxical: that higher forms of happiness could be achieved by privileging duty over happiness in the usual senses (Kant) or by altruistically privileging the happiness of others over one's own welfare (the Utilitarians).

### Happiness through Reason

For Socrates and Plato, happiness consisted in moral virtue, not pleasure. "The happy are happy because they possess justice and temperance, and the unhappy, are so because they possess evil," Plato wrote in the *Gorgias* (508b). For Aristotle, however, moral virtue was only one part of the good life. He offered a formal and two material definitions for happiness that scholars have struggled to reconcile. Formally, happiness was simply that which all men seek. Materially, it was either the pursuit of the highest good, namely wisdom, or else a bundle of activities each of which is valuable for its own sake as well as instrumental to the pursuit of wisdom. The Greek word that he used, *eudaimonia*, literally means "to have a good spirit" and is variously translated into English as "living well" and "human flourishing" as well as—most commonly—"happiness."

### Happiness through Pleasure

Epicurus and other hedonist philosophers understood the good life as the search for pleasure, but insisted that the search be carried out under the guidance of reason. We should, they thought, limit our desires whenever possible and prefer the pleasures of the mind to those of the body.

### Happiness through Domination of Pain and the Passions

Roman Stoic philosophers such as Marcus Aurelius retrieved from early Greek philosophy an important ethical ideal for Western culture, according to which the concept of the good life was reduced to the absence of pain, disquiet, and frustration. Moral perfection for the Stoic is *apatheia,* which is to say the absence of passion. It is interesting to note that a few centuries earlier Buddhist philosophy had developed a similar idea, according to which the solution to the problem of suffering was to eliminate all desire from one's life.

### Happiness through Duty

In modern times Kant developed a new moral paradigm in which happiness was subordinated to duty. One should do one's duty not in order to bring happiness to oneself or others, but to prescribe laws for ourselves that express the autonomy of the will. For Kant and those inspired by him, the functional equivalent of happiness is the exercise of one's free will.

### Happiness through Altruism

Inspired by Jean-Jacques Rousseau's idea of the common will, classical modern philosophers such as A. Smith, J. Bentham, and J.S. Mill claimed that individual happiness was intrinsically linked to the happiness of others, which was formulated by the Utilitarians as "the greatest happiness for the greatest number." Contemporary versions of this idea that one achieves happiness through relations with other persons are found in the works of E. Levinas and M. Buber.

### Conclusion

The various conceptions of the good life are all attempts to answer the question, "how should we live?" Each answer has its own framework and amounts to a very particular knowledge, one that no science explains, no demonstration proves, no laboratory can verify or discover, and no diploma accredits.

*Further Reading:* Hill, T.E. (2004). *The philosophy of the good life.* Lewiston, NY: Edwin Mellen Press. Savater, F. (2002). *The questions of life.* London: Polity Press.

*Juan Gerardo Garza Treviño and Thomas Wren*

## Good Life Reasoning

Philosophers and social critics have promoted different conceptions of the good human life for some 2,600 years. Such philosophical conceptions always included, or relied entirely on models of good psychological functioning or mental health. In contrast, psychologists only recently entered the debate about the Good Life. It was not until the nineteenth century that theorists, such as Sigmund Freud, began to articulate models of mental and psychological health. These models can be understood as attempts to define (in part) a good human life. Contemporary television and the lyrics of popular songs reveal an interest in the nature of a good human life. Yet, many believe that there are as many conceptions of the Good Life as there are persons who seek it (for example, Rawls, 1971). Our research has shown, however, that although the sources of conceptions differ widely across time and culture, the number of actual views of the Good Life may be finite. Despite 2,000 years having passed between the work of the ancient philosophers and that of early psychologists, both of these groups produced some strikingly similar ideas about the Good Life. Similarly, there is dramatic commonality between the Good Life concepts of many current philosophers and the work of contemporary developmental psychologists. Finally, adults, in general, who have studied neither philosophy nor psychology, also construct similar good life concepts.

It is difficult to appreciate many of the substantial theoretical and empirical commonalities in this area between philosophical and psychological studies, as well as among developmental studies themselves. Researchers working in different disciplines and subdisciplines are often unfamiliar with one another's work. There are so many models, findings, and assertions about the development of reasoning about values, it can be difficult to see the forest for the trees. The empirical work and philosophical justification provided by investigations of good life reasoning represent an advance in understanding some core commonalities. A general, developmental model of value reasoning about the Good Life can incorporate many of these typically separate findings.

The good life reasoning model described here was initially developed through a 13-year longitudinal study of children and adults who were asked to describe not only the ideal human life, but also their ideal friendship, intimate relationship, form of work, education, and other dimensions of life. In addition, they were asked to describe the underlying reasoning that gave their idea notions value.

In addition to the developmental perspective of the good life reasoning model, traditional philosophy helped to inform the data analysis. In the initial model building of the Good Life stage model (Armon, 1984), it was found that the material adult subjects offered when describing the Good Life, particularly at higher stages, was similar to professional philosophers' views. Thus, traditional philosophies of the Good Life were used to categorize adult subjects' responses. Responses were separated as either Perfectionistic or Hedonistic. Perfectionist theories define good living as the development and expression of inherent human talents and capacities. Hedonistic theories define the Good Life as the successful acquisition and appreciation of pleasure—the ultimate intrinsic value. In Hedonism, the means to pleasure are secondary. Achieving the result, drawing pleasure from an object or activity, is key.

This model relies primarily on the works of three perfectionists, Aristotle, Spinoza, and Dewey, and two hedonists, Epicurus and Mill. Though these are leading theorists in their persuasions, others could have been chosen to exemplify these ethical views.

In addition to the philosophical orientations, the ethical nature of good-life judgments were differentiated. The domain of the Good Life is conceptualized as broad, including the moral good (e.g., ethical dimensions of persons, relationships) and nonmoral good (for example, nonmoral aspects of work, family, community, and objects). Again, categories were developed from accepted philosophical works. The first category consists of judgment of the moral good, including both aretaic judgments (judgments of character, the good person) and judgments of welfare consequences, such as the consequences of actions taken on moral motives. The former resides in the person and is concerned with the moral worth of individuals, or traits of character. The latter may appear nonmoral, such as a group of children receiving an enriched education. It becomes a morally good consequence, however, if it occurred as a result of moral motives. The second category is intrinsic, nonmoral good, and contains judgments about generally accepted human values, for example, knowledge, sociality, or artistic expression, which in themselves are nonmoral. The final category is extrinsic, nonmoral good, which contains judgments about "goods" that people value because of what they bring or do, not because of what they are in themselves. This category would include cars, pencils, or houses. These are sometimes referred to as "means values" or "instrumental values."

After the first longitudinal study, the good life stage model was tested with a number of other groups, particularly adults. The first stage begins in early childhood with an egocentric conception of the Good Life derived primarily from pleasure-seeking fantasy (for example, "the Good Life is having my birthday party every day"), moves through a conventional social role orientation (for example, "the Good Life is being a good husband and enjoying my family"), and culminates with a complex conception of the Good Life that encompasses complex criteria, including a necessary societal dimension ("the Good Life is the worthy life. It is the integrated life—bringing the various facets of experience into balance with my interests and talents. It is also constructed in a social context. To be good, it must move the society forward in some way"). The stages are most easily observed in individuals' constructions of their evaluative criteria, that is, the standards the subject uses to decide whether a person, idea, state, objective, or activity is good.

The longitudinal and cross-sectional data also supported the invariant sequence stage model of reasoning about the Good Life. Many subjects, including adults, demonstrated development (stage change) during the longitudinal study and, when they did, it was always toward the next stage in the sequence. The Good Life Scoring Manual, developed in 1984, continues to demonstrate high inter-rater and test-retest reliability. Newer forms of analyses, for example, Rasch, also continue support for the model. The general findings provide robust support for a structural-developmental model of value reasoning about the Good Life.

A general model of value reasoning about the Good Life will tell only a part of the story of human valuing. Nevertheless, it goes beyond the value relativism and subjectivism so prevalent in contemporary society in general and in psychology in particular. From homelessness to adolescent homicide, contemporary social problems are, in part, a consequence of adult value reasoning. A stage model of value reasoning about the Good Life can inform our understanding as to some of the origins of such problems and contribute to education and intervention models that attempt to address them.

*Further Reading:* Armon, C. (1984). Ideals of the good life and moral judgment: a cross-sectional/longitudinal study of evaluative reasoning in children and adults. *Moral Education Forum, 9*(2). Armon, C., & Dawson, T. (2004). A longitudinal study of adult value reasoning about the good life. In J. Demick (Ed.), *Handbook of adult development*. New York: Plenum. Rawls, J. (1971). *A theory of justice*. Cambridge, MA: Belknap Press.

*Cheryl Armon*

## Goodlad, John I.

John Goodlad is one of the most influential educational researchers and theorists of his time. He is a past president of the American Educational Research Association and received the Association's prestigious award for "Distinguished Research" in 1993. A courageous advocate of school reform, a champion of the teaching profession, and a staunch proponent for moral and civic education, he has been the conscience of public education for the past 20 years.

One of two sons born to William James and Mary (Inkster) Goodlad in British Columbia in 1917, John I. Goodlad grew up during the Great Depression. Identifying himself and his family as part of the low economic class, Goodlad's early education took place in a small, six-room school. Not expected to pursue university studies, he completed a fifth year of high school and one year of normal school so that he could earn a provisional teaching certificate in elementary education. Later he earned a permanent teaching certificate after completing summer school for two years. He continued his education by attending summer sessions and taking correspondence courses, and earned his bachelor's and master's degrees at the University of British Columbia. Eventually Goodlad moved to the United States, completed work for a doctoral degree, and was awarded a Ph.D. from the University of Chicago.

Goodlad began his teaching career in a one-room school in Vancouver. During his professional career in education, he held numerous positions as principal, teacher educator, curriculum coordinator, and dean. He is a founder of the Center for Educational Renewal at the University of Washington and is currently professor emeritus and president of the Institute for Educational Inquiry there.

Goodlad is credited with writing close to 200 articles in professional journals and encyclopedias, and 100 books singularly and collaboratively, including the celebrated *A Place Called School* (one of the largest studies of schools ever conducted and a winner of the Outstanding Writing Award from the American Association of Colleges for Teacher Education), *Teachers for Our Nation's Schools,* and *In Praise of Education*. More recent books include *Education for Everyone: Agenda for Education in a Democracy,* written with Corinne Mantle-Bromley and Stephen J. Goodlad; *The Teaching Career,* coedited with Timothy J. McMannon, and *Romances with Schools: A Life of Education*.

Goodlad espouses the idea that while the individual school is the key unit for change in the improvement of the education of its students, it cannot do everything by itself. He and his colleagues have proposed that schools form networks. In "The Twelve Major Goals for American Schools" (1979), Goodlad's vision for educational reform includes fostering the mastery of fundamental skills for participation in the activities of society and promoting a commitment to truth, moral integrity, and moral conduct (Goodlad, 1976). The abstract provided for his article entitled, "One Narrative in Changing Contexts" (1999), captures the moral imperative central to Goodlad's thought: "It is not enough to simply inquire into the conditions of schooling. . . . To improve education, people must become increasingly aware of their connections and responsibilities to human and natural contexts" (p. i).

Goodlad began work with the Center for Educational Renewal in 1985 with the articulation of an Agenda for Education in a Democracy. Therein it is stated that better schools require better teachers, but better teachers require better teacher preparation programs heavily dependent on early and often practical experiences in the classroom. Originally the Agenda included 19 postulates on conditions necessary for healthy and vigorous teacher education programs. In 1992 Goodlad established the Institute for Educational Inquiry to work together with the Center for Educational Renewal on the Agenda. A twentieth postulate, focusing on teacher retention, was added and is discussed in Goodlad, Mantle-Bromley, and Goodlad's 2004 publication of *Education for Everyone: Agenda for Education in a Democracy.*

**Further Reading:** Goodlad, J.I. (1976). *Facing the future: Issues in education and schooling.* New York: McGraw-Hill. Goodlad, J.I. (1977). *In praise of education.* New York: Teachers College Press. Goodlad, J.I. (1994). *Educational renewal: Better teachers, better schools.* San Francisco: Jossey-Bass. Goodlad, J.I. (1999). One narrative in changing contexts. *Journal of Thought, 34*(4), 97–107. Goodlad, J.I. (2004). *A place called school: Twentieth anniversary edition.* New York: McGraw-Hill. Goodlad, J.I., Mantle-Bromley, C., & Goodlad, S.J. (2004). *Education for everyone: Agenda for education in a democracy.* San Francisco: Jossey-Bass. Goodlad, J.I., Soder, R., & Sirotnik, K.A. (1990). *The moral dimensions of teaching.* San Francisco: Jossey-Bass.

*Kathleen Roney*

# H

## Habituation

As its "-ion" suffix suggests, the word "habituation" refers to the process by which habits are formed. But since there are different sorts of habits, it is reasonable to assume that they are formed in different ways. There are at least four sorts of habits: physiological, motor, psychological, and moral. In the first three cases, the degree of self-consciousness decreases as the habit becomes established, so that at the end of the habituation process one is able to engage in the relevant activity "without thinking about it," except in the most peripheral sense. (1) Physiological habituation is the increasingly regular response to repeated stimulants, which over time not only becomes automatic but also creates an "acquired need" for the stimulus itself (for example, addiction). (2) Unlike the relatively passive process of habituation that forms the first sort of habits, the formation of motor habits—which are skills involving mastery of a complex organization of movements— consists in repeated practice that does not necessarily create an acquired need for more stimulation or for exercising the skill in question (for example, riding a bicycle). (3) The third sort of habituation, which creates psychological habits, involves both acquired needs and mastery skills: one feels restless if unable to perform habitual actions even though these habits are not identical with the skills with which they are associated (for example, keeping a tidy workplace). (4) The fourth sort of habituation, which produces moral habits or virtues, corresponds to what in contemporary educational contexts is often called "character education," though there is no single sense in which the latter term is used. The rest of this article focuses on this fourth category.

### Ethics as Habituation

The Greek word *ethos,* from which our word "ethics" is derived, is an inherently social concept, referring to a group's customs or, considered collectively, its habits and by extension the social expectations in terms of which standards of behavior are calibrated. As for the word "habit" and its modern cognates, the root meaning is from the Latin words *habito* and *habitation,* which originally had the sense of settling oneself in a physical place or settling into a particular way of life. Thus, it is not surprising that when the scholastic philosophers of the Middle Ages discovered Aristotle's long-lost *Nicomachean Ethics* and other works, they would use the word *habitus* to translate his Greek word *hexis,* that is, the settled attitude or disposition that a thing or person has as one of its enduring qualities. But Aristotle's *hexis* is much different from the contemporary notion of habit. It is an active tendency, a state of readiness in which a human being must hold itself. Its effect is to enhance a consciousness of what he or she is doing, not to reduce it.

For this reason it is best to read Aristotle's discussions of moral habituation reflexively, as the specifically human action of making oneself develop a particular way of living, one that is congruent with the norms and traditions of one's society as well as with the more general criteria of rationality as such. It is true that in his discussions of virtue acquisition Aristotle laid great emphasis on the power of example and the importance of repeated practice, but it would be wrong to link his view too closely with the recent social learning literature on modeling, imitation, and behavior shaping. For Aristotelians interested in character formation it is not enough that a person has had a good upbringing, unless it included conscious self-regulation. In other words, moral learners must make themselves part of the habituation process, consciously making themselves do the right thing until virtuous activity becomes "second nature."

### Character and Cross-Situational Consistency

In approaches to moral education inspired by the Aristotelian tradition, what is important is primarily what sort of person one is, and only secondarily what sort of acts one does. But this contrast should not be pushed too hard, since it is also part of both traditions that good character and good deeds are correlated in real life, such that one cannot have one without the other. Which is logically or psychologically prior is a matter of debate, which over the centuries has had many intermediate and extreme positions ranging from Thomas Aquinas's essentialist natural law theory to Jean-Paul Sartre's existentialism. However, in recent years psychologists such as Walter Mischel, along with a few philosophers such as Gilbert Harman, have called into question the very ideas of character and character traits. Citing experiments in social psychology that seem to show that we tend to react to the same situations in the same way, regardless of what personality traits —including the so-called moral virtues—we are supposed to have, they argue that moral behavior is most reliably produced by changing the features of a situation in which people find themselves, rather than changing their alleged characters by various habit formation strategies. Buried within this critique is the unexamined assumption that habituation leading to moral virtue is no different from the third type of habituation discussed at the outset of this article and only marginally different from the first and second ones. There is no recognition of the possibility that a moral habit might include, as an integral part of its exercise, the essentially cognitive ability to interpret situations in specific moral terms.

### Habituation as Habitat

In addition to the Aristotelian, Kantian, and social learning theory approaches already mentioned, another conception of (moral) habituation has recently received much attention in the Spanish-speaking world. Playing on the shared meaning of "being settled" associated with words such as "habit" and "habitat," philosophers such as Xavier Zubiri have argued that human beings without a functioning morality are not in possession of their true selves: they stand outside themselves and are metaphysically as well as mentally unbalanced. If to habituate is to accustom oneself to doing things in a certain way and for a concrete moral reason or a specific code of values, then one avoids habituation only at great spiritual loss and demoralization (loss of morality). This view is conservative in the metaphysical sense that habituation maintains a person's very being. It understands habituation as a constant and dynamic act, one that forms part of the human psyche and by its very exercise renders moral consciousness capable of self-renewal.

*Further Reading:* Aristotle. (1999). *Nicomachean ethics* (Terence Irwin, Trans.). Indianapolis: Hackett Publishing. Harman, G. (2000). The nonexistence of character traits. *Proceedings of the Aristotelian Society, 100,* 223–26. Mischel, W. (1968). *Personality and assessment.* New York: Wiley. Zubiri, X. (1986). *Sobre el hombre.* Madrid: Alianza.

*Thomas Wren and Adán Pérez-Treviño*


## Hartshorne, Hugh

Hugh Hartshorne (November 13, 1885–December 13, 1967) was co-director with Mark A. May of the Character Education Inquiry, a massive research study sponsored by the Institute for Social and Religious Research and the Religious Education Association. (For more on the Character Education Inquiry, see the entry at May, Mark A.) Prior to his co-direction of that study, Hartshorne was a pioneer in the development of large-scale social-psychological research studies, and specifically noted for applying these tools to religious education. Hartshorne received his bachelor's degree in 1907 from Amherst and his Ph.D. in 1913 in education from Columbia University. He was also ordained in 1913 as a congregational minister. A follower of George Albert Coe, Hartshorne was active in the Religious Education Association from its founding in 1903 until the 1930s, when he served as its president (Schmidt, 1983). Hartshorne was a research associate at Teachers College during the Character Education Inquiry, and in 1929 became a research associate in religion at Yale University. In 1951, he was appointed as a professor of the psychology of religion at Yale. He retired in 1954.

As a liberal theologian, Hartshorne was a strong believer in the possibilities of using science to understand religion and to build a foundation for religious education, and he became a proponent of the use of progressive education methods in Sunday schools. Later, he became an advocate of enhanced training and stronger credentials for religious educators.

With Milton C. Froyd, Hartshorne conducted a study in the 1940s of the ministry of the Northern (now American) Baptist Convention, in part as an answer to May's earlier study of the ministry. Hartshorne and Froyd came to echo May's earlier conclusion that there was a considerable lack of consensus about what ministers should do and how they should be trained, caused, in part, by changing social needs.

*Further Reading:* Hartshorne, H., & May, M. (1928). *Studies in the nature of character. Vol. I: Studies in deceit.* New York: MacMillan. Hartshorne, H., & May, M., with Shuttleworth, F. K. (1930a). *Studies in the nature of character. Vol. III: Studies in the organization of character.* New York: MacMillan.

*Craig A. Cunningham*

## Health Education

Health education is any combination of planned learning experiences based on sound theories that provide individuals, groups, and communities the opportunity to acquire information and the skills needed to make quality health decisions (Report of the 2000 Joint Committee on Health Education and Promotion Terminology, 2001). Quality health education empowers individuals to adopt or maintain behaviors conducive to health. It involves not just the individual but also their support system, environment, and community. Health education should not be coercive, but, rather, should motivate the individual to voluntarily take responsibility for his/her own health. Health educators conduct needs assessments; plan, implement, evaluate, and administer health education programs; serve as a health education resource person; and communicate and advocate for health and health education.

There are many settings in which to conduct health education. These include school, community, work site, and medical care settings. Health education may have different topical emphases and configurations depending upon the setting in which it is conducted. For example, schools often implement what is called a coordinated school health program of which comprehensive school health education is one of eight components. The eight components include comprehensive school health education; a healthy school environment; school nutrition services; school health services; physical education; school counseling, psychological, and social services; family and community involvement in school health; and school site health promotion for staff (Report of the 2000 Joint Committee, 2001). These components of the school health program are most effective when they coordinate their efforts to provide consistent health messages to students, faculty, and staff.

School health education addresses a variety of health topics. Some of these topical areas have been identified by the Centers for Disease Control and Prevention as "priority areas." These priority areas are indicated by asterisks below:

- Alcohol and Other Drugs*
- Injury Prevention*
- Nutrition*
- Physical Activity*
- Family Health and Sexuality*
- Tobacco Prevention*
- Community and Environmental Health
- Mental Health
- Personal and Consumer Health

Comprehensive school health education can improve knowledge and attitudes about health issues and also teach students needed skills such as refusal skills, decision making, problem solving, and communication. National Health Education Standards for prekindergarten through grade 12 were developed by representatives of several professional health education organizations working in concert. These standards often are comprised in the content of comprehensive school health education.

Public and community health education involves health department personnel at local and state health departments, and health educators at voluntary agencies such as the American Cancer Society and the American Red Cross. Public health educators often work on objectives identified in a document called "Healthy People." "Healthy People

2010" (HP 2010) is the most recent version of this document although the Healthy People initiative has been operating for over two decades in the United States. HP 2010 presents baseline data on the current health status of the public and sets objectives for improving health in the subsequent decade. The "Healthy People 2010" document has identified the following 10 leading health indicators that are major health concerns in the United States and the focus of public health education programs:

- Physical Activity
- Overweight and Obesity
- Tobacco Use
- Substance Abuse
- Responsible Sexual Behavior
- Mental Health
- Injury and Violence
- Environmental Quality
- Immunization
- Access to Health Care

Health education in the work site setting typically includes programming for illnesses and conditions facing workers such as stress management, injury prevention, diet and exercise, and smoking cessation. While some work sites have their own health education programs on site, others hire wellness companies and consultants to conduct health education programs in work site settings. Work site health promotion has been shown to increase worker productivity and decrease employee absenteeism and turnover.

Medical care settings provide health education through patient education programs or health promotion programs. In these settings health education is often secondary or tertiary prevention after a patient has suffered ill health. These patients are typically very motivated to make behavior changes conducive to health. In recent years there has been an increase in hospitals providing wellness or health education centers to address primary prevention and promote patient health.

Health education is also a profession. Universities and colleges offer health education programs that prepare professionals to work in the field of health education. These programs often have school health, community health, or public health emphases. Many health educators earn the Certified Health Education Specialist (CHES) Credential. This entry-level credential is administered by the National Commission on Health Education Credentialing. To obtain the CHES credential, one must take approved coursework in health education and pass a national standardized test. In order to maintain the credential, a number of approved continuing education credits must be earned in a given time period.

*Further Reading:* American Association for Health Education. (2001). Report of the 2000 joint committee on health education and promotion terminology. *American Journal of Health Education, 32*(2).

*Dianne L. Kerr*

## Heteronomy

Should we do the right thing for its own sake for purely moral motives? Or is it permissible to recruit a range of motivations when taking the high road? Should we educate students to be morally idealistic? Or should we insist that they conform to basic moral norms by whatever motivational means necessary, from brainwashed fears to direct threats of punishment?

"Heteronomy" is normally used as a technical term, referring to something more distinct in our motivations. It involves taking moral ends as something conditional like our personal interests or desires. If we think our moral duty might be overridden or traded off to avoid certain costs, then we are adopting a heteronomous approach to moral obligations.

To a morally minded person, this bald representation of "moral discretion" can seem outrageous. Morality is usually considered a matter of duty and obligation that is binding to us. One should not wonder, "Do I want to be ethical in this situation, or am I feeling a bit 'gangster?'" But many of us think in this discretionary way. Many of us seem to mix our motives in a way that amounts to something similar, even when we do the right thing.

Relying on mixed motives invokes heteronomous thinking in different degrees. We feel heteronomy is acceptable so long as the ethical motivation is there, or primarily there, so long as we are merely boosting its strength through alliance with more powerful interests.

For some of us, ethics need not be pure to be ethical. What is wrong with rallying other interests in support of doing the right thing? Indeed, any other approach to being ethical seems infeasible or unnecessarily difficult. It seems overly upright and uptight, giving the temptations of immorality too much of an edge. Such approaches make moral upbringing and education too difficult a task, especially at younger ages. Distinctly moral motivations simply are not that strong in themselves, but are invoked to oppose some of the strongest desires or "temptations" we experience. This is not a fair fight. And it is no wonder then that we sink so often into moral failure—hypocrisy, selfishness, a succumbing to temptation.

Motivationally, morality is a hard sale, obliging us to do what we do not want to do. Morality is an especially hard sale in the classroom to children who think primarily in terms of personal interests rather than by reflective principles and self-chosen ideals. Not mixing motives sabotages moral education where it is needed most—where temptations in the other direction are strongest, where children live in such morally hostile environments that taking the high road is the hardest road of all.

The Christian tradition, rationalized by influential ethicists like Immanuel Kant, reserves moral credit for the pure of heart. Kantians wish morality was kept distinct as a logic, a social practice or institution, and as a set of motivations we engender in people. Why admire or see merit in someone doing what they should when they wish to do it anyway and need put in no effort, no sacrifice? Even those who have argued for identifying one's moral duties and interests (from Confucius to Mother Teresa) wish that process to arise by effortful development and choice. We must evolve gradually toward the love of being kind, and struggle with responsibility. Only this arduous path of rising above our ego desires strengthens us sufficiently for the real moral work of aiding the poor and comforting the forlorn and afflicted. Indeed, this tradition sees the ideal of moral education and development as nurturing a zeal for doing good—being wildly attracted to goodness in all its forms and as the passion of one's life. Many religious see God this way, as simply the embodiment of goodness or love. They urge us to love as the highest moral ideal, spreading it wherever possible.

But purity of heart, paradoxically, runs the risk of heteronomy in these traditions. Consider a tortured soul like St. Francis, by contrast, who even at the moment of death fended off praise of his virtue by noting that his formidable sex drive might still cause him to fornicate before facing his Final Judgment. This is where credit should go most—to the tortured soul who does the right thing for no other reason than it is right, and against all odds. Next best may come the ordinary person who chooses to resist temptation time and time each day, doing his duty, doing the right thing, when it feels like something he'd sooner avoid. The purehearted may go too far, struggling to bond with the good so strongly that they bond with it, in fact, transferring their desires, passions, and lusts to it, and thereby besmirching their relationship with it.

**Further Reading:** Aune, B. (1979). *Kant's theory of morals.* Princeton, NJ: Princeton University Press. Reath, A. (2006). *Agency and autonomy in Kant's moral theory.* New York: Oxford University Press. Wood, A. (1999). *Kant's ethical thought.* New York: Cambridge University Press.

*Bill Puka*

## Hidden Curriculum

The implicit or hidden curriculum refers to those values, attitudes, and concepts that are taught and communicated by schools through the structure of the institution and the behaviors of the faculty and staff. Distinguished from the formal curriculum, the hidden curriculum is not written or articulated in an official way. Rather, it is part of the culture of the school, is the climate of the building, and is conveyed in the ordinary events of a school day.

Researchers maintain that the hidden curriculum is a function of the implicit values held by the institution as a whole. There are certain values and behaviors that people learn simply by being a part of the organization and by experiencing its normal course of operations, including daily activities, crises, or special events, as well as dealing with stress, challenges to authority, and the disposition of resources. Analyzing and evaluating both the positive and the negative aspects of the hidden curriculum is common to organizations such as schools, hospitals, social services agencies, and human resource departments.

In education, school leaders are concerned about the values implicit in classrooms and in school management. Various studies have focused on identifying the hidden curriculum in K–12 classrooms. Among those values and attitudes that students are exposed to and learn through the culture of schools are the following: athletics are more important than academics; grades are valued more than learning; troublesome behavior in school merits more attention from faculty and staff than honorable behavior; and males and females have different natural proclivities for certain subjects and sports.

What makes a value or attitude a part of the hidden curriculum is that no one directly teaches it or addresses it. It is not a part of the written, formal scope and sequence of things that are supposed to be taught in school. Rather, by the attention given to sports programs and to student athletes, for example, students learn that athletic participation is valued more than academic performance.

The existence of a hidden curriculum in schools has been a major focus of educational theorists, sociologists, and policy makers for many years. The concept is a useful tool in helping to examine the social implications of school organization, the political ramifications of the evaluating and sorting of people that schools typically provide, and the overall contributions of schools to modern culture. The presence of a hidden curriculum indicates that schools do much more than simply present knowledge and transmit facts in a neutral way. Instead, the hidden curriculum shows the overall culture of the school and helps to shed light on the sociology of education—the relationships, values, hierarchies, and biases present in complex organizations.

The hidden curriculum has prompted the question, what is the ultimate purpose of schooling? From a philosophical perspective, this question has received many answers. For example, beyond the teaching of the basic skills of literacy, ought schools provide a reinforcement of the social mores or a challenge to them? Are there assumptions about knowledge, social order, power, and ethics that are part of the hidden curriculum? Should such assumptions be protected or dismantled?

Some studies have found that schools are instrumental in preparing their students for certain arenas, often defined by their socioeconomic class. The hidden curriculum communicates that students are destined for professional occupations—health care, law, business, and politics. Classes, rules of behavior, and even extracurricular activities are ordered to this end. Other schools are more on the vocational track, teaching students via the formal and implicit curriculum that their lot is the service industry and vocational occupations (Anyon, 1980).

A strong challenge to the status quo in education is found in the school of thought known as critical pedagogy or critical theory. Critical pedagogy examines the assumptions built into the educational enterprise as currently structured and uncovers those unspoken values communicated by school structures and then enshrined by society. Paulo Freire's *Pedagogy of the Oppressed* (1972) is a foundational work in this area, helping to explain the propensity of the dominant class to make decisions and enact policies that will serve to perpetuate their dominance and the success of their offspring. Critical theory makes a strong critique of K–12 schooling in as much as schools function as a great social sorting ground, which, by use of grades, labels, and social recognition, the orderly transmission of power and the maintenance of the social order is ensured. A critical pedagogy would challenge such assumptions, help the poor and oppressed to understand why they are so, and support them in finding the knowledge, tools, and skills to overcome their oppression.

Public education has often been lauded for providing a universal experience of pro-democratic ideals for all students (Dewey, 1916). This notion has supported the idea of the common school as a great equalizer, as a place where cultural mores are modeled, taught, and transmitted. This idea, too, has received much criticism as schools come under more scrutiny for the content of the hidden curriculum (Gatto, 1992).

Religious and private schools struggle with the content of the hidden curriculum as well, but have the advantage of being able to incorporate teachings from their religious or private traditions, moral codes, and history into school life. Whatever the context, complex organizations such as schools must be attentive not only to the success of the formal curriculum but also to those unspoken values and attitudes found in the hidden curriculum.

**Further Reading:** Anyon, J. (1980). Social class and the hidden curriculum of work. *Journal of Education, 163,* 67–92. Dewey, J. (1916). *Democracy and education: An introduction to the philosophy of education.* New York: Macmillan. Freire, P. (1972). *Pedagogy of the oppressed.* New York: Penguin. Gatto, J. T. (1992). *Dumbing us down: The hidden curriculum of compulsory schooling.* Philadelphia: New Society.

*Ronald J. Nuzzi*

## Homosexuality

The concept of "homosexuality," an identity characterized by sexual attraction toward and sexual behavior among members of the same sex, is understood by scholars as a recent social construct. Throughout much of Western history, same-sex sexual behavior was not associated with any particular identity or stable erotic orientation, but rather considered an act that anyone lacking moral integrity could commit. While the quality and degree of attention it received as well as the extent to which it was regarded a moral transgression varied over time, homosexuality was largely scorned in the Western world. Current attitudes toward homosexuality, however, seem to be changing fast.

In ancient Greece, pederasty, a sexual liaison between an older and a younger male, was not entirely acceptable according to social norms, although it was regarded as a natural variation on human sexual behavior. During this period, a person who engaged in same-sex sexual behavior was not identified as "homosexual," or any other variation of sexual miscreant. Rather, a person who consistently lacked the fortitude to fend from a universal gravity toward the opposite end of the gender continuum was known as a *kinaidos,* or "scary image." The act of receptive sex was merely an example of this gender deficiency. Pederasty, in general, however, functioned not only as an indulgence of erotic desire, but an expression of love between teacher and student, where a younger man is a devoted pupil of a presumably wise and experienced mentor. As opposed to same-sex receptive behavior, same-sex penetration was, to an extent, held in esteem.

The Western moral proscription against same-sex sexual behavior might have developed with the conception of Judeo-Christian values. In line with a proposition that the first testament is not a God-given proclamation, a number of biblical scholars have proposed that early Jewish religious laws evolved from a need to establish a culture that would protect monotheism from the influence of more polytheistic cultures. That is, while Greek society, a culture of polytheism, did not decry same-sex sexual behavior as deviant, Israelites set rules about sexual behavior that would distinguish and protect them as a culture and monotheistic form of worship. Dietary restrictions are often cited as a method by which early Jews attempted to separate themselves and their people from the influence of other cultures (for example, a calf boiled in its mother's milk was a popular Greek dish at the time). This cultural insulation protected their beliefs from outside influence and held over time. Consistent with this theory, biblical passages suggesting that same-sex sexual behavior precipitated the destruction of Sodom and Gomorrah at the hands of God were developed in order to render the act of "sodomy" immoral.

It was only after the industrial revolution, the birth of the medical profession, and the field of psychiatry to follow, that homosexuality evolved to become a recognized social construct. Prior to the industrial revolution, the principal economic unit was the family, around which all social and communal life operated. A husband and wife worked primarily in the home on some entrepreneurial venture from which a means of subsistence could be generated. After the industrial revolution and the resulting urbanization of society, men and women began working in factories and urban centers. This afforded individuals social opportunities that were never before available. For example, if a man who worked outside the home was interested in sexual liaisons with other men, he could find taverns or cafes in which other men with similar interests congregated. He could build a lifestyle by participating in the social life of these locations as frequently as desired. Individuals engaging regularly in same-sex sexual behavior could now be classified on the basis of such behavior.

During the late nineteenth century, the Victorian era, a person who engaged in sodomy became a "sodomite," predecessor to the homosexual. As sexual repression was characteristic of the period, sodomy was scandalous and also illegal. A person who engaged in these acts was worthy of shame and could be subject to prosecution. The famous trial of Oscar Wilde marked the first against such a person. Witty, flamboyant, and aesthetically oriented, Wilde himself is often regarded as the epitome, if not the source of the stereotyped image of the contemporary male homosexual.

With the rise of the medical profession, the social category of "homosexual" came into being, and, absorbed into the domain of medicine, quickly became associated with pathology. While Freud himself did not consider it an illness, the field of psychiatry began to catalog homosexuality in its *Diagnostic and Statistical Manual* (*DSM*), a text outlining the taxonomy of mental disorders, from which it was not removed until 1973. Homosexuality was a medical condition that could be cured. A homosexual now had a stable individual identity, a permanent status as morally bereft, and a mental illness. During the decades to follow, men and women with same-sex attractions were categorically homosexuals and thus compelled to seek psychological treatment, regardless of their behavior. This further compounded the stigma attached to the already stigmatized identity. To this day, long after it was removed from the *DSM,* the stigma lingers.

In response to years of ongoing police harassment in public meeting spaces, the 1969 uprising of homosexuals at the Stonewall bar in New York City catalyzed the beginning of the modern gay and lesbian movement. Leaders of the early movement reclaimed the homosexual identity by adapting identifying labels with more positive associations. The terms "gay," meaning happy, and "lesbian," eponymic of the same-sex oriented poet Sappho from the Greek *Isle of Lesbos,* were adopted as the new terms with which they could identify and take pride. Perhaps a result of the movement, most recently the gay identity is losing its derogated moral and mental health status. All over the Western world sodomy laws are being dismantled and same-sex unions are established in their place. Homosexuality is slowly evolving to become a legitimate, acceptable, and even, at times, appreciated social identity.

*Ethan Haymovitz*

## Honesty

Honesty is the disposition to be truthful in dealings with other people, and by extension with oneself. The paradigm or prototypical situation is one in which a person states the truth in response to an inquiry, when a lie would be more convenient or gratifying, stating the truth in a way that provides adequate information for the purposes at hand and frames the presentation of the information so that the audience will correctly apprehend what is being stated.

Dishonesty can involve lying but also cheating, even when nothing false is said. Since cheating succeeds through a misrepresentation in which one presents oneself and appears to play by the rules but, in fact, violates the rules or shared understandings, cheating is a nonverbal form of misrepresentation and hence a form of dishonesty. Honesty is more than not lying or cheating, however, because it involves good judgment about how much of the truth to tell in the circumstances and also about how to frame the telling of it for a particular audience on a specific occasion.

Honesty with oneself involves acknowledging one's weaknesses, or in a specific situation recognizing one's questionable motives or wrongful intentions. Because we have imperfect conscious access to our real motives, and because we have an interest in maintaining a positive impression of ourselves, discernment and frankness about ourselves is sometimes difficult.

Honesty is a disposition to act in a certain way rather than an individual act. An honest person might sometimes lie or cheat, acting out of character and making a mistake, not thereby ceasing to be a person genuinely in the habit of being honest. The more interesting ethical question may be whether an honest person could ever lie or cheat in a way that is in character and not a mistake.

Immanuel Kant argued that lying is always wrong because no one would will that he/she be lied to in the same circumstances in which he/she is considering lying. Furthermore, if one held that lying would be acceptable in such-and-such circumstances, and by extension that everyone could feel free to lie in those circumstances, then we could not trust anyone to tell the truth in those circumstances. But if we did not trust anyone in those circumstances, then a lie could not succeed, since a lie deceives only if the liar is trusted to be telling the truth. The only way one could will to lie, then, is to will that one make an exception for oneself on a particular occasion, and that, Kant argued, was to will an inconsistency, which is contrary to the laws of logic, or in this sort of case, of practical rationality. Thus, it is always one's duty not to lie.

John Stuart Mill rejected Kant's position. He argued that "all moralists" acknowledge that the rule against lying,

> sacred as it is, admits of possible exceptions...the chief of which is when the withholding of some fact (as of information from a malefactor, or of bad news from an individual dangerously ill) would save an individual (especially an individual other than oneself) from great and unmerited evil, and when the withholding can only be effected by denial. (*Utilitarianism*, 1861, Chapter II)

When the police unjustly seek an innocent fugitive from an evil regime who is hiding in your attic, and the only way to turn them away is to deny you are harboring the fugitive, a denial can be permissible. When someone dangerously ill, and with a poor prognosis, would have a substantially improved chance of survival if he/she believed, falsely, that his/her condition is serious but that there is a good chance he/she will fully recover, it can be permissible to deny that he/she is as badly off as he/she is.

Mill's view was that it is possible in exceptional circumstances such as these to delimit acceptable variance from the rule against lying so that "utility" is maximized, that is, so that the greatest happiness is obtained for the greatest number of people. In effect, Mill agreed with Kant about the importance of maintaining a reasonable reliance on veracity but rejected Kant's employment of the criterion of universalizability. For Kant, the crucial thing was avoiding inconsistency, regardless of the consequences. For Mill, the crucial thing was maximizing happiness, even if this required inconsistency. If the gravely ill person or the police pursuing the fugitive can successfully be deceived, utility is maximized, and no universalizability test is necessary, because the actual (rather than "logical") consequences of these two particular acts will not, in fact, reduce the socially useful reliance on veracity enough to outweigh the benefit of the lies.

According to an Aristotelian point of view, both Kant and Mill incorrectly attempt to establish the ultimate standard of moral conduct in general and of truth telling in particular by reference to an abstract rule or principle of morality. For Aristotle, the standard or reference point is not a rule or principle but what a person of good practical judgment would do. Such a person has good judgment about the worthy purposes of human life and about what type of life and which actions in specific cases contribute to accomplishing those purposes. Concrete situations are so various that rules and principles must be interpreted by reference to such purposes, which constitute the "spirit of the law." So Mill was right to suppose that consequences matter, but Kant was right to suppose that momentary feeling states such as pleasure are not the ultimate goal.

From Kantian and utilitarian points of view, the question is whether lying is ever permissible. From an Aristotelian point of view, the question is whether a lie might in some specific set of circumstances be the least bad alternative, given the purposes of human life and the requirements of the way of life which, in one's situation, best promotes those purposes.

**Further Reading:** Bok, S. (1978). *Lying: Moral choice in public and private life.* New York: Pantheon. Bok, S. (1982). *Secrets: On the ethics of concealment and revelation.* New York: Pantheon. Ekman, P. (1985). *Telling lies: Clues to deceit in the marketplace, politics, and marriage.* New York: Norton. Frankfurt, H.G. (2005). *On bullshit.* Princeton, NJ: Princeton University Press.

*Don Collins Reed*

## Honor

To be a person of honor is to be someone who can be trusted to uphold a specific agreement or a general code of conduct. The paradigm or prototypical situation is one in which a person is not under surveillance and in which there is no enforcement mechanism in place to ensure conformity but in which he/she is on his/her own recognizance to perform a task or role. For instance, one might be on one's honor to refrain from an improper use of sources while completing a take-home examination at one's residence, or to make a personal contribution in support of a meal provided to the group, or to remain faithful sexually to one's spouse.

The nature of honor thus depends on the nature of the agreement or shared code. When a people shares an extensive understanding of proper and ideal conduct in a variety of areas of life and reasonably trusts its members to uphold this understanding, honor is a socially important personal characteristic within the society. A shared ethic of honor can optimize cooperation for the common good and maximize willingness to sacrifice for the group.

Moreover, in such a society, more is expected from those to whom more is entrusted, and retaining one's honor may be vital to retaining one's place within a society. The more with which one is entrusted, the greater may be one's honor, and hence the higher one's rank. In such circumstances, to have one's honor impugned by an insult may be experienced as a grave offense. Similarly, to dishonor oneself or one's family may have grave consequences for one's dependents and oneself.

When a people does not share an extensive understanding of proper and ideal conduct or does not trust its members to uphold such a code, honor can be a personal characteristic only quite limited in scope and importance. It may be confined to specific agreements with particular individuals on definite occasions. Honor, that is, may become a wholly private matter, where public matters are guarded by surveillance and enforcement mechanisms. Or honor may be confined to quasi-private subgroups within a society, within which shared understanding and trust can be maintained.

In such a larger society, wealth and/or power may replace honor as measures of personal worth and markers of social status. Being trustworthy may be only marginally significant in the public eye, because being rich and influential may have displaced being honorable. And since to honor someone is to acknowledge their worth or status, to accord someone the honor due him may have come to have little or nothing to do with whether he is an honorable person.

The notion that there is or may be honor among thieves is the idea that a subpopulation operating outside the legal system, where surveillance and enforcement are required, may be able to maintain a shared understanding of proper and/or ideal conduct with respect to each other. In the case of "thieves," this may be possible as much because of the power of fear as of trust, for a group or set of groups already operating outside the law may maintain order through vengeance and retaliation, which are forbidden by the formal legal system. The penalty for violating the code may be so severe, and the certainty of retaliation so high, that shared official mechanisms of surveillance and enforcement are not necessary.

For the same reasons, societies that do not have formal legal systems may both depend on honor and rely on personal vengeance and retaliation to address violations. In such societies, lacking official mechanisms of surveillance and enforcement, personal feelings of shame and/or fear of retaliation perform the function performed by public findings of guilt in societies with formal legal systems. That is, in societies without formal legal systems, honor may be a public phenomenon and policing may be a private affair, whereas the reverse may be the case in societies with formal legal systems that have lost a shared understanding of proper and ideal conduct.

To uphold an antique code or an understanding of proper and ideal conduct that is no longer widely shared may be noble, in circumstances in which the social good could still be done by minority adherence to the code, especially when personal sacrifice is required. But it may be more absurd than noble if the moral or cultural climate of the society has changed in ways that render the antique code either maladaptive or offensive.

*Further Reading:* Bowman, J. (2006). *Honor: A history.* New York: Encounter Books. Kekes, J. (2002). *The art of life.* New York: Cornell University Press. Stewart, F.H. (1994). *Honor.* Chicago: University of Chicago Press.

*Don Collins Reed*

## Humanistic Education

Humanistic education was developed in the 1970s as a movement in American education in response to what some educators perceived as the detrimental learning environment of many of America's classrooms. Proponents of humanistic education believed that education in America had become indoctrinistic and impersonal; schools and teachers damaged, thwarted, and stifled the natural capacity of children to learn and grow. Advocates of humanistic education promoted teaching students not just the basics but also things such as conflict management, cooperation, compassion, honesty, and self-knowledge. These last qualities were thought to be characteristics of what Abraham Maslow identified as "the self-actualized person."

The Humanistic Education Movement began as a reaction by educational professionals to the predominance of the psychology of behaviorism in the American educational system. Rooted in the humanistic or "Third Force" psychology of Carl Rogers and Abraham Maslow, this movement attempted to break away from what it called the manipulative indoctrination or imposition of ideas/thoughts/values on the young person. In contrast, humanistic education attempted to attend to the freedom of the human person and to promote self-realization for the students.

In the field of education in the 1970s, humanistic education was the subject of considerable interest and controversy. The term meant many different things to different people. Generally speaking, educators who used the term humanistic education meant one or more of three things:

1. Humanistic education taught a wide variety of skills needed to function in the world—basic skills such as reading, writing, and computation, as well as skills in communicating, thinking, decision making, problem solving, and knowing oneself.
2. Humanistic education was a humane approach to education—one that helped students believe in themselves and their potential, that encouraged compassion and understanding, and that fostered self-respect and respect for others.
3. Humanistic education dealt with basic human concerns—with the issues throughout history that are of concern to human beings trying to improve the quality of life—to pursue knowledge, to grow, to love, to find meaning for one's existence.

Humanistic education no longer exists as an element in the American educational system. There are four main reasons for this:

1. *Back to Basics Movement.* The movement to get back to the basics—reading, writing, and arithmetic—has labeled humanistic education tenets as problematic and distractive to the primary reasons for education. It is widely assumed that concern with affective development and human relationships in the classroom (humanistic psychology would focus in upon these) is in conflict with cognitive development.
2. *Misguided Values Clarification Programs.* In some places, poor judgment was used by school personnel in selecting materials for values clarification issues. Beyond this, however, is the resistance of teachers and parents to any attempt to introduce discussion of values in the school.
3. *Identification with Secular Humanism.* Opponents of humanistic education have aligned it with secular humanism, thinking that humanistic education attempts to infiltrate the schools to undermine ethics, morals, and religion. Proponents of humanistic education have been labeled atheists.
4. *Games, Gimmicks and Techniques.* Practitioners of humanistic education frequently demonstrated its essentials with games and exercises. Many teachers felt unqualified to use these kinds of experiences in the classroom or came to think of them as soft, shallow, or a waste of class time.

Elements of humanistic education continue to be a part of the American educational system. For example, the current trend toward "character education" displays certain aspects of humanistic education. The character education programs demonstrate elements of humanistic education when they transform educational structures to allow children to reflect upon moral issues and affect children in a more holistic way to help them function more effectively.

**Further Reading:** Kohn, A. (1996). *Beyond discipline: From compliance to community.* Alexandria, VA: Association for Supervision and Curriculum Development. Kozol, J. (1967). *Death at an early age.* Boston: Houghton Mifflin. Maslow, A. (1970). *Motivation and personality.* New York: Harper and Row. Patterson, C.H. (1973). *Humanistic education.* Englewood Cliffs, NJ: Prentice-Hall. Rogers, C. (1969). *Freedom to learn.* Columbus, OH: Merrill Publishing.

*Edward T. Hastings*

# I

## Identity

The concept of identity has been debated and defined in ways that attempt to understand how one's psychology, biology, and environment influence one's unique view of oneself. Various terms have been used to describe identity to include self, I, me, ego, and, of course, identity. Regardless of the terminology, the underlying theme is that a person's self-concept and relationships are multifaceted.

Erik Erikson, considered the first to bring attention to the scientific and popular study of identity, believed that one's identity is continually reformulated throughout the life span. Although one's identity evolves, there is also a need for consistency in who one is and how one presents oneself to others. Some describe this sameness as being genuine or authentic.

There are typically three converging parts of an individual that influence and are influenced by one another, thus creating identity. The physiological or biological makeup consists of gender, physical abilities and limitations, and personal appearance. These characteristics change over time, thereby continually tapping our psychological structures to make sense of the changes. A person's psyche houses his/her emotions, interests, attitudes, and personality. What contributes to the complexity of identity development is that psychological attributes can change, too, over time. The third area of influence is the social structures in which a person participates. This can include immediate and extended family, peers, school, and community. Within the social structures a person has the opportunity to initiate and respond to his/her environment. The feedback one receives is then used to either reinforce or change one's self-concept and related thoughts, feelings, and behaviors.

Part of the process of developing one's identity is a willingness to accept that changes do occur. Change is necessary for a person's ego to become mature with a sense of security in who he/she is and what others know about him/her. Erikson also suggested that achieving a mature identity requires a person to consider various choices as related to such issues as political ideology, religious orientation, vocational opportunities, and interpersonal relations. After exploring one's options, then a meaningful commitment should be made. A commitment in vocational choice, for instance, should be made with an understanding of one's interests, values, personality, abilities, and experiences. This type of self-awareness provides a solid platform to make an informed decision about compatible occupational choices. To accept a position on an issue without considering the options would be considered identity foreclosure and may simply represent a superficial commitment to the choice. An implication to a foreclosed decision may be career dissatisfaction once the person begins the career and finds incompatible qualities between the career and his/her own interests, personality, or values.

Basically, identity development involves an understanding of and participation in one's psychological, physiological, and social development over the life span. The identification of one's ethnicity also plays a role in building a mature identity structure. Major components to an ethnic identity are feelings of belonging and commitment with shared attitudes and values. To develop a positive ethnic identity requires a desire from the individual as opposed to simply having it bestowed upon them.

There are other theories of identity development beyond the psychosocial model. Structural stage theories suggest that internal psychological filters of how one makes sense of the world change and evolve over time. Loevinger (1976) proposed that individuals interpreted information and made decisions based on their level of ego development and moved from an impulsive, self-serving strategy to an integrated approach involving self and other considerations. Kegan (1982) had a similar philosophy, but focused on the development of a moral identity. Some individuals, however, may remain static in methods of interpreting their environment, while others may progress through the various stages of development.

Sociocultural theories focus on an individual's identity development through their interactions with others. The social dynamic influences one's self-concept by how one interprets feedback received from others. Additionally, the feedback one receives from others may be real or imagined. For instance, a child on the playground may notice a group of children who turn their backs when approached. The lone child may interpret this nonverbal behavior as a slight toward their friendship and in turn feel unwanted. Sociocultural theorists believe that only through our interactions do we develop a sense of personal identity.

Narrative approaches to identity imply that individuals shape their identities based on the stories they create and the decisions they make to live out those stories. The manner in which stories are developed are as much a part of a person's response to life events as his/her perceptions of how things should be.

Regardless of the approach that one takes to understand identity development, it is essential to note that identity is a personal and social construct that evolves over the life span.

***Further Reading:*** Erikson, E. H. (1963). *Identity: Youth and crisis.* New York: Norton. Kegan, R. (1982). *The evolving self: Problem and process in human development.* Cambridge, MA: Harvard University Press. Kroger, J. (2000). *Identity development: Adolescence through adulthood.* Thousand Oaks, CA: Sage Publications. Loevinger, J. (1976). *Ego development: Conceptions and theories.* San Francisco: Jossey-Bass. Phinney, J. S. (1990). Ethnic identity in adolescents and adults: Review of research. *Psychological Bulletin, 10*(3), 499–514.

*Scott E. Hall*

## Implementation

In general school reform literature, the school characteristics that promote academic achievement are well known. Schools with high achievement are orderly and safe; they are respectful and provide students with moral and personal support while expecting them to achieve. Achieving schools have a strong sense of community (sense of belonging among students) and high academic press (strong norms and high expectations for achievement). Interestingly, these characteristics overlap with characteristics that nurture prosocial development (Solomon, Watson, & Battistich, 2002).

Although we know what makes schools work empirically, what works is rarely implemented successfully in practice. The reasons for this are many. The failure can be due to multiple reasons such as insufficient staff development, lack of commitment on the part of the teacher, competing responsibilities, lack of school leadership, insufficient school infrastructure such as time or funding, and community opposition. Even if these areas are successfully addressed, implementation can fail at the point of institutionalization. Even when a program is implemented as designed, its sustainability can be thwarted by many of the same problems and, most especially, by a lack of resources such as personnel or a change in leadership.

Implementation fidelity has been a long-standing issue in educational reform but has rarely been studied in character education evaluations (Laud & Berkowitz, 1999). Laud and Berkowitz suggest that the complications of implementation evaluation may be due to the multilevel reform sought by character education programs, levels that include the hidden curriculum, the explicit curriculum, as well as school atmosphere. It is difficult to assess or even know how to assess some of these aspects.

Michael Fullan (1999) has developed the most comprehensive approach to school reform, building on theories from dynamic systems and institutional change. One of the key elements is a change in the internal dynamics of a school, or "reculturing." Reculturing means that educators develop an orientation of learning on the job and helping each other make improvements in practice. For example, schools that are successful in raising student achievement have staffs who, on a continual basis, develop a professional learning community, address student work through assessment, and change practices to improve results. Schools with professional learning communities that focus on assessment and pedagogy, making changes to improve both, are those that successfully improve climate and student achievement. Professional learning communities (whose characteristics were reviewed earlier) create the environment and culture for student achievement and student character development. Although a single teacher can make a difference in the life of a child, the power of a community of teachers cultivating character is unparalleled.

School professionals can build a learning community in which instructional and ethical skill development is fostered among all members of the community, including school staff, parents, and neighborhoods. The cultivation of a professional learning community within a school is key to school reform efforts. Professional learning communities (PLC) that focus on achievement have particular characteristics. These same characteristics are important in professional learning communities that also address ethical character. PLC have five primary characteristics. First, they take the time to develop a shared vision and mutually held values that focus on student learning and foster norms for improving practice. Leadership is democratic, shared among teachers and administrators. The entire staff seeks and shares knowledge, skills, and strategies to improve practice. The school structure supports an environment that is collaborative, trusting, positive, and caring.

Peers open their classrooms to the feedback and suggestions of others in order to improve student achievement and promote individual and community growth. These same practices can also be used to increase student moral development as well as student achievement.

The quality of implementation is related to disparate outcomes as well. Schools with a broader (across more classrooms and by more teachers) and deeper (more frequent and focused) implementation are typically more successful, a finding corroborated by multiple programs. According to Michael Fullan, it takes on average three years for a school reform to influence student performance in primary schools, six years for secondary schools. This is when things go well, meaning that adoption was wholehearted and deep, and implementation was faithful to the design.

In order to earn respect, a program is expected to be replicable. A simple definition of replicability is "successful implementation in more than one school" (from the Comprehensive School Reform Demonstration). Replicability is a sign that the program is well-described, user-friendly, sufficiently trained, worthwhile to educators, and providing measurable results.

One project that challenged the traditional view of replicability was the Minnesota Community Voices and Character Education project (Integrative Ethical Education). Instead of using a universal curriculum, the emphasis was on local adaptation of a research-based road map of character skills and developmentally appropriate pedagogy. Each local educator team was at liberty to follow the road map in a way that was suitable to local needs, replicating the same collaborative process across sites.

*Further Reading:* Fullan, M. (1999). *Change forces: The sequel.* London: Falmer Press. Laud, L., & Berkowitz, M. (1999). Challenges in evaluating character education programs. *Journal of Research in Education, 9,* 66–72 Solomon, D., Watson, M., & Battistich, V. (2002). Teaching and schooling effects on moral/prosocial development. In V. Richardson (Ed.), *Handbook of research on teaching* (pp. 566–603). Washington, D.C.: American Educational Research Association.

*Darcia Narvaez*


## Inclusion

Inclusion refers to an approach to education and administration that calls for all of the assets and resources of a school to be available to all students, regardless of special needs, disability, or developmental differences. Inclusion has its roots in early efforts to exclude certain students from mainstream classroom education. Because of manifest needs, disabilities, and learning differences, some students were once thought to be better served in a special, freestanding educational environment, having been pulled out of the typical classroom. Inclusion challenges that approach and calls for all students, regardless of abilities, to be educated with their age-appropriate peers whenever possible.

"Special education" is the term used to identify the freestanding, pull-out programs that are especially designed and staffed to meet the needs of students with extraordinary needs. Special education programs for students with disabilities have been in operation since at least the 1800s (Lipsky & Gartner, 1997). It was not until 1975, however, that federal law mandated that all children with disabilities must be educated. Congress passed PL 94-142, the Education for All Handicapped Children Act.

This initial legislation was reauthorized in 1990 as PL 101-476, the Individuals with Disabilities Education Act. This new law has ensured that all students with disabilities have access to publicly supported educational programs. Such special education programs currently serve more than 6 million students in the United States, with total costs now surpassing $25 billion.

While the number of students served increased with the passage of the 1975 law, the placement of students with disabilities remained the same. On average, a third of students are educated in a typical classroom, an additional third in pull-out programs, and a final third in special classes or programs. This distribution and its continuance after funding are at the source of the movement toward inclusion.

Special education programs have an appeal in that curriculum and instructional strategies can arguably be adapted to meet the needs of learners. Regular classrooms benefit from the more homogeneous ability level shaped there by the departure of students with special needs. Such an approach has been present in U.S. educational history since 1823 with the opening of schools for children who were deaf.

In the 1960s, researchers began to question the effectiveness of special education programs and their impact on students with special needs (Dunn, 1968). Regular classroom education was found to be effective in educating students with special needs, and few benefits were discovered for those students in special education programs. Self-contained classrooms for students with mental retardation also resulted in increased segregation for African American children who were disproportionately enrolled in special education programs because of an exclusive reliance on IQ testing for placement. Labels that accompanied special education students, such as "retarded" and "dumb," were increasingly stigmatizing.

A provocative aspect of the 1975 law is what is known as the least restrictive environment (LRE) principle. This principle required that whatever services were made available to students, the students must be placed in such a way as to maximize their participation in educational programming and that such placement respect the full range of their abilities. The LRE principle clearly focused on the normalization of educational services to students with disabilities and suggested that the existence of a disability ought not to require a special educational program or the removal of students with disabilities from the regular classroom.

Inclusion as an educational philosophy has numerous advocates, including many in the private sector. Inclusion has been interpreted as a theological construct in many private schools, attributing inclusive behaviors to God and to Jesus (Eiesland, 1994). Private school educators in religiously affiliated institutions have adopted this theological approach and often look to the Bible, especially the examples of Jesus and the Old Testament prophets, for examples of inclusive behaviors and the need to be welcoming of all. Although there is not ample evidence in theological literature to support disability-specific pedagogical approaches, the example of many biblical protagonists seems to support a welcoming posture toward all those who are marginalized by society, physically disabled or not (Weiss Block, 2002).

Other researchers see in disability studies the opportunity to renew and reconstruct educational priorities for the new postindustrial, information age economy. Inclusion is seen as an evolutionary step along a continuum of change that will eventually result in a more critical, equitable, and democratic approach to the education of all citizens (Skrtic, 1995).

**Further Reading:** Dunn, L.M. (1968). Special education for the mildly retarded: Is much of it justifiable? *Exceptional Children, 35,* 5–22. Eiesland, N. (1994). *The disabled God: Toward a liberatory theology of disability.* Nashville, TN: Abingdon Press. Lipsky, D.K., & Gartner, A. (1997). *Inclusion and school reform: Transforming America's classrooms.* Baltimore, MD: Paul H. Brookes. Skrtic, T.M. (Ed.). (1995). *Democracy and disability: Reconstructing [special] education for postmodernity.* New York: Teachers College Press. Weiss Block, J. (2002). *Copious hosting: A theology of access for people with disabilities.* New York: Continuum.

*Ronald J. Nuzzi*

## Indoctrination

Indoctrination refers, in a neutral sense, to successfully teaching or transmitting a specific doctrine or belief to a learner or novice. Frequently and historically, when used in this way the doctrine taught is religious in nature and the speakers approve of the doctrine to be transmitted to the learner.

In contemporary usage, indoctrination is typically used as a pejorative and refers to a type of instruction that results in a learner holding a belief either (a) uncritically and/or (b) tenaciously in a way that the belief cannot be shaken by reason, evidence, or experience. The context could be a dyad, a classroom, a school, a special-interest group, or—particularly in a time of war and via the use of mass media and propaganda—an entire nation.

In U.S. history, several arguments have been advanced that textbooks or a political bias among professors has the effect of indoctrinating students. A claim that a teacher is indoctrinating students usually raises questions about: (1) the soundness and defensibility of the doctrine, (2) the motives (as self-interested or resulting from self-deceptions or the result of the teacher having been indoctrinated by someone else), and (3) the ability of the learner to exercise autonomous judgment. Indoctrination is usually described as an intentional act, but there is nothing inherently self-contradictory to the claim that a student was unintentionally indoctrinated—in the sense of not being able to consider evidence contradicting a belief they came to hold—despite a teacher's attempt to be nonindoctrinative.

Indoctrination, in its current dominant use, is an anathema in moral education. That does not prevent—explicitly or implicitly—the claim to be made in internecine debates within the field of moral education. For example, Lawrence Kohlberg's cognitive-developmental theory of moral education emphasizes the process of reaching a moral decision and acting accordingly. Kohlberg was skeptical of the traditional character education approach of instilling virtues and habits as the primary means of moral education and raised the question of whether such approaches are indoctrinative. Carol Gilligan and other advocates of a caring approach to moral education criticized Kohlberg's focus on justice reasoning and excluding women and racial/ethnic minorities in the longitudinal sample of adolescents upon which he developed his stages of moral development. The effect might be characterized as indoctrinative and the claim made that because of the approach, moral educators and psychologists could not recognize the "different voice" of care. The point here is that indoctrination is usually attributed to those with whom one disagrees rather than a positive descriptor of one's own motives, methods, and outcomes.

To avoid indoctrination—independent of the tradition(s) on moral education a teacher supports and uses—teachers should be aware of their position of authority and the possibility that unintentional indoctrination is possible, and always provide reasons for positions advanced (both in the moral domain, but all others as well). Teachers must also allow those reasons to be questioned and challenged in a climate where students will be safe in raising those questions and challenges. Further, students should be expected to offer reasons for beliefs and claims that they make, in short, creating an environment of shared inquiry.

***Further Reading:*** Gilligan, C. (1982). *In a different voice: Psychological theory and women's development.* Cambridge, MA: Harvard University Press. Kohlberg L. (1981). *Essays on moral development, Vol. I. The philosophy of moral development.* San Francisco: Harper & Row. Loewen, J. (2005). *Lies my teacher told me: Everything your history textbook got wrong.* New York: New Press. (Original work published in 1996.) Ravitch, D. (2003). *The language police: How pressure groups restrict what students learn.* New York: Knopf. Siegel, H. (Ed.). (1997). *Reason and education: Essays in honor of Israel Scheffler.* New York: Springer.

*Robert W. Howard*

## Inductive Discipline

Inductive discipline is a parenting strategy that uses reasoning to help children understand the ways that their actions affect others. During inductive discipline, parents explain to children why certain behaviors are wrong or potentially harmful. By elaborating why an action is problematic and emphasizing how a wrongdoing can impact others negatively, the parent helps the child to create an induction.

According to inductive logic, many specific examples lead to a general conclusion. During inductive discipline, a parent uses specific instances of a behavior to illustrate a more general principle of what is right or wrong. The parent then communicates the reasoning process to the child verbally. For instance, when a parent sees a child bite his/her brother, the parent might remove the misbehaving child from the situation and explain, "Please do not bite your brother, because when you bite him, he gets hurt. Look at how his arm is red, and he is crying. He is probably crying because his arm hurts and because he is sad that you have acted meanly toward him." In this example, the parent is using the child's specific offense to illustrate a general principle that biting is wrong because it can hurt someone else both physically and emotionally. Inductive discipline typically focuses on transgressions toward others.

Proponents of inductive discipline believe that these methods stimulate positive moral development by helping children internalize messages about why specific actions are right or wrong. This means that children hear messages about how their actions affect others so often that the children begin to adopt societal values as their own. Grusec and Goodnow (1994) provide a more complete explanation of how disciplinary strategies can promote the internalization of moral values. Once messages are internalized, children begin to think automatically about whether their behavior will affect someone else, even when the parent is no longer there to tell them. In this way, the parent uses inductive discipline to model his or her belief system for the child.

Inductive reasoning can be contrasted with deductive methods, where a general rule is established, and punishment occurs after the rule is disobeyed. A parent using a deductive method might tell the same child, "Mommy and Daddy make the rules, and the rule in this house is that we do not bite." This statement is an example of *power-assertive discipline,* where the adult establishes authority over the child in order to increase the child's compliance with the desired behavior (not biting). Although power-assertive discipline can increase short-term compliance, some believe that its effectiveness results from fear of punishment without understanding the reason behind the punishment. If a child is fearful, he or she may conform immediately, but might be less likely to act in accordance with a rule when no authority figure is present. Additionally, some researchers believe that the child may become angry because the punishment does not make sense to him/her. Similar feelings of fear and anger can result from *love withdrawal,* another disciplinary strategy endorsed in the 1960s. During love withdrawal, obedience increases once the child realizes that good behavior can earn parental affection. Again, if the child does not understand the punishment, he or she may become mystified at why love is being withheld and become distrustful of the punishing parent. Unlike deductive methods of power assertion and love withdrawal, reasoning strategies such as inductive discipline remove confusion in the child. When parents clearly explain the reason for punishment, fear and anger are lessened. Most parents use a combination of inductive and deductive methods.

Inductive discipline is considered a critical component in Hoffman's theory of socialization. In this view, parental use of inductive reasoning, as opposed to power assertion or love withdrawal, leads to children's prosocial behavior, such as helpfulness or willingness to share. According to Hoffman (1979), the socialization process occurs when parental use of inductive reasoning helps children develop empathy. The mediating factor of empathy then prompts increasingly prosocial behavior. Krevans and Gibbs (1996) have shown recent evidence for the relationship between inductive discipline and children's prosocial behavior via increased empathy. Hoffman (1979) has explained that parents who show high levels of affection alongside inductive disciplinary methods are most likely to promote moral thinking and behavior because of the trust and emotional security that arise from high warmth combined with good communication. Again, parental modeling of inductive reasoning assists children with internalizing the rationale behind moral behavior.

Similar inductive strategies are used by teachers in classroom settings. Teachers, like parents, scaffold children to create inductions. School is a logical setting to extend moral principles established at home because peer interactions occur frequently. Factors that influence the effectiveness of inductive disciplinary methods both at home and at school include child age, child gender, parent gender, and type of misbehavior.

*Further Reading:* Grusec, J.E., & Goodnow, J.J. (1994). Impact of parental discipline methods on the child's internalization of values: A reconceptualization of current points of view. *Developmental Psychology, 30,* 4–19. Hoffman, M.L. (1979). Development of moral thought, feeling, and behavior. *American Psychologist, 34*(10), 958–66. Horton, N.K., Ray, G.E., & Cohen, R. (2001). Children's evaluations of inductive discipline as a function of transgression type and induction orientation. *Child Study Journal, 31*(2), 71–93. Krevans, J., & Gibbs, J.C. (1996). Parents' use of inductive discipline: Relations to children's empathy and prosocial behavior. *Child Development, 67,* 3263–3277.

*Carol E. Akai*

## Inquiry-Discovery Approach

Inquiry-discovery approach is a pedagogical technique that involves designing learning activities so that students are engaged in their own learning and make sense of facts and principles for themselves, rather than relying on textbooks or on teacher explanations. It is often referred to as inquiry learning, discovery learning, or inquiry-discovery learning.

To contrast the approach with more traditional forms of classroom instruction, inquiry learning encourages the students to investigate, ask critical questions, and investigate more. It is highly dependent on process and on the self-directed processing of new information gathered from experiments, problem solving, and problem-based learning activities. The inquiry method is perhaps best described as the way people learn when left alone to investigate and research whatever it is they want to learn.

Some scholars believe that this approach has its roots in the educational philosophy of John Dewey, who believed in the active engagement of students in their own learning and is considered the author of progressivism in educational theory (Dewey, 1902; 1916). Dewey was highly critical of classroom practices that were subject-driven at the expense of student learning. He advocated for a more student-centered approach that considered both the unique needs of the student learner and the demands of the subject area under discussion.

Modern educational theory remains highly focused on inquiry learning. The advent of multiple technologies, computer-assisted learning, the Internet, electronic resources, and distance learning opportunities all help to expand the self-discovery required in inquiry approaches. Supported by such classroom technology, students can more readily develop their critical thinking skills, experience the passion and excitement of original research, and engage in problem solving in a collaborative learning environment.

J. Richard Suchman (1959) proposed a general framework for inquiry learning, delineating a series of six rules and accompanying procedures to guide classroom practice.

Rule 1: Questions. The questions by the students should be phrased in such a way that they can be answered "yes" or "no." While this takes practice and coaching, it has the salutary effect of shifting the thinking responsibility to the students.

Rule 2: Freedom to ask questions. Students may ask as many questions as they like. This encourages students to think critically and to use previous questions to formulate new ones to pursue a reasonable theory.

Rule 3: Teacher response to statements of theory. When students suggest a theory, the teacher should refrain from evaluating it. The teacher might simply record the theory, or ask a question about the student's theory.

Rule 4: Testing theories. Students should be allowed to test their theories at any time.

Rule 5: Cooperation. Students should be encouraged to work in teams in order to confer and discuss their theories.

Rule 6: Experimenting. The teacher should provide resources such as materials for experiments, texts, online tools, and reference books so that the students can explore their ideas.

Research has generally supported the usefulness of inquiry approaches, especially in the teaching of science. However, more traditional pedagogies continue to insist on a basic or essentialistic approach to certain skills sets, believing that there are certain facts that all students must learn and some that they must simply commit to memory. Modern technologies and computer-supported activities can assist teachers in implementing more inquiry and discovery approaches, but they can also be used as a simple replacement for teacher-driven, rather than student-driven, pedagogical approaches. Inquiry-discovery approaches still require significant preparation on the part of teachers and a high degree of familiarity with both the content of the subject matter and the available resources in print and electronic form. When thoughtfully and properly implemented, inquiry-discovery approaches can be effective in adult and higher education in addition to K–12 applications.

**Further Reading:** Campbell, J. (1995). *Understanding John Dewey: Nature and cooperative intelligence*. Chicago: Open Court. Dewey, J. (1902). *The child and the curriculum*. Chicago: University of Chicago Press. Dewey, J. (1916). *Democracy and education: An introduction to the philosophy of education*. New York: Macmillan. Dykhuizen, G. (1973). *The life and mind of John Dewey*. Carbondale: Southern Illinois University Press. Garrison, J. (Ed.). (1995). *The new scholarship on Dewey*. Dordrecht: Kluwer Academic Publishers. Issues in problem-based learning. *Journal on Excellence in College Teaching, 11,* Special Double Issue no. 2. Mierson, S., with Parikh, A.A. (2000). Stories from the field: Problem-based learning from a teacher's and a student's perspective. *Change, 32*(1), 21–27. Nelson, C.E. (1989). Skewered on the unicorn's horn: The illusion of tragic tradeoff between content and critical thinking in the teaching of science. In Linda W. Crow (Ed.), *Enhancing critical thinking in the sciences* (pp. 17–27). Washington, D.C.: Society of College Science Teachers, National Science Teachers Association. Novak, G.M. (1999). *Just in time teaching: Blending active learning with web technology*. Upper Saddle River, NJ: Prentice-Hall. Suchman, J.R. (1959). *Observation and analysis in child development: A laboratory manual*. New York: Harcourt, Brace and Company.

*Ronald J. Nuzzi*


## Integrative Ethical Education

The Integrative Ethical Education model (IEE; Narvaez, 2006) provides a framework for moral character development that can be used at all age levels. It is integrative in several senses and offers a step-by-step approach to character education. IEE integrates the character ethics or virtue approach to character education (represented by Aristotle) with the rule ethics or rational approach to moral education (represented by Lawrence Kohlberg). Each maps roughly onto the two general types of human mentality, deliberative reasoning and intuition, which are educated in the IEE approach.

The Integrative Ethical Education model is built on research literatures of several kinds. First is the notion of expertise development. Expertise refers to a refined, deep understanding that is evident in practice and action. Moral experts demonstrate holistic orientations in one or more of the four processes: ethical sensitivity, ethical judgment, ethical focus, and ethical action. Moral expertise can be built systematically using a holistic immersion approach that enlists both the deliberative mind and the intuitive mind. IEE suggests to educators four levels of knowledge for student development: (1) *identification knowledge,* developed through immersion and exposure to prototypical examples; (2) *elaboration knowledge,* developed through attention to key facts and specific detail in the domain in order to elaborate on their initial intuitions about the domain; (3) *procedural knowledge* of how to carry out tasks in the domain; (4) *execution knowledge,* a fine-tuning of declarative, procedural, and conditional knowledge applied to problems of different kinds in varied contexts.

A second research literature underpinning IEE is that of human memory and learning. Human understanding can be split into two forms, that of the *adaptive unconscious,* which learns automatically without effort, and that of the *deliberative mind,* which learns through effortful processing. Educators should address both "minds." The intuitive mind learns easily through the patterns of the culture or climate of a school or classroom. The deliberative mind can develop more sophisticated reasoning and understanding from direct teaching.

Based on these and other literatures, IEE suggests five steps educators can take for a holistic approach to student character development. These are presented in a logical order but ideally are done simultaneously.

*Step 1: Establish a caring relationship with each student.* A caring relationship forms the bridge from adult to child through which mutual influence can take place. In a caring classroom, discipline is not punishment but is coached character development (Watson, 2003). A child who is cared for will likely care for others and engage as a citizen in the moral life of the community.

*Step 2: Foster a supportive climate for moral behavior and high achievement.* Caring school climates encourage social and emotional bonding and promote positive interpersonal experiences, providing the minimum necessary grounding for the formation of character. Moreover, in schools where there is a strong perception of communal organization there is less student misconduct and lower rates of drug use and delinquency. A caring classroom (and school) climate with high expectations for achievement and behavior is related both to high achievement and to moral behavior (Zins et al., 2004).

*Step 3: Cultivate ethical skills.* The Four Component Model offers a toolkit for character education. Narvaez and colleagues identified seven skills in each of the four components that could be taught in public schools during academic instruction. For example, skills in moral sensitivity include taking the perspectives of others and controlling prejudice; skills in moral judgment include identifying ethical codes and reflecting on decisions and actions; ethical focus includes skills such as cultivating conscience and valuing traditions; ethical action skills include assertiveness for justice and resolving conflicts peacefully.

*Step 4: Use an apprenticeship approach to instruction (novice-to-expert guided practice).* Teaching for expertise involves direct instruction through role modeling, expert demonstration, and thinking aloud. It also requires extensive opportunities to practice skills and procedures in the four levels described earlier. Learning involves an active and interactive process of transforming conceptual structures through selective attention and by relating new information to prior knowledge. IEE identifies four levels of instruction: immersion, attention to facts and skills, practice procedures, and integration across contexts.

*Step 5: Nurture self-regulation skills.* Plato understood human existence to be a problem to the self. In other words, the final responsibility for character development lies with the individual. Learners must eventually act independently with the skills they have developed. Individuals can be coached not only in skills and expertise but in domain-specific self-efficacy and self-regulation. With guided practice students learn to monitor their own progress in skill development.

The IEE model was successfully implemented during the Minnesota Community Voices and Character Education Project (Narvaez et al., 2004). Local teams of educators and community members implemented the framework of skills and pedagogy according to the needs of the students and community. Those who implemented the program in homeroom/advisory, academic, and schoolwide activities were most successful.

**Further Reading:** Narvaez, D. (2006). Integrative ethical education. In M. Killen & J. Smetana (Eds.), *Handbook of moral development* (pp. 703–33). Mahwah, NJ: Erlbaum. Narvaez, D., Bock, T.S., Endicott, L., & Lies, J. (2004). Minnesota's community voices and character education project. *Journal of Research in Character Education, 2,* 89–112. Lapsley, D.K., & Narvaez, D. (2006). Character education. In W. Damon & R. Lerner (Series Eds.) & A. Renninger & I. Siegel (Vol. Eds.), *Handbook of child psychology* (Vol. 4, pp. 248–96). New York: Wiley. Watson, M.

(2003). *Learning to trust.* San Francisco: Jossey-Bass. Zins, J.E., Weissberg, R.P., Wang, M.C., & Walberg, H.J. (2004). *Building academic success on social and emotional learning.* New York: Teachers College Press.

*Darcia Narvaez*

## Integrity

Integrity appeared in the English language around A.D. 1500 to communicate the wholeness or completeness of a physical object, such as a castle wall. During the seventeenth and eighteenth centuries, Renaissance scholars borrowed the integrity concept to describe the psychological self. Like a castle with surrounding walls of integrity, the self was increasingly described as a coherent, autonomous system that defended itself from the forces of circumstance. After 500 years of use, integrity now represents a fuzzy set of four personal characteristics, including commitment, honesty, fortitude, and benevolence.

### Commitment

Beleaguered theologian Martin Luther proclaimed, "Here I stand; I can do no other." Noncontroversial persons of integrity take a principled—and often unpopular—stand on social issues. At great risk to their reputations and lives, Mahatma Gandhi and Martin Luther King Jr. steadfastly engaged in nonviolent protest to force social change in their countries. In contrast, a person who lacks integrity is "wishy-washy" and vacillates on the issues depending on the preferences of his or her current audience.

Young children tend to expediently obey the rules of their parents and teachers in order to maximize their pleasure-to-pain ratios, but a mature person of integrity does not seem to select among ethical actions based on an uncritical obedience to authority. Instead, persons of integrity engage in a deliberate, conscious form of ethical decision making to discern right actions from wrong actions. Once actions are differentiated into their proper moral domain, the person of integrity conforms to right action and avoids wrong action in his or her public and private lives, irrespective of the current pleasure-to-pain ratio. When necessary, the person of integrity can justify an ethical behavior based on his or her understanding of the moral domain. Thus, a central element of integrity is thinking critically about human actions in terms of morality and then committing to a course of right action in daily life.

### Honesty

Characteristic honesty involves accurately communicating one's thoughts, desires, and emotions to self and others at all times, even when those thoughts or feelings are negative or aversive. Relative to a person who focuses on his or her positive or negative aspects, a person who balances his or her self-descriptions with both positive and negative facets is typically regarded by audiences as more sincere, authentic, and likable. Even unpopular persons of integrity are often respected as "straight shooters" who commit to a moral position and honestly disclose that belief system to others.

In addition to conforming to right action, behaving honestly requires avoiding wrong actions, typically defined as lying, cheating, or stealing. In the business sector, for example, job applicants fill out "integrity tests" that predict office supply theft and other forms of workplace dishonesty. In contrast to an expedient employee, a principled "whistle-blower" demonstrates integrity—a sense of personal conscience and responsibility—by reporting corporate wrongdoings despite considerable pressure to remain silent.

### Fortitude

Integrity denotes resistance to pressure. A bridge with structural integrity resists shifting environmental pressures such as changes in wind speed and vibrations in the earth. When applied to a person, integrity denotes a self-system that resists internal or external pressures to alter its shape—a person who does not "cave in" under pressure. How does the self possess this quality of fortitude? People spend their entire lives forging personal identities in the crucible of social interaction. An identity is a theory of self, a collection of images that people project to their important audiences in order to accomplish interpersonal goals. Healthy adults seem to possess a crystallized identity structure—a strong sense of "me"—that allows them to work efficiently and prepares them for a reality that will someday not include them. Devoid of structural integrity, the self-system tends to focus on itself and spiral into identity confusion, characterized by negative emotions including regret, dread, and despair. In contrast, older adults who possess integrity are regarded as blissful, self-actualized people who focus their attention outward to the welfare of others.

### Benevolence

Honesty can be hurtful. In addition to a developed sense of fairness and justice, a person of integrity tries to avoid harming others. More likely, the person of integrity is known by friends and admirers to go out of his or her way to help others in distress. Unlike the expedient person who helps others to maximize personal welfare, there is a sense of selflessness and humility in the actions of a person of integrity. Instead of a strict "me" orientation to life, a person of integrity effectively balances the interdependence of "we" against the personals needs of coherence and autonomy.

**Further Reading:** Carter, S.L. (1996). *Integrity.* New York: Basic Books. Halfon, M.S. (1989). *Integrity: A philosophical inquiry.* Philadelphia: Temple Press. Peterson, C., & Seligman, M.E. (2004). *Character strengths and virtues: A handbook and classification.* Oxford: Oxford Press.

*Scott Wowra*


# Internalization

Internalization is generally defined as the process through which social conventions and moral values (among other things) that initially are external to the self become part of the self (something that one knows, knows how to do, and regards important to do). Internalization primarily takes place through social interactions; that is, we first experience something in interaction with others and then, subsequently, within ourselves (a part of our understanding, skill set, and belief system). However, one may also internalize norms or values through self-socialization (independent exploration and reflection) or through vicarious interactions (by observing others) or virtual interactions (for example, playing computer games).

As a process, internalization occurs over time, often through repeated or similar interactions. As such, it has been conceptualized as a part of a broader progression of development. In their self-determination theory, for example, Deci and Ryan (1985) make an important distinction between intrinsic and extrinsic motivation (that is, between doing something because it is inherently interesting or enjoyable and doing something because it leads to a separate outcome, a reward, or an avoidance of punishment). The former, by definition, is already internalized (a part of the self's needs or desires), whereas the latter begins as external to or outside the self. For Deci and Ryan, these external regulations (sociomoral norms and values) become a part of the self through a progression of three processes: introjection, internalization, and integration.

*Introjection* is a process whereby individuals replicate or mimic the attitudes, values, and norms of their surrounding social worlds, but do so because of the external "voice" (incorporated unconsciously into the psyche) telling them that they "should" or "must not" behave in a certain manner. During *internalization* these attitudes, values, and norms begin to become a consciously incorporated part of the self, and the reason or motivation for expressing them is now internal (emanating from within). However, for Deci and Ryan, it is only after the process of *integration* is complete that societal norms or moral values truly and fully become ones' own self or identity. At this point, one believes and behaves with *self-determination,* involving a full sense of volition and personal commitment (just as one does when intrinsically motivated).

In their book, *Some Do Care,* Colby and Damon (1992) trace the biographies of several contemporary individuals who have developed extraordinary personal commitments to moral values. Many have endured what most of us would consider great sacrifices, though they would not see it that way. For these individuals, for whom morality and sense of self have become so fully integrated, their actions are not cast in terms of costs or even choice but rather a deep sense of obligation to act and even an inability to imagine not acting. In her recent longitudinal study, Kochanska (2002) sheds light on internalization and development of a moral self during early childhood. Boys who exhibited *committed compliance* (eagerly obeying maternal commands to do or not do something) as opposed to *situational compliance* (obeying to get a reward or avoid punishment) over the first four years of life were more likely to internalize moral norms and integrate them into their own sense of selves as morally "good" children. This sense of moral self mediated the relationship between moral internalization and moral conduct at 56 months.

Finally, it is important to reiterate that internalization is not a simple process of understanding and acquiring a regulation or norm once external to self, but is one of truly owning, valuing, and preferring it. In other words, one may understand moral values or principles such as fairness, due process, or the golden mean, but not have internalized them (that is, made them part of one's personal value system and identity). This, in part, explains the oft-observed incongruity between moral judgment and moral action (Blasi, 1980). This gap, however, is not surprising when you consider that the dominant model of moral judgment (Kohlberg, 1969) deals with cognitive development (that is, the increasing ability to reason in a morally principled manner) and not necessarily with changes of one's preference for or valuing of moral principles. In short, while cognitive development affects one's ability to make moral principles and judgments, internalization affects one's commitment to and behavioral enactment of those principles and judgments.

**Further Reading:** Blasi, A. (1980). Bridging moral cognition and moral action: A critical review of the literature. *Psychological Bulletin, 88,* 1–45. Colby, A., & Damon, W. (1992). *Some do care: Contemporary lives of moral commitment.* New York: Free Press. Deci, E., & Ryan, R. (1985). *Intrinsic motivation and self-determination in human behavior.* New York: Academic Press. Kochanska, G. (2002). Committed compliance, moral self, and internalization: A mediational model.

*Developmental Psychology, 38*(3), 339–51. Kohlberg, L. (1969). Stage and sequence: The cognitive-developmental approach to socialization. In D.A. Goslin (Ed.), *Handbook of socialization theory and research* (pp. 347–480). Chicago: Rand McNally.

*Jason M. Stephens*

## Interpersonal Relationships

Interpersonal relationships are the building blocks of society. Our interpersonal relationships are composed of those we encounter regularly in our personal environments, such as home, school, workplace, and place of worship. At the most basic level, our interpersonal relationships are composed of those in our home life, such as spouses, children, parents, family members, and friends, and fan outward to encompass those in our places of work, houses of worship, and larger community. The quality of our interpersonal relationships in many ways mirrors our overall quality of life and mental and emotional well-being.

Because interpersonal relationships are central in the lives of human beings, they are studied by scholars in a variety of disciplines, including clinical psychology, social psychology, developmental psychology, marriage and family therapy, sociology, and linguistics, to name a few. In addition to being the focal point of the lives of individual people, relationships between people are the focus of politics, current events, art, drama, and writing. For centuries people have worked to understand how and why we build relationships with one another.

Interpersonal relationships, especially those with individuals outside of our family of origin, develop over time. People begin as acquaintances, and if they determine that it would be beneficial to maintain their connection to one another, then a relationship develops. Altman's Social Penetration Theory (1973) is one model for understanding how people build interpersonal relationships, and it asserts that we build interpersonal relationships with others as time passes and as we share more and more intimate details about our lives with each other. The theory states that our communication with others becomes more intimate and personal as time goes on, thus creating deeper connections, or relationships.

Interpersonal relationships fill a basic human need. Maslow (1962) created a hierarchy of personal needs and theorized that a person cannot meet higher needs, such as esteem needs and self-actualization, until he/she has met more basic needs such as being loved and feeling a sense of belongingness with others. Interpersonal relationships help people meet those basic needs by creating a sense of connection with others. People suffer when their basic needs are not met. Just as our physical health will rapidly decline if we do not have adequate food, water, or shelter from extremes in weather, our mental, emotional, and spiritual health will decline if we either are isolated from others or have abusive or unhealthy interpersonal relationships.

The support that people receive from their interpersonal relationships can help them cope with a variety of stressors and can sometimes help protect them from physical illness. One study conducted by Kamarck et al. (1990) found that women showed signs of lowered cardiac stress when doing a math problem in the presence of a female friend than when performing the task alone. In another study focusing on how interpersonal support mediates physical stress, House (1981) found that the presence of interpersonal support may help reduce the feeling or perception that a situation is stressful and therefore reduce the need for the body to produce a heightened response. It is evident from these and many other studies that supportive interpersonal relationships improve overall health and well-being and enable the body to handle stress more effectively.

Healthy, authentic interpersonal relationships require mutual respect, trust, and clear communication. One way that people build trust in interpersonal relationships is by being open and honest with one another. When people lie to or deceive others, they erode the foundations on which their relationships are built. When a conflict arises, people in authentic, healthy relationships address their differences with respect and caring, and are willing to make behavioral changes and compromises to improve their relationships. And when people are unable to resolve their conflicts themselves, they often seek the help of an outside professional such as a counselor, mediator, or religious advisor for help and support.

Building and maintaining healthy interpersonal relationships requires learning and practicing prosocial skills, such as respect, openness, sharing, honesty, kindness, and self-lessness. Such skills are often first encountered in families, in which parents or caregivers teach and model socialization skills to children. Socialization skills are also taught and practiced in social settings such as schools, religious institutions, and community organizations. When children do not receive positive modeling of prosocial behaviors, they often have difficulty creating and maintaining interpersonal relationships throughout adolescence and adulthood.

*Further Reading:* Altman, I., & Taylor, D. (1973). *Social penetration: The development of interpersonal relationships.* New York: Holt, Rinehart and Winston. House, J.S. (1981). *Work, stress, and social support.* Reading, MA: Addison-Wesley. Kamarck, T.W., Manuck, S.B., & Jennings, J.R. (1990). Social support reduces cardiovascular reactivity to psychological challenge: A laboratory model. *Psychosomatic Medicine, 54,* 42–58. Maslow, A.H. (1962). *Toward a psychology of being.* Princeton, NJ: Van Nostrand.

*Michelle E. Flaum*

## Intrapersonal Intelligence

Intrapersonal intelligence is the ability to understand one's own thoughts, feelings, motivations, decisions, behavior, and place in the world. Unlike the intelligence that deals with how smart a person is thought to be, intrapersonal intelligence is more difficult to measure and is best displayed through a person's relationships with others. It differs from interpersonal intelligence in that the goal of intrapersonal intelligence is to understand the self, not to understand the thoughts, feelings, or behaviors of others. Intrapersonal intelligence is self-awareness. It is best expressed in the old adage, "Know thyself."

Gardner (1983) was one of the first to study and describe multiple types of intelligence, and his theory is applied in nearly every educational and behavioral science setting today. Gardner's original theory includes seven types of intelligence: logical-mathematical intelligence, which enables one to think logically and use deductive reasoning; linguistic intelligence, which enables one to express oneself through language; spatial intelligence, which enables one to create mental images for problem solving; musical intelligence, which fosters one's ability to create and recognize musical pitch, tone, and rhythm; bodily kinesthetic intelligence, which enables one to coordinate bodily movements; and personal intelligences—interpersonal intelligence, which is the ability to understand the feelings and motivations of others, and intrapersonal intelligence, which is the ability to understand oneself. Gardner argues that the seven intelligences are interrelated and complement one another to help people solve problems.

Intrapersonal intelligence is linked to identity development, or the process through which one defines who he or she is in relation to the rest of the world. Steinberg (1985) posits there are five major developmental milestones we must achieve as we develop our own personal identities. These milestones span from childhood into adulthood and include the development of our own identity or sense of self and an acceptance of our uniqueness in the world; the development of autonomy, or becoming an independent individual who makes his/her own decisions; the establishing of interpersonal relationships that are intimate and based on trust; the development of one's own sexual identity; and the need for achievement and personal/professional recognition. Intrapersonal intelligence, or self-awareness, helps one navigate through developmental milestones and meet the tasks required to develop into a healthy, fully functioning adult.

Erikson (1968) studied the psychosocial development of individuals and described the development of identity using a stage model. In forming our unique identity, Erikson asserts that we must first survey all possible identities available to us and then choose the identity that best fits our own perception of who we are or who we would like to be. We draw conclusions from those around us, or our role models. In order to be successful in this task, we must possess knowledge and understanding of our selves, or intrapersonal intelligence.

Just as logical-mathematical intelligence can vary greatly from individual to individual, intrapersonal intelligence differs from person to person, and its development can be based on many contributing factors. A person's background, including family of origin, level of familial and parental support, birth order, gender, culture, levels of intelligence in other areas, interpersonal relationships, genetic makeup, and personality, can all contribute to his/her level of intrapersonal intelligence, or ability to understand his/her own thoughts, feelings, motivations, and behaviors. Research has shed some light on how these differences in background impact a person's level of intrapersonal intelligence. In one such study, Furnham (1999) found differences in how people perceive their level of intrapersonal intelligence based on gender. The researchers postulate that these differences in self-perception could relate to gender stereotyping and that, just as men as a group are assumed to have higher levels of mathematical intelligence, women are thought to have higher levels of personal intelligences, both intrapersonal and interpersonal. Most studies either have failed to prove that such differences exist or have shown only slight differences between men and women with respect to all types of intelligence. Today, intelligence of all types is known to be highly individualized and a product of heredity, nurturance, and environment, not of gender, race, or religious affiliation.

The concept of intrapersonal intelligence has become critical in our understanding of our own thoughts, feelings, and behavior. Tests and scales that measure intrapersonal intelligence help professionals understand how self-knowledge can affect a person's functioning in groups, and improve relationships between individuals by helping people boost their self-understanding.

***Further Reading:*** Erikson, E. (1968). *Identity: Youth and crisis.* New York: Norton. Furnham, A., & Rawles, R. (1999). Correlations between self-estimated and psychometrically measured IQ. *Journal of Social Behavior and Personality, 10,* 741–45. Gardner, H. (1983). *Frames of mind.* New York: Basic Books Inc. Gardner, H., & Hatch, T. (1989). Multiple intelligences go to school: Educational implications of the theory of multiple intelligences. *Educational Researcher, 18*(8), 4–9. Steinberg, L. (1985). *Adolescence.* New York: Knopf.

*Michelle E. Flaum*

# J

## Jung, Carl

Carl Jung was born July 26, 1875, in Kesswil, Switzerland. His family included several clergymen, all of whom were well educated in ancient languages and literature. As a result, the young Carl was reading Latin by the time he was six years old, which contributed to his lifelong interest in the role of languages and symbolism in literature and psychology. He went to boarding school in Basel, Switzerland, and then studied medicine at the University of Basel. After working with Swiss neurologist Richard von Krafft-Ebing, he settled on psychiatry as his career and established a private practice in Zurich, where he also taught classes at the University of Zurich. Jung was an admirer of Sigmund Freud, whom he met in Vienna in 1907. The admiration was mutual, and Freud reportedly envisioned Jung as the new voice of psychoanalysis. However, their friendship would later be irrevocably strained by crucial differences of opinion, and they ended their professional relationship just a few years later. After World War I ended, Jung traveled extensively and visited Africa, America, and India. In 1946 he retired from his professional duties, and mostly retreated from public attention after his wife died in 1955. Carl Jung died on June 6, 1961, in Zurich, Switzerland.

The most popular component of Jungian psychology is his distinction between introversion and extroversion as applied to personality types. Jung's personality typology describes an introvert as one who prefers his/her own internal world of thoughts, feelings, and dreams, while an extrovert prefers the external world of people, places, and things. In addition to his distinction between introversion and extroversion as the two dominant personality types, Jung argues that there are essentially four different ways that both introverts and extroverts interpret the world around us. These four functions (as he called them) are sensing, thinking, intuiting, and feeling. The first function, sensing, alludes to the ways we get information through our five sensory perceptions: hearing, seeing, smelling, touching, and tasting. Jung referred to sensing as an irrational function because it does not involve any rational or logical thought process.

The second function is thinking, which is, of course, a rational process because it involves intentional judgment and decision making. The third function, intuiting, is more difficult to explain because it involves a complex integration of all our collective sense perceptions. Jung's final function, or way of dealing with the world, is feeling. Interestingly, he suggests that feeling is a rational function because it involves an evaluation of information and gauging emotional response. According to Jung's theory, we all have these four functions, but each of us has them in different degrees. Most of us fully develop only one or two of these functions, but ideally we should hope to develop all four, to some degree, since each function serves its purpose in helping us to better understand our world. Jung's two personality types and four functions were the primary inspiration for the Myers-Briggs Type Indicator, which is an assessment test to evaluate people's personality type. This paper and pencil test has about 125 questions, and on the basis of your responses, you are placed in one of 16 types, or somewhere between two or three types. The Myers-Briggs Type Indicator is one tool for exploring personality types in a nonjudgmental way.

Unlike Freudian and behavioral psychologists, Jungian psychologists believe that we are meant to become qualitatively better persons (in a moral sense) and not just to adapt and react to environmental stimuli or unconscious motivation. Jung's idea of self-realization is clearly similar to self-actualization, and influenced Maslow's theory. According to Jung, there are some common experiences that may be interpreted as resulting from the collective unconscious, such as near death experiences, the immediate recognition of certain symbols, and the meanings of certain myths. He believed these experiences could be understood as the immediate synthesis of outer reality (the actual physical world we are encountering at that moment) and the inner reality of this collective unconscious. Other examples are the creative experiences shared by artists and musicians all over the world, and the spiritual experiences of persons of all religious traditions.

Often, events occur that are completely unrelated causally, yet seem to have some meaningful connection in our lives. For example, we pick up the phone to dial a friend and she is already on the line, or we dream about the death of a loved one and learn of his passing the next morning. Such events are usually explained as mere coincidence, but Jung believed that they were evidence of our deeper connection to nature and to our fellow human beings. He described such phenomena as synchronicity, the occurrence of two events that are not causally linked but yet are still meaningfully related through the collective unconscious. Jung suggested that when we are in a dreaming or meditative state, our personal unconscious comes closer and closer to our true selves, which he called the collective unconscious. In such transcendent states of being, we are more open to receiving communications from other egos and understanding the universal archetypes of human expression. This idea of synchronicity makes Jung's theory one of the rare ones that is not only compatible with parapsychological phenomena but also offers an explanation for such events.

The contents of the collective unconscious are called archetypes, which act as tools to achieve some mental organization of all our experiences. Jungian archetypes capture what are supposed to be universal rubrics of our human experience. Transcending culture and historical place, Jung's archetypes are meant to act as standard metaphors for our various individual modes of self-expression. What Jung suggested is that there are only so many ways to express ourselves, and we keep reinventing the articulation of those forms of expression through stories and myths that represent universal, archetypal structures of the human mind. The idea of Jungian archetypes holds a special appeal to many writers, artists, musicians, filmmakers, theologians, and clergy of all denominations; some noteworthy examples are Joseph Campbell, C.S. Lewis, J.R. Tolkien, and filmmaker George Lucas. The writings of Carl Jung are more often explored in university humanities departments than in research-dominated schools of psychology and psychiatry. This reflects not only the depth of Jung's commitment to spirituality, but also the reticence on the part of researchers to explore levels of human experience that go beyond external, observable behavior. Educators interested in promoting creativity and spirituality in their classrooms will find inspiration in reading Jung.

*Further Reading:* Breggin, P.R. (1994). *Toxic psychiatry: Why therapy, empathy and love must replace the drugs, electroshock, and biochemical theories of the "new psychiatry."* New York: St. Martin's. Campbell, J. (2004). *Pathways to bliss: Mythology and personal transformation.* New York: New World Library. Johnson, R.A. (1989). *Inner work: Using dreams and creative imagination for personal growth and integration.* San Francisco, CA: Harper. Jung, C.G. (1955). *Modern man in search of a soul.* New York: Harvest HBJ Books. Samuels, A. (1986). *Critical dictionary of Jungian analysis.* London: Taylor & Francis Books, Ltd.

*Monalisa M. Mullins*

## Just Community

The term "just community" comes out of the cognitive developmental tradition of moral education. Beginning with his dissertation in 1958, Lawrence Kohlberg argued forcefully that the most effective means of moral education was through the institutional setting. In one of his best-known educational essays, Kohlberg (1970) described the ideal school as "a little Republic" dedicated to virtue. In Kohlberg's view, while most schools paid lip service to building character, they were almost exclusively preoccupied with academic achievement. Like Jean Piaget and John Dewey, Kohlberg argued forcefully that schools dedicated to justice should involve all students in decision making. After visiting an Israeli kibbutz in the summer of 1969, Kohlberg added the collectivist notion of community to his vision of democratic schools. In addition to giving students a role in governance, the kibbutz set high expectations for group solidarity and shared responsibility for the common good. Kohlberg turned to Emile Durkheim's sociology of education to elaborate the implications of such a group-oriented approach.

The term "just community" thus refers to a group-oriented educational approach that employs democratic processes of governance to foster a culture of community. Kohlberg and colleagues (Hickey & Scharf, 1980) established the first just community program at Niantic State Farm, a women's correctional facility in Connecticut. They began working at the prison by conducting discussions of moral dilemmas. They soon became frustrated with their observations that the prison environment discouraged attempts to act on the higher stage of reasoning that the dilemma discussions often elicited. After successfully negotiating with correction officials, they received permission to establish a just community in one of the cottages. The Niantic inmates and staff welcomed the opportunity to build a very different kind of cottage climate. With assistance from Kohlberg, Hickey, and Scharf, they made cottage rules and enforced them. More importantly, they learned how to listen to each others' problems and offer each other support, building a sense of mutual care that few of them had ever experienced.

Not long after opening the just community cottage in Niantic, Kohlberg was asked to join a planning committee for a new alternative high school in Cambridge, which was called Cluster School. Actually the new school would be a less than half-day school-within-a-school. Students would take a double-period core course, which combined social studies and English. The committee agreed to Kohlberg's proposal that the school be governed by a weekly community meeting in which students and teachers would have a single vote. Kohlberg did not require that Cluster's faculty make any explicit commitment to apply his moral stage theory. All that he required was that faculty abide by the democratic process.

With the exception of its highly diverse student body, Cluster looked like many of the alternative schools, which opened in the late 1960s and 1970s with the goal of liberating students from the constraints of authoritarian discipline and highly didactic teaching practices. Cluster teachers, like so many alternative school teachers at the time, believed that students would flourish in a permissive atmosphere, which emphasized self-expression, choice, and personal responsibility.

Kohlberg, seasoned by his kibbutz visit and Niantic experience, had a very different vision for Cluster. Far from being a "free school," Kohlberg proposed Cluster be a community that took pride in its commitment to fairness and discipline. He emphasized that democracy was to be more than an occasion to vent about problems or to recreate the conventional rules in the parent school. Kohlberg urged the faculty to guide the democratic process so that students would first "own" problems, such as stealing and cutting class, and then work together to solve them. Students and faculty had a far more difficult time taking community responsibility for the violations of a few "bad apples." For example, after an initial incident of stealing in the school, many students responded that stealing concerned only the victim and the thief. Kohlberg insisted that the stealing was everyone's business and a stealing rule should represent a shared commitment to discourage stealing. Faculty as well as students found Kohlberg's attention to community to be a far cry from the romantic individualism they expected. The sometimes chaotic early days of Cluster convinced them that building community would be an immensely challenging task.

The Cluster School and the Just Community Programs that followed adopted a set of institutions and practices that define the Just Community approach (Power, Higgins, & Kohlberg, 1989). Key to the approach is a weekly community meeting, which lasts from one to two class periods of about 50 minutes each. The community meeting brings together all faculty and students to deliberate upon matters of common concern. All voting is done within the community meeting. Concerned that students might rush to a vote before adequate discussion, Kohlberg and his colleagues required that a "straw vote" be taken in advance of binding votes and that the discussion prior to the vote be conducted along the lines of a moral dilemma discussion with a focus on the values and reasons being advanced in defense of a particular position. Before the community meetings, smaller teacher-student advisor group meetings were held to prepare students for the community meeting in a small group atmosphere. The advisor group meetings were also the occasion for students to build closer relationships with each other and their teachers and to share more personal concerns in a more intimate setting. Community and advisor group meetings were generally preceded by a faculty planning meeting. Chronic disciplinary problems and disputes were referred to the discipline or fairness committee. This committee was made up a rotating group of faculty and students selected by lot.

*Further Reading:* Kohlberg, L. (1970). Education for justice: A modern restatement of the Platonic view. In N. Sizer & T. Sizer (Eds.), *Moral education: Five lectures.* Cambridge, MA: Harvard University Press. Hickey, J., & Scharf, P. (1980). *Toward a just correctional system.* San Francisco: Jossey-Bass. Power, F. C., Higgins, A., & Kohlberg, L. (1989). *Lawrence Kohlberg's approach to moral education.* New York: Columbia University Press.

*F. Clark Power*

# Justice

Justice may be understood as a principle of morality or as one of the chief or cardinal virtues of a good person. In both cases, the paradigm or prototypical situation is one in which a judgment is rendered in a dispute between conflicted parties or competing interests.

As an abstract principle, justice has been understood recently, under the sway of Kantian and J. S. Mill's utilitarian metaethical theories, to require impartiality and universalizability. A judgment is impartial if it does not show preference for, or confer privileges upon, some over others in arbitrary ways. For instance, one's family members or friends should not be more likely to receive jobs or contracts than others equally or better suited to perform the same services. A judgment is universalizable if it would be considered valid in all relevantly similar circumstances. One should not deliberately mislead one's audience in a particular case, for example, unless it would be appropriate for anyone to deliberately mislead one's audience in all relevantly similar cases.

Three main types of justice have been discussed. Distributive justice concerns the allocation of goods or benefits among members of a society or group. Retributive justice concerns the assignment and imposition of penalties for wrongdoing. And procedural justice concerns the equitable implementation of laws and policies, such as in the administration of the functions of government.

On this account of justice, it has not been surprising that some have supposed that justice is a matter of impersonal relations between anonymous persons, for justice has seemed to require us to treat every person and each situation as if it were not special either to us or in itself.

Alternatively, a just judgment can be construed as one that satisfies the conditions of equality and reciprocity. A person who renders a just judgment treats like cases alike and gives to each what is owed.

To reciprocate is to return a favor (or analogously to repay one wrong with another). In a reciprocal relationship (excluding vendettas or other relationships of retribution), people exchange benefits over time and become indebted to each other. For instance, a friend of yours may pay for lunch one day, and you may return the favor by covering cab fare when you travel across town together, where the cab fare is about the same cost as the earlier lunch. People keep track of who is ahead to the extent necessary to know when one is falling behind.

One's reciprocal relationships may be one-with-one or interpersonal. In the latter, each contributes to the group by benefiting group members indiscriminately and does not keep track of one-with-one debts, though one keeps track of what one owes to and is owed by the group. Or, third, one may be engaged in a social reciprocal relationship, where each performs an assigned role within a cooperative team or community that is seeking a common good. One owes in role performance some benefit comparable to what one receives in sharing in the common good.

Somewhat more expansively, the principle of justice has sometimes been called "the Golden Rule." We should treat others as we wish to be treated by them. What is owed to another is specified by reference to what one would prefer to receive, were one in a reciprocal relationship with that person or persons. This goes beyond concrete one-with-one, interpersonal, and social reciprocity insofar as it includes those with whom one has not established reciprocal relationships.

A question of justice, then, is one in which there is a dispute or conflict in which someone claims to be owed something they are being denied. A reciprocal relationship has broken down. The criteria of impartiality and universalizability can be seen to presuppose abstract or hypothetical reciprocal relationships that extend beyond one-with-one, interpersonal, and social relationships. Such presupposed abstract reciprocal relationships include indirect relationships within a large urban, national, or international society. Hypothetical reciprocal relationships posit a hypothetical association between persons who are not both members of an identifiable society.

In this light, we can see that the so-called "justice-care debate" of the 1980s gets off the ground only if justice is misconstrued exclusively to concern impartial, universalizable judgments between persons who are not bound in concrete reciprocal relationships and/ or who are anonymous to each other. If, on the other hand, justice is grounded in concrete reciprocity and then extended to abstract or hypothetical reciprocal relationships, then justice presupposes care, insofar as responsiveness to the concrete needs of others with whom one is in relationship is part of what we owe to friends or to those with whom we are otherwise bound in a reciprocal relationship.

As a virtue, rather than as a moral principle, justice is the discernment and tendency to judge justly and to carry out these judgments, that is, in ways that treat like cases alike and give to each what is owed.

To think that all morality boils down to one or another term of justice is to suppose that all morality is essentially a matter of conflict resolution. By contrast, to think that justice is one among several important virtues is to suppose that conflict resolution is one among several situations of human interaction and choice in which we must do well to fare well in life. Others include situations in which we face danger in defense of a worthy cause (requiring courage), or in which we must choose wisely how to satisfy our appetites (requiring temperance or moderation), or in which we need to solve practical problems by employing our wits and learning (requiring prudence or practical wisdom).

**Further Reading:** Kohlberg, L. (1981). Justice as reversibility: The claim to moral adequacy of a highest stage of moral judgment. In *The philosophy of moral development*. New York: Harper & Row. MacIntyre, A. (1989). *Whose justice? Which rationality?* Notre Dame, IN: University of Notre Dame. Dame Press. Rawls, J. (1971). *A theory of justice*. Cambridge, MA: Harvard University Press. Walzer, M. (1983). *Spheres of justice*. New York: Basic Books, Inc.

*Don Collins Reed*

## Justice Reasoning

The term justice reasoning is a broad one with different meanings depending on the context. Within Lawrence Kohlberg's cognitive developmental framework, justice reasoning is synonymous with moral reasoning. Kohlberg believed that the function of moral reasoning was to resolve conflicting claims among or between individuals in a way that was fair or just. Following Jean Piaget, Kohlberg thought of justice reasoning as achieving reciprocity or equilibrium among those whose interests were in conflict. Justice reasoning in its broadest sense may thus be defined as a specific kind of social reasoning that has as its aim the resolution of social conflicts in a way that all parties find fair.

Key to justice reasoning and its development is perspective or role taking. Conflict resolution depends upon application of the golden rule: to treat others as you would have them treat you. This means getting into the shoes of other people and understanding their claims. The stages of moral reasoning may be understood as progressively more adequate ways of freeing oneself from an exclusive preoccupation with one's own interests (egocentrism) and taking into account the interests of others. The higher stages of justice reasoning also include taking into account the justice of social institutions and the relationship between one's rights and duties as a member of society.

Carol Gilligan criticized Kohlberg's moral psychology for its exclusive focus on justice and individual rights, which she believed represented a male oriented morality. In response, Gilligan proposed a female oriented morality of care. Kohlberg acknowledged that care may be distinguished from justice, but he did not agree that justice and care represented two different moralities with two different kinds of reasoning. He argued that care was based on justice but went beyond justice in two ways. First, whereas justice is concerned with giving persons their due, care is concerned with benevolence, which means giving others what is good for them. Second, whereas justice seeks a balance or equality between the interests of the self and the interests of others, care entails a willingness to sacrifice one's legitimate self-interest for the good of the other. Gilligan and other critics have countered that Kohlberg's understanding of morality misses the irreducible relational qualities identified within a morality of care.

The debate over the relationship between justice and care raised a related issue at the heart of moral psychology. Gilligan maintained that the justice orientation was based on an abstract and individualistic conception of rights as opposed to responsibilities. She noted that, in contrast, the care orientation was based on a contextually dependent experience of responsibility within a relationship. From a different angle, Augusto Blasi criticized Kohlberg for focusing only on reasoning about the justice of actions and failing to take into account the moral agent's sense of responsibility. Appropriating insights from Gilligan and Blasi, while reflecting on research data from the just community schools, Kohlberg came to see responsibility as mediating the relationship between justice reasoning and moral action.

Some cognitive developmental psychologists, such as William Damon, have found Kohlberg's focus on justice reasoning to be too broad and have followed a long tradition of moral philosophy in distinguishing among different kinds of justice. Distributive justice involves how goods, such as money and status should be allocated. For example, should they be divided according to status, merit, or need or should all good be distributed equally? Retributive justice concerns the apportionment of punishment. Should punishments fit the crime or should the severity of a punishment depend on its effectiveness as a deterrent? Perhaps punishment should be corrective and serve to rehabilitate the offender? Procedural justice concerns what processes should be used to make and implement decisions? Do individuals convicted of a crime have a right to a fair trial? Should public policies be enacted without the advice and consent of the public or their representatives? Attending to procedural justice is important not only for guaranteeing a justice result (substantive justice) but also appears to be morally required in its own right. Individuals are more likely to accept policies with which they disagree if the procedures used to arrive at them are fair. Research indicates that, as expected, these concepts of justice involve somewhat distinctive patterns of reasoning and paths of development.

*Further Reading:* Blasi, A. (1980). Bridging moral cognition and moral action: A critical review of the literature. *Psychological Bulletin, 88,* 1–45. Damon, W. (1990). *The moral child: Nurturing children's natural moral growth.* New York: The Free Press. Gilligan, C. (1982). *In a different voice: Psychological theory and women's development.* Cambridge, MA: Harvard University Press. Kohlberg, L. (1981). *Essays in moral development, Volume 1: The philosophy of moral development.* New York: Harper and Row. Kohlberg, L. (1984). *Essays in moral development, Volume 2: The psychology of moral development.* New York: Harper and Row.

*F. Clark Power*

# K

## Kant, Immanuel

Immanuel Kant was born in 1724 in Königsberg, a city that was then part of East Prussia. Kant reportedly never traveled more than 50 miles beyond his home in Königsberg, where he studied at the university and subsequently taught philosophy for over 40 years. He was held in high regard by his neighbors and colleagues for his degree of self-discipline and his strong work ethic. His most important works are considered to be the *Critique of Pure Reason,* in which he suggests that human knowledge must be mediated by our rational minds (Abela, 2002), and *Groundwork of the Metaphysics of Morals,* in which he posits the "Categorical Imperative" as a universal moral law. Immanuel Kant died at the age of 60, in 1804.

Kant's moral theory is based on the assumption that we are rational thinkers with the power to logically discern what is morally correct behavior. His statement of the Categorical Imperative suggests that we must always act in such a way that we can will that our actions are also dictated for all other persons as well. In other words, we are morally obliged to perform actions that others should also perform. Likewise, if we cannot apply the obligation of an action to all other persons, then we should not consider that action as appropriate for ourselves. For example, suppose that I have an urgent need for information from a reference book in the library, and the copy machine is broken. Could I justify tearing out pages from the book because of the urgency of my need? If I apply the Categorical Imperative as my standard rule of thumb to answer this question, then I will understand that I cannot justify this action because it would violate the moral law. In this case, the violation is clear; I cannot justify this act because I would not want everyone else to do the same thing. My action cannot be universalized for others; therefore it cannot be a morally acceptable action.

This makes the Kantian Categorical Imperative sound very much like the Christian understanding of the golden rule: Do unto others as you would have them do unto you. However, Kant's Categorical Imperative requires that we always treat others as we would have them treat us, even if we do not want to do this. In other words, while the golden rule points to the reciprocity of mutual respect as a standard for moral action, the Kantian

Categorical Imperative requires this moral obligation even when others do not reciprocate our respect.

For Kant, the categorical imperative is the single most important standard of rationality from which our moral obligations are derived. As an imperative, this rational standard is a rule that has the power of a law, in the sense that we are "duty bound" to obey this rule. Futhermore, it is a categorical imperative because we cannot violate it without also being irrational. Thus, for Kant, the most essential aspect of morality is our rational free will, which binds us to act as an autonomous moral agent. If we choose to ignore this autonomous power within ourselves, then we are acting as if we did not have the power to think clearly; that is, we are acting irrationally.

The Kantian notion of a free and autonomous will is also an idea that figures predominantly in Christian moral thought as well (Sullivan, 1994). However, for Kant, the only conceptual framework for morality that is good without qualification is this notion of a "good will" that serves as our absolute moral compass. If we are cognizant of this good will within us, then we will be guided to choose the right moral action. To do otherwise would be unthinkable, insofar as we understand ourselves to be morally obliged to always do the right thing.

This notion of the power of an autonomous good will is representative of an idealized version of human nature, to say the least. However, Kant does concede that we are not always inclined to do the right thing; indeed, it is at those times when we are least inclined to follow our moral obligations that we find ourselves in a moral dilemma. Nonetheless, he believes that if we follow the categorical imperative as our moral guide for action then we will see clearly how we ought to behave, and the moral dilemma will be dissolved. Being inclined to do the right thing is never the proper reason to act morally unless one is following the sense of moral duty that requires the rational obligation to obey the categorical imperative.

The distinction between actions performed from inclination and those performed from a sense of moral duty is an interesting aspect of Kantian moral theory because it creates a rather bizarre scale for measuring the moral worth of an action. For example, if I follow the categorical imperative, then I am morally obliged to treat others with respect and never only as means to an end. Now, this action is morally obligatory and therefore always the right moral action. However, if I am also inclined to do this, to treat others with respect and never just as means to some end, then the moral worth of my action is weakened by my concurrent inclination. The same action would carry greater moral worth if I still did treat others with respect and not only as means to an end, but I was not so inclined. In this latter case, I did not really want to do the right thing, but I did anyway because I recognized my moral duty to do so. In the former case, I did the right thing, but doing so was an easy task because I was inclined by my nature to behave in this manner.

This scale for measuring the moral worth of an action is Kant's way of recognizing that it is not always easy to do the right thing. So, for example, it is easy for me not to cheat on a test if I am also inclined not to cheat because I am a very bright student. Perhaps the student sitting next to me is not as naturally talented and is having difficulty answering the questions on the test. She might be inclined to consider cheating, but if she resists this inclination and refuses to cheat then her action has more moral worth than my action. Cheating is morally wrong because it is a violation of the Categorical Imperative to act only in such a way that you could will for everyone else to do the same thing. In this case, we both did the right thing because neither one of us cheated. Yet, it was clearly much easier for me to do the right thing than it was for my peer, and therefore her moral action receives greater moral worth than mine. We both acted upon our sense of moral duty just as we were both rationally obliged to do, but the level of difficulty in meeting that obligation was relative to our individual personal inclinations. In this way, we see that an application of the Kantian moral principle to follow the categorical imperative carries an obligation to also understand the weight of the moral worth attached to doing the right thing.

**Further Reading:** Abela, P. (2002). *Kant's empirical realism.* Oxford, England: Oxford University Press. Guyer, P. (Ed.). (1997). *Kant's groundwork of the metaphysics of morals: Critical essays.* New York: Rowman & Littlefield. Kitcher, P. (Ed.). (1998). *Kant's critique of pure reason: Critical essays.* New York: Rowman & Littlefield. Sullivan, R.J. (1994). *An introduction to Kant's ethics.* Cambridge, England: Cambridge University Press.

*Monalisa M. Mullins*

## Kirschenbaum, Howard

Howard Kirschenbaum (1944– ) received his B.A. at the New School for Social Research in 1966. In 1968 he received his M.S. degree and, in 1975, the Ed.D. from Temple University in Philadelphia where he also served as an instructor from 1969 to 1971. Additionally, he has taught undergraduate and graduate courses in education, educational psychology, counseling, and human relations at several universities including the New School for Social Research, Temple University (1969–1971), SUNY Brockport (1992–97), and the University of Rochester (1997). In 2000 he became the chair of the Department of Counseling and Human Development at the Margaret Warner Graduate School of Education and Human Development. In 2006, after serving six years as the department chair, he was designated Professor Emeritus.

For some 30 years Kirschenbaum has been an international and national educational consultant focusing on values and character education, humanistic education, human relations, grading practices, sex education, communication, and environmental stewardship. He has served as the Executive Director of the National Humanistic Education Center, Upper Jay, New York (1971–1977), at the Sagamore Institute, Raquette Lake, New York (1977–1990), and as the president of Values Associates in Rochester, New York (1990–1997).

He has authored or co-authored 23 books on diverse subjects within the disciplines of education, psychology, and history. In particular, he has been recognized as a leading scholar of the life and work of Carl Rogers. He has had over 80 works appear in an array of publications including but not limited to *Phi Delta Kappan, Journal of Counseling and Development, Principal, Practitioner, Elementary School Guidance and Counseling, Group & Organizational Studies,* and *Moral Education Forum.*

Along with Louis Raths, Merrill Harmin, and Sidney Simon, Kirschenbaum was a strong advocate of the values clarification (VC) movement of the late 1960s, 1970s, and 1980s (see "Values Clarification"). *Values and Teaching: Working with Values in the Classroom* (1966), by Raths, Harmin, and Simon, provided a strong rationale for the inclusion of direct and explicit attention paid to student values in classroom practice. While not one of the original proponents, Kirschenbaum joined Simon and Leland Howe for the publication of *Values Clarification: A Handbook of Practical Strategies for Teachers and Students* (1972/1978), a work that emphasized values clarification as an approach through which individuals come to understand and develop their own value systems in order to better analyze and clarify what is important to them. In *Readings in Values Clarification* (1973), Kirschenbaum and Simon placed VC within the broader category of humanistic education and advocated a new concept of "life skills." There is little argument about the initial popularity of VC. Kirschenbaum writes that 40 books emphasizing values clarification were published during the 1970s with the 1972/1978 handbook selling more than 600,000 copies—"almost unheard of in the field of education" (1992, p. 2).[1] However, just as popular was a growing reaction to VC from a variety of perspectives (see "Values Clarification"). To counter these criticisms, Kirschenbaum in *Advanced Value Clarification* (1977), after crediting Louis E. Raths as the originator of VC, set out to reconcile the oppositional views with praise coming from "thousands of teachers, parents, counselors and others" (p. 3). After citing evidence from 33 studies, he concluded that they

> lend considerable face validity to the hypothesis that: if reasonable receptive teachers go through a competently led experience in value-clarification training their energy and enthusiasm for teaching will be increased, and a large percentage will return to their classrooms and implement the approach so that their students will be positively influenced on various dimensions of personal and/or academic growth. (p. 37)

Yet the criticism continued to have a strong impact and by the early 1980s VC, in Kirschenbaum's words, had fallen from academic grace and popular acclaim. He cites five reasons for the decline: changing times, faddism, stagnation, erratic implementation, and the assumption that VC by itself was sufficient to influence student moral behavior. The recognition of this major flaw in the theory resulted in Kirschenbaum embracing the rapidly expanding fields of moral and character education both in theory and practice. In *Comprehensive Model for Values Education and Moral Education* (1992), he argued for a four element position that includes all value-related issues from the personal to the ethical, incorporates various methodologies (including the discussion of moral dilemmas), takes place throughout the school rather than being classroom bound, and expands to the community beyond the confines of the school. He continued his comprehensive approach in *One Hundred Ways to Enhance Values and Morality in Schools and Youth Settings* (1995). Here he combines the old with the new, the traditional to inculcate and model the best values and moral traditions of the culture and the progressive to develop capacity for personal value development and moral literacy.

In *From Values Clarification to Character Education* (2000) Kirschenbaum reiterates his belief that the fatal theoretical flaw of VC was that it took for granted students' moral foundation and thus assumed their value choices would be good and responsible and thereby moral; VC was not a complete program but was only a part of a more comprehensive understanding of value and character development. His move to character education, now seemingly complete, can be inferred by noting the missing word "clarification" in his recent writings (undated):

> as I came to better understand the strengths and limitation of the values clarification approach, I became and remain active in the character education movement of the 90s

through today. I developed a comprehensive approach to values education that includes values realization, character education, citizenship education and moral education.[2]

Clarification may be gone, yet Kirschenbaum's interest in values education has not wavered. He continues to develop a character-based, comprehensive approach to sex education for teenagers as well as explore the work and life of Carl Rogers, whom he cites as one of the most influential psychologists and psychotherapists in history (Kirschenbaum 1979; Kirschenbaum & Henderson, 1989).

## Notes

1. The cover of the new and revised (1995) handbook, now renamed workbook, states "over 900,000 copies in print."

2. Howard, Berkowitz, and Schaeffer (2004, p. 94) write: "One indication of the nadir of values clarification is the fact that an author of one of the major values clarification book could in 1995 write a history of character education that never mentions *value clarification* by name." The book referred to is Kirschenbaum's (1995) *One Hundred Ways*.

***Further Reading:*** Howard, R., Berkowitz, M., & Schaeffer, E. (2004). Politics of character education. *Educational Policy, 18*(1), 188–215. Kirschenbaum, H., & Simon, S.B. (Eds.). (1973). *Readings in values clarification*. Minneapolis, MN: Winston Press. Kirschenbaum, H. (1977). *Advanced value clarification*. La Jolla, CA: University Associates. Kirschenbaum, H. (1979). *On becoming Carl Rogers*. New York: Delacorte/Delta Press. Kirschenbaum, H., & Henderson,V. (Eds.). (1989). *The Carl Rogers reader*. Boston: Houghton Mifflin. Kirschenbaum, H. (1992). A comprehensive model for values and moral education. *Phi Delta Kappan, 73*(10), 771–76. Kirschenbaum, H. (1995). *One hundred ways to enhance values and morality in schools and youth settings*. Needham Heights, MA: Allyn and Bacon. Kirschenbaum, H. (2000). From values clarification to character education: A personal journey. *Journal of Humanistic Counseling, Education and Development, 39*(1), 4–20. Kirschenbaum, H. (undated). Howard Kirschenbaum. Accessed on April 23, 2007, at http://www.rochester.edu/warner/faculty/kirschenbaum/values.html. Raths, L., Harmin, M., & Simon, S. (1966). *Values and teaching: Working with values in the classroom*. Columbus, OH: Charles E. Merrill. Simon, S., Howe, L., & Kirschenbaum, H. (1972/1978). *Values clarification: A handbook of practical strategies for teachers and students*. New York: Hart Publishing. Simon, S., Howe, L., & Kirschenbaum, H. (1995). *Values clarification: A practical, action-directed workbook*. New York: Warner Books.

*Tom Wilson*

## Kohlberg, Lawrence

Lawrence Kohlberg was born in 1927 in Bronxville, New York. After his high school graduation, Kohlberg chose to put college on hold in order to help European war refugees trying to resettle in Israel. Later he earned his doctorate from the University of Chicago, and joined the faculty there from 1962 to 1968. Kohlberg subsequently moved to Harvard University in 1969, where he remained until his death in 1987. Kohlberg is best known for his stage theory of moral development, which suggests that children undergo significant changes in moral reasoning abilities around the ages of 10 or 11. He argued that older children (post-10 through 12 years) will begin to judge moral worth as a function of intentions rather than consequences, and he views this as the mark of progress toward full moral maturity.

Kohlberg's theory of moral development originally involved six (later revised to five) stages of moral skills orientation that he attributes to three distinct levels of cognitive development. The first of these levels Kohlberg labeled Preconventional insofar as actions are guided primarily by concern for the consequences of those actions. The Preconventional Level (Level I) of moral development includes the first two stages of moral skills orientation; in stage one, children are inclined to act based primarily on their perceptions of degrees of punishment or other negative consequences. One of Kohlberg's earliest research projects involved interviews with 10-, 13-, and 16-year-old boys who were given hypothetical moral dilemmas such as the following fictional scenario: Mrs. Heinz was near death from a special kind of cancer. There was one drug that the doctors thought might save her, but it was very expensive and Mr. Heinz could not afford to purchase it. He told the druggist that his wife was dying and asked him to sell it cheaper or let him pay later. The druggist refused, so Heinz got desperate and broke into the man's store to steal the drug for his wife. Should the husband have done that?

The point of these interviews was to understand how the boys justified their responses to these questions; that is, Kohlberg was interested in assessing the level of moral reasoning skills demonstrated by the subjects. For example, after presenting the children with this hypothetical moral dilemma, the interviewers would ask if Mr. Heinz was entitled to the medicine, or if Mr. Heinz violated the rights of the drugstore owner. The children were asked to explain their responses so their stage of moral development could be better understood. In Kohlberg's first stage, obedience to rules will simply reflect deference to authority. Children at this first stage of development usually say that Mr. Heinz should not have stolen the drug because that would be against the law. When asked to explain their response further, the children offered the elaboration in terms of the consequences of Heinz's actions, for example, that stealing is bad because of the risk of punishment.

In the second stage of the Preconventional Level, children still exhibit an egocentric preoccupation with satisfying their own needs, but also begin to recognize a multiplicity of viewpoints. For example, they see that Mr. Heinz thinks it is right to take the drug, but point out that the druggist would not agree. Even at this second stage of moral development, the children are still reasoning from the preconventional perspective of consequences and benefits; they see moral answers mostly in terms of what those persons in positions of authority say they must do.

The second level of moral development, the Conventional Level, reflects a child's growing concern for approval from others and an increased interest in maintaining social order. In stage three of the Conventional Level, the children begin to see Heinz's motives as good and the druggist's motives to be bad, and indicate that we should behave in "good" ways. When pressed to elaborate, children at stage three defined good behavior as having good motives and interpersonal feelings such as love, trust, and concern for others. According to Kohlberg, these stage three responses are "conventional" because they have the expectation that these judgments would be shared by the entire community, and that anyone would be right to do what Mr. Heinz did.

The need to seek approval eventually yields to Kohlberg's fourth stage, in which the child becomes increasingly motivated to act from a sense of duty and respect for social convention. Actions may now be oriented more toward the child's perception of "doing the right thing" even if it should conflict with the popular choice of the group. In this last stage of the Conventional Level, we see the emergence of moral reasoning that attaches strong value to the maintenance of social order and respect for laws as being necessary for society as a whole. According to Kohlberg, it is this universal perspective that advances the child's moral reasoning skills to a higher level.

Kohlberg's last level of moral development is the Postconventional Level. In response to the Heinz dilemma, children in stage five do not generally approve of breaking laws because laws are social contracts that we must honor or change through the democratic process. However, in this stage, children also begin to view the wife's right to live as an intrinsic moral right that should be protected by society. They begin to reflect on the essential elements of a good society, and they make moral judgments based on these considerations regarding the nature of a good society. In the final stage of moral development, one's individual principles of moral conscience would presumably yield judgments based on the principle of universality. Like Immanuel Kant, Kohlberg believes that the highest order of moral reasoning is that stage at which one chooses to act in a way that reflects a universal principle of action, and he argues that reaching that highest level requires a reflective and autonomous scrutiny of moral options.

There have been strong critics to Kohlberg's theory of moral development, most notably from Carol Gilligan, who argues that Kohlberg's stages are based on a male conception of morality that neglects to appreciate the "different voice" in a female conception of morality. Whatever questions might remain concerning the efficacy of Kohlberg's theory, his influence has nonetheless been tremendous in the field of developmental psychology. The implications of Kohlberg's stages of moral development for educational practice remain critical points for discussion, not only for early childhood programs but for adolescent programs as well. There is certainly much room to explore further the connections between Kantian ethical frameworks and Kohlberg's Postconventional Level of moral development.

**Further Reading:** Benninga, J.S. (1991). Moral and character education in the elementary school: An introduction. In J.S. Benninga (Ed.), *Moral, character, and civic education in the elementary school.* New York: Teachers College Press. Berkowitz, M.W. (1985). The role of discussion in moral education. In M.W. Berkowitz & F. Oser (Eds.), *Moral education: Theory and application.* Hillsdale, NJ: L. Erlbaum. Gibbs, J.C. (1991). Toward an integration of Kohlberg's and Hoffman's theories of morality. In W.M. Kurtines & J.L. Gewirtz (Eds.), *Handbook of moral behavior and development.* Hillsdale, NJ: L. Erlbaum. Kohlberg, L. (1979). Moral stages and moralization: The cognitive-developmental approach. In T. Lickona (Ed.), *Moral development and behavior: Theory, research and social issues.* New York: Holt Rinehart & Winston. Peters, R.S. (1981). *Moral development and moral education.* London: George Allen & Unwin.

*Monalisa M. Mullins*

# L

## Leming, James Stanley

James Stanley Leming (1941– ), Carl A. Gerstacker Chair in Education, Saginaw Valley State University, chronicler of both the research and history of character education, and advocate for objectivity in its reporting, is the author or editor of four books and over 60 book chapters, articles in professional journals, and reports related in the main to social studies and moral and character education.

Born in Champaign, Illinois, Leming received his B.A. (1964) and M.A. (1966) from the University of Illinois in Social Studies Education and his Ph.D. (1973) from the University of Wisconsin in Curriculum and Instruction. Shortly after receiving his doctorate, he accepted a faculty position at SUNY Stony Brook, and four years later, in 1977, he accepted a position at Southern Illinois University where he remained for 23 years. In 2000 he was offered his current position, an endowed chair in education. In May 2001 he was awarded the Distinguished Alumni Award from the College of Education at the University of Wisconsin–Madison.

A focus of Leming's academic work has coupled the measurement and statistical analysis of moral and character education programs in schools with its contextual setting in twentieth century educational history. In doing so he has clarified understanding of both the application and research of moral and character education in particular, and the social studies in general.

His empirical research extends over four decades and includes, for example, research relating moral reasoning and political activism among adolescents (1974), moral reasoning and cheating behaviors (1978), cooperative learning (1985), and the evaluation of a literature-based character education program for children (2000). In addition, since 1988, he has authored or co-authored no fewer than 15 separate technical evaluation reports on projects related to character education, teaching ethics to adults and adolescents, and teaching character to children. In 2000 Leming authored *What Works in Character Education,* a comprehensive review of research, the foundation for the "Character Assessment and Program Evaluation Index" published by the Character Education Partnership's Assessment Committee that he chaired.

Leming has had a continuing interest in the history of character education and has produced a series of publications and papers on the topic. His work has clarified the status of the significance of the H. Hartshorne and M.A. May research in the 1920s as well as the effects of research on the practice of values clarification and moral education (1997). With regard to Hartshorne and May, Leming notes both the "meticulous and careful" research undertaken, yet its lack of significance on educational practice. Conversely, he documents that the values clarification movement had considerable impact of educational practice despite "vigorous research" to the contrary. Indeed, he writes, research findings "seem to have little impact on practice" in education.

Leming is highly regarded for his work documenting the evidence of program effectiveness in character education. His first such published review (1993) covered research on values clarification and moral education as well as ancillary research on sex and drug education, methods for improving school climate, and contemporary character education. He concluded that didactic methods alone have little impact on character, that moral discussions have little impact on the moral behavior of middle and high school students, and that a "social web or environment" of both limits and supports shape the behaviors of students. He recommended an inclusive perspective on subsequent character education research that integrated appropriate research from sociology, philosophy, and child development. A second review (1999) evaluated ten specific character education programs and drew further research implications. These reviews have become the standard for other such summaries (e.g., Berkowitz and Bier, 2005).

Concurrent with his academic efforts in moral and character education, Leming has been actively engaged as a participant and critic of social studies education. From 1964 to 1969 he was a teacher of high school social studies and mathematics in Des Plaines, Illinois. He is a former member of the board of the National Council for the Social Studies (1995–1998) and past president of the Social Science Education Consortium (1993–1994).

From that practical and conceptual foundation, Leming has criticized modern social studies education for its specific lack of emphasis on American history and government, and for its general lack of attention to geography and economics. In 2003 he and co-editors Lucien Ellington and Kathleen Porter published their critique in a book, *Where Did Social Studies Go Wrong?* Its thesis was that "the state of social studies education at the turn of the twenty-first century...is moribund," due to the dominance of conflicting politicized and often superficial topics. Leming concluded that such misdirected focus has led to "the abandonment of the mission of teaching good quality content" (p. 138).

*Further Reading:* Leming, J.S. (1993). Synthesis of research: In search of effective character education. *Educational Leadership, 51*(3), 63–71. Leming, J.S. (1997). Research and practice in character education: A historical perspective. In A. Molnar (Ed.), *The construction of children's character,* 96th Yearbook of the National Society for the Study of Education, Part II (pp. 31–44). Chicago: University of Chicago Press. Leming, J.S. (2003). Ignorant activists. In J.S. Leming, L. Ellington, & K. Porter, *Where did social studies go wrong?* Washington, D.C.: Thomas Fordham Foundation.

*References:* Berkowitz, M.W., & Bier, M. (2005). *What works in character education.* Washington, D.C.: Character Education Partnership. Leming, J.S. (1974). Moral reasoning, sense of control, and social-political activism among adolescents. *Adolescence, 9,* 507–529. Leming, J.S. (1978). Cheating behavior, situational influence and moral development. *Journal of Educational Research, 71,* 214. Leming, J.S. (1993). Synthesis of research: In search of effective character education. *Educational Leadership, 51*(3), 63–71. Leming, J.S. (1997). Research and practice in character education: A historical perspective. In A. Molnar (Ed.), *The construction of children's character*, 96th Yearbook of the National Society for the Study of Education, Part II (pp. 31–44). Chicago: University of Chicago Press. Leming, J.S. (1999). Current evidence regarding program effectiveness in character education: A brief review. In M. Williams & E. Schapps (Eds.), *Character education: The Foundation of Teacher Education—Report of the National Commission on Character Education* (pp. 50–54). Washington, D.C.: Character Education Partnership. Leming, J.S. (2000). Tell me a story: An evaluation of a literature-based character education program. *Journal of Moral Education, 29*(4), 413–27. Leming, J.S. (2000). *What works in character education: A review of the research in the field.* Washington, D.C.: The Character Education Partnership. Leming, J.S. (2003). Ignorant activists. In J.S. Leming, L. Ellington, & K. Porter (Eds.), *Where did social studies go wrong?* Washington, D.C.: Thomas Fordham Foundation. Leming, J.S., Ellington, L., & Porter, K. (2003). *Where did social studies go wrong?* Washington, D.C.: Thomas Fordham Foundation. Leming, J.S., & Hollifield, J. (1985). Cooperative learning: A research success story. *Educational Researcher, 14,* 29–30.

*Jacques S. Benninga*

## Lickona, Thomas

Thomas Lickona, Ph.D. (born 1943), is a developmental psychologist and professor in the Childhood/Early Childhood Education Department at the State University of New York College at Cortland, where he founded and directs the Center for the 4th and 5th Rs (Respect & Responsibility). Since 1994, the Center has trained approximately 5,000 educators from 35 states and 16 countries through its annual Summer Institute in Character Education. Lickona married his wife, Judith, in 1966. They have two children and eleven grandchildren.

As a boy in his neighborhood, Lickona was known as a passionate advocate for fairness, frequently acting as a "player-referee" in sandlot baseball games. Later, in high school, a weekly sports column for his town paper fostered an early desire to become a sportswriter and a lifelong passion for writing.

A bachelor's degree (Siena College, 1964) and master's degree (Ohio University, 1965) in English honed his skills as a clear and concise writer. In his doctoral studies, Lickona focused his attention on Jean Piaget's research on the moral judgment of the child. Lickona's interest in Piaget led him to Lawrence Kohlberg's work on stages in the development of moral reasoning, and from 1978 to 1980 Lickona joined Kohlberg at Harvard University's Center for Moral Education and Ralph Mosher at Boston University to work with Boston-area schools on the development of democratic classrooms and participatory school governance.

When Lickona's passion for moral development met his passion for writing a good story simply and well, he found his life's work: character education. As he has often described it, he sees himself as a reporter drawing on the experiences of practitioners to tell the unfolding story of character education.

His editorial strengths and his interest in the real-world applications of moral development theory were featured in *Moral Development and Behavior* (1976), an interdisciplinary handbook that brought together leading scholars in the fields of moral psychology, social learning theory, and sociology.

In *Raising Good Children* (1983), Lickona took the framework of Kohlberg's stages of moral development and used the experiences of parents (including, in the spirit of Piaget, many observations of his own children) to create a user-friendly, how-to guide for child rearing. The style of the book became classic Lickona: rigorous and faithful translation of scholarly research, illustrated with stories, and distilled into a series of take-away strategies for putting theory and research into practice.

The style and substance of *Raising Good Children* was extended from homes into schools in Lickona's 1991 classic, *Educating for Character.* A book that is largely credited with launching the modern character education movement and that earned Lickona recognition as the "father of modern character education," *Educating for Character* outlined his 12-point comprehensive approach to character education. This model features a broad blueprint of classroom and schoolwide strategies, substantiated by research and illustrated with real-life examples. Within the classroom, Lickona's approach calls upon teachers to act as caregivers, models, and mentors; create a moral community; practice moral discipline; create a democratic classroom; teach values through the curriculum; use cooperative learning; develop the "conscience of craft"; encourage moral reflection; and teach conflict resolution. The approach calls upon the school to foster caring beyond the classroom; create a positive moral culture; and recruit parents and community as partners.

In 1995, on behalf of the Character Education Partnership (CEP), Lickona took the lead, along with Eric Schaps and Catherine Lewis, in authoring the *Eleven Principles of Effective Character Education.* These principles became the blueprint for comprehensive character education in the United States and have been used as criteria in CEP's National Schools of Character awards program, which annually recognizes schools for exemplary work in character education.

In 2005, Lickona partnered with his long-time colleague, Matthew Davidson, in publishing a research report on high school character education, *Smart & Good High Schools: Integrating Excellence & Ethics for Success in School, Work, and Beyond* (www.cortland.edu/character). This work is credited with providing a more adequate framework for conducting character education at the high school level, where character education had historically made few inroads. The *Smart & Good Schools* report introduced new theoretical ideas to the field of character education, including performance character, 8 Strengths of Character, Ethical Learning Community, and Professional Ethical Learning Community. Working with the Institute for Excellence & Ethics, the Center for the 4th and 5th Rs has begun a four-year project, funded by the John Templeton Foundation, to advance the Smart & Good vision and to conduct systematic research on its impact.

Over his career, Lickona's public writing and presenting on issues such as abortion and abstinence-based sex education have led some to regard him as controversial and even to view his stances as religiously motivated. Lickona freely acknowledges that he is a practicing Roman Catholic. However, while many in the field of character education have avoided these controversial topics as politically charged, potentially divisive, and even detrimental to the work of character education, Lickona views these as character-based (not sectarian) issues with deep societal impact, requiring deep and clear thinking and practical guidelines for those who work with youth.

Lickona is the recipient of numerous honors and awards, including a Christopher Award (for *Educating for Character*) and a "Sandy Award" for Lifetime achievement in Character Education (presented by the Character Education Partnership).

***Further Reading:*** Lickona, T. (Ed.) (1976). *Moral development and behavior.* New York: Holt, Rinehart, & Winston. Lickona, T. (1983). *Raising good children.* New York: Bantam. Lickona, T. (1991). *Educating for character.* New York: Bantam. Lickona, T. (2004). *Character matters: How to help our children develop good judgment, integrity, and other essential virtues.* New York: Simon and Schuster. Lickona, T., & Davidson, M. (2005). *Smart & good schools: Integrating excellence and ethics for success in school, work, and beyond.* Cortland, NY: Center for the 4th and 5th Rs (Respect & Responsibility). Washington, D.C.: Character Education Partnership. Lickona, T., Lickona, J., & Boudreau, W. (1994). *Sex, love and you: Making the right decision.* Notre Dame, IN: Ave Maria Press.

*Matthew L. Davidson*